Statistics for Social and Behavioral Sciences

Advisors:

S.E. Fienberg   W.J. van der Linden

Statistics for Social and Behavioral Sciences

Scott M. Lynch

Introduction to Applied Bayesian Statistics and Estimation for Social Scientists

With 89 Figures

 Springer

Scott M. Lynch
Department of Sociology and
   Office of Population Research
Princeton University
Princeton, NJ 08544
slynch@princeton.edu

Series Editors:

Stephen E. Fienberg
Department of Statistics
Carnegie Mellon University
Pittsburgh, PA 15213–3890
USA

Wim J. van der Linden
Department of Measurement
   and Data Analysis
Faculty of Behavioral Sciences
University of Twente
7500 AE Enschede
The Netherlands

Library of Congress Control Number: 2007929729

ISBN 978-0-387-71264-2   e-ISBN 978-0-387-71265-9

SAS® and all other SAS Institute Inc. product or service names are registered trademarks or trademarks
of SAS Institute Inc. in the USA and other countries.

STATA® and STATA® logo are registered trademarks of StataCorp LP.

Printed on acid-free paper.

9 8 7 6 5 4 3 2 1

springer.com

For my Barbara

Preface

This book was written slowly over the course of the last five years. During that time, a number of advances have been made in Bayesian statistics and Markov chain Monte Carlo (MCMC) methods, but, in my opinion, the market still lacks a *truly* introductory book written explicitly for social scientists that thoroughly describes the actual process of Bayesian analysis using these methods. To be sure, a variety of introductory books are available that cover the basics of the Bayesian approach to statistics (e.g., Gill 2002 and Gelman et al. 1995) and several that cover the foundation of MCMC methods (e.g., beginning with Gilks et al. 1996). Yet, a highly applied book showing how to use MCMC methods to complete a Bayesian analysis involving typical social science models applied to typical social science data is still sorely lacking. The goal of this book is to fill this niche.

The Bayesian approach to statistics has a long history in the discipline of statistics, but prior to the 1990s, it held a marginal, almost cult-like status in the discipline and was almost unheard of in social science methodology. The primary reasons for the marginal status of the Bayesian approach include (1) philosophical opposition to the use of "prior distributions" in particular and the subjective approach to probability in general, and (2) the lack of computing power for completing realistic Bayesian analyses. In the 1990s, several events occurred simultaneously to overcome these concerns. First, the explosion in computing power nullified the second limitation of conducting Bayesian analyses, especially with the development of sampling based methods (e.g., MCMC methods) for estimating parameters of Bayesian models. Second, the growth in availability of longitudinal (panel) data and the rise in the use of hierarchical modeling made the Bayesian approach more appealing, because Bayesian statistics offers a natural approach to constructing hierarchical models. Third, there has been a growing recognition both that the enterprise of statistics is a subjective process in general and that the use of prior distributions need not influence results substantially. Additionally, in many problems, the use of a prior distribution turns out to be advantageous.

The publication of Gelfand and Smith's 1990 paper describing the use of MCMC simulation methods for summarizing Bayesian posterior distributions was the watershed event that launched MCMC methods into popularity in statistics. Following relatively closely on the heels of this article, Gelman et al.'s (1995) book, *Bayesian Data Analysis*, and Gilks et al.'s (1996) book, *Markov Chain Monte Carlo in Practice*, placed the Bayesian approach in general, and the application of MCMC methods to Bayesian statistical models, squarely in the mainstream of statistics. I consider these books to be classics in the field and rely heavily on them throughout this book.

Since the mid-1990s, there has been an explosion in advances in Bayesian statistics and especially MCMC methodology. Many improvements in the recent past have been in terms of (1) monitoring and improving the performance of MCMC algorithms and (2) the development of more refined and complex Bayesian models and MCMC algorithms tailored to specific problems. These advances have largely escaped mainstream social science.

In my view, these advances have gone largely unnoticed in social science, because purported introductory books on Bayesian statistics and MCMC methods are not truly introductory for this audience. First, the mathematics in introductory books is often too advanced for a mainstream social science audience, which begs the question: "introductory *for whom?*" Many social scientists do not have the probability theory and mathematical statistics background to follow many of these books beyond the first chapter. This is not to say that the material is impossible to follow, only that more detail may be needed to make the text and examples more readable for a mainstream social science audience.

Second, many examples in introductory-level Bayesian books are at best foreign and at worst irrelevant to social scientists. The probability distributions that are used in many examples are not typical probability distributions used by social scientists (e.g., Cauchy), and the data sets that are used in examples are often atypical of social science data. Specifically, many books use small data sets with a limited number of covariates, and many of the models are not typical of the regression-based approaches used in social science research. This fact may not seem problematic until, for example, one is faced with a research question requiring a multivariate regression model for 10,000 observations measured on 5 outcomes with 10 or more covariates. Nonetheless, research questions involving large-scale data sets are not uncommon in social science research, and methods shown that handle a sample of size 100 measured on one or two outcomes with a couple of covariates simply may not be directly transferrable to a larger data set context. In such cases, the analyst without a solid understanding of the linkage between the model and the estimation routine may be unable to complete the analysis. Thus, some discussion tailored to the practicalities of *real* social science data and computing is warranted.

Third, there seems to be a disjunction between introductory books on Bayesian theory and introductory books on applied Bayesian statistics. One of the greatest frustrations for me, while I was learning the basics of Bayesian statistics and MCMC estimation methods, was (and is) the lack of a book that links the theoretical aspects of Bayesian statistics and model development with the application of modern estimation methods. Some examples in extant books may be substantively interesting, but they are often incomplete in the sense that discussion is truncated after model development without adequate guidance regarding how to estimate parameters. Often, suggestions are made concerning how to go about implementing only certain aspects of an estimation routine, but for a person with no experience doing this, these suggestions are not enough.

In an attempt to remedy these issues, this book takes a step back from the most recent advances in Bayesian statistics and MCMC methods and tries to bridge the gap between Bayesian theory and modern Bayesian estimation methods, as well as to bridge the gap between Bayesian statistics books written as "introductory" texts for statisticians and the needs of a mainstream social science audience. To accomplish this goal, this book presents very little that is new. Indeed, most of the material in this book is now "old-hat" in statistics, and many references are a decade old (In fact, a second edition of Gelman et al.'s 1995 book is now available). However, the trade-off for not presenting much new material is that this book explains the process of Bayesian statistics and modern parameter estimation via MCMC simulation methods in great depth. Throughout the book, I painstakingly show the modeling process from model development, through development of an MCMC algorithm to estimate its parameters, through model evaluation, and through summarization and inference.

Although many introductory books begin with the assumption that the reader has a solid grasp of probability theory and mathematical statistics, I do not make that assumption. Instead, this book begins with an exposition of the probability theory needed to gain a solid understanding of the statistical analysis of data. In the early chapters, I use contrived examples applied to (sometimes) contrived data so that the forest is not lost for the trees: The goal is to provide an understanding of the issue at hand rather than to get lost in the idiosyncratic features of real data. In the latter chapters, I show a Bayesian approach (or approaches) to estimating some of the most common models in social science research, including the linear regression model, generalized linear models (specifically, dichotomous and ordinal probit models), hierarchical models, and multivariate models.

A consequence of this choice of models is that the parameter estimates obtained via the Bayesian approach are often very consistent with those that could be obtained via a classical approach. This may make a reader ask, "then what's the point?" First, there are many cases in which a Bayesian approach and a classical approach will not coincide, but from my perspective, an introductory text should establish a foundation that can be built upon, rather than beginning in unfamiliar territory. Second, there are additional benefits to taking a Bayesian approach beyond the simple estimation of model parameters. Specifically, the Bayesian approach allows for greater flexibility in evaluating model fit, comparing models, producing samples of parameters that are not directly estimated within a model, handling missing data, "tweaking" a model in ways that cannot be done using canned routines in existing software (e.g., freeing or imposing constraints), and making predictions/forecasts that capture greater uncertainty than classical methods. I discuss each of these benefits in the examples throughout the latter chapters.

Throughout the book I thoroughly flesh out each example, beginning with the development of the model and continuing through to developing an MCMC algorithm (generally in R) to estimate it, estimating it using the algorithm, and presenting and summarizing the results. These programs should be straightforward, albeit perhaps tedious, to replicate, but some programming is inherently required to conduct Bayesian analyses. However, once such programming skills are learned, they are incredibly freeing to the researcher and thus well worth the investment to acquire them. Ultimately, the point is that the examples are thoroughly detailed; nothing is left to the imagination or to guesswork, including the mathematical contortions of simplifying posterior distributions to make them recognizable as known distributions.

A key feature of Bayesian statistics, and a point of contention for opponents, is the use of a prior distribution. Indeed, one of the most complex things about Bayesian statistics is the development of a model that includes a prior and yields a "proper" posterior distribution. In this book, I do not concentrate much effort on developing priors. Often, I use uniform priors on most parameters in a model, or I use "reference" priors. Both types of priors generally have the effect of producing results roughly comparable with those obtained via maximum likelihood estimation (although not in interpretation!). My goal is not to minimize the importance of choosing appropriate priors, but instead it is not to overcomplicate an introductory exposition of Bayesian statistics and model estimation. The fact is that most Bayesian analyses explicitly attempt to minimize the effect of the prior. Most published applications to date have involved using uniform, reference, or otherwise "noninformative" priors in an effort to avoid the "subjectivity" criticism that historically has been levied against Bayesians by classical statisticians. Thus, in most Bayesian social science research, the prior has faded in its importance in differentiating the classical and Bayesian paradigms. This is not to say that prior distributions are unimportant—for some problems they may be very important or useful—but it is to say that it is not necessary to dwell on them.

The book consists of a total of 11 chapters plus two appendices covering (1) calculus and matrix algebra and (2) the basic concepts of the Central Limit Theorem. The book is suited for a highly applied one-semester graduate level social science course. Each chapter, including the appendix but excluding the introduction, contains a handful of exercises at the end that test the understanding of the material in the chapter at both theoretical and applied levels. In the exercises, I have traded quantity for quality: There are relatively few exercises, but each one was chosen to address the essential material in the chapter. The first half of the book (Chapters 1-6) is primarily theoretical and provides a generic introduction to the theory and methods of Bayesian statistics. These methods are then applied to common social science models and data in the latter half of the book (Chapters 7-11). Chapters 2-4 can each be covered in a week of classes, and much of this material, especially in Chapters 2 and 3, should be review material for most students. Chapters 5 and 6 will most likely each require more than a week to cover, as they form the nuts and bolts of MCMC methods and evaluation. Subsequent chapters should each take 1-2 weeks of class time. The models themselves should be familiar, but the estimation of them via MCMC methods will not be and may be difficult for students without some programming and applied data analysis experience. The programming language used throughout the book is R, a freely available and common package used in applied statistics, but I introduce the program WinBugs in the chapter on hierarchical modeling. Overall, R and WinBugs are syntactically similar, and so the introduction of WinBugs is not problematic. From my perspective, the main benefit of WinBugs is that some derivations of conditional distributions that would need to be done in order to write an R program are handled automatically by WinBugs. This feature is especially useful in hierarchical models. All programs used in this book, as well as most data, and hints and/or solutions to the exercises can be found on my Princeton University website at: www.princeton.edu/~slynch.

Acknowledgements

I have a number of people to thank for their help during the writing of this book. First, I want to thank German Rodriguez and Bruce Western (both at Princeton) for sharing their advice, guidance, and statistical knowledge with me as I worked through several sections of the book. Second, I thank my friend and colleague J. Scott Brown for reading through virtually all chapters and providing much-needed feedback over the course of the last several years. Along these same lines, I thank Chris Wildeman and Steven Shafer for reading through a number of chapters and suggesting ways to improve examples and the general presentation of material. Third, I thank my statistics thesis advisor, Valen Johnson, and my mentor and friend, Ken Bollen, for all that they have taught me about statistics. (They cannot be held responsible for the fact that I may not have learned well, however). For their constant help and tolerance, I thank Wayne Appleton and Bob Jackson, the senior computer folks at Princeton University and Duke University, without whose support this book could not have been possible. For their general support and friendship over a period including, but not limited to, the writing of this book, I thank Linda George, Angie O'Rand, Phil Morgan, Tom Espenshade, Debby Gold, Mark Hayward, Eileen Crimmins, Ken Land, Dan Beirute, Tom Rice, and John Moore. I also thank my son, Tyler, and my wife, Barbara, for listening to me ramble incessantly about statistics and acting as a sounding board during the writing of the book. Certainly not least, I thank Bill Mc-Cabe for helping to identify an egregious error on page 364. Finally, I want to thank my editor at Springer, John Kimmel, for his patience and advice, and I acknowledge support from NICHD grant R03HD050374-01 for much of the work in Chapter 10 on multivariate models.

Despite having all of these sources of guidance and support, all the errors in the book remain my own.

Princeton University   *Scott M. Lynch*
                                                                      April 2007

Contents

List of Figures

List of Tables

1

Introduction

The fundamental goal of statistics is to summarize large amounts of data with a few numbers that provide us with some sort of insight into the process that generated the data we observed. For example, if we were interested in learning about the income of individuals in American society, and we asked 1,000 individuals "What is your income?," we would probably not be interested in reporting the income of all 1,000 persons. Instead, we would more likely be interested in a few numbers that summarized this information—like the mean, median, and variance of income in the sample—and we would want to be able to use these sample summaries to say something about income in the population. In a nutshell, "statistics" is the process of constructing these sample summaries and using them to infer something about the population, and it is the inverse of probabilistic reasoning. Whereas determining probabilities or frequencies of events—like particular incomes—is a *deductive* process of computing probabilities given certain parameters of probability distributions (like the mean and variance of a normal distribution), statistical reasoning is an *inductive* process of "guessing" best choices for parameters, given the data that have been observed, and making some statement about how close our "guess" is to the real population parameters of interest. Bayesian statistics and classical statistics involving maximum likelihood estimation constitute two different approaches to obtaining "guesses" for parameters and for making inferences about them. This book provides a detailed introduction to the Bayesian approach to statistics and compares and contrasts it with the classical approach under a variety of statistical models commonly used in social science research.

Regardless of the approach one takes to statistics, the process of statistics involves (1) formulating a research question, (2) collecting data, (3) developing a probability model for the data, (4) estimating the model, and (5) summarizing the results in an appropriate fashion in order to answer the research question—a process often called "statistical inference." This book generally assumes that a research question has been formulated and that a random sample of data has already been obtained. Therefore, this book focuses on model development, estimation, and summarization/inference. Under a classical approach to statistics, model estimation is often performed using canned procedures within statistical software packages like SAS®, STATA®, and SPSS®. Under the Bayesian approach, on the other hand, model estimation is often performed using software/programs that the researcher has developed using more general programming languages like R, C, or C++. Therefore, a substantial portion of this book is devoted to explaining the mechanics of model estimation in a Bayesian context. Although I often use the term "estimation" throughout the book, the modern Bayesian approach to statistics typically involves simulation of model parameters from their "posterior distributions," and so "model estimation" is actually a misnomer.

In brief, the modern Bayesian approach to model development, estimation, and inference involves the following steps:

1. Specification of a "likelihood function" (or "sampling density") for the data, given the model parameters.
2. Specification of a "prior distribution" for the model parameters.
3. Derivation of the "posterior distribution" for the model parameters, given the likelihood function and prior distribution.
4. Simulation of parameters to obtain a sample from the "posterior distribution" of the parameters.
5. Summarization of these parameter samples using basic descriptive statistical calculations.

Although this process and its associated terminology may seem foreign at the moment, the goal of this book is to thoroughly describe and illustrate these steps. The first step—as well as the associated parameter estimation method of maximum likelihood—is perhaps well understood by most quantitative researchers in the social sciences. The subsequent steps, on the other hand, are not, especially Step 4. Yet advances in Step 4 have led to the recent explosion in the use of Bayesian methods. Specifically, the development of Markov chain Monte Carlo (MCMC) sampling methods, coupled with exponential growth in computing capabilities, has made the use of Bayesian statistics more feasible because of their relative simplicity compared with traditional numerical methods. When approximation methods of estimation were more common, such methods generally relied on normality assumptions and asymptotic arguments for which Bayesians often criticize classical statistics. With the advent of MCMC sampling methods, however, more complicated and realistic applications can be undertaken, and there is no inherent reliance on asymptotic arguments and assumptions. This has allowed the benefits of taking a Bayesian approach over a classical approach to be realized.

1.1 Outline

For this book, I assume only a familiarity with (1) classical social science statistics and (2) matrix algebra and basic calculus. For those without such a background, or for whom basic concepts from these subjects are not fresh in memory, there are two appendices at the end of the book. Appendix A covers the basic ideas of calculus and matrix algebra needed to understand the concepts of, and notation for, mathematical statistics. Appendix B briefly reviews the Central Limit Theorem and its importance for classical hypothesis testing using a simulation study.

The first several chapters of this book lay a foundation for understanding the Bayesian paradigm of statistics and some basic modern methods of estimating Bayesian models. Chapter 2 provides a review of (or introduction to) probability theory and probability distributions (see DeGroot 1986, for an excellent background in probability theory; see Billingsley 1995 and Chung and AitSahlia 2003, for more advanced discussion, including coverage of Measure theory). Within this chapter, I develop several simple probability distributions that are used in subsequent chapters as examples before jumping into more complex real-world models. I also discuss a number of real univariate and multivariate distributions that are commonly used in social science research.

Chapter 2 also reviews the classical approach to statistical inference from the development of a likelihood function through the steps of estimating the parameters involved in it. Classical statistics is actually a combination of at least two different historical strains in statistics: one involving Fisherian maximum likelihood estimation and the other involving Fisherian and Neyman and Pearsonian hypothesis testing and confidence interval construction (DeGroot 1986; Edwards 1992; see Hubbard and Bayarri 2003 for a discussion of the confusion regarding the two approaches). The approach commonly followed today is a hybrid of these traditions, and I lump them both under the term "classical statistics." This chapter spells out the usual approach to deriving parameter estimates and conducting hypothesis tests under this paradigm.

Chapter 3 develops Bayes' Theorem and discusses the Bayesian paradigm of statistics in depth. Specifically, I spend considerable time discussing the concept of prior distributions, the classical statistical critique of their use, and the Bayesian responses. I begin the chapter with examples that use a point-estimate approach to applying Bayes' Theorem. Next, I turn to more realistic examples involving probability distributions rather than points estimates. For these examples, I use real distributions (binomial, poisson, and normal for sampling distributions and beta, gamma, and inverse gamma for prior distributions). Finally, in this chapter, I discuss several additional probability distributions that are not commonly used in social science research but are commonly used as prior distributions by Bayesians.

Chapter 4 introduces the rationale for MCMC methods, namely that sampling quantities from distributions can help us produce summaries of them that allow us to answer our research questions. The chapter then describes some basic methods of sampling from arbitrary distributions and then develops the Gibbs sampler as a fundamental method for sampling from high-dimensional distributions that are common in social science research.

Chapter 5 introduces an alternative MCMC sampling method that can be used when Gibbs sampling cannot be easily employed: the Metropolis-Hastings algorithm. In both Chapters 4 and 5, I apply these sampling methods to distributions and problems that were used in Chapters 2 and 3 in order to exemplify the complete process of performing a Bayesian analysis *up to, but not including,* assessing MCMC algorithm performance and evaluating model fit.

Chapter 6 completes the exemplification of a Bayesian analysis by showing (1) how to monitor and assess MCMC algorithm performance and (2) how to evaluate model fit and compare models. The first part of the chapter is almost entirely devoted to technical issues concerning MCMC implementation. A researcher must know that his/her estimation method is performing acceptably, and s/he must know how to use the output to produce appropriate estimates. These issues are generally nonissues for most classical statistical analyses, because generic software exists for most applications. However, they are important issues for Bayesian analyses, which typically involve software that is developed by the researcher him/herself. A benefit to this additional step in the process of analysis—evaluating algorithm performance—is that it requires a much more intimate relationship with the data and model assumptions than a classical analysis, which may have the potential to lull researchers into a false sense of security about the validity of parameter estimates and model assumptions.

The second part of the chapter is largely substantive. All researchers, classical or Bayesian, need to determine whether their models fit the data at hand and whether one model is better than another. I attempt to demonstrate that the Bayesian paradigm offers considerably more information and flexibility than a classical approach in making these determinations. Although I cannot and do not cover all the possibilities, in this part of the chapter, I introduce a number of approaches to consider.

The focus of the remaining chapters (7-10) is substantive and applied. These chapters are geared to developing and demonstrating MCMC algorithms for specific models that are common in social science research. Chapter 7 shows a Bayesian approach to the linear regression model. Chapter 8 shows a Bayesian approach to generalized linear models, specifically the dichotomous and ordinal probit models. Chapter 9 introduces a Bayesian approach to hierarchical models. Finally, Chapter 10 introduces a Bayesian approach to multivariate models. The algorithms developed in these chapters, although fairly generic, should not be considered endpoints for use by researchers. Instead, they should be considered as starting points for the development of algorithms tailored to user-specific problems.

In contrast to the use of sometimes contrived examples in the first six chapters, almost all examples in the latter chapters concern real probability distributions, real research questions, and real data. To that end, some additional beneficial aspects of Bayesian analysis are introduced, including the ability to obtain posterior distributions for parameters that are not directly estimated as part of a model, and the ease with which missing data can be handled.

1.2 A note on programming

Throughout the text, I present R programs for virtually all MCMC algorithms in order to demystify the linkage between model development and estimation. R is a freely available, downloadable programming package and is extremely well suited to Bayesian analyses (www.r-project.org). However, R is only one possible programming language in which MCMC algorithms can be written. Another package I use in the chapter on hierarchical modeling is WinBugs. WinBugs is a freely available, downloadable software package that performs Gibbs sampling with relative ease (www.mrc-bsu.cam.ac.uk/bugs). I strongly suggest learning how to use WinBugs if you expect to routinely conduct Bayesian analyses. The syntax of WinBugs is very similar to R, and so the learning curve is not steep once R is familiar. The key advantage to WinBugs over R is that WinBugs derives conditional distributions for Gibbs sampling for you; the user simply has to specify the model. In R, on the other hand, the conditional distributions must be derived mathematically by the user and then programmed. The key advantage of R over WinBugs, however, is that R—as a generic programming language—affords the user greater flexibility in reading data from files, modeling data, and writing output to files. For learning how to program in R, I recommend downloading the various documentation available when you download the software. I also recommend Venables and Ripley's books for S and S-Plus® programming (1999, 2000). The S and S-Plus languages are virtually identical to R, but they are not freely available.

I even more strongly recommend learning a generic programming language like C or C++. Although I show R programs throughout the text, I have used UNIX-based C extensively in my own work, because programs tend to run *much* faster in UNIX-based C than in any other language. First, UNIX systems are generally faster than other systems. Second, C++ is the language in which many software packages are written. Thus, writing a program in a software package's language when that language itself rests on a foundation in C/C++ makes any algorithm in that language inherently slower than it would be if it were written directly in C/C++.

C and C++ are not difficult languages to learn. In fact, if you can program in R, you can program in C, because the syntax for many commands is close to identical. Furthermore, if you can program in SAS or STATA, you can learn C very easily. The key differences between database programming languages like SAS and generic programming languages like C are in terms of how elements in arrays are handled. In C, each element in an array must be handled; in database and statistics programming languages, commands typically apply to an entire column (variable) at once. For example, recoding gender in a database or statistics package requires only a single command that is systematically applied to all observations automatically. In a generic programming language, on the other hand, one has to apply the command repeatedly to every row (usually using a loop). R combines both features, as I exemplify throughout the examples in the text: Elements in arrays may be handled one-at-a-time, or they may be handled all at once.

Another difference between generic programming languages like C and database packages is that generic languages do not have many functions built into them. For example, simulating variates from normal distributions in R, SAS, and STATA is easy because these languages have built-in functions that can be used to do so. In a generic language like C, on the other hand, one must either write the function oneself or find a function in an existing library. Once again, although this may seem like a drawback, it takes very little time to amass a collection of functions which can be used in all subsequent programs.

If you choose to learn C, I recommend two books: *Teach Yourself C in 24 Hours* (Zhang 1997) and *Numerical Recipes in C* (Press et al. 2002). *Teach Yourself C* is easy to read and will show you practically everything you need to know about the language, with the exception of listing all the built-in functions that C-compilers possess. *Numerical Recipes* provides a number of algorithms/functions for conducting various mathematical operations, such as Cholesky decomposition, matrix inversion, etc.

1.3 Symbols used throughout the book

A number of mathematical symbols that may be unfamiliar are used throughout this book. The meanings of most symbols are discussed upon their first appearance, but here I provide a nonexhaustive summary table for reference. Parts of this table may not be helpful *until* certain sections of the book have been read; the table is a summary, and so some expressions/terms are used here but are defined within the text (e.g., density function).

As for general notation that is not described elsewhere, I use lowercase letters, generally from the end of the alphabet (e.g., x), to represent random variables and uppercase versions of these letters to represent vectors of random variables or specific values of a random variable (e.g., X). I violate this general rule only in a few cases for the sake of clarity. Greek letters are reserved for distribution parameters (which, from a Bayesian view, can also be viewed as random variables). In some cases, I use $p()$ to represent probabilities; in other cases, for the sake of clarity, I use $pr()$.

Table 1.1. Some Symbols Used Throughout the Text

Symbol or Expression	Meaning	Explanation
$\forall$	"for all"	Used to summarily define all elements in a set.
$\in$	"in" or "is an element of"	Set notation symbol that means that the item to its left is a member of the set to its right.
$\sum_{i=1}^{n} x_i$	Repeated, discrete summation	Shorthand for representing that all elements x_i are to be summed together.
$f(x)$	Generic continuous function	Used to represent a generic function of the random variable x. Mostly used to represent an algebraic probability density function for a continuous variable.
$p(x)$	Generic discrete function or probability	Used to represent a generic function of a discrete random variable x. Also used to represent "the probability of x." In a discrete sample space, these are equivalent, given that the function yields the probability for a specified value of x.
$\int_a^b f(x)dx$	Integration (continuous summation)	Calculus symbol that is the continuous analog to $\sum$. Implies continuous summation of the function $f(x)$ over the interval $[a,b]$. In multiple dimensional problems, multiple integration may be used (e.g., $\int_a^b \int_c^d \ldots$). See Appendix A.
$F(x)$	Cumulative distribution function	Used to represent $\int_{-\infty}^{X} f(x)dx$.
$\propto$	"is proportional to"	Used to indicate that the object to its left is proportional to (differs only by a multiplicative constant compared to) the object on its right.
$\sim$	"is distributed as"	Used to indicate that the random variable or parameter on its left follows the distribution on its right.
$A \otimes B$	Kronecker product	A special type of matrix multiplication in which each element of A is replaced by itself multiplied by the entirety of $B : A_{ij}B, \forall i,j$.

2

Probability Theory and Classical Statistics

Statistical inference rests on probability theory, and so an in-depth understanding of the basics of probability theory is necessary for acquiring a conceptual foundation for mathematical statistics. First courses in statistics for social scientists, however, often divorce statistics and probability early with the emphasis placed on basic statistical modeling (e.g., linear regression) in the absence of a grounding of these models in probability theory and probability distributions. Thus, in the first part of this chapter, I review some basic concepts and build statistical modeling from probability theory. In the second part of the chapter, I review the classical approach to statistics as it is commonly applied in social science research.

2.1 Rules of probability

Defining "probability" is a difficult challenge, and there are several approaches for doing so. One approach to defining probability concerns itself with the frequency of events in a long, perhaps infinite, series of trials. From that perspective, the reason that the probability of achieving a heads on a coin flip is 1/2 is that, in an infinite series of trials, we would see heads 50% of the time. This perspective grounds the classical approach to statistical theory and modeling. Another perspective on probability defines probability as a subjective representation of uncertainty about events. When we say that the probability of observing heads on a single coin flip is 1/2, we are really making a series of assumptions, including that the coin is fair (i.e., heads and tails are in fact equally likely), and that in prior experience or learning we recognize that heads occurs 50% of the time. This latter understanding of probability grounds Bayesian statistical thinking. From that view, the language and mathematics of probability is the natural language for representing uncertainty, and there are subjective elements that play a role in shaping probabilistic statements.

Although these two approaches to understanding probability lead to different approaches to statistics, some fundamental axioms of probability are important and agreed upon. We represent the probability that a particular event, E, will occur as $p(E)$. All possible events that can occur in a single trial or experiment constitute a sample space (S), and the sum of the probabilities of all possible events in the sample space is 1[1]:

$$\sum_{\forall E \in S} p(E) = 1. \tag{2.1}$$

As an example that highlights this terminology, a single coin flip is a trial/experiment with possible events "Heads" and "Tails," and therefore has a sample space of $S = \{\text{Heads, Tails}\}$. Assuming the coin is fair, the probabilities of each event are $1/2$, and—as used in social science—the record of the outcome of the coin-flipping process can be considered a "random variable."

We can extend the idea of the probability of observing one event in one trial (e.g., one head in one coin toss) to multiple trials and events (e.g., two heads in two coin tosses). The probability assigned to multiple events, say A and B, is called a "joint" probability, and we denote joint probabilities using the disjunction symbol from set notation ($\cap$) or commas, so that the probability of observing events A and B is simply $p(A, B)$. When we are interested in the occurrence of event A *or* event B, we use the union symbol ($\cup$), or simply the word "or": $p(A \cup B) \equiv p(A \text{ or } B)$.

The "or" in probability is somewhat different than the "or" in common usage. Typically, in English, when we use the word "or," we are referring to the occurrence of one or another event, but not both. In the language of logic and probability, when we say "or" we are referring to the occurrence of either event or both events. Using a Venn diagram clarifies this concept (see Figure 2.1).

In the diagram, the large rectangle denotes the sample space. Circles A and B denote events A and B, respectively. The overlap region denotes the joint probability $p(A, B)$. $p(A \text{ or } B)$ is the region that is A only, B only, and the disjunction region. A simple rule follows:

$$p(A \text{ or } B) = p(A) + p(B) - p(A, B). \tag{2.2}$$

$p(A, B)$ is subtracted, because it is added twice when summing $p(A)$ and $p(B)$.

There are two important rules for joint probabilities. First:

$$p(A, B) = p(A)p(B) \tag{2.3}$$

iff (if and only if) A and B are independent events. In probability theory, independence means that event A has no bearing on the occurrence of event B. For example, two coin flips are independent events, because the outcome of the first flip has no bearing on the outcome of the second flip. Second, if A and B are not independent, then:

---

[1] If the sample space is continuous, then integration, rather than summation, is used. We will discuss this issue in greater depth shortly.

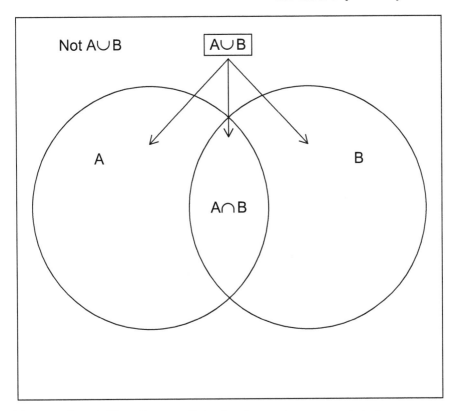

Fig. 2.1. Sample Venn diagram: Outer box is sample space; and circles are events A and B.

$$p(A, B) = p(A|B)p(B). \tag{2.4}$$

Expressed another way:

$$p(A|B) = \frac{p(A, B)}{p(B)}. \tag{2.5}$$

Here, the "|" represents a conditional and is read as "given." This last rule can be seen via Figure 2.1. $p(A|B)$ refers to the region that contains A, given that we know B is already true. Knowing that B is true implies a reduction in the total sample space from the entire rectangle to the circle B only. Thus, $p(A)$ is reduced to the (A, B) region, given the reduced space B, and $p(A|B)$ is the proportion of the new sample space, B, which includes A. Returning to the rule above, which states $p(A, B) = p(A)p(B)$ iff A and B are independent, if A and B are independent, then knowing B is true in that case does not reduce the sample space. In that case, then $p(A|B) = p(A)$, which leaves us with the first rule.

Although we have limited our discussion to two events, these rules generalize to more than two events. For example, the probability of observing three independent events A, B, and C, is $p(A, B, C) = p(A)p(B)p(C)$. More generally, the joint probability of n independent events, $E_1, E_2 \ldots E_n$, is $\prod_{i=1}^{n} p(E_i)$, where the $\prod$ symbol represents repeated multiplication. This result is very useful in statistics in constructing likelihood functions. See DeGroot (1986) for additional generalizations. Surprisingly, with basic generalizations, these basic probability rules are all that are needed to develop the most common probability models that are used in social science statistics.

2.2 Probability distributions in general

The sample space for a single coin flip is easy to represent using set notation as we did above, because the space consists of only two possible events (heads or tails). Larger sample spaces, like the sample space for 100 coin flips, or the sample space for drawing a random integer between 1 and 1,000,000, however, are more cumbersome to represent using set notation. Consequently, we often use functions to assign probabilities or relative frequencies to all events in a sample space, where these functions contain "parameters" that govern the shape and scale of the curve defined by the function, as well as expressions containing the random variable to which the function applies. These functions are called "probability density functions," if the events are continuously distributed, or "probability mass functions," if the events are discretely distributed. By continuous, I mean that all values of a random variable x are possible in some region (like $x = 1.2345$); by discrete, I mean that only some values of x are possible (like all integers between 1 and 10). These functions are called "density" and "mass" functions because they tell us where the most (and least) likely events are concentrated in a sample space. We often abbreviate both types of functions using "pdf," and we denote a random variable x that has a particular distribution $g(.)$ using the generic notation: $x \sim g(.)$, where the "$\sim$" is read "is distributed as," the g denotes a particular distribution, and the "." contains the parameters of the distribution g.

If $x \sim g(.)$, then the pdf itself is expressed as $f(x) = \ldots$, where the "$\ldots$" is the particular algebraic function that returns the relative frequency/probability associated with each value of x. For example, one of the most common continuous pdfs in statistics is the normal distribution, which has two parameters—a mean (μ) and variance (σ^2). If a variable x has probabilities/relative frequencies that follow a normal distribution, then we say $x \sim N(\mu, \sigma^2)$, and the pdf is:

$$f(x) = \frac{1}{\sqrt{2\pi\sigma^2}} \exp\left\{-\frac{(x - \mu)^2}{2\sigma^2}\right\}.$$

We will discuss this particular distribution in considerable detail throughout the book; the point is that the pdf is simply an algebraic function that, given particular values for the parameters μ and σ^2, assigns relative frequencies for all events x in the sample space.

I use the term "relative frequencies" rather than "probabilities" in discussing continuous distributions, because in continuous distributions, technically, 0 probability is associated with any particular value of x. An infinite number of real numbers exist between any two numbers. Given that we commonly express the probability for an event E as the number of ways E can be realized divided by the number of possible equally likely events that can occur, when the sample space is continuous, the denominator is infinite. The result is that the probability for any particular event is 0. Therefore, instead of discussing the probability of a particular event, we may discuss the probability of observing an event within a specified range. For this reason, we need to define the cumulative distribution function.

Formally, we define a "distribution function" or "cumulative distribution function," often denoted "cdf," as the sum or integral of a mass or density function from the smallest possible value for x in the sample space to some value X, and we represent the cdf using the uppercase letter or symbol that we used to represent the corresponding pdf. For example, for a continuous pdf $f(x)$, in which x can take all real values $(x \in R)$,

$$p(x < X) = F(x < X) = \int_{-\infty}^{X} f(x) \, dx. \tag{2.6}$$

For a discrete distribution, integration is replaced with summation and the "$<$" symbol is replaced with "$\leq$," because some probability is associated with every discrete value of x in the sample space.

Virtually *any* function can be considered a probability density function, so long as the function is real-valued and it integrates (or sums) to 1 over the sample space (the region of allowable values). The latter requirement is necessary in order to keep consistent with the rule stated in the previous section that the sum of all possible events in a sample space equals 1. It is often the case, however, that a given function will not integrate to 1, hence requiring the inclusion of a "normalizing constant" to bring the integral to 1. For example, the leading term outside the exponential expression in the normal density function $(1/\sqrt{2\pi\sigma^2})$ is a normalizing constant. A normalized density—one that integrates to 1—or a density that *can* integrate to 1 with an appropriate normalizing constant is called a "proper" density function. In contrast, a density that cannot integrate to 1 (or a finite value), is called "improper." In Bayesian statistics, the propriety of density functions is important, as we will discuss throughout the remainder of the book.

Many of the most useful pdfs in social science statistics appear complicated, but as a simple first example, suppose we have some random variable x that can take any value in the interval (a, b) with equal probability. This is called a uniform distribution and is commonly denoted as $U(a, b)$, where a and b are the lower and upper bounds of the interval in which x can fall. If $x \sim U(a, b)$, then

$$f(x) = \begin{cases} c & \text{if } a < x < b \\ 0 & \text{otherwise.} \end{cases} \qquad (2.7)$$

What is c? c is a constant, which shows that any value in the interval (a, b) is equally likely to occur. In other words, regardless of which value of x one chooses, the height of the curve is the same. The constant must be determined so that the area under the curve/line is 1. A little calculus shows that this constant must be $1/(b - a)$. That is, if:

$$\int_a^b c \, dx = 1,$$

then

$$c \, x \big|_a^b = 1,$$

and so

$$c = \frac{1}{(b - a)}.$$

Because the uniform density function does not depend on x, it is a rectangle. Figure 2.2 shows two uniform densities: the $U(-1.5, .5)$ and the $U(0, 1)$ densities. Notice that the heights of the two densities differ; they differ because their widths vary, and the total area under the curve must be 1.

The uniform distribution is not explicitly used very often in social science research, largely because very few phenomena in the social sciences follow such a distribution. In order for something to follow this distribution, values at the extreme ends of the distribution must occur as often as values in the center, and such simply is not the case with most social science variables. However, the distribution is important in mathematical statistics generally, and Bayesian statistics more specifically, for a couple of reasons. First, random samples from other distributions are generally simulated from draws from uniform distributions—especially the standard uniform density $[U(0, 1)]$. Second, uniform distributions are commonly used in Bayesian statistics as priors on parameters when little or no information exists to construct a more informative prior (see subsequent chapters).

More often than not, variables of interest in the social sciences follow distributions that are either peaked in the center and taper at the extremes, or they are peaked at one end of the distribution and taper away from that end (i.e., they are skewed). As an example of a simple distribution that exhibits the latter pattern, consider a density in which larger values are linearly more (or less) likely than smaller ones on the interval (r, s):

$$f(x) = \begin{cases} c(mx + b) & \text{if } r < x < s \\ 0 & \text{otherwise.} \end{cases} \qquad (2.8)$$

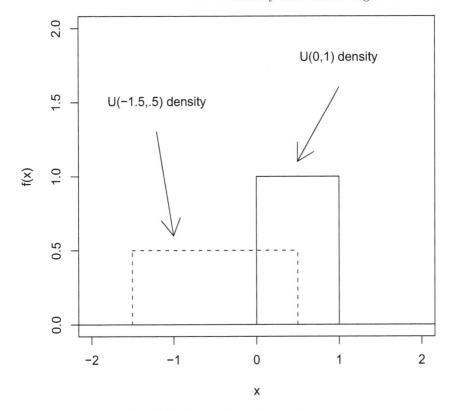

Fig. 2.2. Two uniform distributions.

This density function is a line, with r and s as the left and right boundaries, respectively. As with the uniform density, c is a constant—a normalizing constant—that must be determined in order for the density to integrate to 1. For this generic linear density, the normalizing constant is (see Exercises):

$$c = \frac{2}{(s-r)[m(s+r)+2b]}.$$

In this density, the relative frequency of any particular value of x depends on x, as well as on the parameters m and b. If m is positive, then larger values of x occur more frequently than smaller values. If m is negative, then smaller values of x occur more frequently than larger values.

What type of variable might follow a distribution like this in social science research? I would argue that many attitudinal items follow this sort of distribution, especially those with ceiling or floor effects. For example, in the 2000 General Social Survey (GSS) special topic module on freedom, a question was asked regarding the belief in the importance of being able to express unpopular views in a democracy. Figure 2.3 shows the histogram of responses for this item with a linear density superimposed. A linear density appears to fit fairly well (of course, the data are discrete, whereas the density function is continuous).

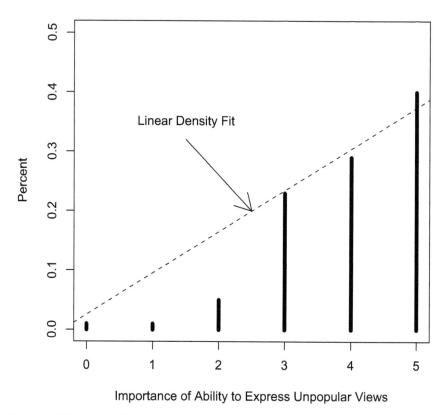

Fig. 2.3. Histogram of the importance of being able to express unpopular views in a free society (1 = Not very important...6 = One of the most important things).

To be sure, we commonly treat such attitudinal items as being normally distributed and model them accordingly, but they may follow a linear distribution as well as, or better than, a normal distribution. Ultimately, this is a question we will address later in the book under model evaluation.

Figure 2.4 shows a particular, arbitrary case of the linear density in which $m = 2$, $b = 3$; the density is bounded on the interval $(0, 5)$; and thus $c = 1/40$. So:

$$f(x) = \begin{cases} (1/40)(2x + 3) & 0 < x < 5 \\ 0 & \text{otherwise.} \end{cases} \tag{2.9}$$

Notice that the inclusion of the normalizing constant ultimately alters the slope and intercept if it is distributed through: The slope becomes 1/20 and the intercept becomes 3/40. This change is not a problem, and it highlights the notion of "relative frequency": The *relative* frequency of values of x are unaffected. For example, the ratio of the height of the original function at $x = 5$ and $x = 0$ is $13/3$, whereas the ratio of the new function at the same values is $\frac{13/40}{3/40} = 13/3$.

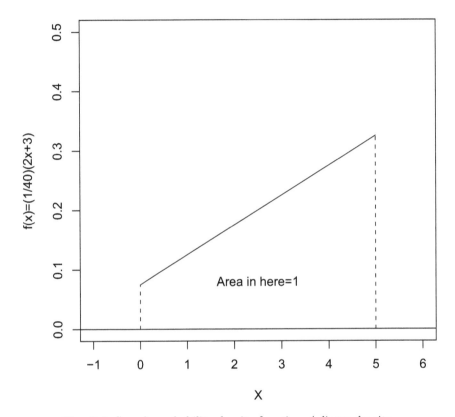

Fig. 2.4. Sample probability density function: A linear density.

2.2.1 Important quantities in distributions

We generally want to summarize information concerning a probability distribution using summary statistics like the mean and variance, and these quantities can be computed from pdfs using integral calculus for continuous distributions and summation for discrete distributions. The mean is defined as:

$$\mu_x = \int_{x \in S} x \times f(x) dx, \qquad (2.10)$$

if the distribution is continuous, and:

$$\mu_x = \sum_{x \in S} x \times p(x), \tag{2.11}$$

if the distribution is discrete. The mean is often called the "expectation" or expected value of x and is denoted as $E(x)$. The variance is defined as:

$$\sigma_x^2 = \int_{x \in S} (x - \mu_x)^2 \times f(x)dx, \tag{2.12}$$

if the distribution is continuous, and:

$$\sigma_x^2 = \sum_{x \in S} (x - \mu_x)^2 p(x), \tag{2.13}$$

if the distribution is discrete. Using the expectation notation introduced for the mean, the variance is sometimes referred to as $E((x - \mu_x)^2)$; in other words, the variance is the expected value of the squared deviation from the mean.[2]

Quantiles, including the median, can also be computed using integral calculus. The median of a continuous distribution, for example, is obtained by finding Q that satisfies:

$$.5 = \int_{-\infty}^{Q} f(x)dx. \tag{2.14}$$

Returning to the examples in the previous section, the mean of the $U(a, b)$ distribution is:

$$E(x) = \mu_x = \int_a^b x \times \left(\frac{1}{b - a}\right) dx = \frac{b + a}{2},$$

and the variance is:

$$E((x - \mu_x)^2) = \int_a^b \frac{1}{b - a}(x - \mu_x)^2 \, dx = \frac{(b - a)^2}{12}.$$

For the linear density with the arbitrary parameter values introduced in Equation 2.9 ($f(x) = (1/40)(2x + 3)$), the mean is:

$$\mu_x = \int_0^5 x \times (1/40)(2x + 3)dx = (1/240)(4x^3 + 9x^2)dx \Big|_0^5 = 3.02.$$

The variance is:

---

[2] The sample mean, unlike the population distribution mean shown here, is estimated with $(n - 1)$ in the denominator rather than with n. This is a correction factor for the known bias in estimating the population variance from sample data. It becomes less important asymptotically (as $n \to \infty$.)

$$\text{Var}(x) = \int_0^5 (x - 3.02)^2 \times (1/40)(2x + 3)dx = 1.81.$$

Finally, the median can be found by solving for Q in:

$$.5 = \int_0^Q (1/40)(2x + 3)dx.$$

This yields:

$$20 = Q^2 + 3Q,$$

which can be solved using the quadratic formula from algebra. The quadratic formula yields two real roots—3.22 and -6.22—only one of which is within the "support" of the distribution (3.22); that is, only one has a value that falls in the domain of the distribution.

In addition to finding particular quantiles of the distribution (like quartile cutpoints, deciles, etc.), we may also like to determine the probability associated with a given range of the variable. For example, in the $U(0,1)$ distribution, what is the probability that a random value drawn from this distribution will fall between .2 and .6? Determining this probability also involves calculus[3]:

$$p(.2 < x < .6) = \int_{.2}^{.6} \frac{1}{1-0}dx = x\Big|_{.2}^{.6} = .4.$$

An alternative, but equivalent, way of conceptualizing probabilities for regions of a density is in terms of the cdf. That is, $p(.2 < x < .6) = F(x = .6) - F(x = .2)$, where F is $\int_0^X f(x)dx$ [the cumulative distribution function of $f(x)$].

2.2.2 Multivariate distributions

In social science research, we routinely need distributions that represent more than one variable simultaneously. For example, factor analysis, structural equation modeling with latent variables, simultaneous equation modeling, as well as other methods require the simultaneous analysis of variables that are thought to be related to one another. Densities that involve more than one random variable are called joint densities, or more commonly, multivariate distributions. For the sake of concreteness, a simple, arbitrary example of such a distribution might be:

$$f(x,y) = \begin{cases} c(2x + 3y + 2) & \text{if} \quad 0 < x < 2, \, 0 < y < 2 \\ 0 & \text{otherwise.} \end{cases} \tag{2.15}$$

Here, the x and y are the two dimensions of the random variable, and $f(x,y)$ is the height of the density, given specific values for the two variables. Thus,

---

[3] With discrete distributions, calculus is not required, only summation of the relevant discrete probabilities.

$f(x, y)$ gives us the relative frequency/probability of particular values of x and y. Once again, c is the normalizing constant that ensures the function of x and y is a proper density function (that it integrates to 1). In this example, determining c involves solving a double integral:

$$c \int_0^2 \int_0^2 (2x + 3y + 2) \, dx \, dy \ = 1.$$

For this distribution, $c = 1/28$ (find this).

Figure 2.5 shows this density in three dimensions. The height of the density represents the relative frequencies of particular *pairs* of values for x and y. As the figure shows, the density is a partial plane (bounded at 0 and 2 in both x and y dimensions) that is tilted so that larger values of x and y occur more frequently than smaller values. Additionally, the plane inclines more steeply in the y dimension than the x dimension, given the larger slope in the density function.

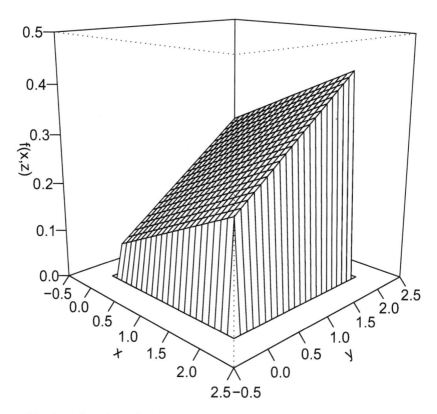

Fig. 2.5. Sample probability density function: A bivariate plane density.

What pair of variables might follow a distribution like this one (albeit with different parameters and domains)? Realistically, we probably would not use this distribution, but some variables might actually follow this sort of pattern. Consider two items from the 2000 GSS topic module on freedom: the one we previously discussed regarding the importance of the ability to express unpopular views in a free society, and another asking respondents to classify the importance of political participation to freedom. Table 2.1 is a cross-tabulation of these two variables. Considered separately, each variable follows a linear density such as discussed earlier. The proportion of individuals in the "Most Important" category for each variable is large, with the proportion diminishing across the remaining categories of the variable. Together, the variables appear to some extent to follow a planar density like the one above. Of course, there are some substantial deviations in places, with two noticeable 'humps' along the diagonal of the table.

Table 2.1. Cross-tabulation of importance of expressing unpopular views with importance of political participation.

Political Participation	Express Unpopular Views						
	1	2	3	4	5	6	
1	361	87	39	8	2	2	36%
2	109	193	51	13	2	3	27%
3	45	91	184	25	4	5	26%
4	15	17	35	17	4	2	7%
5	10	4	9	5	2	0	2%
6	11	9	4	3	1	5	2%
	40%	29%	23%	5%	1%	1%	100%

Note: Data are from the 2000 GSS special topic module on freedom (variables are expunpop and partpol). 1 = One of the most important parts of freedom ... 6 = Not so important to freedom.

Figure 2.6 presents a three-dimensional depiction of these data with an estimated planar density superimposed. The imposed density follows the general pattern of the data but fits poorly in several places. First, in several places the planar density substantially underestimates the true frequencies (three places along the diagonal). Second, the density tends to substantially overestimate frequencies in the middle of the distribution. Based on these problems, finding an alternative density is warranted. For example, a density with exponential or quadratic components may be desirable in order to allow more rapid declines in the expected relative frequencies at higher values of the variables. Furthermore, we may consider using a density that contains a parameter— like a correlation—that captures the relationship between the two variables, given their apparent lack of independence (the "humps" along the diagonal).

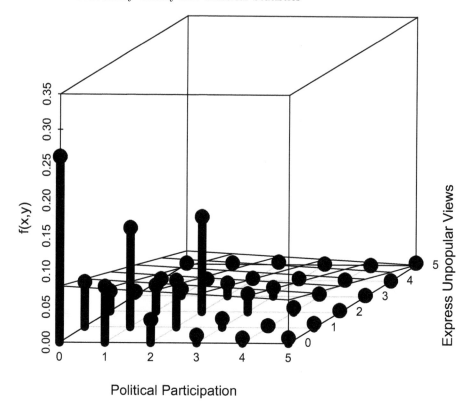

Fig. 2.6. Three-dimensional bar chart for GSS data with "best" planar density superimposed.

In multivariate continuous densities like this planar density, determining the probability that x and y fall in particular regions of the density is determined via integration, just as in univariate densities. That is, the concept of cumulative distribution functions extends to multivariate densities:

$$p(x < X \,,\, y < Y) = F(x,y) = \int_{-\infty}^{X} \int_{-\infty}^{Y} f(x,y) \; dx \; dy. \qquad (2.16)$$

Considering the planar density with parameters arbitrarily fixed at 2 and 3, for example, the probability that $x < 1$ and $y < 1$ is:

$$\int_{0}^{1} \int_{0}^{1} (1/28)(2x + 3y + 2) \; dx \; dy = \frac{9}{56}.$$

This region is presented in Figure 2.7, with the shadow of the omitted portion of the density shown on the $z = 0$ plane.

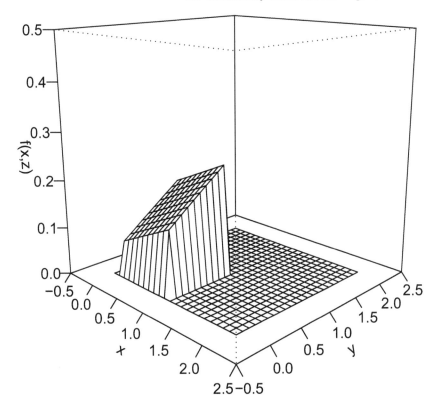

Fig. 2.7. Representation of bivariate cumulative distribution function: Area under bivariate plane density from 0 to 1 in both dimensions.

2.2.3 Marginal and conditional distributions

Although determining the probabilities for particular regions of multivariate densities is important, we may be interested in only a subset of the dimensions of a multivariate density. Two types of "subsets" are frequently needed: marginal distributions and conditional distributions. The data contained in Table 2.1 help differentiate these two types of distributions.

The marginal distribution for the "Express unpopular views" item is the row at the bottom of the table: It is the distribution of this variable summing across the categories of the other variable (or integrating, if the density were continuous). The conditional distribution of this item, on the other hand, is the row of the table corresponding to a particular value for the political participation variable. For example, the conditional distribution for expressing unpopular views, *given* the value of "1" for political participation, consists of the data in the first row of the table (361, 87, 39, 8, 2, and 2, or in renormalized percents: 72%, 17%, 8%, 2%, .4%, and .4%).

Thus, we can think of marginal distributions for a variable as being the original distribution "flattened" in one dimension, whereas the conditional distribution for a variable is a "slice" through one dimension.

Finding marginal and conditional distributions mathematically is conceptually straightforward, although often difficult in practice. Although Equation 2.5 was presented in terms of discrete probabilities, the rule also applies to density functions. From Equation 2.5, a conditional distribution can be computed as:

$$f(x|y) = \frac{f(x, y)}{f(y)} \tag{2.17}$$

This equation says that the conditional distribution for x given y is equal to the joint density of x and y divided by the *marginal* distribution for y, where a marginal distribution is the distribution of one variable, integrating/summing over the other variables in the joint density. Thus:

$$f(y) = \int_{x \in S} f(x, y) dx. \tag{2.18}$$

In terms of our bivariate distribution above ($f(x, y) = (1/28)(2x+3y+2)$), the marginal distributions for x and y can be found as:

$$f(x) = \int_{y=0}^{2} (1/28)(2x + 3y + 2) dy = (1/28)(4x + 10)$$

and

$$f(y) = \int_{x=0}^{2} (1/28)(2x + 3y + 2) dx = (1/28)(6y + 8).$$

The conditional distributions can then be found as:

$$f(x|y) = \frac{(1/28)(2x + 3y + 2)}{\int_{x=0}^{2}(2x + 3y + 2)dx} = \frac{(1/28)(2x + 3y + 2)}{(1/28)(6y + 8)}$$

and

$$f(y|x) = \frac{(1/28)(2x + 3y + 2)}{\int_{y=0}^{2}(2x + 3y + 2)dy} = \frac{(1/28)(2x + 3y + 2)}{(1/28)(4x + 10)}.$$

Observe how the marginal distributions for each variable exclude the other variable (as they should), whereas the conditional distributions do not. Once a specific value for x or y is chosen in the conditional distribution, however, the remaining function will only depend on the variable of interest. Once again, in other words, the conditional distribution is akin to taking a slice through one dimension of the bivariate distribution.

As a final example, take the conditional distribution $f(x|y)$, where $y = 0$, so that we are looking at the slice of the bivariate distribution that lies on the x axis. The conditional distribution for that slice is:

$$f(x|y=0) = \frac{2x + 3(y=0) + 2}{6(y=0) + 8} = (1/8)(2x + 2).$$

With very little effort, it is easy to see that this result gives us the formula for the line that we observe in the x, z plane when we set $y = 0$ in the original unnormalized function and we exclude the constant $1/8$. In other words:

$$(1/8)(2x + 2) \propto (1/28)(2x + 3y + 2)$$

when $y = 0$. Thus, an important finding is that the conditional distribution $f(x|y)$ is proportional to the joint distribution for $f(x, y)$ evaluated at a particular value for y [expressed $f(x|y) \propto f(x, y)$], differing only by a normalizing constant. This fact will be useful when we discuss Gibbs sampling in Chapter 4.

2.3 Some important distributions in social science

Unlike the relatively simple distributions we developed in the previous section, the distributions that have been found to be most useful in social science research appear more complicated. However, it should be remembered that, despite their sometimes more complicated appearance, they are simply algebraic functions that describe the relative frequencies of occurence for particular values of a random variable. In this section, I discuss several of the most important distributions used in social science research. I limit the discussion at this point to distributions that are commonly applied to random variables as social scientists view them. In the next chapter, I discuss some additional distributions that are commonly used in Bayesian statistics as "prior distributions" for parameters (which, as we will see, are also treated as random variables by Bayesians). I recommend Evans, Hastings, and Peacock (2000) for learning more about these and other common probability distributions.

2.3.1 The binomial distribution

The binomial distribution is a common discrete distribution used in social science statistics. This distribution represents the probability for x successes in n trials, given a success probability p for each trial. If $x \sim Bin(n, p)$, then:

$$pr(x|n, p) = \binom{n}{x} p^x (1 - p)^{n-x}. \tag{2.19}$$

Here, I change the notation on the left side of the mass function to "pr" to avoid confusion with the parameter p in the function. The combinatorial, $\binom{n}{x}$, at the front of the function, compensates for the fact that the x successes can come in any order in the n trials. For example, if we are interested in the probability of obtaining exactly 10 heads in 50 flips of a fair coin [thus, $pr(x = 10 \mid n = 50, p = .5)$], the 10 heads could occur back-to-back, or several may appear in a row, followed by several tails, followed by more heads, etc. This constant is computed as $n!/(x!(n - x)!)$ and acts as a normalizing constant to ensure the mass under the curve sums to 1. The latter two terms in the function multiply the independent success and failure probabilities, based on the observed number of successes and failures. Once the parameters n and p are chosen, the probability of observing any number x of successes can be computed/deduced. For example, if we wanted to know the probability of *exactly* $x = 10$ heads out of $n = 50$ flips, then we would simply substitute those numbers into the right side of the equation, and the result would tell us the probability. If we wanted to determine the probability of obtaining *at least* 10 heads in 50 flips, we would need to sum the probabilities from 10 successes up to 50 successes. Obviously, in this example, the probability of obtaining more heads than 50 or fewer heads than 0 is 0. Hence, this sample space is bounded to counting integers between 0 and 50, and computing the probability of at least 10 heads would require summing 41 applications of the function (for $x = 10$, $x = 11$, ..., $x = 50$).

The mean of the binomial distribution is np, and the variance of the binomial distribution is $np(1 - p)$. When $p = .5$, the distribution is symmetric around the mean. When $p > .5$, the distribution is skewed to the left; when $p < .5$, the distribution is skewed to the right. See Figure 2.8 for an example of the effect of p on the shape of the distribution ($n = 10$). Note that, although the figure is presented in a histogram format for the purpose of appearance (the densities are presented as lines), the distribution is discrete, and so 0 probability is associated with non-integer values of x.

A normal approximation to the binomial may be used when p is close to .5 and n is large, by setting $\mu_x = np$ and $\sigma_x = \sqrt{np(1 - p)}$. For example, in the case mentioned above in which we were interested in computing the probability of obtaining 10 or more heads in a series of 50 coin flips, computing 41 probabilities with the function would be tedious. Instead, we could set $\mu_x = 25$, and $\sigma_x = \sqrt{50(.5)(1 - .5)} = 3.54$, and compute a z-score as $z = (10 - 25)/(3.54) = -4.24$. Recalling from basic statistics that there is virtually 0 probability in the tail of the z distribution to the left of -4.24, we would conclude that the probability of obtaining at least 10 heads is practically 1, using this approximation. In fact, the actual probability of obtaining at least 10 heads is .999988.

When $n = 1$, the binomial distribution reduces to another important distribution called the Bernoulli distribution. The binomial distribution is often used in social science statistics as a building block for models for dichotomous outcome variables like whether a Republican or Democrat will win an upcoming election, whether an individual will die within a specified period of time, etc.

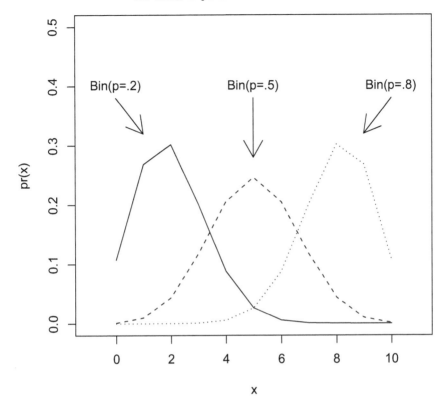

Fig. 2.8. Some binomial distributions (with parameter $n = 10$).

2.3.2 The multinomial distribution

The multinomial distribution is a generalization of the binomial distribution in which there are more than two outcome categories, and thus, there are more than two "success" probabilities (one for each outcome category). If $x \sim Multinomial(n, p_1, p_2, \ldots, p_k)$, then:

$$pr(x_1 \ldots x_k \mid n, p_1 \ldots p_k) = \frac{n!}{x_1! \, x_2! \, \ldots \, x_k!} \, p_1^{x_1} \, p_2^{x_2} \, \ldots \, p_k^{x_k}, \qquad (2.20)$$

where the leading combinatorial expression is a normalizing constant, $\sum_{i=1}^{k} p_i = 1$, and $\sum_{i=1}^{k} x_i = n$. Whereas the binomial distribution allows us to compute the probability of obtaining a given number of successes (x) out of n trials, given a particular success probability (p), the multinomial distribution allows us to compute the probability of obtaining particular sets of successes, given n trials and given different success probabilities for each member of the set. To make this idea concrete, consider rolling a pair of dice. The sample space for possible outcomes of a single roll is $S = \{2, 3, 4, 5, 6, 7, 8, 9, 10, 11, 12\}$, and we can consider the number of occurrences in multiple rolls of each of these outcomes to be represented by a particular x (so, x_1 represents the number of times a 2 is rolled, x_2 represents the number of times a 3 is rolled, etc.). The success probabilities for these possible outcomes vary, given the fact that there are more ways to obtain some sums than others. The vector of probabilities $p_1 \ldots p_{11}$ is $\{\frac{1}{36}, \frac{2}{36}, \frac{3}{36}, \frac{4}{36}, \frac{5}{36}, \frac{6}{36}, \frac{5}{36}, \frac{4}{36}, \frac{3}{36}, \frac{2}{36}, \frac{1}{36}\}$. Suppose we roll the pair of dice 36 times. Then, if we want to know the probability of obtaining one "2", two "3s", three "4s", etc., we would simply substitute $n = 36$, $p_1 = \frac{1}{36}, p_2 = \frac{2}{36}, \ldots, p_{11} = \frac{1}{36}$, and $x_1 = 1, x_2 = 2, x_3 = 3, \ldots$ into the function and compute the probability.

The multinomial distribution is often used in social science statistics to model variables with qualitatively different outcomes categories, like religious affiliation, political party affiliation, race, etc, and I will discuss this distribution in more depth in later chapters as a building block of some generalized linear models and some multivariate models.

2.3.3 The Poisson distribution

The Poisson distribution is another discrete distribution, like the binomial, but instead of providing the probabilities for a particular number of successes out of a *given* number of trials, it essentially provides the probabilities for a given number of successes in an infinite number of trials. Put another way, the Poisson distribution is a distribution for count variables. If $x \sim Poi(\lambda)$, then:

$$p(x|\lambda) = \frac{e^{-\lambda}\lambda^x}{x!}. \tag{2.21}$$

Figure 2.9 shows three Poisson distributions, with different values for the λ parameter. When λ is small, the distribution is skewed to the right, with most of the mass concentrated close to 0. As λ increases, the distribution becomes more symmetric and shifts to the right. As with the figure for the binomial distribution above, I have plotted the densities as if they were continuous for the sake of appearance, but because the distribution is discrete, 0 probability is associated with non-integer values of x

The Poisson distribution is often used to model count outcome variables, (e.g., numbers of arrests, number of children, etc.), especially those with low expected counts, because the distributions of such variables are often skewed to the right with most values clustered close to 0. The mean and variance of the Poisson distribution are both λ, which is often found to be unrealistic for many count variables, however. Also problematic with the Poisson distribution is the fact that many count variables, such as the number of times an individual is arrested, have a greater frequency of 0 counts than the Poisson density predicts. In such cases, the negative binomial distribution (not discussed here) and mixture distributions (also not discussed) are often used (see Degroot 1986

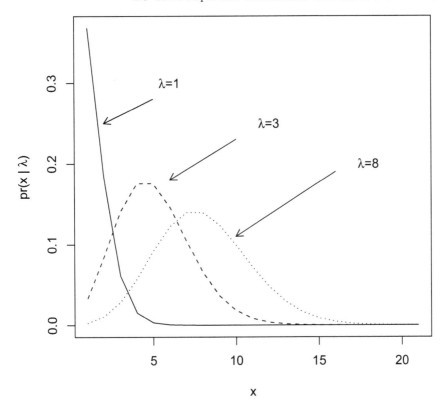

Fig. 2.9. Some Poisson distributions.

for the development of the negative binomial distribution; see Long 1997 for a discussion of negative binomial regression modeling; see Land, McCall, and Nagin 1996 for a discussion of the use of Poisson mixture models).

2.3.4 The normal distribution

The most commonly used distribution in social science statistics and statistics in general is the normal distribution. Many, if not most, variables of interest follow a bell-shaped distribution, and the normal distribution, with both a mean and variance parameter, fits such variables quite well. If $x \sim N(\mu, \sigma^2)$, then:

$$f(x|\mu, \sigma) = \frac{1}{\sqrt{2\pi\sigma^2}} \exp\left\{-\frac{(x-\mu)^2}{2\sigma^2}\right\}. \qquad (2.22)$$

In this density, the preceding $(\sqrt{2\pi\sigma^2})^{-1}$ is included as a normalizing constant so that the area under the curve from $-\infty$ to $+\infty$ integrates to 1. The latter half of the pdf is the "kernel" of the density and gives the curve its location and shape. Given a value for the parameters of the distribution, μ and σ^2, the curve shows the relative probabilities for every value of x. In this case, x can range over the entire real line, from $-\infty$ to $+\infty$. Technically, because an infinite number of values exist between any two other values of x (ironically making $p(x = X) = 0, \forall X$), the value returned by the function $f(x)$ does not reveal the probability of x, unlike with the binomial and Poisson distribution above (as well as other discrete distributions). Rather, when using continuous pdfs, one must consider the probability for regions under the curve. Just as above in the discussion of the binomial distribution, where we needed to sum all the probabilities between $x = 10$ and $x = 50$ to obtain the probability that $x \geq 10$, here we would need to integrate the continuous function from $x = a$ to $x = b$ to obtain the probability that $a < x < b$. Note that we did not say $a \leq x \leq b$; we did not for the same reason mentioned just above: The probability that x equals any number q is 0 (the area of a line is 0). Hence $a < x < b$ is equivalent to $a \leq x \leq b$.

The case in which $\mu = 0$ and $\sigma^2 = 1$ is called the "standard normal distribution," and often, the z distribution. In that case, the kernel of the density reduces to $\exp\{-x^2/2\}$, and the bell shape of the distribution can be easily seen. That is, where $x = 0$, the function value is 1, and as x moves away from 0 in either direction, the function value rapidly declines.

Figure 2.10 depicts three different normal distributions: The first has a mean of 0 and a standard deviation of 1; the second has the same mean but a standard deviation of 2; and the third has a standard deviation of 1 but a mean of 3.

The normal distribution is used as the foundation for ordinary least squares (OLS) regression, for some generalized linear models, and for many other models in social science statistics. Furthermore, it is an important distribution in statistical theory: The Central Limit Theorem used to justify most of classical statistical testing states that sampling distributions for statistics are, in the limit, normal. Thus, the z distribution is commonly used to assess statistical "significance" within a classical statistics framework. For these reasons, we will consider the normal distribution repeatedly throughout the remainder of the book.

2.3.5 The multivariate normal distribution

The normal distribution easily extends to more than one dimension. If $X \sim MVN(\mu, \Sigma)$, then:

$$f(X|\mu, \Sigma) = (2\pi)^{-\frac{k}{2}}|\Sigma|^{-\frac{1}{2}} \exp\left\{-\frac{1}{2}(X - \mu)^T \Sigma^{-1}(X - \mu)\right\}, \qquad (2.23)$$

where X is a vector of random variables, k is the dimensionality of the vector, μ is the vector of means of X, and Σ is the covariance matrix of X. The multivariate normal distribution is an extension of the univariate normal in

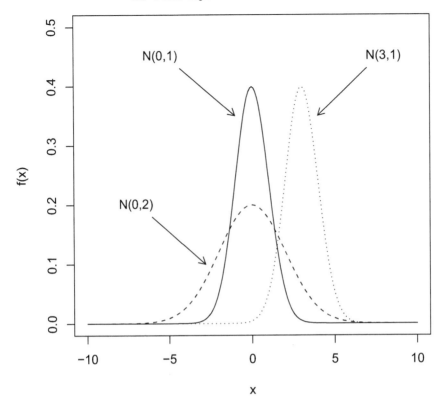

Fig. 2.10. Some normal distributions.

which x is expanded from a scalar to a k-dimensional vector of variables, $x_1, x_2, \ldots, x_k$, that are related to one another via the covariance matrix Σ. If X is multivariate normal, then each variable in the vector X is normal. If Σ is diagonal (all off-diagonal elements are 0), then the multivariate normal distribution is equivalent to k univariate normal densities.

When the dimensionality of the MVN distribution is equal to two, the distribution is called the "bivariate normal distribution." Its density function, although equivalent to the one presented above, is often expressed in scalar form as:

$$f(x_1, x_2) = \frac{1}{2\pi\sigma_1\sigma_2\sqrt{1-\rho^2}} \exp\left[-\frac{1}{2(1-\rho^2)}(Q - R + S)\right], \qquad (2.24)$$

where

$$Q = \frac{(x_1 - \mu_1)^2}{\sigma_1^2}, \qquad (2.25)$$

$$R = \frac{2\rho(x_1 - \mu_1)(x_2 - \mu_2)}{\sigma_1\sigma_2}, \qquad (2.26)$$

and

$$S = \frac{(x_2 - \mu_2)^2}{\sigma_2^2}.$$

(2.27)

The bivariate normal distribution, when the correlation parameter ρ is 0, looks like a three-dimensional bell. As ρ becomes larger (in either positive or negative directions), the bell flattens, as shown in Figure 2.11. The upper part of the figure shows a three-dimensional view and a (top-down) contour plot of the bivariate normal density when $\rho = 0$. The lower part of the figure shows the density when $\rho = .8$.

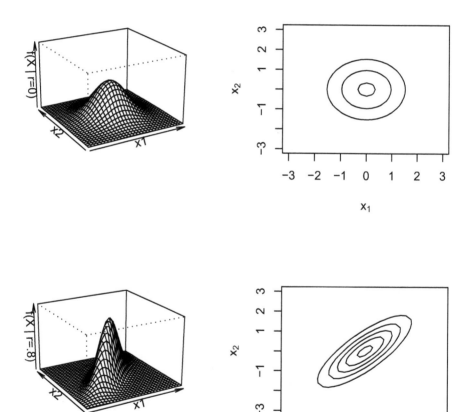

Fig. 2.11. Two bivariate normal distributions.

   The multivariate normal distribution is used fairly frequently in social science statistics. Specifically, the bivariate normal distribution is used to model simultaneous equations for two outcome variables that are known to be related, and structural equation models rely on the full multivariate normal distribution. I will discuss this distribution in more depth in later chapters describing multivariate models.

2.3.6 t and multivariate t distributions

The t (Student's t) and multivariate t distributions are quite commonly used in modern social science statistics. For example, when the variance is unknown in a model that assumes a normal distribution for the data, with the variance following an inverse gamma distribution (see subsequent chapters), the marginal distribution for the mean follows a t distribution (consider tests of coefficients in a regression model). Also, when the sample size is small, the t is used as a robust alternative to the normal distribution in order to compensate for heavier tails in the distribution of the data. As the sample size increases, uncertainty about σ decreases, and the t distribution converges on a normal distribution (see Figure 2.12). The density functions for the t distribution appears much more complicated than the normal. If $x \sim t(\mu, \sigma, v)$, then:

$$f(x) = \frac{\Gamma((v+1)/2)}{\Gamma(v/2)\sigma\sqrt{v\pi}} \left(1 + v^{-1}\left(\frac{x-\mu}{\sigma}\right)^2\right)^{-(v+1)/2}, \qquad (2.28)$$

where μ is the mean, σ is the standard deviation, and v is the "degrees of freedom." If X is a k-dimensional vector of variables $(x_1 \ldots x_k)$, and $X \sim mvt(\mu, \Sigma, v)$, then:

$$f(X) = \frac{\Gamma((v+d)/2)}{\Gamma(v/2)v^{k/2}\pi^{k/2}} \mid \Sigma \mid^{-1/2} \left(1 + v^{-1}(X-\mu)^T \Sigma^{-1}(X-\mu)\right)^{-(v+k)/2},$$

$$(2.29)$$

where μ is a vector of means, and Σ is the variance-covariance matrix of X.
   We will not explicitly use the t and multivariate t distributions in this book, although a number of marginal distributions we will be working with will be implicitly t distributions.

2.4 Classical statistics in social science

Throughout the fall of 2004, CNN/USAToday/Gallup conducted a number of polls attempting to predict whether George W. Bush or John F. Kerry would win the U.S. presidential election. One of the key battleground states was Ohio, which ultimately George Bush won, but all the polls leading up

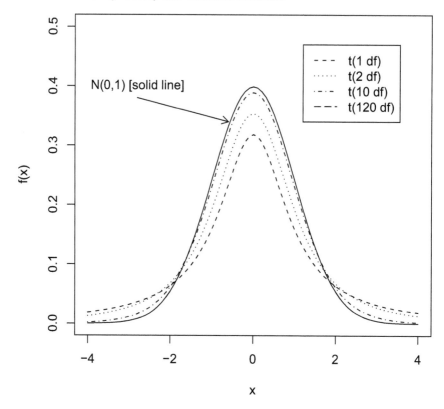

Fig. 2.12. The $t(0, 1, 1)$, $t(0, 1, 10)$, and $t(0, 1, 120)$ distributions (with an $N(0, 1)$ distribution superimposed).

to the election showed the two candidates claiming proportions of the votes that were statistically indistinguishable in the state. The last poll in Ohio consisted of 1,111 likely voters, 46% of whom stated that they would vote for Bush, and 50% of whom stated that they would vote for Kerry, but the poll had a margin of error of ±3%.[4]

In the previous sections, we discussed probability theory, and I stated that statistics is essentially the inverse of probability. In probability, once we are given a distribution and its parameters, we can deduce the probabilities for events. In statistics, we have a collection of events and are interested in

---

[4] see http://www.cnn.com/ELECTION/2004/special/president/showdown/OH/ polls.html for the data reported in this and the next chapter. Additional polls are displayed on the website, but I use only the CNN/USAToday/Gallup polls, given that they are most likely similar in sample design. Unfortunately, the proportions are rounded, and so my results from here on are approximate. For example, in the last poll, 50% planned to vote for Kerry, and 50% of 1,111 is 556. However, the actual number could range from 550 to 561 given the rounding.

determining the values of the parameters that produced them. Returning to the polling data, determining who would win the election is tantamount to determining the population parameter (the proportion of actual voters who will vote for a certain candidate) given a collection of events (a sample of potential votes) thought to arise from this parameter and the probability distribution to which it belongs.

Classical statistics provides one recipe for estimating this population parameter; in the remainder of this chapter, I demonstrate how. In the next chapter, I tackle the problem from a Bayesian perspective. Throughout this section, by "classical statistics" I mean the approach that is most commonly used among academic researchers in the social sciences. To be sure, the classical approach to statistics in use is a combination of several approaches, involving the use of theorems and perspectives of a number of statisticians. For example, the most common approach to model estimation is maximum likelihood estimation, which has its roots in the works of Fisher, whereas the common approach to hypothesis testing using p-values has its roots in the works of both Neyman and Pearson and Fisher—each of whom in fact developed somewhat differing views of hypothesis testing using p-values (again, see Hubbard and Bayarri 2003 or see Gill 2002 for an even more detailed history).

2.5 Maximum likelihood estimation

The classical approach to statistics taught in social science statistics courses involves two basic steps: (1) model estimation and (2) inference. The first step involves first determining an appropriate probability distribution/model for the data at hand and then estimating its parameters. Maximum likelihood (ML) is the most commonly used method of estimating parameters and determining the extent of error in the estimation (steps 1 and 2, respectively) in social science statistics (see Edwards 1992 for a detailed, theoretical discussion of likelihood analysis; see Eliason 1993 for a more detailed discussion of the mechanics of ML estimation).

The fundamental idea behind maximum likelihood estimation is that a good choice for the estimate of a parameter of interest is the value of the parameter that makes the observed data most likely to have occurred. To do this, we need to establish some sort of function that gives us the probability for the data, and we need to find the value of the parameter that maximizes this probability. This function is called the "likelihood function" in classical statistics, and it is essentially the product of sampling densities—probability distributions—for each observation in the sample. The process of estimation thus involves the following steps:

1. Construct a likelihood function for the parameter(s) of interest.
2. Simplify the likelihood function and take its logarithm.
3. Take the partial derivative of the log-likelihood function with respect to each parameter, and set the resulting equation(s) equal to 0.

4. Solve the system of equations to find the parameters.

This process seems complicated, and indeed it can be. Step 4 can be quite difficult when there are lots of parameters. Generally, some sort of iterative method is required to find the maximum. Below I detail the process of ML estimation.

2.5.1 Constructing a likelihood function

If $x_1, x_2 \ldots x_n$ are independent observations of a random variable, x, in a data set of size n, then we know from the multiplication rule in probability theory that the joint probability for the vector X is:

$$f(X|\theta) \equiv L(\theta \mid x) = \prod_{i=1}^{n} f(x_i \mid \theta). \qquad (2.30)$$

This equation is the likelihood function for the model. Notice how the parameter and the data switch places in the $L(.)$ notation versus the $f(.)$ notation. We denote this as $L(.)$, because from a classical standpoint, the parameter is assumed to be fixed. However, we are interested in estimating the parameter θ, given the data we have observed, so we use this notation. The primary point of constructing a likelihood function is that, given the data at hand, we would like to solve for the value of the parameter that makes the occurence of the data most probable, or most "likely" to have actually occurred.

As the right-hand side of the equation shows, the construction of the likelihood function first relies on determining an appropriate probability distribution $f(.)$ thought to generate the observed data. In our election polling example, the data consist of 1,111 potential votes, the vast majority of which were either for Bush or for Kerry. If we assume that candidates other than these two are unimportant—that is, the election will come down to whom among these two receives more votes—then the data ultimately reduce to 556 potential votes for Kerry and 511 potential votes for Bush. An appropriate distribution for such data is the binomial distribution. If we are interested in whether Kerry will win the election, we can consider a vote for Kerry a "success," and its opposite, a vote for Bush, a "failure," and we can set up our likelihood function with the goal of determining the success probability p. The likelihood function in this case looks like:

$$L(p|X) = \binom{1067}{556} p^{556}(1 - p)^{511}.$$

As an alternative view that ultimately produces the same results, we can consider that, at the individual level, each of our votes arises from a Bernoulli distribution, and so our likelihood function is the product of $n = 1,067$ Bernoulli distributions. In that case:

$$L(p|X) = \prod_{i=1}^{n=1067} p^{x_i}(1-p)^{1-x_i}. \tag{2.31}$$

Given that we know nothing about our potential voters beyond for whom they plan to vote, we can consider the individuals "exchangeable," and after carrying out the multiplication across individuals, this version of the likelihood function is proportional to the first one based on the binomial distribution, only differing by a combinatorial expression. This expression simply scales the curve, and so it is ultimately unimportant in affecting our estimate. Figure 2.13 shows this result: The upper figure shows the likelihood function based on the binomial distribution; the lower figure shows the likelihood function based on the Bernoulli distribution. The only difference between the two functions can be found in the scale of the y axis.

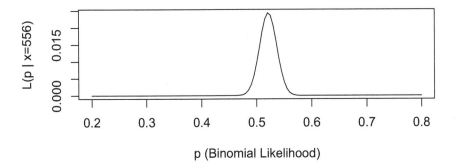

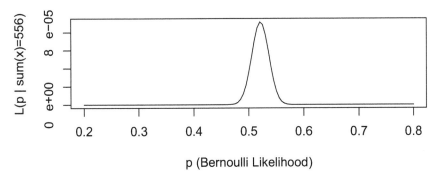

Fig. 2.13. Binomial (top) and Bernoulli (bottom) likelihood functions for the OH presidential poll data.

2.5.2 Maximizing a likelihood function

How do we obtain the estimates for the parameters after we set up the likelihood function? Just as many pdfs are unimodal and slope away from the mode of the distribution, we expect the likelihood function to look about the same. So, what we need to find is the peak of this curve. From calculus we know that the slope of the curve should be 0 at its peak. Thus, we should take the derivative of the likelihood function with respect to the parameter, set it equal to 0, and find the x coordinate (the parameter value) for which the curve reaches a maximum.

We generally take the logarithm of the likelihood function before we differentiate, because the log function converts the repeated multiplication to repeated addition, and repeated addition is much easier to work with. The log-likelihood reaches a maximum at the same point as the original function. Generically:

$$\text{Log-Likelihood} \equiv LL(\theta \mid X) = \sum_{i=1}^{n} \ln\left(f(x_i \mid \theta)\right). \tag{2.32}$$

For our specific problem:

$$LL(p|x) \propto 556 \ln p + 511 \ln(1-p).$$

To find the value of p where this log-likelihood function reaches a maximum, we need to take the derivative of the function with respect to p, set it equal to 0, and solve for p. Generically, the derivative of a binomial log-likelihood function is:

$$\frac{dLL}{dp} = \frac{\sum x_i}{p} - \frac{n - \sum x_i}{1-p}. \tag{2.33}$$

If we set this derivative equal to 0 and solve for p, we obtain:

$$\frac{n - \sum x_i}{1-p} = \frac{\sum x_i}{p}.$$

Simplifying yields:

$$\hat{p} = \frac{\sum x_i}{n}. \tag{2.34}$$

This result shows that the maximum likelihood estimate for p is simply the observed proportion of successes. In our example, this is the proportion of potential votes for Kerry, out of those who opted for either Kerry or Bush (here, $556/1067 = .521$). Given that this value for p is an estimate, we typically denote it $\hat{p}$, rather than p.

Figure 2.14 displays this process of estimation graphically. The figure shows that both the likelihood function and the log-likelihood functions peak at the same point. The horizontal lines are the tangent lines to the curve

where the slopes of these lines are 0; they are at the maximum of the functions. The corresponding x coordinate where the curves reach their maximum
is the maximum likelihood estimate (MLE).

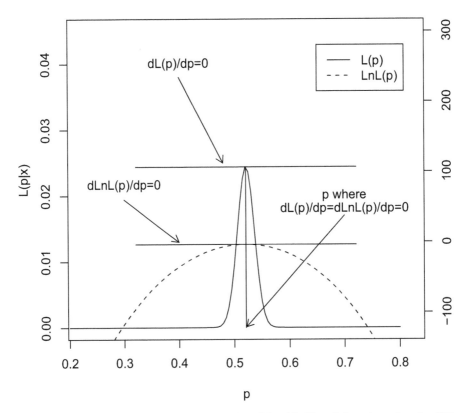

Fig. 2.14. Finding the MLE: Likelihood and log-likelihood functions for the OH
presidential poll data.

2.5.3 Obtaining standard errors

$\hat{p}$ is an estimate and is not guaranteed to equal the population parameter p in
any particular sample. Thus, we need some way to quantify our uncertainty
in estimating p with $\hat{p}$ from our sample. A nice additional feature of the
log-likelihood is that a function of the second derivative of the log-likelihood
function can be used to estimate the variance of the sampling distribution
(the square root of which is called the "standard error").[5] Specifically, we

---

[5] See Appendix B for a discussion of the Central Limit Theorem and the basis for
classical inference.

must take the inverse of the negative expected value of the second derivative of the log-likelihood function. Mathematically:

$$I(\theta)^{-1} = \left(-E\left(\frac{\partial^2 LL}{\partial\theta\partial\theta^T}\right)\right)^{-1}, \tag{2.35}$$

where θ is our parameter or vector of parameters and $I(\theta)$ is called the "information matrix." The square root of the diagonal elements of this matrix are the parameter standard errors. $I(\theta)^{-1}$ can be computed using the following steps:

1. Take the second partial derivatives of the log-likelihood. In multiparameter models, this produces a matrix of partial derivatives (called the Hessian matrix).
2. Take the negative of the expectation of this matrix to obtain the "information matrix" $I(\theta)$.
3. Invert this matrix to obtain estimates of the variances and covariances of parameters (get standard errors by square-rooting the diagonal elements of the matrix).

The fact that $I(\theta)^{-1}$ contains the standard errors is not intuitive. But, if you recall that the first derivative is a measure of the slope of a function at a point (the rate of change in the function at that point), and the second derivative is a measure of the rate of change in the slope, we can think of the second derivative as indicating the rate of curvature of the curve. A very steep curve, then, has a very high rate of curvature, which makes its second derivative large. Thus, when we invert it, it makes the standard deviation small. On the other hand, a very shallow curve has a very low rate of curvature, which makes its second derivative small. When we invert a small number, it makes the standard deviation large. Note that, when we evaluate the second derivative, we substitute the MLE estimate for the parameter into the result to obtain the standard error at the estimate.

Returning to our data at hand, the second partial derivative of the generic binomial log-likelihood function with respect to p is:

$$\frac{\partial^2 LL}{\partial p^2} = \frac{\sum x}{p^2} - \frac{n - \sum x}{(1-p)^2}. \tag{2.36}$$

Taking expectations yields:

$$E\left(\frac{\partial^2 LL}{\partial p^2}\right) = E\left[-\frac{\sum x}{p^2} - \frac{n - \sum x}{(1-p)^2}\right].$$

The expectation of these expressions can be computed by realizing that the expectation of $\sum x/n$ is p (put another way: $E(\hat{p}) = p$). Thus:

$$E\left(\frac{\partial^2 LL}{\partial p^2}\right) = -\frac{np}{p^2} - \frac{n - np}{(1-p)^2}.$$

Some simplification yields:

$$E\left(\frac{\partial^2 LL}{\partial p^2}\right) = -\frac{n}{p(1-p)}.$$

At this point, we can negate the expectation, invert it, and evaluate it at the MLE ($\hat{p}$) to obtain:

$$I(p)^{-1} = \frac{\hat{p}(1-\hat{p})}{n}. \qquad (2.37)$$

Taking the square root of this yields the estimated standard error. In our polling data case, the standard error is $\sqrt{(.521 \times .479)/1067} = .015$.

Recall that our question is whether Kerry would win the vote in Ohio. Our estimate for the Ohio population proportion to vote for Kerry (versus Bush) was .521, which suggests he would win the popular vote in Ohio (discounting third party candidates). However, the standard error of this estimate was .015. We can construct our usual confidence interval around the maximum likelihood estimate to obtain a 95% interval for the MLE. If we do this, we obtain an interval of $[.492, .550]$ ($CI = \hat{p} \pm 1.96 \times s.e.(\hat{p})$). Given that the lower bound on this interval is below .5, we can conclude that we cannot rule out the possibility that Kerry would not win the popular vote in Ohio.

An alternative to the confidence interval approach to answering this question is to construct a t test, with a null hypothesis $H_0 : p < .5$. Following that approach:

$$t = \frac{(.521 - .5)}{.015} = 1.4.$$

This t value is not large enough to reject the null hypothesis (that Kerry's proportion of the vote is less than .5), and thus, the conclusion we would reach is the same: We do not have enough evidence to conclude that Kerry will win (see Appendix B for more discussion of null hypotheses, confidence intervals, and t tests).

Note that this result is consistent with the result I stated at the beginning of this section: The results of the original poll suggested that the vote was too close to call, given a $\pm 3\%$ margin of error. Here, I have shown essentially from where that margin of error arose. We ended up with a margin of error of .0294, which is approximately equal to the margin of error in the original poll.

2.5.4 A normal likelihood example

Because the normal distribution is used repeatedly throughout this book and throughout the social sciences, I conclude this chapter by deriving parameter estimates and standard errors for a normal distribution problem. I keep this example at a general level; in subsequent chapters, we will return to this likelihood function with specific problems and data.

Suppose you have n observations $x_1, x_2, \ldots, x_n$ that you assume are normally distributed. Once again, if the observations are assumed to be independent, a likelihood function can be constructed as the multiple of independent normal density functions:

$$L(\mu, \sigma \mid X) = \prod_{i=1}^{n} \frac{1}{\sqrt{2\pi\sigma^2}} \exp\left\{ -\frac{(x_i - \mu)^2}{2\sigma^2} \right\}. \tag{2.38}$$

We can simplify the likelihood as:

$$L(\mu, \sigma \mid X) = (2\pi\sigma^2)^{-\frac{n}{2}} \exp\left\{ -\frac{1}{2\sigma^2} \sum_{i=1}^{n} (x_i - \mu)^2 \right\}.$$

The log of the likelihood is:

$$LL(\mu, \sigma \mid X) \propto -n\ln(\sigma) - \frac{1}{2\sigma^2} \sum_{i=1}^{n} (x_i - \mu)^2. \tag{2.39}$$

In the above equation, I have eliminated the $-\frac{n}{2}\ln(2\pi)$, an irrelevant constant. It is irrelevant, because it does not depend on either parameter and will therefore drop once the partial derivatives are taken. In this example, we have two parameters, μ and σ, and hence the first partial derivative must be taken with respect to each parameter. This will leave us with two equations (one for each parameter). After taking the partial derivatives with respect to each parameter, we obtain the following:

$$\frac{\partial LL}{\partial \mu} = \frac{n(\bar{x} - \mu)}{\sigma^2}$$

and

$$\frac{\partial LL}{\partial \sigma} = -\frac{n}{\sigma} + \frac{1}{\sigma^3} \sum_{i=1}^{n} (x_i - \mu)^2.$$

Setting these partial derivatives each equal to 0 and doing a little algebra yields:

$$\hat{\mu} = \bar{x} \tag{2.40}$$

and

$$\hat{\sigma}^2 = \frac{\sum_{i=1}^{n} (x_i - \mu)^2}{n}. \tag{2.41}$$

These estimators should look familiar: The MLE for the population mean is the sample mean; the MLE for the population variance is the sample variance.[6] Estimates of the variability in the estimates for the mean and standard deviation can be obtained as we did in the binomial example. However, as

---

[6] The MLE is known to be biased, and hence, a correction is added, so that the denominator is $n - 1$ rather than n.

noted above, given that we have two parameters, our second derivate matrix will, in fact, be a matrix. For the purposes of avoiding taking square roots until the end, let $\tau = \sigma^2$, and we'll construct the Hessian matrix in terms of τ. Also, let θ be a vector containing both μ and τ. Thus, we must compute:

$$\frac{\partial^2 LL}{\partial\theta\partial\theta^T} = \begin{bmatrix} \frac{\partial^2 LL}{\partial\mu^2} & \frac{\partial^2 LL}{\partial\mu\partial\tau} \\ \frac{\partial^2 LL}{\partial\tau\partial\mu} & \frac{\partial^2 LL}{\partial\tau^2} \end{bmatrix}. \tag{2.42}$$

Without showing all the derivatives (see Exercises), the elements of the Hessian matrix are then:

$$\frac{\partial^2 LL}{\partial\theta\partial\theta^T} = \begin{bmatrix} \frac{-n}{\tau} & -\frac{n(\bar{x}-\mu)}{\tau^2} \\ -\frac{n(\bar{x}-\mu)}{\tau^2} & \frac{n}{2\tau^2} - \frac{\sum_{i=1}^{n}(x_i-\mu)^2}{\tau^3} \end{bmatrix}.$$

In order to obtain the information matrix, which can be used to compute the standard errors, we must take the expectation of this Hessian matrix and take its negative. Let's take the expectation of the off-diagonal elements first. The expectation of $\bar{x} - \mu$ is 0 (given that the MLE is unbiased), which makes the off-diagonal elements of the information matrix equal to 0. This result should be somewhat intuitive: There need be no relationship between the mean and variance in a normal distribution.

The first element, $(-n/\tau)$, is unchanged under expectation. Thus, after substituting σ^2 back in for τ and negating the result, we obtain n/σ^2 for this element of the information matrix.

The last element, $(n/2\tau^2) - (\sum_{i=1}^{n}(x_i - \mu)^2)/\tau^3$, requires a little consideration. The only part of this expression that changes under expectation is $\sum_{i=1}^{n}(x_i - \mu)^2$. The expectation of this expression is $n\tau$. That is, $E(x_i - \mu)^2 = \tau$, and we are taking this value n times (notice the summation). Thus, this element, after a little algebraic manipulation, negation, and substitution of σ^2 for τ, becomes: $n/2\sigma^4$. So, our information matrix appears as:

$$I(\theta) = \begin{bmatrix} \frac{n}{\sigma^2} & 0 \\ 0 & \frac{n}{2\sigma^4} \end{bmatrix}. \tag{2.43}$$

To obtain standard errors, we need to (1) invert this matrix, and (2) take the square root of the diagonal elements (variances) to obtain the standard errors. Matrix inversion in this case is quite simple, given that the off-diagonal elements are equal to 0. In this case, the inverse of the matrix is simply the inverse of the diagonal elements.

Once we invert and square root the elements of the information matrix, we find that the estimate for the standard error for our estimate $\hat{\mu}$ is $\hat{\sigma}/\sqrt{n}$, and our estimate for the standard error for $\hat{\sigma}^2$ is $\hat{\sigma}^2\sqrt{2/n}$. The estimate for the standard error for $\hat{\mu}$ should look familiar: It is the standard deviation of the sampling distribution for a mean based on the Central Limit Theorem (see Appendix B).

2.6 Conclusions

In this chapter, we have reviewed the basics of probability theory. Importantly, we have developed the concept of probability distributions in general, and we have discussed a number of actual probability distributions. In addition, we have discussed how important quantities like the mean and variance can be derived analytically from probability distributions. Finally, we reviewed the most common approach to estimating such quantities in a classical setting—maximum likelihood estimation—given a collection of data thought to arise from a particular distribution. As stated earlier, I recommend reading De-Groot (1986) for a more thorough introduction to probability theory, and I recommend Billingsley (1995) and Chung and AitSahlia (2003) for more advanced and detailed expositions. For a condensed exposition, I suggest Rudas 2004. Finally, I recommend Edwards (1992) and Gill (2002) for detailed discussions of the history and practice of maximum likelihood (ML) estimation, and I suggest Eliason (1993) for a highly applied perspective on ML estimation. In the next chapter, we will discuss the Bayesian approach to statistics as an alternative to this classical approach to model building and estimation.

2.7 Exercises

2.7.1 Probability exercises

1. Find the normalizing constant for the linear density in Equation 2.8.
2. Using the binomial mass function, find the probability of obtaining 3 heads in a row with a fair coin.
3. Find the probability of obtaining 3 heads in a row with a coin weighted so that the probability of obtaining a head is .7.
4. What is the probability of obtaining 3 heads OR 3 tails in a row with a fair coin?
5. What is the probability of obtaining 3 heads and 1 tail (order irrelevant) on four flips of a fair coin?
6. Using a normal approximation to the binomial distribution, find the probability of obtaining 130 or more heads in 200 flips of a fair coin.
7. Plot a normal distribution with parameters $\mu = 5$ and $\sigma = 2$.
8. Plot a normal distribution with parameters $\mu = 2$ and $\sigma = 5$.
9. Plot the $t(0, 1, df = 1)$ and $t(0, 1, df = 10)$ distributions. Note: Γ is a function. The function is: $\Gamma(n) = \int_0^\infty e^{-u} u^{n-1} du$. For integers, $\Gamma(n) = (n-1)!$. Thus, $\Gamma(4) = (4-1)! = 6$. However, when the argument to the function is not an integer, this formula will not work. Instead, it is easier to use a software package to compute the function value for you.

10. Show that the multivariate normal density function reduces to the univari-
    ate normal density function when the dimensionality of the distribution
    is 1.

2.7.2 Classical inference exercises

1. Find the MLE for p in a binomial distribution representing a sample in
   which 20 successes were obtained out of 30 trials.
2. Based on the binomial sample in the previous question, if the trials involved coin flips, would having 20 heads be sufficient to question the fairness of the coin? Why or why not?
3. Suppose a sample of students at a major university were given an IQ test,
   which resulted in a mean of 120 and a standard deviation of 10. If we
   know that IQs are normally distributed in the population with a mean of
   100 and a standard deviation of 16, is there sufficient evidence to suggest
   that the college students are more intelligent than average?
4. Suppose a single college student were given an IQ test and scored 120. Is
   there sufficient evidence to indicate that college students are more intelligent than average based on this sample?
5. What is the difference (if any) between the responses to the previous two
   questions?
6. Derive the Hessian matrix for the normal distribution example at the end
   of the chapter.
7. Derive the MLE for λ from a sample of n observations from a Poisson
   distribution.
8. Derive the standard error estimate for λ from the previous question.

3

Basics of Bayesian Statistics

Suppose a woman believes she may be pregnant after a single sexual encounter, but she is unsure. So, she takes a pregnancy test that is known to be 90% accurate—meaning it gives positive results to positive cases 90% of the time—and the test produces a positive result.[1] Ultimately, she would like to know the probability she is pregnant, given a positive test ($p(\text{preg} \mid \text{test} +)$); however, what she knows is the probability of obtaining a positive test result if she is pregnant ($p(\text{test} + \mid \text{preg})$), and she knows the result of the test.

In a similar type of problem, suppose a 30-year-old man has a positive blood test for a prostate cancer marker (PSA). Assume this test is also approximately 90% accurate. Once again, in this situation, the individual would like to know the probability that he has prostate cancer, given the positive test, but the information at hand is simply the probability of testing positive if he has prostate cancer, coupled with the knowledge that he tested positive.

Bayes' Theorem offers a way to reverse conditional probabilities and, hence, provides a way to answer these questions. In this chapter, I first show how Bayes' Theorem can be applied to answer these questions, but then I expand the discussion to show how the theorem can be applied to probability distributions to answer the type of questions that social scientists commonly ask. For that, I return to the polling data described in the previous chapter.

3.1 Bayes' Theorem for point probabilities

Bayes' original theorem applied to point probabilities. The basic theorem states simply:

$$p(B|A) = \frac{p(A|B)p(B)}{p(A)}. \tag{3.1}$$

---

[1] In fact, most pregnancy tests today have a higher accuracy rate, but the accuracy rate depends on the proper use of the test as well as other factors.

In English, the theorem says that a conditional probability for event B given event A is equal to the conditional probability of event A given event B, multiplied by the marginal probability for event B and divided by the marginal probability for event A.

Proof: From the probability rules introduced in Chapter 2, we know that $p(A, B) = p(A|B)p(B)$. Similarly, we can state that $p(B, A) = p(B|A)p(A)$. Obviously, $p(A, B) = p(B, A)$, so we can set the right sides of each of these equations equal to each other to obtain:

$$p(B|A)p(A) = p(A|B)p(B).$$

Dividing both sides by $p(A)$ leaves us with Equation 3.1.

The left side of Equation 3.1 is the conditional probability in which we are interested, whereas the right side consists of three components. $p(A|B)$ is the conditional probability we are interested in reversing. $p(B)$ is the unconditional (marginal) probability of the event of interest. Finally, $p(A)$ is the marginal probability of event A. This quantity is computed as the sum of the conditional probability of A under all possible events B_i in the sample space: Either the woman is pregnant or she is not. Stated mathematically for a discrete sample space:

$$p(A) = \sum_{B_i \in S_B} p(A \mid B_i)p(B_i).$$

Returning to the pregnancy example to make the theorem more concrete, suppose that, in addition to the 90% accuracy rate, we also know that the test gives false-positive results 50% of the time. In other words, in cases in which a woman is *not* pregnant, she will test positive 50% of the time. Thus, there are two possible events B_i: $B_1 =$ preg and $B_2 =$ not preg. Additionally, given the accuracy and false-positive rates, we know the conditional probabilities of obtaining a positive test under these events: $p(\text{test } +|\text{preg}) = .9$ and $p(\text{test } +|\text{not preg}) = .5$. With this information, combined with some "prior" information concerning the probability of becoming pregnant from a single sexual encounter, Bayes' theorem provides a prescription for determining the probability of interest.

The "prior" information we need, $p(B) \equiv p(\text{preg})$, is the marginal probability of being pregnant, not knowing anything beyond the fact that the woman has had a single sexual encounter. This information is considered prior information, because it is relevant information that exists prior to the test. We may know from previous research that, without any additional information (e.g., concerning date of last menstrual cycle), the probability of conception for any single sexual encounter is approximately 15%. (In a similar fashion, concerning the prostate cancer scenario, we may know that the prostate cancer incidence rate for 30-year-olds is .00001—see Exercises). With this information, we can determine $p(B \mid A) \equiv p(\text{preg}|\text{test } +)$ as:

$$p(\text{preg} \mid \text{test} +) = \frac{p(\text{test} + \mid \text{preg})p(\text{preg})}{p(\text{test} + \mid \text{preg})p(\text{preg}) + p(\text{test} + \mid \text{not preg})p(\text{not preg})}.$$

Filling in the known information yields:

$$p(\text{preg} \mid \text{test} +) = \frac{(.90)(.15)}{(.90)(.15) + (.50)(.85)} = \frac{.135}{.135 + .425} = .241.$$

Thus, the probability the woman is pregnant, given the positive test, is only .241. Using Bayesian terminology, this probability is called a "posterior probability," because it is the estimated probability of being pregnant obtained *after* observing the data (the positive test). The posterior probability is quite small, which is surprising, given a test with so-called 90% "accuracy." However, a few things affect this probability. First is the relatively low probability of becoming pregnant from a single sexual encounter (.15). Second is the extremely high probability of a false-positive test (.50), especially given the high probability of not becoming pregnant from a single sexual encounter ($p = .85$) (see Exercises).

If the woman is aware of the test's limitations, she may choose to repeat the test. Now, she can use the "updated" probability of being pregnant ($p = .241$) as the new $p(B)$; that is, the prior probability for being pregnant has now been updated to reflect the results of the first test. If she repeats the test and again observes a positive result, her new "posterior probability" of being pregnant is:

$$p(\text{preg} \mid \text{test} +) = \frac{(.90)(.241)}{(.90)(.241) + (.50)(.759)} = \frac{.135}{.135 + .425} = .364.$$

This result is still not very convincing evidence that she is pregnant, but if she repeats the test again and finds a positive result, her probability increases to .507 (for general interest, subsequent positive tests yield the following probabilities: test 4 = .649, test 5 = .769, test 6 = .857, test 7 = .915, test 8 = .951, test 9 = .972, test 10 = .984).

This process of repeating the test and recomputing the probability of interest is the basic process of concern in Bayesian statistics. From a Bayesian perspective, we begin with some prior probability for some event, and we update this prior probability with new information to obtain a posterior probability. The posterior probability can then be used as a prior probability in a subsequent analysis. From a Bayesian point of view, this is an appropriate strategy for conducting scientific research: We continue to gather data to evaluate a particular scientific hypothesis; we do not begin anew (ignorant) each time we attempt to answer a hypothesis, because previous research provides us with *a priori* information concerning the merit of the hypothesis.

3.2 Bayes' Theorem applied to probability distributions

Bayes' theorem, and indeed, its repeated application in cases such as the example above, is beyond mathematical dispute. However, Bayesian statistics
typically involves using probability *distributions* rather than point probabilities for the quantities in the theorem. In the pregnancy example, we assumed
the prior probability for pregnancy was a known quantity of exactly .15. However, it is unreasonable to believe that this probability of .15 is in fact this
precise. A cursory glance at various websites, for example, reveals a wide range
for this probability, depending on a woman's age, the date of her last men-
strual cycle, her use of contraception, etc. Perhaps even more importantly,
even if these factors were not relevant in determining the prior probability
for being pregnant, our knowledge of this prior probability is not likely to be
perfect because it is simply derived from previous samples and is not a known
and fixed population quantity (which is precisely why different sources may
give different estimates of this prior probability!). From a Bayesian perspective, then, we may replace this value of .15 with a distribution for the prior
pregnancy probability that captures our prior uncertainty about its true value.
The inclusion of a prior probability distribution ultimately produces a posterior probability that is also no longer a single quantity; instead, the posterior
becomes a probability distribution as well. This distribution combines the
information from the positive test with the prior probability distribution to
provide an updated distribution concerning our knowledge of the probability
the woman is pregnant.

Put generally, the goal of Bayesian statistics is to represent prior uncertainty about model parameters with a probability distribution and to update
this prior uncertainty with current data to produce a posterior probability distribution for the parameter that contains less uncertainty. This perspective
implies a subjective view of probability—probability represents uncertainty—
and it contrasts with the classical perspective. From the Bayesian perspective,
any quantity for which the true value is uncertain, including model parameters, can be represented with probability distributions. From the classical
perspective, however, it is unacceptable to place probability distributions on
parameters, because parameters are assumed to be fixed quantities: Only the
data are random, and thus, probability distributions can only be used to represent the data.

Bayes' Theorem, expressed in terms of probability distributions, appears
as:

$$f(\theta|\text{data}) = \frac{f(\text{data}|\theta)f(\theta)}{f(\text{data})}, \tag{3.2}$$

where $f(\theta|\text{data})$ is the posterior distribution for the parameter θ, $f(\text{data}|\theta)$
is the *sampling density* for the data—which is proportional to the Likeli-
hood function, only differing by a constant that makes it a proper density
function—$f(\theta)$ is the prior distribution for the parameter, and $f(\text{data})$ is the

marginal probability of the data. For a continuous sample space, this marginal probability is computed as:

$$f(\text{data}) = \int f(\text{data}|\theta) f(\theta) d\theta,$$

the integral of the sampling density multiplied by the prior over the sample space for θ. This quantity is sometimes called the "marginal likelihood" for the data and acts as a normalizing constant to make the posterior density proper (but see Raftery 1995 for an important use of this marginal likelihood). Because this denominator simply scales the posterior density to make it a proper density, and because the sampling density is proportional to the likelihood function, Bayes' Theorem for probability distributions is often stated as:

$$\text{Posterior} \propto \text{Likelihood} \times \text{Prior}, \tag{3.3}$$

where the symbol "$\propto$" means "is proportional to."

3.2.1 Proportionality

As Equation 3.3 shows, the posterior density is proportional to the likelihood function for the data (given the model parameters) multiplied by the prior for the parameters. The prior distribution is often—but not always—normalized so that it is a true density function for the parameter. The likelihood function, however, as we saw in the previous chapter, is not itself a density; instead, it is a product of densities and thus lacks a normalizing constant to make it a true density function. Consider, for example, the Bernoulli versus binomial specifications of the likelihood function for the dichotomous voting data. First, the Bernoulli specification lacked the combinatorial expression to make the likelihood function a true density function for either the data or the parameter. Second, although the binomial representation for the likelihood function constituted a true density function, it only constituted a true density *for the data* and not for the parameter p. Thus, when the prior distribution for a parameter is multiplied by the likelihood function, the result is also not a proper density function. Indeed, Equation 3.3 will be "off" by the denominator on the right side of Equation 3.2, in addition to whatever normalizing constant is needed to equalize the likelihood function and the sampling density $p(\text{data} \mid \theta)$.

Fortunately, the fact that the posterior density is only proportional to the product of the likelihood function and prior is not generally a problem in Bayesian analysis, as the remainder of the book will demonstrate. However, a note is in order regarding what proportionality actually means. In brief, if a is proportional to b, then a and b only differ by a multiplicative constant. How does this translate to probability distributions? First, we need to keep in mind that, in a Bayesian analysis, model parameters are considered random quantities, whereas the data, having been already observed, are considered fixed quantities. This view is completely opposite that assumed under the classical approach. Second, we need to recall from Chapter 2 that potential density functions often need to have a normalizing constant included to make them proper density functions, but we also need to recall that this normalzing constant only has the effect of scaling the density—it does not fundamentally change the relative frequencies of different values of the random variable. As we saw in Chapter 2, the normalizing constant is sometimes simply a true constant—a number—but sometimes the constant involves the random variable(s) themselves.

As a general rule, when considering a univariate density, any term, say Q (no matter how complicated), that can be factored away from the random variable in the density—so that all the term(s) involving the random variable are simply multiples of Q—can be considered an irrelevant proportionality constant and can be eliminated from the density without affecting the results.

In theory, this rule is fairly straightforward, but it is often difficult to apply for two key reasons. First, it is sometimes difficult to see whether a term can be factored out. For example, consider the following function for θ:

$$f(\theta) = e^{-\theta+Q}.$$

It may not be immediately clear that Q here is an arbitrary constant with respect to θ, but it is. This function can be rewritten as:

$$f(\theta) = e^{-\theta} \times e^{Q},$$

using the algebraic rule that $e^{a+b} = e^a e^b$. Thus, if we are considering $f(\theta)$ as a density function for θ, e^Q would be an arbitrary constant and could be removed without affecting inference about θ. Thus, we could state without loss of information that:

$$f(\theta) \propto e^{-\theta}.$$

In fact, this particular function, without Q, is an exponential density for θ with parameter $\beta = 1$ (see the end of this chapter). With Q, it is proportional to an exponential density; it simply needs a normalizing constant of e^{-Q} so that the function integrates to 1 over the sample space $S = \{\theta : \theta > 0\}$:

$$\int_0^\infty e^{-\theta+Q} \, d\theta = -\frac{1}{e^{\infty-Q}} + e^Q = e^Q.$$

Thus, given that this function integrates to e^Q, e^{-Q} renormalizes the integral to 1.

A second difficulty with this rule is that multivariate densities sometimes make it difficult to determine what is an irrelevant constant and what is not. With Gibbs sampling, as we will discuss in the next chapter and throughout the remainder of the book, we generally break down multivariate densities into univariate conditional densities. When we do this, we can consider all terms not involving the random variable to which the conditional density applies to be proportionality constants. I will show this shortly in the last example in this chapter.

3.3 Bayes' Theorem with distributions: A voting example

To make the notion of Bayes' Theorem applied to probability distributions concrete, consider the polling data from the previous chapter. In the previous chapter, we attempted to determine whether John F. Kerry would win the popular vote in Ohio, using the most recent CNN/USAToday/Gallup polling data. When we have a sample of data, such as potential votes for and against a candidate, and we assume they arise from a particular probability distribution, the construction of a likelihood function gives us the joint probability of the events, conditional on the parameter of interest: $p(\text{data}|\text{parameter})$. In the election polling example, we maximized this likelihood function to obtain a value for the parameter of interest—the proportion of Kerry voters in Ohio—that maximized the probability of obtaining the polling data we did. That estimated proportion (let's call it K to minimize confusion) was .521. We then determined how uncertain we were about our finding that $K = .521$. To be more precise, we determined under some assumptions how far K may reasonably be from .521 and still produce the polling data we observed.

This process of maximizing the likelihood function ultimately simply tells us how probable the data are under different values for K—indeed, that is precisely what a likelihood function *is* —but our ultimate question is really whether Kerry will win, given the polling data. Thus, our question of interest is "what is $p(K > .5)$," but the likelihood function gives us $p(\text{poll data} | K)$— that is, the probability of the data given different values of K.

In order to answer the question of interest, we need to apply Bayes' Theorem in order to obtain a posterior distribution for K and then evaluate $p(K > .5)$ using this distribution. Bayes' Theorem says:

$$f(K|\text{poll data}) \propto f(\text{poll data}|K)f(K),$$

or verbally: The posterior distribution for K, given the sample data, is proportional to the probability of the sample data, given K, multiplied by the prior probability for K. $f(\text{poll data}|K)$ is the likelihood function (or sampling density for the data). As we discussed in the previous chapter, it can be viewed as a binomial distribution with $x = 556$ "successes" (votes for Kerry) and $n - x = 511$ "failures" (votes for Bush), with $n = 1,067$ total votes between the two candidates. Thus,

$$f(\text{poll data}|K) \propto K^{556}(1 - K)^{511}.$$

What remains to be specified to complete the Bayesian development of the model is a prior probability distribution for K. The important question is: How do we do construct a prior?

3.3.1 Specification of a prior: The beta distribution

Specification of an appropriate prior distribution for a parameter is the most substantial aspect of a Bayesian analysis that differentiates it from a classical analysis. In the pregnancy example, the prior probability for pregnancy was said to be a point estimate of .15. However, as we discussed earlier, that specification did not consider that that prior probability is not known with complete certainty. Thus, if we wanted to be more realistic in our estimate of the posterior probability of pregnancy, we could compute the posterior probability under different values for the prior probability to obtain a collection of possible posterior probabilities that we could then consider and compare to determine which estimated posterior probability we thought was more reasonable. More efficiently, we could replace the point estimate of .15 with a probability distribution that represented (1) the plausible values of the prior probability of pregnancy and (2) their relative merit. For example, we may give considerable prior weight to the value .15 with diminishing weight to values of the prior probability that are far from .15.

Similarly, in the polling data example, we can use a distribution to represent our prior knowledge and uncertainty regarding K. An appropriate prior distribution for an unknown proportion such as K is a beta distribution. The pdf of the beta distribution is:

$$f(K \mid \alpha, \beta) = \frac{\Gamma(\alpha + \beta)}{\Gamma(\alpha)\Gamma(\beta)} K^{\alpha-1}(1 - K)^{\beta-1},$$

where $\Gamma(a)$ is the gamma function applied to a and $0 < K < 1$.[2] The parameters α and β can be thought of as prior "successes" and "failures," respectively. The mean and variance of a beta distribution are determined by these parameters:

$$E(K \mid \alpha, \beta) = \frac{\alpha}{\alpha + \beta}$$

and

$$\text{Var}(K \mid \alpha, \beta) = \frac{\alpha\beta}{(\alpha + \beta)^2(\alpha + \beta + 1)}.$$

This distribution looks similar to the binomial distribution we have already discussed. The key difference is that, whereas the random variable is x and the key parameter is K in the binomial distribution, the random variable is K and the parameters are α and β in the beta distribution. Keep in mind, however, from a Bayesian perspective, all unknown quantities can be considered random variables.

---

[2] The gamma function is the generalization of the factorial to nonintegers. For integers, $\Gamma(a) = (a - 1)!$. For nonintegers, $\Gamma(a) = \int_0^\infty x^{a-1} e^{-x} dx$. Most software packages will compute this function, but it is often unnecessary in practice, because it tends to be part of the normalizing constant in most problems.

How do we choose α and β for our prior distribution? The answer to this question depends on at least two factors. First, how much information prior to this poll do we have about the parameter K? Second, how much stock do we want to put into this prior information? These are questions that all Bayesian analyses must face, but contrary to the view that this is a limitation of Bayesian statistics, the incorporation of prior information can actually be an advantage and provides us considerable flexibility. If we have little or no prior information, or we want to put very little stock in the information we have, we can choose values for α and β that reduce the distribution to a uniform distribution. For example, if we let $\alpha = 1$ and $\beta = 1$, we get

$$f(p|\alpha = 1, \beta = 1) \propto K^{1-1=0}(1-K)^{1-1=0} = 1,$$

which is proportional to a uniform distribution on the allowable interval for K ([0,1]). That is, the prior distribution is flat, not producing greater *a priori* weight for any value of K over another. Thus, the prior distribution will have little effect on the posterior distribution. For this reason, this type of prior is called "noninformative."[3]

At the opposite extreme, if we have considerable prior information and we want it to weigh heavily relative to the current data, we can use large values of α and β. A little algebraic manipulation of the formula for the variance reveals that, as α and β increase, the variance decreases, which makes sense, because adding additional prior information *ought* to reduce our uncertainty about the parameter. Thus, adding more prior successes and failures (increasing both parameters) reduces prior uncertainty about the parameter of interest (K). Finally, if we have considerable prior information but we do not wish for it to weigh heavily in the posterior distribution, we can choose moderate values of the parameters that yield a mean that is consistent with the previous research but that also produce a variance around that mean that is broad.

Figure 3.1 displays some beta distributions with different values of α and β in order to clarify these ideas. All three displayed beta distributions have a mean of .5, but they each have different variances as a result of having α and β parameters of different magnitude. The most-peaked beta distribution has parameters $\alpha = \beta = 50$. The least-peaked distribution is actually flat— uniform—with parameters $\alpha = \beta = 1$. As with the binomial distribution, the beta distribution becomes skewed if α and β are unequal, but the basic idea is the same: the larger the parameters, the more prior information and the narrower the density.

Returning to the voting example, CNN/USAToday/Gallup had conducted three previous polls, the results of which could be treated as prior information.

---

[3] Virtually all priors, despite sometimes being called "noninformative," impart some information to the posterior distribution. Another way to say this is that claiming ignorance is, in fact, providing some information! However, flat priors generally have little weight in affecting posterior inference, and so they are called noninformative. See Box and Tiao 1973; Gelman et al. 1995; and Lee 1989.

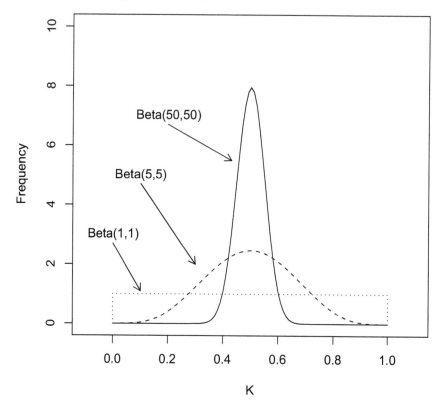

Fig. 3.1. Three beta distributions with mean $\alpha/(\alpha + \beta) = .5$.

These additional polling data are shown in Table 3.1.[4] If we consider these previous polls to provide us prior knowledge about the election, then our prior information consists of 1,008 (339 + 325 + 344) votes for Bush and 942 votes for Kerry (346 + 312 + 284) out of a total of 1,950 votes.

This prior information can be included by using a beta distribution with parameters $\alpha = 942$ and $\beta = 1008$:

$$f(K \mid \alpha, \beta) \propto K^{942-1}(1 - K)^{1008-1}.$$

---

[4] The data appear to show some trending, in the sense that the proportion stating that they would vote for Bush declined across time, whereas the proportion stating that they would vote for Kerry increased. This fact may suggest consideration of a more complex model than discussed here. Nonetheless, given a margin of error of ±4% for each of these additional polls, it is unclear whether the trend is meaningful. In other words, we could simply consider these polls as repeated samples from the same, unchanging population. Indeed, the website shows the results of 22 polls taken by various organizations, and no trending is apparent in the proportions from late September on.

Table 3.1. CNN/USAToday/Gallup 2004 presidential election polls.

Date	n	% for Bush	$\approx n$	% for Kerry	$\approx n$
Oct 17-20	706	48%	339	49%	346
Sep 25-28	664	49%	325	47%	312
Sep 4-7	661	52%	344	43%	284
TOTAL	2,031		1,008		942

Note: Proportions and candidate-specific sample sizes may not add to 100% of total sample n, because proportions opting for third-party candidates have been excluded.

After combining this prior with the binomial likelihood for the current sample, we obtain the following posterior density for K:

$$p(K \mid \alpha, \beta, x) \propto K^{556}(1 - K)^{511} K^{941}(1 - K)^{1007} = K^{1497}(1 - K)^{1518}.$$

This posterior density is also a beta density, with parameters $\alpha = 1498$ and $\beta = 1519$, and highlights the important concept of "conjugacy" in Bayesian statistics. When the prior and likelihood are of such a form that the posterior distribution follows the same form as the prior, the prior and likelihood are said to be conjugate. Historically, conjugacy has been very important to Bayesians, because, prior to the development of the methods discussed in this book, using conjugate priors/likelihoods with known forms ensured that the posterior would be a known distribution that could be easily evaluated to answer the scientific question of interest.

Figure 3.2 shows the prior, likelihood, and posterior densities. The likelihood function has been normalized as a proper density for K, rather than x. The figure shows that the posterior density is a compromise between the prior distribution and the likelihood (current data). The prior is on the left side of the figure; the likelihood is on the right side; and the posterior is between, but closer to the prior. The reason the posterior is closer to the prior is that the prior contained more information than the likelihood: There were 1,950 previously sampled persons and only 1,067 in the current sample.[5]

With the posterior density determined, we now can summarize our updated knowledge about K, the proportion of voters in Ohio who will vote for Kerry, and answer our question of interest: What is the probability that Kerry would win Ohio? A number of summaries are possible, given that we have a posterior distribution with a known form (a beta density). First, the mean of K is $1498/(1498 + 1519) = .497$, and the median is also .497 (found using the qbeta function in R). The variance of this beta distribution is .00008283 (standard deviation=.0091). If we are willing to assume that this beta distribution is approximately normal, then we could construct a 95% interval based on a normal approximation and conclude that the proportion of Ohio voters

---

[5] This movement of the posterior distribution away from the prior and toward the likelihood is sometimes called "Bayesian shrinkage" (see Gelman et al. 1995).

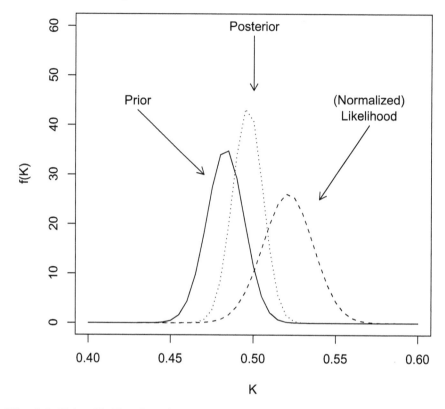

Fig. 3.2. Prior, likelihood, and posterior for polling data example: The likelihood function has been normalized as a density for the parameter K.

who would vote for Kerry falls between .479 and .515 (.497±1.96×.0091). This interval is called a "credible interval," a "posterior probability interval," or a "probability interval," and it has a simpler interpretation than the classical confidence interval. Using this interval, we can say simply that the proportion K falls in this interval with probability .95.

If, on the other hand, we are not willing to assume that this posterior density is approximately normal, we can directly compute a 95% probability interval by selecting the lower and upper values of this beta density that produce the desired interval. That is, we can determine the values of this beta density below which 2.5% of the distribution falls and above which 2.5% of the distribution falls. These values are .479 and .514, which are quite close to those under the normal approximation.

These results suggest that, even with the prior information, the election may have been too close to call, given that the interval estimate for K captures .5. However, the substantive question—what is the probability that Kerry would win—can also be answered within the Bayesian framework. This probability is the probability that Kerry will get more than half of the votes, which is simply the probability that $K > .5$. This probability can be directly computed from the beta distribution as the integral of this density from .5 to 1 (the mass of the curve to the right of .5; see Figure 3.3). The result is .351, which means that Kerry did not have a favorable chance to win Ohio, given the complete polling data.

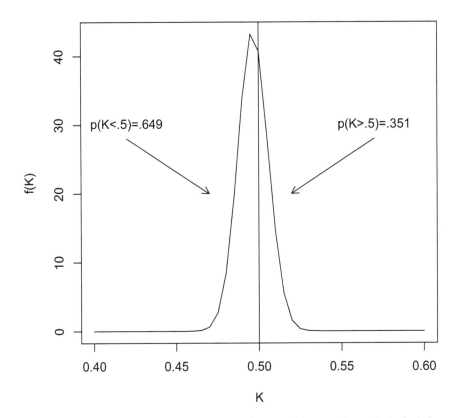

Fig. 3.3. Posterior for polling data example: A vertical line at $K = .5$ is included to show the area needed to be computed to estimate the probability that Kerry would win Ohio.

In fact, Kerry did not win Ohio; he obtained 48.9% of the votes cast for either Kerry or Bush. The classical analysis did not yield this conclusion: It simply suggested that the results were too close to call. The Bayesian analysis, on the other hand, while recognizing that the election would be close, suggested that there was not a very high probability that Kerry would win. The price that had to be paid for reaching this conclusion, however, was (1) we had to be willing to specify a prior probability for K, and (2) we had to be willing to treat the parameter of interest as a random, and not a fixed, quantity.

3.3.2 An alternative model for the polling data: A gamma prior/ Poisson likelihood approach

In this section, I repeat the analysis from the previous section. However, instead of considering the problem as a binomial problem with the proportion parameter p, I consider the problem as a Poisson distribution problem with rate parameter λ. As we discussed in the previous chapter, the Poisson distribution is a distribution for count variables; we can consider an individual's potential vote for Kerry as a discrete count that takes values of either 0 or 1. From that perspective, the likelihood function for the 1,067 sample members in the most recent survey prior to the election is:

$$L(\lambda|Y) = \prod_{i=1}^{1067} \frac{\lambda^{y_i} e^{-\lambda}}{y_i!} = \frac{\lambda^{\sum_{i=1}^{1067} y_i} e^{-1067\lambda}}{\prod_{i=1}^{1067} y_i!},$$

where y_i is the 0 (Bush) or 1 (Kerry) vote of the ith individual.

As in the binomial example, we would probably like to include the previous survey data in our prior distribution. A conjugate prior for the Poisson distribution is a gamma distribution. The pdf of the gamma distribution is as follows. If $x \sim \text{gamma}(\alpha, \beta)$, then:

$$f(x) = \frac{\beta^\alpha}{\Gamma(\alpha)} x^{\alpha-1} e^{-\beta x}.$$

The parameters α and β in the gamma distribution are shape and inverse-scale parameters, respectively. The mean of a gamma distribution is α/β, and the variance is α/β^2. Figure 3.4 shows four different gamma distributions. As the plot shows, the distribution is very flexible: Slight changes in the α and β parameters—which can take any non-negative value—yield highly variable shapes and scales for the density.

For the moment, we will leave α and β unspecified in our voting model so that we can see how they enter into the posterior distribution. If we combine this gamma prior with the likelihood function, we obtain:

$$p(\lambda \mid Y) \propto \left(\frac{\beta^\alpha}{\Gamma(\alpha)}\right) \lambda^{\alpha-1} e^{-\beta\lambda} \left(\frac{1}{\prod_{i=1}^{1067} y_i!}\right) \lambda^{\sum_{i=1}^{1067} y_i} e^{-1067\lambda}.$$

This expression can be simplified by combining like terms and excluding the arbitrary proportionality constants (the terms in parentheses, which do not include λ) to obtain:

$$p(\lambda \mid y) \propto \lambda^{\sum_{i=1}^{1067} y_i + \alpha - 1} e^{-(1067+\beta)\lambda}.$$

Given that each y_i is either a 0 (vote for Bush) or 1 (vote for Kerry), $\sum_{i=1}^{1067} y_i$ is simply the count of votes for Kerry in the current sample (=556). Thus, just as in the binomial example, the parameters α and β—at least in this

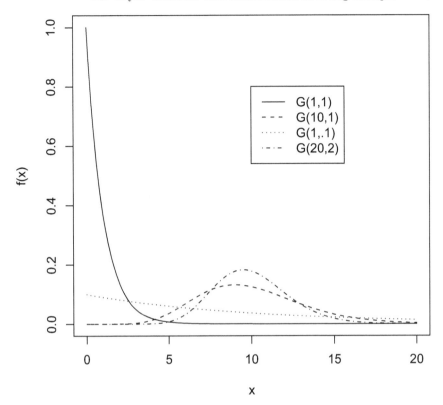

Fig. 3.4. Some examples of the gamma distribution.

particular model—appear to capture prior "successes" and "failures." Specifically, α is the count of prior "successes," and β is the total number of prior observations. The mean of the gamma distribution (α/β) also supports this conclusion. Thus, as in the beta prior/binomial likelihood example, if we want to incorporate the data from previous survey into the prior distribution, we can set $\alpha = 942$ and $\beta = 942 + 1008 = 1950$ to obtain the following posterior:

$$p(\lambda \mid Y) \propto \lambda^{556+942-1}e^{-(1067+1950)\lambda} = \lambda^{1497}e^{-3017\lambda}.$$

Thus, the posterior density is also a gamma density with parameters $\alpha = 1498$ and $\beta = 3017$. Because the gamma density is a known density, we can immediately compute the posterior mean and standard deviation for λ: $\bar{\lambda} = .497$; $\hat{\sigma}_\lambda = .0128$. If we wish to construct a 95% probability/credible interval for λ, and we are willing to make a normal approximation given the large sample size, we can construct the interval as $.497 \pm 1.96 \times .0128$. This result gives us an interval estimate of $[.472, .522]$ for λ. On the other hand, if we wish to compute the interval directly using integration of the gamma density (i.e., the cdf for the gamma distribution), we obtain an interval of $[.472, .522]$.

In this case, the normal-theory interval and the analytically derived interval are the same when rounded to three decimal places.

How does this posterior inference compare with that obtained using the beta prior/binomial likelihood approach? The means for K in the beta/binomial approach and for λ in the gamma/Poisson approach are identical. The intervals are also quite comparable, but the interval in this latter approach is wider—about 42% wider. If we wish to determine the probability that Kerry would win Ohio, we simply need to compute $p(\lambda > .5)$, which equals .390. Thus, under this model, Kerry had a probability of winning of .390, which is still an unfavorable result, although it is a slightly greater probability than the beta/binomial result of .351.

Which model is to be preferred? In this case, the substantive conclusion we reached was comparable for the two models: Kerry was unlikely to win Ohio. So, it does not matter which model we choose. The fact that the two models produced comparable results is reassuring, because the conclusion does not appear to be very sensitive to choice of model. Ultimately, however, we should probably place greater emphasis on the beta/binomial model, because the Poisson distribution is a distribution for counts, and our data, which consisted of dichotomous outcomes, really does not fit the bill. Consider the parameter λ: There is no guarantee with the gamma/Poisson setup that λ will be less than 1. This lack of limit could certainly be problematic if we had less data, or if the underlying proportion favoring Kerry were closer to 1. In such a case, the upper bound on the interval for λ may have exceeded 1, and our results would therefore be suspect. In this particular case, however, we had enough data and prior information that ultimately made the interval width very narrow, and so the bounding problem was not an issue. Nonetheless, the beta/binomial setup is a more natural model for the voting data.

3.4 A normal prior–normal likelihood example with σ^2 known

The normal distribution is one of the most common distributions used in statistics by social scientists, in part because many social phenomena in fact follow a normal distribution. Thus, it is not uncommon for a social scientist to use a normal distribution as the basis for a likelihood function for a set of data. Here, I develop a normal distribution problem, but for the sake of keeping this example general for use in later chapters, I used a contrived scenario and keep the mathematics fairly general. The purpose at this point is simply to illustrate a Bayesian approach with a multivariate posterior distribution.[6]

---

[6] The normal distribution involves two parameters: the mean (μ) and variance (σ^2). When considered as a density for x, it is univariate, but when a normal likelihood and some prior for the parameters are combined, the result is a joint posterior distribution for μ and σ^2, which makes the posterior a multivariate density.

Suppose that we have a class of 30 students who have recently taken a midterm exam, and the mean grade was $\bar{x} = 75$ with a standard deviation of $\sigma = 10$. Note that for now we have assumed that the variance is known, hence, the use of σ rather than s. We have taught the course repeatedly, semester after semester, and past test means have given us an overall mean μ of 70, but the class means have varied from class to class, giving us a standard deviation for the class means of $\tau = 5$. That is, τ reflects how much our class means have varied and does not directly reflect the variability of individual test scores. We will discuss this more in depth momentarily.

Our goal is ultimately to update our knowledge of μ, the unobservable population mean test score with the new test grade data. In other words, we wish to find $f(\mu|x)$. Bayes' Theorem tells us that:

$$f(\mu|X) \propto f(X|\mu)f(\mu),$$

where $f(X|\mu)$ is the likelihood function for the current data, and $f(\mu)$ is the prior for the test mean. (At the moment, I am omitting σ^2 from the notation). If we assume the current test scores are normally distributed with a mean equal to μ and variance σ^2, then our likelihood function for X is:

$$f(X|\mu) \propto L(\mu|X) = \prod_{i=1}^{n} \frac{1}{\sqrt{2\pi\sigma^2}} \exp\left\{-\frac{(x_i - \mu)^2}{2\sigma^2}\right\}.$$

Furthermore, our previous test results have provided us with an overall mean of 70, but we are uncertain about μ's actual value, given that class means vary semester by semester (giving us $\tau = 5$). So our prior distribution for μ is:

$$f(\mu) = \frac{1}{\sqrt{2\pi\tau^2}} \exp\left\{-\frac{(\mu - M)^2}{2\tau^2}\right\},$$

where in this expression, μ is the random variable, with M as the prior mean ($=70$), and τ^2 ($=25$) reflects the variation of μ around M.

Our posterior is the product of the likelihood and prior, which gives us:

$$f(\mu|X) \propto \frac{1}{\sqrt{\tau^2\sigma^2}} \exp\left\{\frac{-(\mu - M)^2}{2\tau^2} + \frac{-\sum_{i=1}^{n}(x_i - \mu)^2}{2\sigma^2}\right\}.$$

This posterior can be reexpressed as a normal distribution for μ, but it takes some algebra in order to see this. First, since the terms outside the exponential are simply normalizing constants with respect to μ, we can drop them and work with the terms inside the exponential function. Second, let's expand the quadratic components and the summations. For the sake of simplicty, I temporarily drop the exponential function in this expression:

$$(-1/2)\left[\frac{\mu^2 - 2\mu M + M^2}{\tau^2} + \frac{\sum x^2 - 2n\bar{x}\mu + n\mu^2}{\sigma^2}\right].$$

Using this expression, any term that does not include μ can be viewed as a proportionality constant, can be factored out of the exponent, and can be dropped (recall that $e^{a+b} = e^a e^b$). After obtaining common denominators for the remaining terms by cross-multiplying by each of the individual denominators and dropping proportionality constants, we are left with:

$$(-1/2)\left[\frac{\sigma^2\mu^2 - 2\sigma^2\mu M - 2\tau^2 n\bar{x}\mu + \tau^2 n\mu^2}{\sigma^2\tau^2}\right].$$

From here, we need to combine terms involving μ^2 and those involving μ:

$$(-1/2)\left[\frac{(n\tau^2 + \sigma^2)\mu^2 - 2(\sigma^2 M + \tau^2 n\bar{x})\mu}{\sigma^2\tau^2}\right].$$

Dividing the numerator and denominator of this fraction by the $(n\tau^2 + \sigma^2)$ in front of μ^2 yields:

$$(-1/2)\left[\frac{\mu^2 - 2\mu\frac{(\sigma^2 M + n\tau^2\bar{x})}{(n\tau^2 + \sigma^2)}}{\frac{\sigma^2\tau^2}{(n\tau^2 + \sigma^2)}}\right].$$

Finally, all we need to do is to complete the square in μ and discard any remaining constants to obtain:

$$(-1/2)\left[\frac{\left(\mu - \frac{(\sigma^2 M + n\tau^2\bar{x})}{(n\tau^2 + \sigma^2)}\right)^2}{\frac{\sigma^2\tau^2}{(n\tau^2 + \sigma^2)}}\right].$$

This result shows that our updated μ is normally distributed with mean $(\sigma^2 M + \tau^2 n\bar{x})/(n\tau^2 + \sigma^2)$ and variance $(\sigma^2\tau^2)/(n\tau^2 + \sigma^2)$. Notice how the posterior mean is a weighted combination of the prior mean and the sample mean. The prior mean is multiplied by the known variance of test scores in the sample, σ^2, whereas the sample mean $\bar{x}$ is multiplied by n and by the prior variance τ^2. This shows first that the sample mean will tend to have more weight than the prior mean (because of the n multiple), but also that the prior and sample variances affect the weighting of the means. If the sample variance is large, then the prior mean has considerable weight in the posterior; if the prior variance is large, the sample mean has considerable weight in the posterior. If the two quantities are equal ($\sigma^2 = \tau^2$), then the calculation reduces to $(M + n\bar{x})/(n+1)$, which means that the prior mean will only have a weight of $1/(n+1)$ in the posterior.

In this particular example, our posterior mean would be:

$$(100 \times 70) + (25 \times 30 \times 75)/(30 \times 25 + 100) = 74.4.$$

Thus, our result is clearly more heavily influenced by the sample data than by the prior. One thing that must be kept in mind but is easily forgotten is that our updated variance parameter (which is 20—the standard deviation is therefore 4.47) reflects our uncertainty about μ. This estimate is smaller than both the prior variance and the sample variance, and it is much closer to τ^2 than to σ^2. Why? Again, this quantity reflects how much μ varies (or, put another way, how much uncertainty we have in knowing M, the true value of μ) and not how much we know about any particular sample. Thus, the fact that our sample standard deviation was 10 does not play a large role in changing our minds about uncertainty in μ, especially given that the sample mean was not that different from the prior mean. In other words, our sample mean is sufficiently close to our prior mean μ so that we are unconvinced that the variance of μ around M should be larger than it was. Indeed, the data convince us that our prior variance should actually be smaller, because the current sample mean is well within the range around M implied by our prior value for τ.

3.4.1 Extending the normal distribution example

The natural extension of the previous example in which the variance σ^2 was considered known is to consider the more realistic case in which the variance is not known. Recall that, ultimately in the previous example, we were interested in the quantity μ—the overall mean test score. Previous data had given us an estimate of μ, but we were still uncertain about its value, and thus, we used τ to represent our uncertainty in μ. We considered σ^2 to be a known quantity (10). In reality, we typically do not know σ^2 any more than we know μ, and thus we have two quantities of interest that we should be updating with new information. A full probability model for μ and σ^2 would look like:

$$f(\mu, \sigma^2 | x) \propto f(x | \mu, \sigma^2) f(\mu, \sigma^2).$$

This model is similar to the one in the example above, but we have now explicitly noted that σ^2 is also an unknown quantity, by including it in the prior distribution. Therefore, we now need to specify a joint prior for both μ and σ^2, and not just a prior for μ. If we assume μ and σ^2 are independent—and this is a reasonable assumption as we mentioned in the previous chapter; there's no reason the two parameters need be related—then we can consider $p(\mu, \sigma^2) = p(\mu)p(\sigma^2)$ and establish separate priors for each.

In the example above, we established the prior for μ to be $\mu \sim N(M, \tau^2)$, where M was the prior mean (70) and τ^2 was the measure of uncertainty we had in μ. We did not, however, specify a prior for σ^2, but we used σ^2 to update our knowledge of τ.[7]

How do we specify a prior distribution for μ and σ^2 in a more general case? Unlike in the previous example, we often do not have prior information about these parameters, and so we often wish to develop noninformative priors for

---

[7] Recall from the CLT that $\bar{x} \sim N(\mu, \sigma^2/n)$; thus σ^2 and τ^2 are related: σ^2/n should be an estimate for τ^2, and so treating σ^2 as fixed yields an updated τ^2 that depends heavily on the new sample data.

them. There are several ways to do this in the normal distribution problem, but two of the most common approaches lead to the same prior. One approach is to assign a uniform prior over the real line for μ and the same uniform prior for $\log(\sigma^2)$. We assign a uniform prior on $\log(\sigma^2)$ because σ^2 is a nonnegative quantity, and the transformation to $\log(\sigma^2)$ stretches this new parameter across the real line. If we transform the uniform prior on $\log(\sigma^2)$ into a density for σ^2, we obtain $p(\sigma^2) \propto 1/\sigma^2$.[8] Thus, our joint prior is: $p(\mu, \sigma^2) \propto 1/\sigma^2$.

A second way to obtain this prior is to give μ and σ^2 proper prior distributions (not uniform over the real line, which is improper). If we continue with the assumption that $\mu \sim N(M, \tau^2)$, we can choose values of M and τ^2 that yield a flat distribution. For example, if we let $\mu \sim N(0, 10000)$, we have a very flat prior for μ. We can also choose a relatively noninformative prior for σ^2 by first noting that variance parameters follow an inverse gamma distribution (see the next section) and then choosing values for the inverse gamma distribution that produce a noninformative prior. If $\sigma^2 \sim IG(a, b)$, the pdf appears as:

$$f(\sigma^2 | a, b) \propto (\sigma^2)^{-(a+1)} e^{-\beta/(\sigma^2)}.$$

In the limit, if we let the parameters a and b approach 0, a noninformative prior is obtained as $1/\sigma^2$. Strictly speaking, however, if a and b are 0, the distribution is improper, but we can let both parameters *approach* 0. We can then use this as our prior for σ^2 (that is, $\sigma^2 \sim IG(0, 0); p(\sigma^2) \propto 1/\sigma^2$). There are other ways to arrive at this choice for the prior distribution for μ and σ, but I will not address them here (see Gelman et al. 1995).

The resulting posterior for μ and σ^2, if we assume a joint prior of $1/\sigma^2$ for these parameters, is:

$$f(\mu, \sigma^2 | X) \propto \frac{1}{\sigma^2} \prod_{i=1}^{n} \frac{1}{\sqrt{2\pi\sigma^2}} \exp\left\{ -\frac{(x_i - \mu)^2}{2\sigma^2} \right\}. \tag{3.4}$$

Unlike in the previous example, however, this is a joint posterior density for two parameters rather than one. Yet we can determine the *conditional* posterior distributions for both parameters, using the rule discussed in the previous chapter that, generally, $f(x|y) \propto f(x, y)$.

Determining the form for the posterior density for μ follows the same logic as in the previous section. First, we carry out the product over all observations. Next, we expand the quadratic, eliminate terms that are constant with respect to μ and rearrange the terms with the μ^2 term first. Doing so yields:

---

[8] This transformation of variables involves a Jacobian, as discussed in the previous chapter. Let $m = \log(\sigma^2)$, and let $p(m) \propto$ constant. Then $p(\sigma^2) \propto$ constant $\times J$, where J is the Jacobian of the transformation from m to σ^2. The Jacobian is then $dm/d\sigma^2 = 1/\sigma^2$. See DeGroot (1986) for a fuller exposition of this process, and see any introductory calculus book for a general discussion of transformations of variables. See Gelman et al. 1995 for further discussion of this prior.

$$f(\mu|X,\sigma^2) \propto \exp\left\{-\frac{n\mu^2 - 2n\bar{x}\mu}{2\sigma^2}\right\}.$$

Next, to isolate μ^2, we can divide the numerator and denominator by n. Finally, we can complete the square in μ to find:

$$f(\mu|X,\sigma^2) \propto \exp\left\{-\frac{(\mu - \bar{x})^2}{2\sigma^2/n}\right\}.$$

This result shows us that the conditional distribution for $\mu|X,\sigma^2 \sim N(\bar{x}, \frac{\sigma^2}{n})$, which should look familiar. That is, this is a similar result to what the Central Limit Theorem in classical statistics claims regarding the sampling distribution for $\bar{x}$.

What about the posterior distribution for σ^2? There are at least two ways to approach this derivation. First, we could consider the conditional distribution for $\sigma^2|\mu, X$. If we take this approach, then we again begin with the full posterior density, but we now must consider all terms that involve σ^2. If we carry out the multiplication in the posterior density and combine like terms, we obtain:

$$f(\mu, \sigma^2) \propto \frac{1}{(\sigma^2)^{n/2+1}} \exp\left\{-\frac{\sum(x_i - \mu)^2}{2\sigma^2}\right\}.$$

Referring back to the above description of the inverse gamma distribution, it is clear that, if μ is considered fixed, the conditional posterior density for σ^2 is inverse gamma with parameters $a = n/2$ and $b = \sum(x_i - \mu)^2/2$.

A second way to approach this problem is to consider that the joint posterior density for μ and σ^2 can be factored using the conditional probability rule as:

$$f(\mu, \sigma^2|X) = f(\mu|\sigma^2, X)f(\sigma^2|X).$$

The first term on the right-hand side we have already considered in the previous example with σ^2 considered to be a known, fixed quantity. The latter term, however, is the *marginal* posterior density for σ^2. Technically, an exact expression for it can be found by integrating the joint posterior density over μ (i.e., $\int f(\mu, \sigma^2)d\mu$.) (see Gelman et al. 1995). Alternatively, we can find an expression proportional to it by factoring Equation 3.4. We know that the distribution for $\mu|\sigma^2, X$ is proportional to a normal density with mean $\bar{x}$ and variance σ^2/n. Thus, if we factor this term out of the posterior, what is left is proportional to the marginal density for σ^2.

In order to factor the posterior, first, expand the quadratic again to obtain:

$$\frac{1}{(\sigma^2)^{n/2+1}} \exp\left\{-\frac{\sum x_i^2 - 2n\bar{x}\mu + n\mu^2}{2\sigma^2}\right\}.$$

Next, rearrange terms to put μ^2 first, and divide the numerator and denominator by n. Once again, complete the square to obtain:

$$\frac{1}{(\sigma^2)^{n/2+1}} \exp\left\{-\frac{(\mu - \bar{x})^2 + \sum x_i^2/n - \bar{x}^2}{2\sigma^2/n}\right\}.$$

We can now separate the two parts of the exponential to obtain:

$$\frac{1}{\sigma} \exp\left\{-\frac{(\mu - \bar{x})^2}{2\sigma^2/n}\right\} \times \frac{1}{(\sigma^2)^{n/2}} \exp\left\{\frac{\sum x_i^2 - n\bar{x}^2}{2\sigma^2}\right\}.$$

The first term is the conditional posterior for μ. The latter term is proportional to the marginal posterior density for σ^2. The numerator in the exponential is the numerator for the computational version of the sample variance, $\sum(x_i - \bar{x})^2$, and so, the result is recognizable as an inverse gamma distribution with parameters $a = (n-1)/2$ and $b = (n-1)\text{var}(x)/2$.

3.5 Some useful prior distributions

Thus far, we have discussed the use of a beta prior for proportion parameter p combined with a binomial likelihood function, a gamma prior for a Poisson rate parameter λ, a normal prior for a mean parameter combined with a normal likelihood function for the case in which the variance parameter σ^2 was assumed to be known, and a reference prior of $1/\sigma^2$—a special case of an inverse gamma distribution—for a normal likelihood function for the case in which neither μ nor σ^2 were assumed to be known. In this section, I discuss a few additional distributions that are commonly used as priors for parameters in social science models. These distributions are commonly used as priors, because they are conjugate for certain sampling densities/likelihood functions. Specifically, I discuss the Dirichlet, the inverse gamma (in some more depth), and the Wishart and inverse Wishart distributions.

One thing that must be kept in mind when considering distributions as priors and/or sampling densities is *what symbols in the density are parameters versus what symbols are the random variables*. For example, take the binomial distribution discussed in Chapter 2. In the binomial mass function, the random variable is represented by x, whereas the parameter is represented by p. However, in the beta distribution, the random variable is represented by p and the parameters are α and β. From a Bayesian perspective, parameters *are* random variables or at least can be treated as such. Thus, what is important to realize is that we may need to change notation in the pdf so that we maintain the appropriate notation for representing the prior distribution for the parameter(s). For example, if we used θ to represent the parameter p in the binomial likelihood function, while p is used as the random variable in the beta distribution, the two distributions, when multiplied together, would contain p, θ, and x, and it would be unclear how θ and p were related. In fact, in the beta-binomial setup, $\theta = p$, but we need to make sure our notation is clear so that that can be immediately seen.

3.5.1 The Dirichlet distribution

Just as the multinomial distribution is a multivariate extension of the binomial distribution, the Dirichlet distribution is a multivariate generalization of the beta distribution. If X is a k-dimensional vector and $X \sim$ Dirichlet$(\alpha_1, \alpha_2, \ldots, \alpha_k)$, then:

$$f(X) = \frac{\Gamma(\alpha_1 + \ldots + \alpha_k)}{\Gamma(\alpha_1) \ldots \Gamma(\alpha_k)} x_1^{\alpha_1 - 1} \ldots x_k^{\alpha_k - 1}.$$

Just as the beta distribution is a conjugate prior for the binomial distribution, the Dirichlet is a conjugate prior for the multinomial distribution. We can see this result clearly, if we combine a Dirichlet distribution as a prior with a multinomial distribution likelihood:

$$
\begin{aligned}
f(p_1 \ldots p_k | X) &\propto f(X | p_1 \ldots p_k) f(p_1 \ldots p_k) \\
&\propto \text{Multinomial}(X | p_1 \ldots p_k) \text{Dirichlet}(p_1 \ldots p_k | \alpha_1 \ldots \alpha_k) \\
&\propto \text{Dirichlet}(p_1 \ldots p_k | \alpha_1 + x_1, \alpha_2 + x_2, \ldots, \alpha_k + x_k) \\
&\propto p_1^{\alpha_1 + x_1 - 1} p_2^{\alpha_2 + x_2 - 1} \ldots p_k^{\alpha_k + x_k - 1}.
\end{aligned}
$$

Notice how here, as we discussed at the beginning of the section, the vector X in the original specification of the Dirichlet pdf has been changed to a vector p. In this specification, p is the random variable in the Dirichlet distribution, whereas $\alpha_1 \ldots \alpha_k$ are the parameters representing prior counts of outcomes in each of the k possible outcome categories.

Also observe how the resulting Dirichlet posterior distribution looks just like the resulting beta posterior distribution, only with more possible outcomes.

3.5.2 The inverse gamma distribution

We have already discussed the gamma distribution in the Poisson/gamma example, and we have briefly discussed the inverse gamma distribution. If $1/x \sim \text{gamma}(\alpha, \beta)$, then $x \sim \text{IG}(\alpha, \beta)$. The density function for the inverse gamma distribution is:

$$f(x) = \frac{\beta^\alpha}{\Gamma(\alpha)} x^{-(\alpha+1)} e^{-\beta/x},$$

with $x > 0$. Just as in the gamma distribution, the parameters α and β affect the shape and scale of the curve (respectively), and both must be greater than 0 to make the density proper.

As discussed earlier, the inverse gamma distribution is used as a conjugate prior for the variance in a normal model. If the normal distribution is parameterized with a precision parameter rather than with a variance parameter, where the precision parameter is simply the inverse of the variance, the gamma distribution is appropriate as a conjugate prior distribution for the precision parameter. In a normal model, if an inverse gamma distribution is used as the prior for the variance, the marginal distribution for the mean is a t distribution.

The gamma and inverse gamma distributions are general distributions; other distributions arise by fixing the parameters to specific values. For example, if α is set to 1, the exponential distribution results:

$$f(x) = (1/\beta)e^{-x/\beta},$$

or, more commonly $f(x) = \beta e^{-\beta x}$, where β is an inverse scale parameter. Under this parameterization, $\beta_{\text{inverse scale}} = 1/\beta_{\text{scale}}$.

If α is set to $v/2$, where v is the degrees of freedom, and β is set to $1/2$, the chi-square distribution results. Setting the parameters equal to the same value in the inverse-gamma distribution yields an inverse-chi-square distribution.

3.5.3 Wishart and inverse Wishart distributions

The Wishart and inverse Wishart distributions are complex in appearance; they are multivariate generalizations of the gamma and inverse gamma distributions, respectively. Thus, just as the inverse gamma is a conjugate prior density for the variance in a univariate normal model, the inverse Wishart is a conjugate prior density for the variance-covariance matrix in a multivariate normal model. With an inverse Wishart distribution for the variance-covariance matrix in a multivariate normal model, the marginal distribution for the mean vector is multivariate t.

If $X \sim \text{Wishart}(S)$, where S is a scale matrix of dimension d, then

$$f(X) \propto |X|^{(v-d-1)/2} \exp\left\{-\frac{1}{2}\text{tr}(S^{-1}X)\right\},$$

where v is the degrees of freedom.

If $X \sim \text{inverse Wishart}(S^{-1})$, then:

$$f(X) \propto |X|^{-(v+d+1)/2} \exp\left\{-\frac{1}{2}\text{tr}(SX^{-1})\right\}.$$

The assumption for both the Wishart and inverse Wishart distributions is that X and S are both positive definite; that is, $z^T X z > 0$ and $z^T S z > 0$ for any non-zero vector z of length d.

3.6 Criticism against Bayesian statistics

As we have seen in the examples, the development of a Bayesian model requires the inclusion of a prior distribution for the parameters in the model. The notion of using prior research or other information to inform a current analysis and to produce an updated prior for subsequent use seems quite reasonable, if not very appropriate, for the advancement of research toward a more refined knowledge of the parameters that govern social processes. However, the Bayesian approach to updating knowledge of parameters has been criticized on philosophical grounds for more than a century, providing one reason its adoption has been relatively limited in mainstream social science research.

What is in philosophical dispute between Bayesians and classical statisticians includes: (1) whether data and hypotheses (which are simply statements about parameters of distributions[9]) can hold the same status as random variables, and (2) whether the use of a prior probability injects too much subjectivity into the modeling process.

The first standard argument presented against the Bayesian approach is that, because parameters are fixed, it is unreasonable to place a probability distribution on them (they simply are what they are). More formally, parameters and data cannot share the same sample space. However, recall that the Bayesian perspective on probability is that probability is a subjective approach to uncertainty. Whether a parameter is indeed fixed, to a Bayesian, is irrelevant, because we are still uncertain about its true value. Thus, imposing a probability distribution over a parameter space is reasonable, because it provides a method to reflect our uncertainty about the parameter's true value.

Bayesians argue that doing so has some significant advantages. First, as we have seen, Bayesian interval estimates have a clearer and more direct interpretation than classical confidence intervals. That is, we can directly conclude that a parameter falls in some interval with some probability. This is a common but incorrect interpretation of classical confidence intervals, which simply reflect the probability of obtaining an interval estimate that contains the parameter of interest under repeated sampling. Second, the Bayesian approach can naturally incorporate the findings of previous research with the prior, whereas the classical approach to statistics really has no coherent means of using previous results in current analyses beyond assisting with the specification of a hypothesis. That is, the Bayesian approach formalizes the process of hypothesis construction by incorporating it as part of the model. Third, the Bayesian approach more easily allows more detailed summaries concerning parameters. Instead of simply obtaining a maximum likelihood estimate and standard error, we have an entire distribution that can be summarized using various measures (e.g., mean, median, mode, and interquartile range).

---

[9] An alternative representation of Bayes' Theorem is $p(\text{Hypothesis} \mid \text{data}) \propto p(\text{data} \mid \text{Hypothesis}) \times p(\text{Hypothesis})$, which shows that, from a Bayesian perspective, we can place a probability (distribution) on a scientific hypothesis. See Jeffreys 1961 for a detailed discussion of the theory of "inverse probability," which describes the Bayesian approach in these terms.

The second general argument that has been advanced against Bayesian analysis is that incorporating a prior injects too much subjectivity into statistical modeling. The Bayesian response to this argument is multifaceted. First, all statistics is subjective. The choice of sampling density (likelihood) to use in a specific project is a subjective determination. For example, when faced with an ordinal outcome, some choose to use a normal likelihood function, leading to the ordinary least squares (OLS) regression model. Others choose a binomial likelihood with a link function, leading to an ordinal logit or probit regression model. These are subjective choices.

Second, the choice of cut-point (α) at which to declare a result "statistically significant" in a classical sense is a purely subjective determination. Also, similarly, the decision to declare a statistically significant result substantively meaningful is a subjective decision.

A third response to the subjectivity criticism is that priors tend to be overwhelmed by data, especially in social science research. The prior distribution generally contributes to the posterior once, whereas data enter into the likelihood function multiple times. As $n \to \infty$, the prior's influence on the posterior often becomes negligible.

Fourth, priors can be quite noninformative, obviating the need for large quantities of data to "outweigh" them. In other words, a prior can be made to contribute little information to the posterior. That is, given that the posterior density is simply a weighted likelihood function, where the weighting is imposed by the prior, we can simply choose a prior distribution for the parameters that assigns approximately equal weight to all possible values of the parameters. The simplest noninformative prior that is often used is thus a uniform prior. Use of this prior yields a posterior density that is proportional to the likelihood function. In that case, the mode of the likelihood function (the maximum likelihood estimate) is the same as the Bayesian *maximum a posteriori* (MAP) estimate, and the substantive conclusions reached by both approaches may be similar, only differing in interpretation.

In defense of the classical criticism, although uniform densities for parameters are often used as priors, transformation from one parameterization of a parameter to another may yield an informative prior. However, alternative approaches have been developed for generating noninformative priors, including the development of Jeffreys priors and other priors. These noninformative priors tend to be based on the information matrix and are invariant under parameter transformation. An in-depth discussion of such priors is beyond the scope of this book, given the goal of a general introduction to estimation. For more details, see Gelman et al. (1995) or see Gill (2002) for a more in-depth discussion of the history of the use and construction of noninformative priors.

A fourth response is that the influence of priors can be evaluated after modeling the data to determine whether posterior inference is reasonable. Ultimately, the results of any statistical analysis, whether Bayesian or classical, must be subjectively evaluated to determine whether they are reasonable, and so, the use of informative priors cannot introduce any more subjectivity than could be included via other means in any analysis. Another response along these lines is that we can use priors to our advantage to examine how powerful the data are at invalidating the prior. For example, we may establish a conservative prior for a regression coefficient that claims that the *a priori* probability for a regression coefficient is heavily concentrated around 0 (i.e., the covariate has no effect on the outcome). We can then examine the strength of the data in rejecting this prior, providing a conservative test of a covariate's effect.

In general, the historical criticisms of Bayesian statistics are philosophical in nature and cannot be conclusively adjudicated. Instead, the rise in the use of Bayesian statistics over the last few decades has largely occurred for pragmatic reasons, including (1) that many contemporary research questions readily lend themselves to a Bayesian approach, and (2) that the development of sampling methods used to estimate model parameters has increased their ease of use. The remaining chapters attempt to demonstrate these points.

3.7 Conclusions

In this chapter, we have developed the basics of the Bayesian approach to statistical inference. First, we derived Bayes' Theorem from the probability rules developed in the previous chapter, and we applied Bayes' Theorem to problems requiring point estimates for probabilities. We then extended the Bayesian approach to handle prior *distributions* for parameters rather than simply point estimates for prior probabilties. The result was that our posterior probability became a distribution, rather than a point estimate. Next, we discussed how to summarize posterior probability distributions, and we demonstrated how to do so using several common examples. Finally, we discussed some common criticisms of the Bayesian approach that have been advanced over the last century, and we reviewed some common Bayesian responses to them. Although the material presented in this chapter is sufficient for gaining a basic understanding of the Bayesian approach to statistics, I recommend several additional sources for more in-depth coverage. I recommend Lee 1989 for an extremely thorough but accessible exposition of the Bayesian paradigm, and I recommend Box and Tiao (1973) for a more advanced exposition.

In the next chapter, we will continue exploring the Bayesian approach to posterior summarization and inference, but we will ultimately focus on multivariate posterior distributions—the most common type of posterior distribution found in social science research—where the multivariate posterior distribution may not be as easy to summarize directly as the univariate posterior densities shown in this chapter.

3.8 Exercises

1. In your own words, state what Bayes' Theorem for point probabilities actually does. For example, refer to Chapter 2 where I defined conditional probability, and use the same sort of discussion to describe how the theorem works.

2. The pregnancy example was completely contrived. In fact, most pregnancy tests today do not have such high rates of false positives. The "accuracy rate" is usually determined by computing the percent of correct answers the test gives; that is, the combined percent of positive results for positive cases and negative results for negative cases (versus false positives and false negatives). Recompute the posterior probability for being pregnant based on an accuracy rate of 90% defined in this manner. Assume that false positives and false negatives occur equally frequently under this 90% rate. What changes in the calculation?

3. Determine the posterior probability that a 30-year-old male has prostate cancer, given (1) a positive PSA test result; (2) a 90% accuracy rate (as defined in the pregnancy example), coupled with a 90% false positive rate; and (3) a prior probability of .00001 for a 30-year-old male having prostate cancer. Based on the result, why might a physician consider *not* testing a 30-year-old male using the PSA test?

4. Find and plot the posterior distribution for a binomial likelihood with $x = 5$ successes out of $n = 10$ trials using at least three different beta prior distributions. Does the prior make a large difference in the outcome—when?

5. Find and plot the posterior distribution for a normal distribution likelihood with a sample mean $\bar{x} = 100$ and variance $\text{var}(x) = 144$ (assume $n = 169$) using at least three different normal priors for the mean. When does the prior make the largest difference in the outcome—when the prior mean varies substantially from the sample mean, or when the prior variance is small or large?

6. Reconsider the pregnancy example from the beginning of the chapter. I showed the posterior probabilities for the second through the tenth subsequent tests. Reproduce these results, using the posterior obtained from the kth test as the prior for the $(k+1)^{\text{st}}$ test. Next, assume the original prior ($p = .15$) and assume the 10 tests were taken simultaneously and all yielded a positive result. What is the posterior probability for pregnancy? Finally, reconduct the pregnancy example with the 10 positive tests treated simultaneously as the current data, and use a beta prior distribution. Interpret the results.

7. In the 2004 U.S. presidential election, surveys throughout the fall constantly reversed the projected victor. As each survey was conducted, would it have been appropriate to incorporate the results of previous surveys as priors and treat the current survey as new data to update the prior in a Bayesian fashion? If so, do you think a more consistent picture of the

winner would have emerged before the election? If a Bayesian approach would not have been appropriate, why not?

8. Give two simple examples showing a case in which a prior distribution would *not* be overwhelmed by data, regardless of the sample size.

9. Show how the multinomial likelihood and Dirichlet prior are simply a multivariate generalization of the binomial likelihood and beta prior.

10. Show how the Wishart distribution reduces to the gamma distribution when the number of dimensions of the random variable is 1.

11. I said throughout the chapter that the inverse gamma distribution was the appropriate distribution for a variance parameter. It could be said that variance parameter could be considered to be distributed as an inverse chi-square random variable. Both of these statements are true. How?

12. Why can a prior distribution that equals a constant be considered proportional to a uniform distribution?

4

Modern Model Estimation Part 1: Gibbs Sampling

The estimation of a Bayesian model is the most difficult part of undertaking a Bayesian analysis. Given that researchers may use different priors for any particular model, estimation must be tailored to the specific model under consideration. Classical analyses, on the other hand, often involve the use of standard likelihood functions, and hence, once an estimation routine is developed, it can be used again and again.

The trade-off for the additional work required for a Bayesian analysis is that (1) a more appropriate model for the data can be constructed than extant software may allow, (2) more measures of model fit and outlier/influential case diagnostics can be produced, and (3) more information is generally available to summarize knowledge about model parameters than a classical analysis based on maximum likelihood (ML) estimation provides. Along these same lines, additional measures may be constructed to test hypotheses concerning parameters not directly estimated in the model.

In this chapter, I first discuss the goal of model estimation in the Bayesian paradigm and contrast it with that of maximum likelihood estimation. Then, I discuss modern simulation/sampling methods used by Bayesian statisticians to perform analyses, including Gibbs sampling. In the next chapter, I discuss the Metropolis-Hastings algorithm as an alternative to Gibbs sampling.

4.1 What Bayesians want and why

As the discussion of ML estimation in Chapter 2 showed, the ML approach finds the parameter values that maximize the likelihood function for the observed data and then produces point estimates of the standard errors of these estimates. A typical classical statistical test is then conducted by subtracting a hypothesized value for the parameter from the ML estimate and dividing the result by the estimated standard error. This process yields a standardized estimate (under the hypothesized value). The Central Limit Theorem states that the sampling distribution for a sample statistic/parameter estimate is asymptotically normal, and so we can use the z (or t) distribution to evaluate the probability of observing the sample statistic we observed under the assumption that the hypothesized value for it were true. If observing the sample statistic we did would be an extremely rare event under the hypothesized value, we reject the hypothesized value.

In contrast to the use of a single point estimate for a parameter and its standard error and reliance on the Central Limit Theorem, a Bayesian analysis derives the posterior distribution for a parameter and then seeks to summarize the entire distribution. As we discussed in Chapter 2, many of the quantities that may be of interest in summarizing knowledge about a distribution are integrals of it, like the mean, median, variance, and various quantiles. Obtaining such integrals, therefore, is a key focus of Bayesian summarization and inference.

The benefits of using the entire posterior distribution, rather than point estimates of the mode of the likelihood function and standard errors, are several. First, if we can summarize the entire posterior distribution for a parameter, there is no need to rely on asymptotic arguments about the normality of the distribution: It can be directly assessed. Second, as stated above, having the entire posterior distribution for a parameter available allows for a considerable number of additional tests and summaries that cannot be performed under a classical likelihood-based approach. Third, as discussed in subsequent chapters, distributions for the parameters in the model can be easily transformed into distributions of quantities that may be of interest but may not be directly estimated as part of the original model. For example, in Chapter 10, I show how distributions for hazard model parameters estimated via Markov chain Monte Carlo (MCMC) methods can be transformed into distributions of life table quantities like healthy life expectancy. Distributions of this quantity cannot be directly estimated from data but instead can be computed as a function of parameters from a hazard model. A likelihood approach that produces only point estimates of the parameters and their associated standard errors cannot accomplish this.

Given the benefits of a Bayesian approach to inference, the key question then is: How difficult is it to integrate a posterior distribution to produce summaries of parameters?

4.2 The logic of sampling from posterior densities

For some distributions, integrals for summarizing posterior distributions have closed-form solutions and are known, or they can be easily computed using numerical methods. For example, in the previous chapter, we determined the expected proportion of—and a plausible range for—votes for Kerry in the 2004 presidential election in Ohio, as well as the probability that Kerry would win Ohio, using known information about integrals of the beta distribution. We also computed several summaries using a normal approximation to the posterior density, and of course, integrals of the normal distribution are well-known.

For many distributions, especially multivariate ones, however, integrals may not be easy to compute. For example, if we had a beta prior distribution on the variance of a normal distribution, the posterior distribution for the variance would not have a known form. In order to remedy this problem, Bayesians often work with conjugate priors, as we discussed in the previous chapter. However, sometimes conjugate priors are unrealistic, or a model may involve distributions that simply are not amenable to simple computation of quantiles and other quantities. In those cases, there are essentially two basic approaches to computing integrals: approximation methods and sampling methods.

Before modern sampling methods (e.g., MCMC) were available or computationally feasible, Bayesians used a variety of approximation methods to perform integrations necessary to summarize posterior densities. Using these methods often required extensive knowledge of advanced numerical methods that social scientists generally do not possess, limiting the usefulness of a Bayesian approach. For example, quadrature methods—which involve evaluating weighted points on a multidimensional grid—were often used. As another example, Bayesians often generated Taylor series expansions around the mode of the log-posterior distribution, and then used normal approximations to the posterior for which integrals are known. For multimodal distributions, Bayesians would often use approximations based on mixtures of normals. All of these approaches were methods of *approximation* and, hence, formed a foundation for criticizing Bayesian analysis. Of course, it is true that a Bayesian Central Limit Theorem shows that *asymptotically* most posterior distributions are normal (see Gelman et al. 1995 for an in-depth discussion of asymptotic normal theory in a Bayesian setting), but reliance on this theorem undermines a key benefit of having a complete posterior distribution: the lack of need to—and, in small samples, the inability to—rely on asymptotic arguments. I do not focus on these methods in this book.

Sampling methods constitute an alternative to approximation methods. The logic of sampling is that we can generate (simulate) a sample of size n from the distribution of interest and then use discrete formulas applied to these samples to approximate the integrals of interest. Under a sampling approach, we can estimate a mean by:

$$\int x f(x) dx \approx \frac{1}{n} \sum x$$

and the variance by:

$$\int (x - \mu)^2 f(x) dx \approx \frac{1}{n} \sum (x - \mu)^2.$$

Various quantiles can be computed empirically by noting the value of x for which $Q\%$ of the sampled values fall below it.

Thus, modern Bayesian inference typically involves (1) establishing a model and obtaining a posterior distribution for the parameter(s) of interest, (2) generating samples from the posterior distribution, and (3) using discrete formulas applied to the samples from the posterior distribution to summarize our knowledge of the parameters. These summaries are not limited to a single quantity but instead are virtually limitless. Any summary statistic that we commonly compute to describe a sample of data can also be computed for a sample from a posterior distribution and can then be used to describe it!

Consider, for example, the voting example from the previous chapter in which we specified a beta prior distribution for K, coupled with a binomial likelihood for the most recent polling data. In that example, the posterior density for K was a beta density with parameters $\alpha = 1498$ and $\beta = 1519$. Given that the beta density is a known density, we computed the posterior mean as $1498/(1498 + 1519) = .497$, and the probability that $K > .5$ as .351. However, assume these integrals could not be computed analytically. In that case, we could simulate several thousand draws from this particular beta density (using x=rbeta(5000,1498,1519) in R, with the first argument being the desired number of samples), and we could then compute the mean, median, and other desired quantities from this sample. I performed this simulation and obtained a mean of .496 for the 5,000 samples (obtained by typing mean(x) in R) and a probability of .351 that Kerry would win (obtained by typing sum(x>.5)/5000).

Notice that the mean obtained analytically (via integration of the posterior density) and the mean obtained via sampling are identical to almost three decimal places, as are the estimated probabilities that Kerry would win. The reason that these estimates are close is that sampling methods, in the limit, are not approximations; instead, they provide exact summaries equivalent to those obtained via integration. A sample of 5,000 draws from this beta distribution is more than sufficient to accurately summarize the density. As a demonstration, Figure 4.1 shows the convergence of the sample-estimated mean for this particular beta distribution as the sample size increases from 1 to 100,000. At samples of size $n = 5,000$, the confidence band around the mean is only approximately .0005 units wide. In other words, our error in using simulation rather than analytic integration is extremely small. As the sample size increases, we can see that the simulation error diminishes even further.

4.3 Two basic sampling methods

In the example shown above, it was easy to obtain samples from the desired beta density using a simple command in R. For many distributions, there are effective routines in existence for simulating from them (some of which ultimately rely on the inversion method discussed below). For other distributions, there may not be an extant routine, and hence, a statistician may need

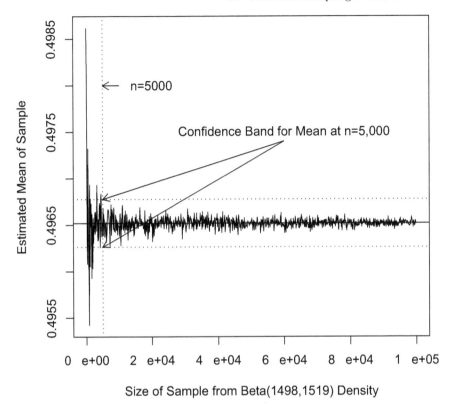

Fig. 4.1. Convergence of sample means on the true beta distribution mean across samples sizes: Vertical line shows sample size of 5,000; dashed horizontal lines show approximate confidence band of sample estimates for samples of size $n = 5,000$; and solid horizontal line shows the true mean.

to create one. Indeed, this is the entire reason for MCMC methods, as we will discuss: Integration of posterior densities is often impossible, and there may not be extant routines for sampling from them either, especially when they are high-dimensional. I first discuss two sampling methods, each of which is important for a basic understanding of MCMC methods. These methods, as well as several others, are described in greater depth in Gilks (1996). For a more detailed exposition on simulation methods, see Ripley (1987).

4.3.1 The inversion method of sampling

For drawing a sample from a univariate distribution $f(x)$, we can often use the inversion method. The inversion method is quite simple and follows two steps:

1. Draw a uniform random number u between 0 and 1 (a $U(0,1)$ random variable).

2. Then $z = F^{-1}(u)$ is a draw from $f(x)$.

In step 1, we draw a $U(0,1)$ random variable. This draw represents the area under the curve up to the value of our desired random draw from the distribution of interest. Thus, we simply need to find z such that:

$$u = \int_L^z f(x)dx,$$

where L is the lower limit of the density f. Put another way, $u = F(z)$. So, phrased in terms of z:

$$z = F^{-1}(u).$$

To provide a concrete example, take the linear density function from Chapter 2: $f(x) = (1/40)(2x+3)$ (with $0 < x < 5$). As far as I know, no routines are readily available that allow sampling from this density, and so, if one needed draws from this density, one would need to develop one. In order to generate a draw from this distribution using the inversion method, we first need to draw $u \sim U(0,1)$ and then compute z that satisfies

$$u = \int_0^z \frac{1}{40}(2x + 3)dx.$$

We can solve this equation for z as follows. First, evaluate the integral:

$$40u = x^2 + 3x\big|_0^z = z^2 + 3z.$$

Second, complete the square in z:

$$40u + \frac{9}{4} = z^2 + 3z + \frac{9}{4} = \left(z + \frac{3}{2}\right)^2.$$

Third, take the square root of both sides and rearrange to find z:

$$z = \frac{-3 \pm \sqrt{160u + 9}}{2}.$$

This result reveals two solutions for z; however, given that z must be between 0 and 5, only the positive root is relevant. If we substitute 0 and 1—the minimum and maximum values for u—we find that the range of z is $[0, 5]$ as it should be.

Figure 4.2 displays the results of an algorithm simulating 1,000 random draws from this density using the inversion method. The figures on the left-hand side show the sequence of draws from the $U(0,1)$ density, which are then inverted to produce the sequence of draws from the density of interest. The right-hand side of the figure shows the simulated and theoretical density functions. Notice how the samples from both densities closely follow, but do not exactly match, the theoretical densities. This error is sampling error, which diminishes as the simulation sample size increases.

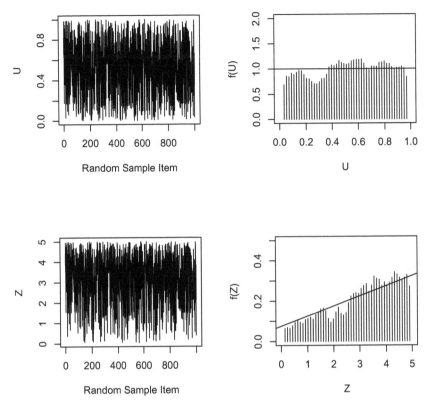

Fig. 4.2. Example of the inversion method: Left-hand figures show the sequence of draws from the $U(0,1)$ density (upper left) and the sequence of draws from the density $f(x) = (1/40)(2x+3)$ density (lower left); and the right-hand figures show these draws in histogram format, with true density functions superimposed.

The following R program was used to generate these draws. The first line simulates 1,000 random draws from the $U(0,1)$ distribution; the second line generates the vector z as the inverse of u :

```
#R program for inversion method of sampling
u=runif(1000,min=0,max=1)
z=(1/2) * (-3 + sqrt(160*u +9))
```

Although the inversion method is very efficient and easy to implement, two key limitations reduce its usability as a general method for drawing samples from posterior densities. First, if the inverse function is impossible to derive analytically, obviously the method cannot be used. For example, the normal integral cannot be directly solved, and hence, the inversion method cannot be used to simulate from the normal distribution.[1] To some extent, this problem

---

[1] Of course, we do have efficient algorithms for computing this integral, but the integral cannot be solved analytically.

begs the question: If we can integrate the density as required by the inversion method, then why bother with simulation? This question will be addressed shortly, but the short answer is that we may not be able to perform integration on a multivariate density, but we can often break a multivariate density into univariate ones for which inversion may work.

The second problem with the inversion method is that the method will not work with multivariate distributions, because the inverse is generally not unique beyond one dimension. For example, consider the bivariate planar density function discussed in Chapter 2:

$$f(x, y) = \frac{1}{28}(2x + 3y + 2),$$

with $0 < x, y < 2$. If we draw $u \sim U(0, 1)$ and attempt to solve the double integral for x and y, we get:

$$28u = yx^2 + \frac{3xy^2}{2} + 2xy,$$

which, of course, has infinitely many solutions (one equation with two unknowns). Thinking ahead, we could select a value for one variable and then use the inversion method to draw from the conditional distribution of the other variable. This process would reduce the problem to one of sampling from univariate conditional distributions, which is the basic idea of Gibbs sampling, as I discuss shortly.

4.3.2 The rejection method of sampling

When $F^{-1}(u)$ cannot be computed, other methods of sampling exist. A very important one is rejection sampling. In rejection sampling, sampling from a distribution $f(x)$ for x involves three basic steps:

1. Sample a value z from a distribution $g(x)$ from which sampling is easy and for which values of $m \times g(x)$ are greater than $f(x)$ at all points (m is a constant).
2. Compute the ratio $R = \frac{f(z)}{m \times g(z)}$.
3. Sample $u \sim U(0, 1)$. If $R > u$, then accept z as a draw from $f(x)$. Otherwise, return to step 1.

In this algorithm, $m \times g(x)$ is called an "envelope function," because of the requirement that the density function $g(x)$ multiplied by some constant m be greater than the density function value for the distribution of interest $[f(x)]$ at the same point for all points. In other words, $m \times g(x)$ *envelops* $f(x)$. In step 1, we sample a point z from the pdf $g(x)$.

In step 2, we compute the ratio of the envelope function $[m \times g(x)]$ evaluated at z to the density function of interest $[f(x)]$ evaluated at the same point.

Finally, in step 3, we draw a $U(0,1)$ random variable u and compare it with R. If $R > u$, then we treat the draw as a draw from $f(x)$. If not, we reject z as coming from $f(x)$, and we repeat the process until we obtain a satisfactory draw.

This routine is easy to implement, but it is not immediately apparent why it works. Let's again examine the density discussed in the previous section and consider an envelope function that is a uniform density on the $[0, 5]$ interval multiplied by a constant of 2. I choose this constant because the height of the $U(0,5)$ density is .2, whereas the maximum height of the density $f(x) = (1/40)(2x + 3)$ is .325. Multiplying the $U(0,5)$ density by two increases the height of this density to .4, which is well above the maximum for $f(x)$ and therefore makes $m \times g(x)$ a true envelope function. Figure 4.3 shows the density and envelope functions and graphically depicts the process of rejection sampling.

In the first step, when we are sampling from the envelope function, we are choosing a location on the x axis in the graph (see top graph in Figure 4.3). The process of constructing the ratio R and comparing it with a uniform deviate is essentially a process of locating a point in the y direction once the x coordinate is chosen and then deciding whether it is *under* the density of interest. This becomes more apparent if we rearrange the ratio and the inequality with u:

$$f(z) \underbrace{<=>}_{?} m \times g(z) \times u.$$

$m \times g(z) \times u$ provides us a point in the y dimension that falls somewhere between 0 and $m \times g(z)$. This can be easily seen by noting that $m \times g(z) \times u$ is really simply providing a random draw from the $U(0, g(z))$ distribution: The value of this computation when $u = 0$ is 0; its value when $u = 1$ is $m \times g(z)$ (see middle graph in Figure 4.3). In the last step, in which we decide whether to accept z as a draw from $f(x)$, we are simply determining whether the y coordinate falls below the $f(x)$ curve (see bottom graph in Figure 4.3). Another way to think about this process is that the ratio tells us the proportion of times we will accept a draw at a given value of x as coming from the density of interest.

The following R program simulates 1,000 draws from the density $f(x) = (1/40)(2x+3)$ using rejection sampling. The routine also keeps a count of how many total draws from $g(x)$ must be made in order to obtain 1,000 draws from $f(x)$.

```
#R program for rejection method of sampling
count=0; k=1; f=matrix(NA,1000)
while(k<1001)
  {
  z=runif(1,min=0,max=5)
  r=((1/40)*(2*z+3))/(2*.2)
```

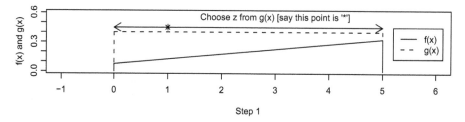

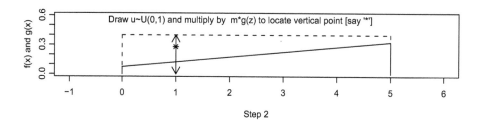

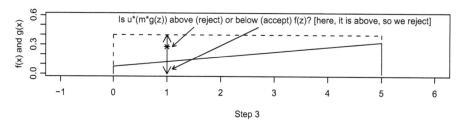

Fig. 4.3. The three-step process of rejection sampling.

```
if(r>runif(1,min=0,max=1))
  {f[k]=z; k=k+1}
count=count+1
}
```

Figure 4.4 shows the results of a run of this algorithm. The histogram of the sample of 1,000 draws very closely matches the density of interest.

Rejection sampling is a powerful method of sampling from densities for which inversion sampling does not work. It can be used to sample from *any* density, and it can be used to sample from multivariate densities. In the multivariate case, we first choose an X—now a random vector, rather than a single point—from a multivariate enveloping function, and then we proceed just as before.

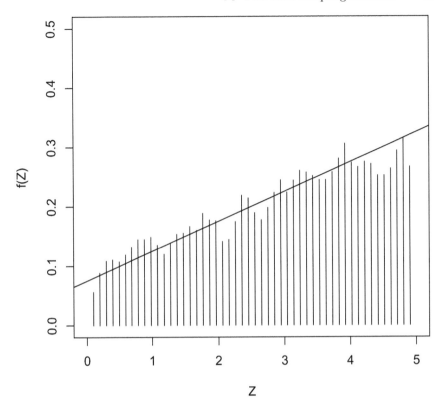

Fig. 4.4. Sample of 1,000 draws from density using rejection sampling with theoretical density superimposed.

Rejection sampling does have some limitations. First, finding an enveloping function $m \times g(x)$ may not be an easy task. For example, it may be difficult to find an envelope with values that are greater at all points of support for the density of interest. Consider trying to use a uniform density as an envelope for sampling from a normal density. The domain of x for the normal density runs from $-\infty$ to $+\infty$, but there is no corresponding uniform density. In the limit, a $U(-\infty, +\infty)$ density would have an infinitely low height, which would make $g(x)$ fall below $f(x)$ in the center of the distribution, regardless of the constant multiple m chosen. Second, the algorithm may not be very efficient. If the enveloping function is considerably higher than $f(x)$ at all points, the algorithm will reject most attempted draws, which implies that an incredible number of draws may need to be made before finding a single value from $f(x)$. In theory, the efficiency of a rejection sampling routine is calculable before implementing it. In the case above, the total area under the enveloping curve is 2 ($5 \times .4$), but the total area under the density of interest is 1 (by definition of a density function). Thus, the algorithm used should accept about 50% of the draws from $g(x)$. In fact, in the case shown and discussed above, it took 2,021 attempts to obtain 1,000 draws from $f(x)$, which is a rejection rate of 50.5%. These two limitations make rejection sampling, although possible, increasingly difficult as the dimensionality increases in multivariate distributions.

4.4 Introduction to MCMC sampling

The limitations of inversion and rejection sampling make the prospects of using these simple methods daunting in complex statistical analyses involving high-dimensional distributions. Although rejection sampling approaches can be refined to be more efficient, they are still not very useful in and of themselves in real-world statistical modeling. Fortunately, over the last few decades, MCMC methods have been developed that facilitate sampling from complex distributions. Furthermore, aside from allowing sampling from complex distributions, these methods provide several additional benefits, as we will be discussing in the remaining chapters.

MCMC sampling provides a method to sample from multivariate densities that are not easy to sample from, often by breaking these densities down into more manageable univariate or multivariate densities. The basic MCMC approach provides a prescription for (1) sampling from one or more dimensions of a posterior distribution and (2) moving throughout the entire support of a posterior distribution. In fact, the name "Markov chain Monte Carlo" implies this process. The "Monte Carlo" portion refers to the random simulation process. The "Markov chain" portion refers to the process of sampling a new value from the posterior distribution, given the previous value: This iterative process produces a Markov chain of values that constitute a sample of draws from the posterior.

4.4.1 Generic Gibbs sampling

The Gibbs sampler is the most basic MCMC method used in Bayesian statistics. Although Gibbs sampling was developed and used in physics prior to 1990, its widespread use in Bayesian statistics originated in 1990 with its introduction by Gelfand and Smith (1990). As will be discussed more in the next chapter, the Gibbs sampler is a special case of the more general Metropolis-Hastings algorithm that is useful when (1) sampling from a multivariate posterior is not feasible, but (2) sampling from the conditional distributions for each parameter (or blocks of them) is feasible. A generic Gibbs sampler follows the following iterative process (j indexes the iteration count):

0. Assign a vector of starting values, S, to the parameter vector: $\Theta^{j=0} = S$.
1. Set $j = j + 1$.
2. Sample $(\theta_1^j \mid \theta_2^{j-1}, \theta_3^{j-1} \ldots \theta_k^{j-1})$.
3. Sample $(\theta_2^j \mid \theta_1^j, \theta_3^{j-1} \ldots \theta_k^{j-1})$.

$\vdots$ $\vdots$

k. Sample $(\theta_k^j \mid \theta_1^j, \theta_2^j, \ldots, \theta_{k-1}^j)$.
k+1. Return to step 1.

In other words, Gibbs sampling involves ordering the parameters and sampling from the conditional distribution for each parameter given the current value of all the other parameters and repeatedly cycling through this updating process. Each "loop" through these steps is called an "iteration" of the Gibbs sampler, and when a new sampled value of a parameter is obtained, it is called an "updated" value.

For Gibbs sampling, the full conditional density for a parameter needs only to be known up to a normalizing constant. As we discussed in Chapters 2 and 3, this implies that we can use the joint density with the other parameters set at their current values. This fact makes Gibbs sampling relatively simple for most problems in which the joint density reduces to known forms for each parameter once all other parameters are treated as fixed.

4.4.2 Gibbs sampling example using the inversion method

Here, I provide a simple example of Gibbs sampling based on the bivariate plane distribution developed in Chapter 2 $f(x, y) = (1/28)(2x + 3y + 2)$. The conditional distribution for x was:

$$f(x \mid y) = \frac{f(x, y)}{f(y)} = \frac{2x + 3y + 2}{6y + 8},$$

and the conditional distribution for y was:

$$f(y \mid x) = \frac{f(x, y)}{f(x)} = \frac{2x + 3y + 2}{4x + 10}.$$

Thus, a Gibbs sampler for sampling x and y in this problem would follow these steps:

1. Set $j = 0$ and establish starting values. Here, let's set $x^{j=0} = -5$ and $y^{j=0} = -5$.
2. Sample x^{j+1} from $f(x \mid y = y^j)$.
3. Sample y^{j+1} from $f(y \mid x = x^{j+1})$.
4. Increment $j = j + 1$ and return to step 2 until $j = 2000$.

How do we sample from these conditional distributions? We know what they are, but they certainly are not standard distributions. Since they are not standard distributions, but since these conditionals are univariate and $F^{-1}()$ can be calculated for each one, we can use an inversion subroutine to sample from each conditional density. How do we find the inverses in this bivariate density? Recall that inversion sampling requires first drawing a $u \sim U(0,1)$ random variable and then inverting this draw using F^{-1}. Thus, to find the inverse of the conditional density for $y|x$, we need to solve:

$$u = \int_0^z \frac{2x + 3y + 2}{4x + 10}$$

for z. Given that this is the conditional density for y, x is fixed and can be treated as a constant, and we obtain:

$$u(4x + 10) = (2x + 2)y + (3/2)y^2 \big|_0^z .$$

Thus:

$$u(4x + 10) = (2x + 2)z + (3/2)z^2.$$

After multiplying through by $(2/3)$ and rearranging terms, we get:

$$(2/3)u(4x + 10) = z^2 + (2/3)(2x + 2)z.$$

We can then complete the square in z and solve for z to obtain:

$$z = \sqrt{(2/3)u(4x + 10) + ((1/3)(2x + 2))^2} - (1/3)(2x + 2).$$

Given a current value for x and a random draw u, z is a random draw from the conditional density for $y|x$. A similar process can be undertaken to find the inverse for $x|y$ (see Exercises).

Below is an R program that implements the Gibbs sampling:

```
#R program for Gibbs sampling using inversion method
x=matrix(-5,2000); y=matrix(-5,2000)
for(i in 2:2000)
  {
  #sample from x | y
  u=runif(1,min=0, max=1)
  x[i]=sqrt(u*(6*y[i-1]+8)+(1.5*y[i-1]+1)*(1.5*y[i-1]+1))
          -(1.5*y[i-1]+1)
  #sample from y | x
  u=runif(1,min=0,max=1)
  y[i]=sqrt((2*u*(4*x[i]+10))/3 +((2*x[i]+2)/3)*((2*x[i]+2)/3))
          - ((2*x[i]+2)/3)
  }
```

This program first sets the starting values for x and y equal to -5. Then, x is updated using the current value of y. Then, y is updated using the just-sampled value of x. (Notice how x[i] is computed using y[i-1], whereas y[i] is sampled using x[i].) Both are updated using the inversion method of sampling discussed above.

This algorithm produces samples from the marginal distributions for both x and y, but we can also treat pairs of x and y as draws from the joint density. We will discuss the conditions in which we can do this in greater depth shortly. Generally, however, of particular interest are the marginal distributions for parameters, since we are often concerned with testing hypotheses concerning one parameter, net of the other parameters in a model. Figure 4.5 shows a "trace plot" of both x and y as well as the marginal densities for both variables. The trace plot is simply a two-dimensional plot in which the x axis represents the iteration of the algorithm, and the y axis represents the simulated value of the random variable at each particular iteration. Heuristically, we can then take the trace plot, turn it on its edge (a 90 degree clockwise turn), and allow the "ink" to fall down along the y-axis and "pile-up" to produce a histogram of the marginal density. Places in the trace plot that are particularly dark represent regions of the density in which the algorithm simulated frequently; lighter areas are regions of the density that were more rarely visited by the algorithm. Thus, the "ink" will pile-up higher in areas for which the variable of interest has greater probability. Histograms of these marginal densities are shown to the right of their respective trace plots, with the theoretical marginal densities derived in Chapter 2 superimposed. Realize that these marginals are unnormalized, because the leading $1/28$ normalizing constant cancels in both the numerator and the denominator.

Notice that, although the starting values were very poor (-5 is not a valid point in either dimension of the density), the algorithm converged very rapidly to the appropriate region—$[0, 2]$. It generally takes a number of iterations for an MCMC algorithm to find the appropriate region—and, more theoretically, for the Markov chain produced by the algorithm to sample from the appropriate "target" distribution. Thus, we generally discard a number of early iterations before making calculations (called the "burn-in"). The marginal densities, therefore, are produced from only the last 1,500 iterations of the algorithm.

The histograms for the marginal densities show that the algorithm samples appropriately from the densities of interest. Of course, there is certainly some error—observe how the histograms tend to be a little too low or high here and there. This reflects sampling error, and such error is reduced by sampling more values (e.g., using 5,000 draws, rather than 2,000); we will return to this issue in the next chapter.

Aside from examining the marginal distributions for x and y, we can also examine the joint density. Figure 4.6 shows a two-dimensional trace plot, taken at several stages. The upper left figure shows the state of the algorithm after 5 iterations; the upper right figure shows the state after 25 iterations; the

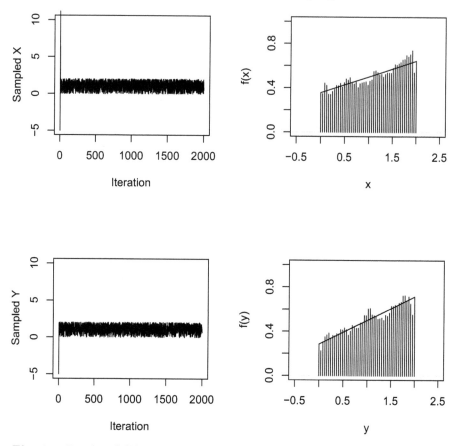

Fig. 4.5. Results of Gibbs sampler using the inversion method for sampling from conditional densities.

lower left figure shows it after 100 iterations; and the lower right figure shows it after the 2,000 iterations. Here again, we see that the algorithm, although starting with poor starting values, converged rapidly to the appropriate two-dimensional, partial plane region represented by $f(x, y)$.

After sampling from the distribution for x and y, we can now summarize our knowledge of the density. The theoretical mean for x can be found by taking the marginal for x $(f(x) = (1/28)(4x + 10))$ and by integrating across all values for x:

$$\mu_x = \int_0^2 x \times f(x)dx = 1.095.$$

A similar calculation for y yields a theoretical mean of 1.143. The empirical estimates of the means, based on the last 1,500 draws from the marginal distributions for the variables (discarding the first 500 as the burn-in) are

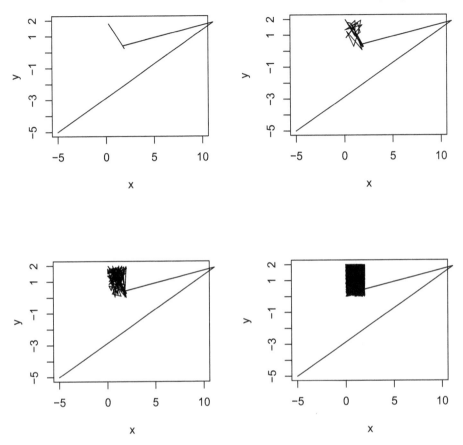

Fig. 4.6. Results of Gibbs sampler using the inversion method for sampling from conditional densities: Two-dimensional view after 5, 25, 100, and 2,000 iterations.

$\bar{x} = 1.076$ and $\bar{y} = 1.158$. The discrepancy between the theoretical and the empirical means is attributable to sampling error in the MCMC algorithm. A longer run would reduce the error, although, even with 1,500 simulated draws, the discrepancies here are minimal (less than 2% for both x and y).

4.4.3 Example repeated using rejection sampling

In the Gibbs sampling algorithm we just discussed, we used the inversion method for sampling from the conditional distributions of x and y. It is often the case that using the inversion method may not be feasible, for several reasons. First, the conditionals in the Gibbs sampler may not be univariate. That is, we do not have to break our conditional distributions into univariate conditional densities; we may choose multivariate conditional densities, as we will see in Chapter 7. Second, $F()^{-1}$ may not be calculable, even in one dimension.

For example, if the distribution were bivariate normal, the conditionals would be univariate normal, and $F()^{-1}$ cannot be analytically computed.[2] Third, even if the inverse of the density is calculable, the normalizing constant in the conditional may not be easily computable. The inversion algorithm technically requires the complete computation of $F()^{-1}$, which, in this case, requires us to know both the numerator and the denominator of the formulas for the conditional distributions. It is often the case that we do not know the exact formula for a conditional distribution, but instead, we know the conditional only up to a normalizing (proportionality) constant. Generally speaking, conditional distributions are proportional to the joint distribution evaluated at the point of conditioning. So, for example, in the example discussed above, if we know $y = q$, then the following is true:

$$f(x \mid y = q) = (1/28) \times \frac{2x + 3q + 2}{6q + 8} \propto 2x + 3q + 2.$$

Notice that $(1/28)(6q + 8)$ is not contained in the final proportionality; the reason is that this factor is simply a constant that scales this slice of the joint density so that its integral is 1. However, this constant is not necessary for Gibbs sampling to work! Why not? Because the Gibbs sampler will only set $y = q$ in direct proportion to its relative frequency in the joint density. Put another way, the Gibbs sampler will visit $y = q$ as often as it should under the joint density. This result is perhaps easier to see in a contingency table; consider the example displayed in Table 4.1.

Table 4.1. Cell counts and marginals for a hypothetical bivariate dichotomous distribution.

	$x = 0$	$x = 1$	$x \mid y = k$
$y = 0$	a	b	$a + b$
$y = 1$	c	d	$c + d$
$y \mid x = m$	$a + c$	$b + d$	$a + b + c + d$

   In this example, if we follow a Gibbs sampling strategy, we would choose a starting value for x and y; suppose we chose 0 for each. If we started with $y = 0$, we would then select $x = 0$ with probability $a/(a + b)$ and $x = 1$ with probability $b/(a + b)$. Once we had chosen our x, if x had been 0, we would then select $y = 0$ with probability $a/(a+c)$ and $y = 1$ with probability $c/(a + c)$. On the other hand, if we had selected $x = 1$, we would then select

---

[2] Again, we *do* have efficient algorithms for computing this integral, but it cannot be directly analytically computed.

$y = 0$ with probability $b/(b+d)$ and $y = 1$ with probability $d/(b+d)$. Thus, we would be selecting $y = 0$ with total probability

$$p(y = 0) = p(y = 0 \mid x = 0)p(x = 0) + p(y = 0 \mid x = 1)p(x = 1).$$

So,

$$p(y = 0) = \left(\frac{a}{a+c}\right)\left(\frac{a+c}{a+b+c+d}\right) + \left(\frac{b}{b+d}\right)\left(\frac{b+d}{a+b+c+d}\right)$$

$$= \frac{a+b}{a+b+c+d}.$$

This proportion reflects exactly how often we should choose $y = 0$, given the marginal distribution for y in the contingency table. Thus, the normalizing constant is not relevant, because the Gibbs sampler will visit each value of one variable in proportion to its relative marginal frequency, which leads us to then sample the other variable, conditional on the first, with the appropriate relative marginal frequency.

Returning to the example at hand, then, we simply need to know what the conditional distribution is proportional to in order to sample from it. Here, if we know $y = q$, then $f(x \mid y = q) \propto 2x + 3q + 2$. Because we do not necessarily always know this normalizing constant, using the inversion method of sampling will not work.[3] However, we can simulate from this density using rejection sampling. Recall from the discussion of rejection sampling that we need an enveloping function $g(x)$ that, when multiplied by a constant m, returns a value that is greater than $f(x)$ for all x. With an unnormalized density, only m must be adjusted relative to what it would be under the normalized density in order to ensure this rule is followed. In this case, if we will be sampling from the joint density, we can use a uniform density on the $[0, 2]$ interval multiplied by a constant m that ensures that the density does not exceed $m \times .5$ (.5 is the height of the U(0,2) density). The joint density reaches a maximum where x and y are both 2; that peak value is 12. Thus, if we set $m = 25$, the $U(0, 2)$ density multiplied by m will always be above the joint density. And, we can ignore the normalizing constants, including the leading $(1/28)$ in the joint density and the $1/(6y + 8)$ in the conditional for x and the $1/(4x + 10)$ in the conditional for y. As exemplified above, the Gibbs sampler will sample from the marginals in the correct proportion to their relative frequency in the joint density. Below is a Gibbs sampler that simulates from $f(x, y)$ using rejection sampling:

---

[3] The normalizing constant must be known one way or another. Certainly, we can perform the integration we need to compute F^{-1} so long as the distribution is proper. However, if we do not know the normalizing constant, the integral will differ from 1, which necessitates that our uniform draw representing the area under the curve be scaled by the inverse of the normalizing constant in order to represent the area under the unnormalized density fully.

```
#R program for Gibbs sampling using rejection sampling
x=matrix(-1,2000); y=matrix(-1,2000)
for(i in 2:2000)
 {
  #sample from x | y using rejection sampling
  z=0
  while(z==0)
   {
    u=runif(1,min=0, max=2)
    if( ((2*u)+(3*y[i-1])+2) > (25*runif(1,min=0,max=1)*.5))
     {x[i]=u; z=1}
   }
  #sample from y | x using rejection sampling
  z=0
  while(z==0)
   {
    u=runif(1,min=0,max=2)
    if( ((2*x[i])+(3*u)+2) > (25*runif(1,min=0,max=1)*.5))
     {y[i]=u; z=1}
   }
 }
```

In this program, the overall Gibbs sampling process is the same as for the inversion sampling approach; the only difference is that we are now using rejection sampling to sample from the unnormalized conditional distributions. One consequence of switching sampling methods is that we have now had to use better starting values (-1 here versus -5 under inversion sampling). The reason for this is that the algorithm will never get off the ground otherwise. Notice that the first item to be selected is $x[2]$. If $y[1]$ is -5, the first conditional statement (if ...) will never be true: The value on the left side of the expression, ((2*u)+(3*y[i-1])+2), can never be positive, but the value on the right, (25*runif(1,min=0,max=1)*.5), will always be positive. So, the algorithm will "stick" in the first while loop.

Figures 4.7 and 4.8 are replications of the previous two figures produced under rejection sampling. The overall results appear the same. For example, the mean for x under the rejection sampling approach was 1.085, and the mean for y was 1.161, which are both very close to those obtained using the inversion method.

4.4.4 Gibbs sampling from a real bivariate density

The densities we examined in the examples above were very basic densities (linear and planar) and are seldom used in social science modeling. In this section, I will discuss using Gibbs sampling to sample observations from a density that *is* commonly used in social science research—the bivariate normal density. As discussed in Chapter 2, the bivariate normal density is a special case of the multivariate normal density in which the dimensionality of the

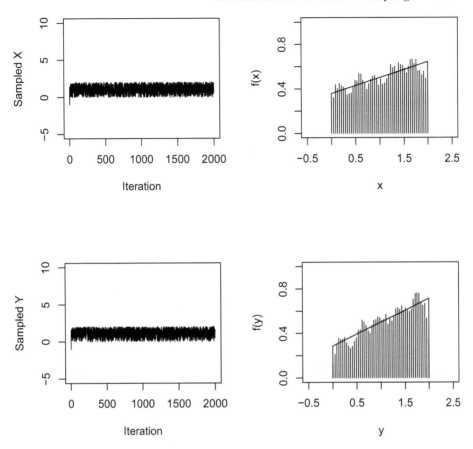

Fig. 4.7. Results of Gibbs sampler using rejection sampling to sample from conditional densities.

density is 2, and the variables—say x and y—in this density are related by the correlation parameter ρ. For the sake of this example, we will use the standard bivariate normal density—that is, the means and variances of both x and y are 0 and 1, respectively—and we will assume that ρ is a known constant (say, .5). The pdf in this case is:

$$f(x, y|\rho) = \frac{1}{2\pi\sqrt{1-\rho^2}} \exp\left\{-\frac{x^2 - 2\rho xy + y^2}{2(1-\rho^2)}\right\}.$$

In order to use Gibbs sampling for sampling values of x and y, we need to determine the full conditional distributions for both x and y, that is, $f(x|y)$ and $f(y|x)$. I have suppressed the conditioning on ρ in these densities, simply because ρ is a known constant in this problem.

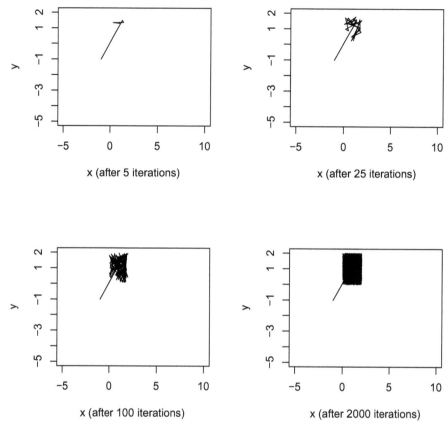

Fig. 4.8. Results of Gibbs sampler using rejection sampling to sample from conditional densities: Two-dimensional view after 5, 25, 100, and 2,000 iterations.

As we discussed above, Gibbs sampling does not require that we know the normalizing constant; we only need to know to what density each conditional density is proportional. Thus, we will drop the leading constant $(1/(2\pi\sqrt{1-\rho^2}))$. The conditional for x then requires that we treat y as known. If y is known, we can reexpress the kernel of the density as

$$f(x|y) \propto \exp\left\{-\frac{x^2 - x(2\rho y)}{2(1-\rho^2)}\right\} \exp\left\{-\frac{y^2}{2(1-\rho^2)}\right\},$$

and we can drop the latter exponential containing y^2, because it is simply a proportionality constant with respect to x. Thus, we are left with the left-hand exponential. If we complete the square in x, we obtain

$$f(x|y) \propto \exp\left\{-\frac{(x^2 - x(2\rho y) + (\rho y)^2 - (\rho y)^2)}{2(1-\rho^2)}\right\},$$

which reduces to

$$f(x|y) \propto \exp\left\{-\frac{(x-\rho y)^2 - (\rho y)^2}{2(1-\rho^2)}\right\}.$$

Given that both ρ and y are constants in the conditional for x, the latter term on the right in the numerator can be extracted just as y^2 was above, and we are left with:

$$f(x|y) \propto \exp\left\{-\frac{(x-\rho y)^2}{2(1-\rho^2)}\right\}.$$

Thus, the full conditional for x can be seen as proportional to a univariate normal density with a mean of ρy and a variance of $(1-\rho^2)$. We can find the full conditional for y exactly the same way. By symmetry, the full conditional for y will be proportional to a univariate normal density with a mean of ρx and the same variance.

Writing a Gibbs sampler to sample from this bivariate density, then, is quite easy, especially given that R (and most languages) have efficient algorithms for sampling from normal distributions (rnorm in R). Below is an R program that does such sampling:

```
#R program for Gibbs sampling from a bivariate normal pdf
x=matrix(-10,2000); y=matrix(-10,2000)
for(j in 2:2000)
  {
  #sampling from x|y
  x[j]=rnorm(1,mean=(.5*y[j-1]),sd=sqrt(1-.5*.5))
  #sampling from y|x
  y[j]=rnorm(1,mean=(.5*x[j]),sd=sqrt(1-.5*.5))
  }
```

This algorithm is quite similar to the Gibbs sampler shown previously for the bivariate planar density. The key difference is that the conditionals are normal; thus, x and y are updated using the rnorm random sampling function.

Figure 4.9 shows the state of the algorithm after 10, 50, 200, and 2,000 iterations. As the figure shows, despite the poor starting values of -10 for both x and y, the algorithm rapidly converged to the appropriate region (within 10 iterations).

Figure 4.10 contains four graphs. The upper graphs show the marginal distributions for x and y for the last 1,500 iterations of the algorithm, with the appropriate "true" marginal distributions superimposed. As these graphs show, the Gibbs sampler appears to have generated samples from the appropriate marginals. In fact, the mean and standard deviation for x are .059 and .984, respectively, which are close to their true values of 0 and 1. Similarly, the mean and standard deviation for y were .012 and .979, which are also close to their true values.

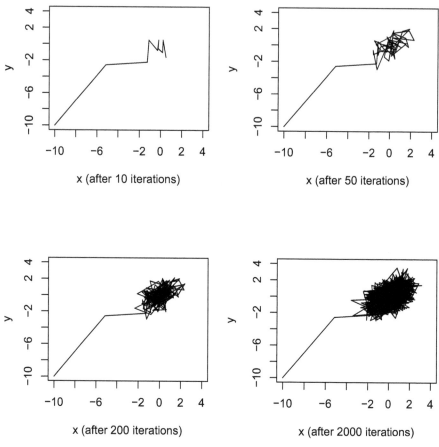

Fig. 4.9. Results of Gibbs sampler for standard bivariate normal distribution with correlation $r = .5$: Two-dimensional view after 10, 50, 200, and 2,000 iterations.

As I said earlier, we are typically interested in just the marginal distributions. However, I also stated that the samples of x and y can also be considered—after a sufficient number of burn-in iterations—as a sample from the joint density for both variables. Is this true? The lower left graph in the figure shows a contour plot for the true standard bivariate normal distribution with correlation $r = .5$. The lower right graph shows this same contour plot with the Gibbs samples superimposed. As the figure shows, the countour plot is completely covered by the Gibbs samples.

4.4.5 Reversing the process: Sampling the parameters *given* the data

Sampling *data* from densities, conditional on the parameters of the density, as we did in the previous section is an important process, but the process of Bayesian statistics is about sampling *parameters* conditional on having data,

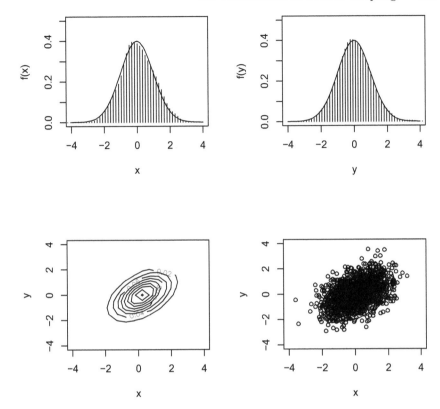

Fig. 4.10. Results of Gibbs sampler for standard bivariate normal distribution: Upper left and right graphs show marginal distributions for x and y (last 1,500 iterations); lower left graph shows contour plot of true density; and lower right graph shows contour plot of true density with Gibbs samples superimposed.

not about sampling *data* conditional on knowing the parameters. As I have repeatedly said, however, from the Bayesian perspective, both data and parameters are considered random quantities, and so sampling the parameters conditional on data is not a fundamentally different process than sampling data conditional on parameters. The main difference is simply in the mathematics we need to apply to the density to express it as a conditional density for the parameters rather than for the data. We first saw this process in the previous chapter when deriving the conditional posterior distribution for the mean parameter from a univariate normal distribution.

Let's first consider a univariate normal distribution example. In the previous chapter, we derived two results for the posterior distributions for the mean and variance parameters (assuming a reference prior of $1/\sigma^2$). In one, we showed that the posterior density could be factored to produce (1) a marginal posterior density for σ^2 that was an inverse gamma distribution, and (2) a conditional posterior density for μ that was a normal distribution:

$$p(\sigma^2|X) \propto IG\left((n-1)/2 \, , \, (n-1)\mathrm{var}(x)/2\right)$$
$$p(\mu|\sigma^2, X) \propto N\left(\bar{x} \, , \, \sigma^2/n\right).$$

In the second derivation for the posterior distribution for σ^2, we showed that the *conditional* (not marginal) distribution for σ^2 was also an inverse gamma distribution, but with slightly different parameters:

$$p(\sigma^2|\mu, X) \propto IG\left(n/2 \, , \, \sum(x_i - \mu)^2/2\right).$$

Both of these derivations lend themselves easily to Gibbs sampling. Under the first derivation, we could first sample a vector of values for σ^2 from the marginal distribution and then sample a value for μ conditional on each value of σ^2 from its conditional distribution. Under the second derivation, we would follow the iterative process shown in the previous sections, first sampling a value for σ^2 conditional on μ, then sampling a value for μ conditional on the new value for σ^2, and so on.

In practice, the first approach is more efficient. However, some situations may warrant the latter approach (e.g., when missing data are included). Here, I show both approaches in estimating the average years of schooling for the adult U.S. population in 2000. The data for this example are from the 2000 National Health Interview Survey (NHIS), a repeated cross-sectional survey conducted annually since 1969. The data set is relatively large by social science standards, consisting of roughly 40,000 respondents in each of many years. In 2000, after limiting the data to respondents 30 years and older and deleting observations missing on education, I obtained an analytic sample of 17,946 respondents. Mean educational attainment in the sample was 12.69 years (s.d. = 3.16 years), slightly below the mean of 12.74 from the 2000 U.S. Census.[4]

Below is an R program that first samples 2,000 values of the variance of educational attainment (σ^2) from its inverse gamma marginal distribution and then, conditional on each value for σ^2, samples μ from the appropriate normal distribution:

```
#R: sampling from marginal for variance and conditional for mean

x<-as.matrix(read.table("c:\\education.dat",header=F)[,1])
sig<-rgamma(2000,(length(x)-1)/2 , rate=((length(x)-1)*var(x)/2))
sig<-1/sig
mu<-rnorm(2000,mean=mean(x),sd=(sqrt(sig/length(x))))
```

---

[4] In calculating the mean from the census, I recoded the census categories for (1) under 9 years; (2) 9-12 years, no diploma; (3) high-school graduate or equivalent; (4) some college, no degree; (5) Associate degree; (6) Bachelor degree; and (4) graduate or professional degree to the midpoint for years of schooling and created a ceiling of 17 years, which is the upper limit for the NHIS.

This program is remarkably short, first reading the data into a vector X and then generating 2,000 draws from a gamma distribution with the appropriate shape and scale parameters. These draws are then inverted, because R has no direct inverse gamma distribution; thus, I make use of the fact that, if $1/x$ is gamma distributed with parameters a and b, then x is inverse gamma distributed with the same parameters. Finally, the program samples μ from its appropriate normal distribution.

Below is the R program for the alternative approach in which μ and σ are sequentially sampled from their conditional distributions:

```
#R: sampling from conditionals for both variance and mean

x<-as.matrix(read.table("c:\\education.dat",header=F)[,1])
mu=matrix(0,2000); sig=matrix(1,2000)
for(i in 2:2000)
 {
  sig[i]=rgamma(1,(length(x)/2),rate=sum((x-mu[i-1])^2)/2)
  sig[i]=1/sig[i]
  mu[i]=rnorm(1,mean=mean(x),sd=sqrt(sig[i]/length(x)))
 }
```

Under this approach, we must select starting values for μ and σ^2; here I use 0 and 1, respectively (assigned when the matrices are defined in R), which are far from their estimates based on the sample means. This approach also necessitates looping, as we saw in the planar density earlier.

Figure 4.11 shows the results of both algorithms. The first 1,000 draws have been discarded from each run, because the poor starting values in the second algorithm imply that convergence is not immediate. In contrast, under the first method, convergence is immediate; the first 1,000 are discarded simply to have comparable sample sizes. As the figure shows, the results are virtually identical for the two approaches.

Numerically, the posterior means for μ under the two approaches were both 12.69, and the posterior means for σ^2 were 10.01 and 10.00, respectively (the means for $\sqrt{\sigma^2}$ were both 3.16). These results are virtually identical to the sample estimates of these parameters, as they should be. A remaining question may be: What are the reasonable values for mean education in the population? In order to answer this question, we can construct a 95% "empirical probability interval" for μ by taking the 25th and 975th sorted values of μ from our Gibbs samples. For both approaches, the resulting interval is [12.64 , 12.73], which implies that the true population mean for years of schooling falls in this interval with probability .95.

4.5 Conclusions

As we have seen in the last two chapters, the Bayesian approach to inference involves simply summarizing the posterior density using basic sample statistics

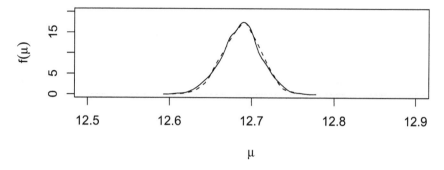

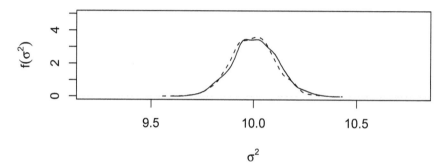

Fig. 4.11. Samples from posterior densities for a mean and variance parameter for NHIS years of schooling data under two Gibbs sampling approaches: The solid lines are the results for the marginal-for-σ^2-but conditional-for-μ approach; and the dashed lines are the results for the full conditionals approach.

like the mean, median, variance, and various quantiles of the distribution. When posterior densities are such that these integral-based statistics cannot be directly computed—e.g., when they are multivariate—modern Bayesian statistics turns to sampling from the posterior density and to computing these quantities just as we would when we have a sample of data.

Gibbs sampling provides a fairly easy method for sampling from multivariate densities, so long as we can derive the appropriate conditional densities. In most problems, this reduces simply to (1) treating other variables as fixed in the joint density, and (2) determining how to sample from the resulting conditional density. Sometimes, the conditional densities take known forms, as they did in our normal distribution example. Other times, the conditional densities may be derivable, but they may take unknown forms, as they did in our linear and planar distributions examples. In the latter case, we may turn to inversion or rejection sampling for sampling from the conditionals with unknown forms.

In some cases, however, inversion of a conditional density may not be possible, and rejection sampling may be difficult or very inefficient. In those cases, Bayesians can turn to another method—the Metropolis-Hastings algorithm. Discussion of that method is the topic of the next chapter. For alternative and more in-depth and theoretical expositions of the Gibbs sampler, I recommend the entirety of Gilks, Richardson, and Spiegelhalter 1996 in general and Gilks 1996 in particular. I also recommend a number of additional readings in the concluding chapter of this book.

4.6 Exercises

1. Find the inverse distribution function (F^{-1}) for $y|x$ in the bivariate planar density; that is, show how a $U(0,1)$ sample must be transformed to be a draw from $y|x$.
2. Develop a rejection sampler for sampling data from the bivariate planar density $f(x) \propto 2x + 3y + 2$.
3. Develop an inversion sampler for sampling data from the linear density $f(x) \propto 5x + 2$. (Hint: First, find the normalizing constant, and then find the inverse function).
4. Develop an appropriate routine for sampling the λ parameter from the Poisson distribution voting example in the previous chapter.
5. Develop an appropriate routine for sampling 20 observations (data points) from an $N(0,1)$ distribution. Then, reverse the process using these data to sample from the posterior distribution for μ and σ^2. Use the noninformative prior $p(\mu, \sigma^2) \propto 1/\sigma^2$, and use either Gibbs sampler described in the chapter. Next, plot the posterior density for μ, and superimpose an appropriate t distribution over this density. How close is the match? Discuss.
6. As we have seen throughout this chapter, computing integrals (e.g., the mean and variance) using sampling methods yields estimates that are not exact in finite samples but that become better and better estimates as the sample size increases. Describe how we might quantify how much sampling error is involved in estimating quantities using sampling methods (Hint: Consider the Central Limit Theorem).

5

Modern Model Estimation Part 2: Metroplis–Hastings Sampling

Gibbs sampling is a very powerful tool, and to date, it has been used by statisticians performing Bayesian analyses perhaps more than any other Markov chain Monte Carlo (MCMC) method. However, Gibbs sampling has several limitations. First, there are cases in which a conditional distribution cannot be easily derived or determined from the joint density. Such cases are rare, as we discussed previously: Conditional densities are proportional to the joint density. Nonetheless, consider the simple generic linear density discussed before:

$$f(x|m, b) = \frac{2(mx + b)}{(s - r)[m(s + r) + 2b]}.$$

With the boundaries s and r as known constants, the likelihood function for m and b would be:

$$L(m, b|X) \propto \prod_{i=1}^{n} \frac{mx_i + b}{m(s + r) + 2b}. \tag{5.1}$$

Even ignoring the denominator, the repeated multiplication of the numerator becomes messy. For example, consider just the first two terms:

$$
\begin{aligned}
L(m, b|X) &\propto \prod_{i=1}^{2} (mx_i + b) \\
&= (mx_1 + b)(mx_2 + b) \\
&= m^2 x_1 x_2 + mx_1 b + mx_2 b + b^2.
\end{aligned}
$$

Given that almost every term contains both m and b, and given that these terms are additive, it would be extremely difficult (if not impossible) to determine the conditionals for either parameter, almost regardless of what type of prior density one chose for the parameters. Fortunately, the most common distributions used in social science research are exponential family distributions (e.g., the normal and Poisson distributions) that do not generally present this type of problem.

A second, more common case in which Gibbs sampling may not be optimal is if a conditional density is not of a known form, inversion sampling from it is impossible, or it is difficult to find an appropriate envelope for rejection sampling. For example, determining the maximum value of a density in a multivariate model may be analytically difficult. We will discuss this case in greater depth below.

A third case in which Gibbs sampling may be limited in its usefulness is if Gibbs sampling is simply inefficient for the problem at hand. We will discuss this case in the next chapter and in Chapter 10, but essentially, there are cases in which sampling from the conditional distributions may lead to very slow "mixing" of the algorithm. That is, rather than converging rapidly to the center of the distribution of interest and sampling rapidly throughout it, the algorithm may stick in a low-density area, moving slowly to the main support of the density and moving slowly within it once it reaches it.

In each of these cases, an alternative to Gibbs sampling is the more generic Metropolis-Hastings (MH) algorithm. In this chapter, I first describe the MH algorithm in some detail. I then apply it to two generic examples in which Gibbs sampling would difficult to implement.

5.1 A generic MH algorithm

The MH algorithm is an algorithm that generates samples from a probability distribution, using the full joint density function (see Hastings 1970 for the original exposition; see Gilks, Richardson, and Spiegelhalter 1996 for a presentation of various MH algorithms). A key advantage to the MH algorithm over other methods of sampling, like inversion and rejection sampling, is that it will work with multivariate distributions (unlike inversion sampling), and we do not need an enveloping function (as in rejection sampling).

A basic MH algorithm consists of the following steps:

1. Establish starting values S for the parameter: $\theta^{j=0} = S$. Set $j = 1$.
2. Draw a "candidate" parameter, θ^c from a "proposal density," $\alpha(.)$.
3. Compute the ratio $R = \frac{f(\theta^c)\alpha(\theta^{j-1}|\theta^c)}{f(\theta^{j-1})\alpha(\theta^c|\theta^{j-1})}$.
4. Compare R with a $U(0,1)$ random draw u. If $R > u$, then set $\theta^j = \theta^c$. Otherwise, set $\theta^j = \theta^{j-1}$.
5. Set $j = j + 1$ and return to step 2 until enough draws are obtained.

In the first step, one must establish starting values for the parameters, just as in Gibbs sampling. Starting values can be obtained via maximum likelihood estimation or via some other (even arbitrary) method. MCMC theory says that the algorithm's stationary distribution—that is, the distribution to which the Markov chain produced by the algorithm converges—will be the posterior distribution of interest, regardless of the starting values chosen (Tierney 1996). However, particularly poor starting values may cause the algorithm to reject many candidates and hence not move quickly toward the main support of the posterior, leading to extremely long run times. We will discuss how to assess and address this problem, as well as others, in the next chapter.

In step 2, a candidate value for the parameter (θ^c) is obtained by simulating a value for it from a proposal density $[\alpha(.)]$. The simulated value is considered a "candidate," because it is not automatically accepted as a draw from the distribution of interest; it must be evaluated for acceptance just as in rejection sampling. Indeed, this step is somewhat akin to drawing a candidate from an enveloping function in rejection sampling, except that the proposal density need not actually envelop the posterior distribution. Instead, a proposal density can take any form that is easy to sample from (normal, uniform, etc.). Given that the proposal density is not the density of interest, we must check to determine whether the candidate parameter can be considered to be from the target distribution, just as we did in rejection sampling.

Often, we may use a symmetric proposal density (e.g., a normal or uniform) centered over the current value of the parameter (θ^{j-1}). For example, using a normal proposal density, the candidate would be drawn from a normal distribution with a mean equal to θ^{j-1} and some variance: $\theta^c = \theta^{j-1} + N(0, c)$, where c is a constant (more on the choice for c later). This approach yields a "random walk Metropolis algorithm," which is the main algorithm discussed/used in this book because of its simplicity and effectiveness.

The use of symmetric proposals centered over the previous value of the parameter is not necessary, but understanding asymmetry in the context of MH algorithms requires some discussion. In the MH algorithm, asymmetry means that $\alpha(\theta^c|\theta^{j-1}) \neq \alpha(\theta^{j-1}|\theta^c)$. In other words, there is greater probability that either the candidate would be proposed when the chain is in state θ^{j-1} than θ^{j-1} would be proposed when the chain is in state θ^c, or vice versa. To clarify this point, see Figure 5.1. The figure shows normal proposal densities centered over both the candidate and the previous values. Because these densities themselves are symmetric and centered over the candidate and previous values, the height of the proposal density at the candidate value, when the proposal is centered over the previous value, is the same as the height of the proposal density at the previous value, when the proposal is centered over the candidate value. This result implies that the chain is just as likely to move from the candidate to the previous value as it is to move from the previous value to the candidate.

When might a proposal density be asymmetric, or how may asymmetry arise? First, we can use proposals that are asymmetric densities, like the lognormal distribution. We have not discussed this distribution, but if $\ln(x) \sim N(\mu, \sigma^2)$, then $x \sim LogN(\mu, \sigma^2)$. The distribution is therefore skewed right (consider the distribution of income and $\ln(\text{income})$, for instance). Consider

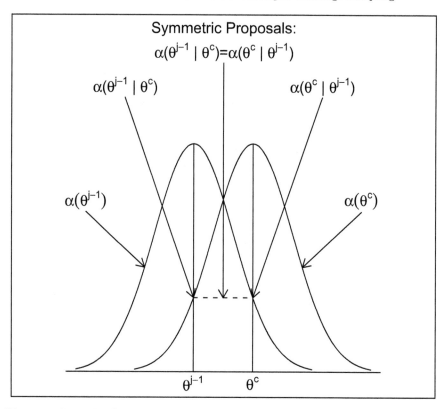

Fig. 5.1. Example of symmetric proposals centered over the previous and candidate values of the parameters.

using a lognormal proposal centered so that θ is the mode of the density.[1] Figure 5.2 shows this case. Given the right-hand skew/asymmetry of the proposal distributions, the probability of moving from θ^{j-1} to θ^c is not the same as moving from θ^c to θ^{j-1}.

A second way in which asymmetry may occur is if we use proposal densities that are fixed, regardless of the current state of the chain. For example, we could specify the proposal distribution to be an $N(0, 100)$ distribution, with this proposal *not changing* from one iteration of the algorithm to the next. In

---

[1] The mode (MO) of a lognormal density is equal to $\exp(\mu-\sigma^2)$, and so the proposal is: $\alpha(\theta^c|\theta^{j-1}) = (\theta^{j-1} - MO) + \mathrm{LogN}(\mu, \sigma^2)$.

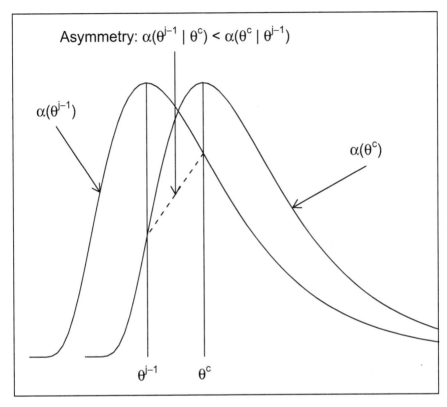

Fig. 5.2. Example of asymmetric proposals centered at the mode over the previous and candidate values of the parameters.

other words, the proposal could remain $N(0, 100)$ regardless of whether θ is currently 12 or 55 (just to pick some random values). This approach would make the algorithm quite similar to a rejection sampler.[2]

A final way in which asymmetry may occur, and one that is most relevant for the types of models discused in this book, is if the density for a parameter is bounded. For example, a variance parameter cannot take a value less than 0. If we are using a uniform proposal to update the parameter, however, it might

---

[2] In fact, this sampler is called the independence sampler and may not work well at all if the posterior density is not enveloped by the proposal—see Gilks, Richardson, and Spiegelhalter (1996).

be possible for an illegal value to be proposed: Whenever the chain wanders toward the boundary, the left-hand side of the proposal density may overlap 0. We may choose to allow the proposal of invalid candidates and simply realize that, when a candidate is selected that is less than 0, $f(\theta^c) = 0$, and so the chain does not move (i.e., we automatically set $\theta^j = \theta^{j-1}$). Alternatively, we may choose to change the proposal density to exclude values below the boundary and thus increase the efficiency of the algorithm (i.e., no illegitimate values will be proposed as candidates). However, if we follow this strategy, we are actually increasing the probability that the algorithm will select values *away* from the boundary more often than it should. To see how asymmetry occurs in this case, refer to Figure 5.3. The figure shows the chain in two states—θ^{j-1} and θ^c. When the chain is in state θ^{j-1}, it can only propose candidates that are greater than 0, and hence, the proposal is both asymmetric around θ^{j-1} and *tall*, because the area under the density must be 1. When the chain is in state θ^c, on the other hand, the boundary constraint is not an issue, and therefore the density is symmetric and *short*. The upside to imposing the boundary constraint is that we will not propose illegitimate candidates. The downside is that we now need to compute the latter half of the ratio R to compensate for the asymmetry.

Generally speaking, with large data sets and with the models discussed in this book, although boundary constraints exist, they generally do not pose much of a problem: It is a rare event when a parameter approaches the boundary. Thus, the efficiency gain by using an asymmetric proposal like in Figure 5.3 is often minimal.

Returning to step 3, when asymmetric proposals are used (or asymmetry arises via the second or third cases), a correction factor in the ratio R helps adjust for the asymmetry. This correction factor is the latter half of the ratio in step 3. The first part of this ratio (called an "importance ratio")— the $f(\theta^c)/f(\theta^{j-1})$—is simply the ratio of the unnormalized posterior density evaluated at the candidate parameter value (θ^c) to the posterior density evaluated at the previous parameter value (θ^{j-1}). The second part of the ratio [the $\alpha(\theta^{j-1}|\theta^c)/\alpha(\theta^c|\theta^{j-1})$] is the ratio of the *proposal* densities evaluated at the candidate and previous points. The $(a|b)$ means the probability (really, the density height of α) that a candidate value a would be proposed, given that the chain is in location b. This ratio adjusts for the fact that, with asymmetric proposals, some candidate values may be selected more often than others, and it makes the algorithm a Metropolis-Hastings algorithm rather than simply a Metropolis algorithm.

In step 4, we simulate a draw u from a $U(0,1)$ density and compare it with our ratio R. If $R > u$, we accept the candidate as a draw from our posterior density $p(.)$. Otherwise, we retain the previous parameter value. Let's consider this step in some detail. An alternative way that this step is often presented is to say "accept the candidate with probability $\min(R, 1)$" (Johnson and Albert 1999). In this representation, the "min" function is included as a formality to indicate that probabilities cannot exceed 1. Thus, again, the comparison

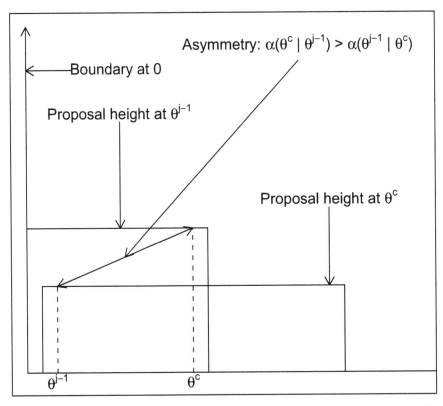

Fig. 5.3. Example of asymmetry in proposals due to a boundary constraint on the parameter space.

is between R and some random probability (hence, the $U(0,1)$ random draw u). If R is greater than 1, then the candidate will be accepted. If R is large, but less than 1, then the candidate will almost certainly be accepted. If R is small, then the candidate will occasionally/rarely be accepted. Finally, if R is 0, the candidate will not be accepted. This step ensures that the accepted candidates come from the distribution of interest, $p(.)$.

5.1.1 Relationship between Gibbs and MH sampling

As you might guess, Gibbs sampling and MH are related approaches to simulation. First, the Gibbs sampler can be viewed as a special case of the MH

algorithm in which the proposal densities for each parameter/random variable
are the full conditionals. In Gibbs sampling, every candidate is selected; there
is no rejection of candidates. The reason is that the ratio R is always 1. Why?
Consider the components of the ratio R:

$$R = \frac{f(\theta^c)\alpha(\theta^{j-1}|\theta^c)}{f(\theta^{j-1})\alpha(\theta^c|\theta^{j-1})}. \tag{5.2}$$

The first term in the numerator is the posterior distribution evaluated at the
candidate value. The second term in the numerator is the posterior probability
of returning to the previous point given that we are at the current point. In the
denominator, the first expression is equivalent to this latter value, because the
proposal density is already the full conditional for the parameter. Similarly,
the second expression in the denominator is equivalent to the first term in the
numerator. Thus $f(\theta^c) = \alpha(\theta^c|\theta^{j-1})$, and vice versa. Since the parameter is
accepted with probability $\min(1, R)$, and it is always true that $R = 1$, every
draw is accepted.

The 100% acceptance rate makes the Gibbs sampler more efficient, and
therefore generally faster than MH algorithms, just as the inversion sampling
method is more efficient than the rejection sampling method. However, as
mentioned previously and discussed later in the book, there are cases in which
the MH algorithm is more efficient, and there are cases in which the difficulty
of implementing Gibbs sampling—in terms of deriving conditionals—overrides
its efficiency. I have sometimes found it easier to use a random walk metropolis
algorithm and to let the computer labor more intensively than for me to labor
more intensively to derive complex conditionals and let the computer work
less!

A second link between Gibbs sampling and MH sampling is that they can
be combined to sample from multivariate densities. Recall that the Gibbs sampler splits the joint density into conditional densities. In the previous chapter,
we sampled from each conditional using the inversion method in one example
and rejection sampling in the next. There is no inherent reason we cannot
use different sampling methods for sampling from different conditionals; for
example, using inversion sampling for sampling from $x|y$ and rejection sam-
pling for sampling from $y|x$. By the same token, there is no inherent reason we
cannot use an MH subalgorithm to sample from one of the conditional distributions. This approach has been termed "Metropolis within Gibbs" sampling
(see Gilks 1996).

We can also view such a hybrid approach as "Gibbs within Metropolis"
sampling, if we view the overall algorithm as an MH algorithm with the component parameters updated one-at-a-time. Indeed, we should recall that Gibbs
sampling is simply a special case of MH sampling in the first place, and so
the entire algorithm is always an MH algorithm!

Because the MH algorithm does not require that all parameters in a problem be updated simultaneously, updating parameters one-at-a-time in an MH
algorithm makes MH sampling *seem* like Gibbs sampling. However, the MH

algorithm differs from the Gibbs sampler in two important ways. First, the candidate parameter is not automatically accepted, because it comes from a proposal density and not from the appropriate conditional distribution. Second, the proposal density is not an enveloping function as in the rejection sampling routine discussed above. In short, all Gibbs sampling is MH sampling, but not all MH sampling is Gibbs sampling.

Some of the algorithms discussed in the later chapters of this book will involve mixtures of Gibbs and MH steps, so it is important to realize that their combination is possible and sometimes even a desirable alternative to one or the other approach. For the models presented in the later chapters, virtually all of the algorithms that involve MH steps technically will be random walk metropolis algorithms involving symmetric proposals.

5.2 Example: MH sampling when conditional densities are difficult to derive

In Chapter 2 I suggested that a linear density may fit the 2000 GSS item regarding the importance of expressing unpopular views ("free speech") better than some other distribution. As we discussed at the beginning of this chapter, it would be quite difficult to determine the conditional distributions for the linear density parameters, m and b, and so Gibbs sampling would not be a good option for sampling from the posterior density. For that matter, a classical analysis involving finding the maximum likelihood estimate of these parameters would be difficult also. Therefore, here I develop an MH algorithm for sampling from the posterior density for m and b. First, I assume uniform prior distributions for the parameters such that $p(m) \propto U(-\infty, \infty)$ and $p(b) \propto U(0, \infty)$. Although these priors are improper (they cannot integrate to 1), the posterior distribution is proper, subject to an important constraint: m and b must be perfectly related. The possible responses to the free speech item range from 0 to 5.[3] Thus, if $b = 0$, m must equal 2 in order for the area under the (sampling) density to equal 1. Similarly, if $b = 5$, m must be -2. More generally, $b = (2 - (s - r)^2 m)/2(s - r)$, (find this) and so, once m is known, b is automatically determined. This finding makes an MH algorithm a simple one-parameter process. Below is a random walk metropolis algorithm that samples from the posterior distribution for m (and by default, b):

```
#R program for Random Walk Metropolis algorithm

m<-matrix(0,5000); b<-matrix(.2,5000); z<-matrix(0,1377)
z[1:17]=0;    z[18:32]=1;    z[33:103]=2
z[104:425]=3; z[426:826]=4; z[827:1337]=5
```

---

[3] The original metric was integers ranging from 1 to 6, but I have recoded to the (0,5) interval and have made a standard assumption that responses are continuously, rather than discretely, distributed for simplicity.

```
acctot=0

for(i in 2:5000)
 {
  m[i]=m[i-1]+rnorm(1,mean=0,sd=.002)
  b[i]=(2-25*m[i])/10
  acc=tot=1
  for(j in 1:1377)
   {tot=tot*((z[j]*m[i]+b[i])/(z[j]*m[i-1]+b[i-1]))}
  if(runif(1,min=0,max=1)>tot || b[i]<0)
   {m[i]=m[i-1]; b[i]=b[i-1]; acc=0}
  acctot=acctot+acc

  if(i%%10==0){print(c(i,m[i],b[i],acctot/i))}
 }
```

The first line of this program establishes (1) the vectors and starting values for the slope (m) and intercept (b) parameters (step 1 of the general MH algorithm described above), and (2) the vector for the data (z). The next two lines constitute the data, with $17/1337$ persons responding "0", $15/1337$ persons responding "1," and so on. The third line sets a variable acctot equal to 0; this variable keeps a tally of the number of candidate parameter values that are accepted over the course of the algorithm. (We will discuss the need for this quantity in some depth later).

The subsequent lines of the program constitute the iterative looping for the MH algorithm. First, at each iteration, a candidate parameter value for m is generated using a normal proposal density centered over the previous value for m (m[i]=m[i-1]+rnorm(1,mean=0,sd=.002)), and b is computed (b[i]=(2-25*m[i])/10), given the candidate value for m (step 2 of the general MH algorithm). The next line sets variables acc and tot equal to 1. acc is an indicator for whether a candidate is accepted. By default, the algorithm assumes the candidate is accepted; acc is set to 0 later in the event the candidate is rejected. tot is initialized at 1; this variable is used to tabulate the ratio R.

The next two lines loop over the data in generating the unnormalized posterior density value at the current and previous values for the parameters. This is the ratio R from step 3 of the general MH algorithm.[4]

In accordance with Step 4 of the general MH algorithm, the following lines (1) compare this ratio to a $U(0,1)$ draw (say u), and (2) set the values of m and b to their previous values if $R < u$ or $b < 0$ (the prior constraint on b).

---

[4] As written, the program computes this ratio one person at a time and sequentially multiplies the results together, because computing the entire posterior density at either the candidate or previous value yields a number too large for the computer to handle. That is, $\prod_{i=1}^{n} A_i / \prod_{i=1}^{n} B_i = \prod_{i=1}^{n} A_i/B_i$, but the former leads to overflows in the numerator and denominator, whereas the latter does not.

At this point, if the candidate values are rejected, the indicator `acc` is set to 0.

For monitoring the acceptance rate, `acc` is then added to `acctot`. The last few lines print the current results to the screen, including the current values of the parameters and the updated acceptance rate.

Figure 5.4 shows the results of the algorithm. The upper graph shows a trace plot of the parameter m across the run of the algorithm. As the figure shows, m converged very rapidly from its poor starting value of 0 to a region around .07. The lower graph is a histogram of the last 3,000 sampled values of m, with a vertical reference line at the mean of m ($\bar{m} = .0697$, s.d. $= .0013$). The mean for b was .0257 (s.d. $= .003$), and the overall acceptance rate of the algorithm was 56%. The posterior mean values for m and b were used in Figure 2.3 to construct the superimposed "best linear fit" line.

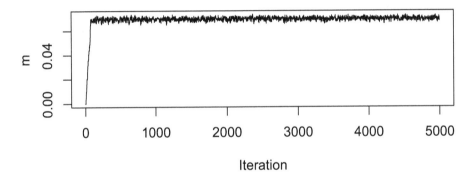

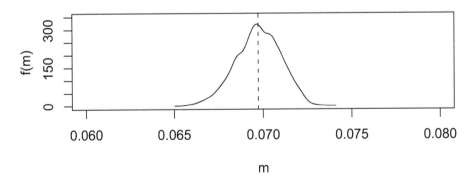

Fig. 5.4. Trace plot and histogram of m parameter from linear density model for the 2000 GSS free speech data.

5.3 Example: MH sampling for a conditional density with an unknown form

In Chapter 2, in addition to suggesting that a linear density may fit the free speech item better than a normal distribution, we also discussed that a planar density may fit the two GSS items concerning the importance of free speech and political participation better than some other distribution. A limitation of the planar density we discussed, however, is that it does not allow us to consider that the two items may be related and to estimate the extent of the relationship. Yet, the two certainly may be related, and they appear to be, given the peaks along the diagonal that the planar density is unable to model.

A density that does allow us to estimate the relationship between the two items is the bivariate normal distribution, which we have discussed in the previous chapter. For this example, we will assume that the data from Table 2.1 follow a bivariate normal distribution, and we will estimate the parameter ρ, which is the correlation between the two variables. In order to keep the mathematics relatively simple at this point, we will standardize the variables and assume that the means (μ_x and μ_y) and variances (σ_x^2 and σ_y^2) for each variable are 0 and 1, respectively. In that case, the likelihood function for the data is:

$$L(\rho|x,y) = \prod_{i=1}^{n} \frac{1}{2\pi\sqrt{1-\rho^2}} \exp\left\{ -\frac{1}{2(1-\rho^2)} \left[x_i^2 - 2\rho x_i y_i + y_i^2\right] \right\}.$$

In order to make the analysis fully Bayesian, we need to specify an appropriate prior distribution for the sole parameter ρ. In the univariate normal distribution, $1/\sigma^2$ is a reference prior; in the bivariate normal distribution, $1/|\Sigma|^{(3/2)}$ is an analogous prior (the Jeffreys prior; see Gelman et al. 1995), where Σ is the covariance matrix of x and y. Given that we have standardized the variables and have assumed each variance parameter is known to be 1, the prior is: $1/(1-\rho^2)^{(3/2)}$. Under this prior, our posterior density for n observations is simply:

$$f(\rho|x,y) \propto \frac{1}{(1-\rho^2)^{(3/2)}} \prod_{i=1}^{n} \frac{1}{2\pi\sqrt{1-\rho^2}} \exp\left\{ -\frac{1}{2(1-\rho^2)} \left[x_i^2 - 2\rho x_i y_i + y_i^2\right] \right\}.$$

This posterior density can be simplified somewhat by carrying out the multiplication and combining like terms as:

$$f(\rho|x,y) \propto \frac{1}{(1-\rho^2)^{(n+3)/2}} \exp\left\{ -\frac{1}{2(1-\rho^2)} \left[\sum x_i^2 - 2\rho \sum x_i y_i + \sum y_i^2\right] \right\}.$$

However, because the $-1/2(1-\rho^2)$ is multiplicative within the exponential, there is nothing more that can be done to simplify the posterior density. As it stands, this posterior density for ρ is not a known form, and so Gibbs sampling is not a straightforward option (but see Albert 1992 for an approach to using Gibbs sampling to sample a correlation parameter via transformation of variables in an unrelated model).[5] Below is an R program that uses MH sampling to sample from the posterior density for ρ. To save space, I have omitted a number of initial lines that define the data (from Table 2.1):

```
#MH algorithm for sampling a correlation parameter
#x and y are the data, already stored in memory

lnpost<-function(r)
 {-690*log(1-r^2)-.5*(sum(x^2)-2*r*sum(x*y)+sum(y^2))/(1-r^2)}

corr=matrix(0,10000); acctot=0
for(i in 2:10000)
  {
   corr[i]=corr[i-1]+runif(1,min=-.07,max=.07)
   acc=1
   if(abs(corr[i])>1){acc=0; corr[i]=corr[i-1]}
   if((lnpost(corr[i])-lnpost(corr[i-1]))
        <log(runif(1,min=0,max=1)))
    {corr[i]=corr[i-1]; acc=0}
   acctot=acctot+acc
   if(i%%100==0){print(c(i,corr[i],acctot/i))}
  }
```

The first line of this program creates a function (lnpost) that evaluates the log of the posterior density, given the data and a specified value for the correlation coefficient (r). Here, I have introduced a new approach—using the log of the posterior density rather than the posterior density. With a sample as large as this one ($n = 1,377$), evaluating the posterior itself would generate an underflow problem because of the large negative exponents involved in the posterior. Evaluating the log of the posterior resolves this problem. However, it requires a change later in the program as I will discuss.

After the matrix corr[] is created to store the samples of ρ, and the acceptance rate total is established, the main loop begins. As with the linear density example in the previous section, the parameter is first updated, here using a uniform proposal density. The candidate is assumed to be accepted (acc=1), but it is then evaluated twice for rejection. It is first evaluated to determine whether it is a legitimate value for a correlation (within the $[-1, 1]$ interval). Next, it is evaluated using the standard step 3 of the generic MH algorithm: If $R < u$, the candidate is rejected. However, given that we are comparing *log* posterior values, the ratio R becomes a subtraction, and it must be compared with the log of a uniform draw, rather than simply a

---

[5] In fact, univariate sampling is really not Gibbs sampling, but this finding—that the conditional is an unknown form—would hold if the mean and variance parameters were being estimated rather than assumed to be known quantities.

uniform draw. As before, the acceptance rate is then updated, and the program occasionally prints some output to the screen for monitoring.

Figure 5.5 provides a graphic display of the results. I show a trace plot of ρ across the 10,000 iterations of the algorithm (upper figure) and a histogram of the last several thousand samples of ρ, with a reference line superimposed at the posterior mean for ρ ($\bar{\rho} = .4504$; s.d.$(\rho) = .02$) (lower figure). As with the m parameter from the linear density example, ρ appears to have rapidly converged from its starting value of 0 to its posterior distribution. The results suggest that there is a moderately strong, positive relationship between people's beliefs in the importance of free speech and of participation in the political process.

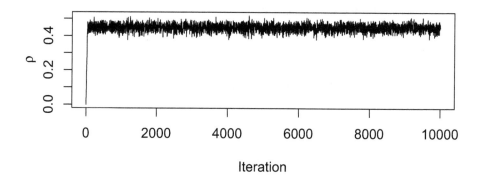

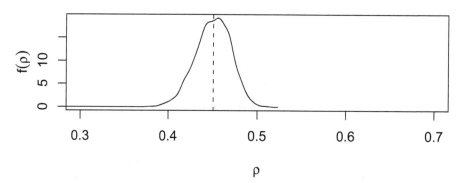

Fig. 5.5. Trace plot and histogram of ρ parameter from bivariate normal density model for the 2000 GSS free speech and political participation data.

5.4 Extending the bivariate normal example: The full multiparameter model

In the preceding section, we standardized the data and assumed the mean and variance parameters in the bivariate normal distribution were known. The result is that our posterior mean estimate for ρ is almost identical to what we would have obtained if we had just computed the Pearson correlation: The Pearson correlation for these data was also .4504. Although I did not present an empirical 95% interval for ρ derived from the MH algorithm above, this interval was $[.408, .485]$. A comparable interval can be constructed for the Pearson correlation. Specifically, the traditional way to construct such an interval is to use Fisher's z transformation of the correlation: $z = .5 \times (\ln(1 + \rho) - \ln(1 - \rho))$. Whereas the correlation is bounded on the $[-1, 1]$ interval and therefore tends to have a skewed distribution, Fisher's z is approximately normal, with an approximate standard deviation of $\sigma_z = 1/\sqrt{n - 3}$. Thus, a 95% interval for z can be constructed as $z \pm 1.96 \times \sigma_z$. Once the interval is obtained, the upper and lower bounds can be transformed back to the original ρ scale (see Snedecor and Cochran 1980). For this particular problem, the resulting interval is $[.407, .492]$, which is a result comparable with but broader than the one we obtained using the MH algorithm.

A key problem with our Bayesian interval estimate is that we have completely ignored uncertainty in the values of the other parameters in the model: μ_x, μ_y, σ_x^2, and σ_y^2. As a result, our interval is almost certainly too small. Given that we are almost certainly not interested in any parameter other than ρ, the other parameters are sometimes called "nuissance parameters." They are not of fundamental interest, but they must be dealt with in order to obtain a valid interval estimate for ρ.

A straightforward solution exists under the Bayesian approach using an MH algorithm. Here, I show how Gibbs sampling steps and MH sampling steps can be combined in order to obtain a more appropriate interval from the marginal posterior distribution of ρ.

Assuming the Jeffreys prior $1/|\Sigma|^{3/2}$ as before, the complete posterior density $f(\rho, \mu_x, \mu_y, \sigma_x^2, \sigma_y^2 | x, y)$ is proportional to:

$$\frac{1}{|\Sigma|^{3/2}} \prod_{i=1}^{n} \frac{1}{2\pi\sigma_x\sigma_y\sqrt{1 - \rho^2}} \times$$

$$\exp\left\{-\frac{1}{2(1 - \rho^2)}\left[\frac{(x_i - \mu_x)^2}{\sigma_x^2} - \frac{2\rho(x_i - \mu_x)(y_i - \mu_y)}{\sigma_x\sigma_y} + \frac{(y_i - \mu_y)^2}{\sigma_y^2}\right]\right\}.$$

This posterior density can be simplified somewhat by carrying out the multiplication:

$$(\sigma_x^2)^{-(3+n)/2}(\sigma_y^2)^{-(3+n)/2}(1 - \rho^2)^{-(3+n)/2} \times$$

$$\exp\left\{-\frac{1}{2(1-\rho^2)}\left[\frac{\sum(x_i-\mu_x)^2}{\sigma_x^2}-\frac{2\rho\sum(x_i-\mu_x)(y_i-\mu_y)}{\sigma_x\sigma_y}+\frac{\sum(y_i-\mu_y)^2}{\sigma_y^2}\right]\right\}.$$

$$\tag{5.3}$$

5.4.1 The conditionals for μ_x and μ_y

In order to develop a Gibbs sampling routine (with MH steps for simulating σ_x^2, σ_y^2, and ρ), we need to derive the conditionals for the parameters in the model. This process is tedious, although not fundamentally difficult. In deriving the conditional for μ_x, as before we can eliminate multiplicative terms that are constant with respect to μ_x. The remaining terms are:

$$p(\mu_x|\mu_y,\sigma_x^2,\sigma_y^2,\rho,x,y)\propto$$

$$\exp\left\{-\frac{1}{2(1-\rho^2)}\left[\frac{\sum(x_i-\mu_x)^2}{\sigma_x^2}-\frac{2\rho\sum(x_i-\mu_x)(y_i-\mu_y)}{\sigma_x\sigma_y}\right]\right\}.$$

This result can be simplified by expanding the quadratic expressions and again eliminating terms that do not involve μ_x as proportionality constants. Following this strategy leaves us with:

$$p(\mu_x|\mu_y,\sigma_x^2,\sigma_y^2,\rho,x,y)\propto$$

$$\exp\left\{-\frac{1}{2(1-\rho^2)}\left[\frac{n}{\sigma_x^2}(\mu_x^2-2\bar{x}\mu_x)-\frac{2n\rho}{\sigma_x\sigma_y}(\mu_x\mu_y-\bar{y}\mu_x)\right]\right\}.$$

In order to conserve space, I do not elaborate on all the remaining steps. However, if we take this expression, (1) factor an n from the numerator, (2) multiply through by $\sigma_x^2\sigma_y$ to eliminate the denominator, and (3) rearrange terms, we obtain:

$$\exp\left\{\left(-\frac{n}{2\sigma_x^2(1-\rho^2)}\right)\left[\mu_x^2-2\mu_x\left(\bar{x}+\frac{\sigma_x\rho}{\sigma_y}(\mu_y-\bar{y})\right)\right]\right\}.$$

As in the previous chapter, we can now complete the square in μ_x, but even without doing this, we may recognize that the conditional for μ_x is:

$$\mu_x|\mu_y,\sigma_x,\sigma_y,\rho,x,y\sim N\left(\bar{x}+\frac{\sigma_x}{\sigma_y}\rho(\mu_y-\bar{y}),\ \frac{\sigma_x^2(1-\rho^2)}{n}\right).$$

Suppose, momentarily that we know $\rho=0$. In that case, the conditional posterior for μ_x would reduce to the posterior for the mean in the previous chapter:

$$\mu_x|\rho=0\sim N\left(\bar{x},\ \sigma_x^2/n\right).$$

By symmetry, we can obtain a comparable conditional distribution for μ_y; only the x and y subscripts must be changed. What remains is determining the conditional distributions for the two variance parameters and the correlation.

5.4.2 The conditionals for σ_x^2, σ_y^2, and ρ

The derivations for the conditional distributions for the variance parameters and correlation parameter are not as straightforward as the derivations for the mean parameters. First, as we noted before, because ρ appears in multiplicative form within the exponential, there are no terms that can be separated from this parameter, and so there is little simplication that can be done to clarify the distribution for ρ. Only the leading terms $(\sigma_x^2)^{(3+n)/2}(\sigma_y^2)^{(3+n)/2}$ outside the exponential can be eliminated as proportionality constants.

Second, using scalar notation with the model parameterized in terms of the correlation parameter ρ rather than the *covariance* parameter σ_{xy}, the univariate conditional distributions for the variance parameters are also difficult to derive. For example, in terms of the conditional for σ_x^2, let's begin with the full posterior density found in Equation 5.3. In this expression, the leading multiplicative terms not involving σ_x^2 can be eliminated as constants, and within the exponential, the additive terms not involving σ_x^2 can be eliminated. This leaves us with the conditional posterior:

$$p(\sigma_x^2 | \mu_x, \mu_y, \sigma_y^2, \rho, x, y) \propto$$

$$(\sigma_x^2)^{-(3+n)/2} \exp\left\{-\frac{1}{2(1-\rho^2)}\left[\frac{\sum(x_i-\mu_x)^2}{\sigma_x^2} - \frac{2\rho\sum(x_i-\mu_x)(y_i-\mu_y)}{\sigma_x\sigma_y}\right]\right\}.$$

Next, we can multiply the terms in the exponential through by $\sigma_x^2\sigma_y$ to eliminate the denominator to obtain (within the exponential):

$$\exp\left\{-\frac{1}{2(1-\rho^2)\sigma_x^2\sigma_y}\left[\sigma_y\sum(x_i-\mu_x)^2 - 2\sigma_x\rho\sum(x_i-\mu_x)(y_i-\mu_y)\right]\right\}.$$

If we rearrange terms a little, we obtain:

$$p(\sigma_x^2 | \mu_x, \mu_y, \sigma_y^2, \rho, x, y) \propto$$

$$(\sigma_x^2)^{-(n+1)/2+1} \exp\left\{-\left[\frac{\sigma_y\sum(x_i-\mu_x)^2 - 2\sigma_x\rho\sum(x_i-\mu_x)(y_i-\mu_y)}{2(1-\rho^2)\sigma_y}\right]/\sigma_x^2\right\}.$$

In this representation, the distribution for σ^2 *almost* appears to be inverse gamma with parameters $\alpha = (n+1)/2$ and β equal to the expression in brackets within the exponential. However, there is an additional σ_x term in the expression that cannot be factored out. A similar expression can be found for σ_y^2. In fact, we could use the matrix representation for the multivariate normal distribution and derive the conditional distribution for the entire covariance matrix Σ, and we will do so in the next section. For now, however, consider that it is simpler, at this point, to use MH steps to update the variance parameters as well as the correlation parameter.

5.4.3 The complete MH algorithm

Below is a hybrid algorithm with Gibbs sampling steps for updating the mean
parameters μ_x and μ_y and with MH steps for updating σ_x^2 and σ_y^2:

```
# R program for simulating parameters from BVN distribution
# x and y are the data, already stored in memory

lnpost<-function(ar,amx,amy,asx,asy,ax,ay,axy)
{return(-690*log((1-ar^2)*asx*asy)
       +(-.5/(1-ar^2))*(ax/asx - 2*ar*axy/sqrt(asx*asy) + ay/asy))}

mnx=mean(x); mny=mean(y); accr=0; accx=0; accy=0
mx=matrix(0,10000); my=matrix(0,10000);
sx=matrix(1,10000); sy=matrix(1,10000); r=matrix(0,10000)

for(i in 2:10000){
#sample mx from normal
mx[i]<-rnorm(1,mean=mnx+(r[i-1]*sx[i-1]*(my[i-1]-mny))/sy[i-1]
             ,sd=sqrt(sx[i-1]*(1-r[i-1]^2)/1377))

#sample my from normal
my[i]<-rnorm(1,mean=mny+(r[i-1]*sy[i-1]*(mx[i]-mnx))/sx[i-1]
             ,sd=sqrt(sy[i-1]*(1-r[i-1]^2)/1377))

#update sums of squares
sx2=sum((x-mx[i])^2); sy2=sum((y-my[i])^2);
sxy=sum((x-mx[i])*(y-my[i]))

#sample sx
sx[i]=sx[i-1]+runif(1,min=-.1,max=.1); acc=1
if(sx[i]<0){acc=0; sx[i]=sx[i-1]}
if((lnpost(r[i-1],mx[i],my[i],sx[i],sy[i-1],sx2,sy2,sxy)
   -lnpost(r[i-1],mx[i],my[i],sx[i-1],sy[i-1],sx2,sy2,sxy))
   <log(runif(1,min=0,max=1)))
{acc=0; sx[i]=sx[i-1]}
accx=accx+acc

#sample sy
sy[i]=sy[i-1]+runif(1,min=-.1,max=.1); acc=1
if(sy[i]<0){acc=0; sy[i]=sy[i-1]}
if((lnpost(r[i-1],mx[i],my[i],sx[i],sy[i],sx2,sy2,sxy)
   -lnpost(r[i-1],mx[i],my[i],sx[i],sy[i-1],sx2,sy2,sxy))
   <log(runif(1,min=0,max=1)))
{acc=0; sy[i]=sy[i-1]}
accy=accy+acc

#sample r from full posterior using MH step
```

```
r[i]=r[i-1]+runif(1,min=-.05,max=.05);  acc=1
if(abs(r[i])>1){acc=0;  r[i]=r[i-1]}
if((lnpost(r[i],mx[i],my[i],sx[i],sy[i],sx2,sy2,sxy)
    -lnpost(r[i-1],mx[i],my[i],sx[i],sy[i],sx2,sy2,sxy))
  <log(runif(1,min=0,max=1)))
{acc=0;  r[i]=r[i-1]}
accr=accr+acc

if(i%%100==0){print(c(i,accr/i,accx/i,accy/i,
                  mx[i],my[i],sx[i],sy[i],r[i]),digits=4)}
```

This program is intimidatingly long. However, if we consider each section of the program separately, it is really fairly simple. For the sake of brevity, I will not discuss the entire program line-by-line; instead, I will briefly describe the separate sections.

At the very beginning of the program, I define the various variables to be used in the program, and I create a function (lnpost) that is used in the MH steps for updating the variance and correlation parameters. This function is the log posterior density, which is evaluated at established values of the data and parameters. Once again, I use the log posterior density, because evaluating the density itself (in this form) produces computational underflow issues.

The next two sections simply sample the mean parameters from appropriate normal distributions derived in the previous section, conditional on the current values of all other parameters in the model. The next, brief section updates the sums of squares (sums of the square deviations of the data from the current values of the mean parameters). The next three sections update the variances and correlation, given the current values for the means, sums of squares, and other remaining parameters. These sections are remarkably similar, except that (1) the candidate generation step changes, and (2) the lnpost function is fed different variables. Notice that I have created separate acceptance rate variables—one for each variance and correlation—and that I use a logged value of a uniform random number to compare with the ratio of the logged posterior densities.

Figure 5.6 shows a trace plot and histogram of the samples from the marginal posterior distribution of the correlation parameter—the key parameter of interest in the model. As the figure shows, the algorithm rapidly converged to the .45 region (the Pearson correlation). Overall, the posterior means for all parameters were very close to their sample counterparts: $\bar{\mu}_x = \bar{x} = 2.19$; $\bar{\mu}_y = \bar{y} = 2.02$; $\sigma_x^2 = s_x^2 = 1.43$; $\sigma_y^2 = s_y^2 = 1.14$; and $\bar{\rho} = r = .450$. Finally, we can construct a new interval estimate for ρ that reflects our uncertainty in all the parameters. This interval is $[.406, .491]$, which is about 10% larger than the estimate we obtained when we assumed the other parameters were fixed at their sample values, and this estimate more closely matches the one obtained using the z transformation of the Pearson correlation.

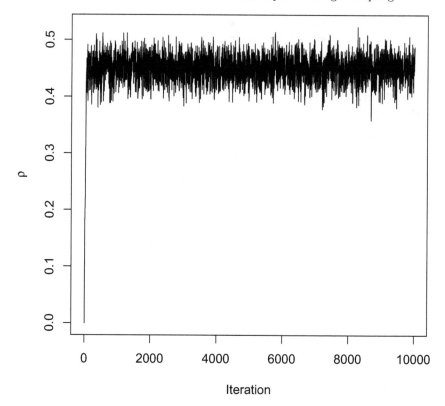

Fig. 5.6. Trace plot and histogram of ρ from bivariate normal model for the 2000 GSS free speech and political participation data.

5.4.4 A matrix approach to the bivariate normal distribution problem

As we discussed, the bivariate normal distribution is simply the multivariate normal distribution with dimensions equal to two. Although I presented a scalar version of the density function, the matrix representation shown in Chapter 2 can also be used to construct the posterior density. Under that approach, given the same prior as used above, the posterior density is:

$$p(\mu, \Sigma | X, Y) \propto$$

$$\frac{1}{|\Sigma|^{3/2}} \prod_{i=1}^{n} \frac{1}{|\Sigma|^{1/2}} \exp\left\{ -\frac{1}{2}[(x_i - \mu_x)\ (y_i - \mu_y)]\Sigma^{-1}[(x_i - \mu_x)\ (y_i - \mu_x)]^T \right\}$$

More succinctly:

$$p(\mu, \Sigma | X, Y) \propto \frac{1}{|\Sigma|^{(n+3)/2}} \exp\left\{ -\frac{1}{2}tr(S\Sigma^{-1}) \right\},$$

where S is the sums of squares matrix $[(X - \mu_x)(Y - \mu_y)]^T[(X - \mu_x)(Y - \mu_y)]$. Note that X and Y are $n \times 1$ column vectors, and so S is 2×2. The diagonal elements of this matrix are the numerators for the variance; the off-diagonal element is the numerator of the *covariance* between x and y.

In this representation of the posterior density, it is clear that, conditional on values of μ_x, μ_y, and the data, the covariance matrix Σ follows an inverse Wishart distribution with n degrees of freedom and scale matrix S.

What are the conditional distributions for the mean parameters? The result we obtained in the previous chapter for the univariate normal distribution problem is extendable. In the univariate case, the posterior density for μ is $N(\bar{x}, \sigma^2/n)$. In the multivariate case, the posterior distribution is $N(\bar{X}, (1/n)\Sigma)$, where $\bar{X}$ is a vector of sample means.

A Gibbs sampler can be established that first samples from the conditional distribution for the mean vector and that second samples from the condtional distribution for the covariance matrix. Below is the R program that performs such sampling. Notice that this program is considerably shorter than the previous one; there are several reasons for this, including the use of R's matrix operators, the use of built-in random sampling functions, and the simultaneous updating of vectors/matrices of parameters.

Once the sample loop begins, the mean parameters (m[]) are sampled from a multivariate normal distribution with a mean vector equal to the sample mean vector and a covariance matrix equal to the current value of the covariance matrix Σ divided by the sample size.[6]

Next, given a value for the means, the sums of squares matrix is constructed, and a value for Σ is generated from the inverse Wishart distribution.

```
#R program for matrix approach to sampling BVN parameters
#matrix d is the data, already stored in memory

m=matrix(0,10000,2)
s=array(1,dim=c(10000,2,2)); s[,1,2]=s[,2,1]=0
sc=matrix(0,2,2)
corr=matrix(0,10000)
e=d
mn=matrix(c(mean(d[,1]),mean(d[,2])),2)

for(i in 2:10000)
  {
    #simulate m
    u=rnorm(2,mean=0,sd=1)
```

---

[6] Sampling from a multivariate normal distribution requires the use of a Cholesky decomposition, which is essentially a square root of the matrix. In R, the function chol returns an upper triangular matrix, which, when multiplied by itself transposed, equals the original matrix. To obtain draws from a multivariate normal distribution, we generate a $k \times 1$ column vector of independent $N(0, 1)$ draws and then multiply this vector by the Cholesky factor.

```
m[i,]=t(mn) + t(u)%*%chol(s[i-1,,]/1377)

#simulate s
e[,1]=d[,1]-m[i,1]; e[,2]=d[,2]-m[i,2]
sc=t(e)%*%(e)
s[i,,]=riwish(1377,sc)

corr[i]=s[i,1,2]/sqrt(s[i,1,1]*s[i,2,2])

if(i%%100==0){print(c(i,corr[i]))}
}
```

The covariance matrix Σ contains the covariance between x and y but not the correlation. Yet we are really interested in the correlation; the covariance is scale-dependent, and so it tells us little about the extent of the relationship between the two survey items. Obtaining a distribution for the correlation, however, is not a problem, given that it is a simple transformation of sampled model parameters: We know that $\rho = \sigma_{xy}/\sigma_x\sigma_y$. So, the next-to-last line in the program computes the correlation at every iteration, which yields a posterior distribution for the correlation. The posterior mean for the correlation using this algorithm was .450, and a 95% probability interval for the correlation was [.408, .491]. These results were quite consistent with those obtained under the univariate approach.

This computation highlights an important feature of Bayesian statistics using MCMC methods: the ability to obtain distributions for quantities that are not directly estimated within a model but are functions of model parameters. We will discuss this process of inference for unestimated parameters in greater depth in the examples in subsequent chapters.

5.5 Conclusions

In this chapter, we discussed the MH algorithm as an alternative approach to Gibbs sampling when Gibbs sampling cannot be easily employed. Some of the examples showed full MH algorithms, while others involved combinations of MH and Gibbs sampling steps. In general, when conditional distributions can be derived, and samples can be directly simulated from them, the Gibbs sampler is faster and more efficient than the MH algorithm. The primary trade-off between the two sampling approaches is that Gibbs sampling involves considerably more mathematical overhead work in deriving the conditional distributions, whereas the MH algorithm involves lengthier programming steps but only requires specification of the unnormalized joint posterior distribution for the parameters.

A secondary trade-off, however, is that the MH algorithm can be difficult to implement because it is sensitive to specification of the proposal densities from which candidate parameters are simulated. The consequence is that monitoring the performance of an MH algorithm—and making adjustments—is, in many ways, more important than monitoring the performance of a Gibbs sampling routine. To be sure, *both* types of algorithms require careful monitoring to ensure that they are "converging" and "mixing" appropriately. The next chapter discusses how to conduct such monitoring and then describes some approaches to evaluating overall model fit before constructing summaries of individual model parameters.

5.6 Exercises

1. In the final example, I introduced a possibly unfamiliar matrix algebra identity in showing the posterior density for Σ. Let A be a $k \times 1$ column vector, and let B be a $k \times k$ matrix. Show that $A^T B A = tr(AB)$ when $k = 3$.

2. Derive the relationship shown between m and b in the linear density as shown in Section 5.2, and show how m can also be represented as a function of b (the opposite approach to that shown in the example). Run the algorithm as it is presented in the text, and then set up the MH algorithm to sample from the posterior for b, rather than m. Compare the results and discuss.

3. Rerun the MH algorithm for the linear density in Section 5.2, but first attempt to allow m and b to *both* be updated independently. That is, ignore the constraint that b is completely determined by m. What happens? Next, continue to allow both parameters to be updated, but change the posterior density by adopting a proper prior distribution. Try independent beta distributions for both parameters, and then try a bivariate normal distribution with correlation $\rho = .5$. What happens? Discuss.

4. Return to the final bivariate normal distribution example. Instead of deriving the conditional distributions for some of the parameters, develop an MH algorithm to sample all the parameters.

5. Develop an MH algorithm to sample the parameters m_x, m_y, and b from the planar density using the data from Table 2.1. Note that a constraint similar to the one imposed in the linear density example needs to be enforced. That is, once two parameters are determined, the third parameter is fixed.

6. The last bivariate normal algorithm presented (the Gibbs sampler) is the multivariate analog to the univariate Gibbs sampler for sampling the mean and variance parameters from a univariate normal distribution. In Chapter 4, I also presented a Gibbs sampler using the *marginal* distribution (not the conditional distribution) for σ^2. In that algorithm, we generated a sequence of draws for σ^2, and then we simulated values for μ conditional on these samples for σ^2. A similar process can be performed in the multivariate case; the only changes include (1) that the scale matrix S

is constructed once, using the sample means rather than the parameters μ_x and μ_y, and (2) the degrees of freedom for the inverse Wishart distribution are one fewer. Construct this Gibbs sampler and compare results with those obtained using the algorithm presented in the chapter.

6

Evaluating Markov Chain Monte Carlo (MCMC) Algorithms and Model Fit

In the previous two chapters, we used Gibbs sampling and Metropolis-Hastings (MH) sampling to make inference for parameters. Making inference, however, should come *after* (1) we have determined that the algorithm worked correctly, and (2) we have decided that the model we chose is acceptable for our purposes. These two issues are the focus of this chapter.

The first part of this chapter addresses the first concern in discussing the convergence and mixing of MCMC algorithms. This part should not be considered an exhaustive exposition of the topic; as I stated, many of the recent advances in MCMC methods have been in this area. However, the approaches I present to evaluating algorithm performance are the most common ones used (see Liu 2001 and Robert and Casella 1999). In the previous chapters, I showed the basics of MCMC implementation, but I left these technical issues unaddressed. However, because software development is largely left to the researcher estimating Bayesian models, assessing how well an MCMC algorithm performs is crucial to conducting a responsible Bayesian analysis and to making appropriate inferences.

The second part of the chapter discusses three approaches to evaluating the fit of models and to selecting a model as "best." Specifically, I discuss posterior predictive distributions, Bayes factors, and Bayesian model averaging. I devote relatively little attention to the latter two methods. Bayes factors require the computation of the marginal likelihood of the data (the denominator of Bayes' full formula for probability distributions), which is a complex integral that is not a by-product of MCMC estimation and is generally quite difficult to compute. Hence, additional methods are needed to compute it, and such is beyond the scope of this book (see Chen, Shao, and Ibrahim 2000). Bayesian model averaging (BMA) avoids the need for selecting models essentially by combining the results of multiple models into a single model. BMA therefore may not be used often in a social science setting in which we are generally interested in testing a single, specific model to evaluate a hypothesis.

6.1 Why evaluate MCMC algorithm performance?

In classical statistics, the estimation routines that are used to produce maximum likelihood or other (e.g., least squares) estimates have already been developed, debugged, tested, and retested, and they are largely out of view of the researcher who uses them. For example, if a researcher is using SAS or STATA to estimate an ordinary least squares (OLS) regression model, the researcher does not need to know how to compute $(X^T X)^{-1}(X^T Y)$ to use the software and obtain the OLS estimates. In contrast, in a Bayesian analysis involving MCMC methods, the researcher does need to know this information. Thus, the researcher must be attuned to programming errors and other issues that are involved in constructing estimation routines. The trade-off for this extra work is that there is much more flexibility in model development, inference, and evaluation of model fit than a classical analysis generally can offer without the researcher investing considerable programming effort.

Aside from basic programming mistakes that can render an MCMC algorithm useless, there are two primary concerns with the implementation of any MCMC algorithm: convergence and mixing. We must make sure that the algorithm produces a Markov chain that "converges" to the appropriate density (the posterior density) and that "mixes" well throughout the support of the density. Unlike routines used to find maximum likelihood estimates, which converge to a point, MCMC algorithms must converge to, and sample thoroughly from, a density. Thus, even if an MCMC algorithm converges to the appropriate region, we must also be sure that the algorithm "moves around" throughout the density once it has converged and samples from all areas of the density as it should before the run of the algorithm ends.

6.2 Some common problems and solutions

Convergence and mixing may be affected by a number of factors, including especially the following:

- The starting values for the parameters.
- The shape of the posterior distribution.
- The choice of proposal density in an MH algorithm.

As with maximum likelihood estimation algorithms, starting values may make a difference in the performance of an MCMC algorithm. Although MCMC theory shows that an MCMC algorithm will, in the limit, converge on the posterior distribution of interest, there is no guarantee that it will in any run of finite length (see Tierney 1996 for discussion of theory relevant to MCMC methods; see Bremaud 1999 for a broader theoretical exposition). For example, if it takes 10,000 iterations for an MCMC algorithm to converge, but the algorithm is only run for 1,000 iterations, the algorithm certainly will not have converged. Furthermore, the algorithm obviously will not have mixed well, either. In brief, if the starting values are particularly poor (e.g., far from the center of the target distribution), the run may end before convergence is even obtained, let alone before the algorithm has thoroughly sampled from the target distribution. In some cases, particularly poor starting values may produce an algorithm that never even "gets off the ground." For example, as I mentioned in Chapter 4, the second Gibbs sampler for the planar density required reasonable starting values in order for the algorithm to begin sampling; without a good starting value, the algorithm could not simulate a single legitimate value for x.

An obvious solution to the problem of having poor starting values is simply to find better ones! This may be easier said than done; however, for most models common in the social sciences, we can generally use maximum likelihood estimates from similar models as our starting values. For example, in the multivariate probit models discussed later in the book, we could use maximum likelihood estimates from univariate probit models as our starting values. A second solution to the problem may be to run the algorithm for more iterations. In the limit, the algorithm should converge on the target distribution.

The shape of the posterior distribution may also affect convergence and mixing. If the posterior is multimodal, for example, an MCMC algorithm may converge rapidly on one mode, but it may not mix well across modes. There are a number of solutions to this problem (some more complicated than others); a simple one might be to expand the width/variance of the proposal density so that it is possible to jump from one mode to another. A second solution may be to find a better model, that is, to incorporate better predictors (assuming the model is a regression model). One cause of multimodality may be the omission of an important variable (like gender). Theoretically, posterior distributions tend to be asymptotically normal, and with the models discussed in this book, multimodality may seldom be a problem if most or all relevant variables are included.

Another feature of a posterior distribution that may slow convergence and mixing is strong posterior correlation of the model parameters. In a simple regression model, for example, the intercept and slope parameters will often be highly negatively correlated. Strong correlations between parameters may cause slow convergence, because it may be difficult—especially when the proposal densities are broad—for the algorithm to move from its starting values. Similarly, if the starting values are very good (e.g., at the maximum likelihood estimates), the algorithm may not mix well, because it may be difficult for the algorithm to move away from them. This problem is often easy to diagnose, because it will yield a very low acceptance rate (see below), but it may not be very easy to remedy. There are essentially three solutions to the problem of highly correlated parameters: transforming the data, reparameterizing the model, and modifying the proposal densities.

In the simple regression model example mentioned above, an easy solution is to transform the data by centering the variables, where centering is simply the process of subtracting the mean of each variable from all of the observations on that variable. Centering often works to reduce posterior correlation of the parameters in regression models as well as hierarchical/growth models. However, in a regression model, centering will only reduce the correlation between the intercept and the slope parameters (and not between slope parameters).

The latter two solutions to the problem of strong posterior correlations between parameters are essentially flip sides of the same coin. Reparameterization is the process of transforming the model parameters so that they are uncorrelated. For example, Gilks and Roberts (1996) show that transforming two highly correlated parameters X_1 and X_2 by constructing new variables $Y_1 = X_1 + X_2$ and $Y_2 = 3(X_1 X_2)$, simulating from the distribution for Y_1 and Y_2, and then transforming the simulated samples back to get samples from the distributions for the original variables, leads to more rapid convergence and mixing. Alternative reparameterizations are possible, of course, so long as the new parameters are uncorrelated or weakly correlated.

Reparameterization may be quite difficult. First, if we are estimating a regression model with a large number of predictors, transforming all the regression coefficients may be extremely tedious, and finding a transformation that reduces or eliminates strong posterior correlations may be a hit-or-miss proposition. Second, when we transform a distribution from one parameterization to another, we must include the Jacobian of the transformation in the new distribution, where the Jacobian is essentially a scalar or matrix that represents how the variables in one space relate to one another relative to how the variables in the original space related to one another. The Jacobian in a high-dimensional transformation will be a matrix, and its derivation may be complex, especially when compared with simply changing the proposal densities (see DeGroot 1986 and/or a calculus text discussing transformations of multivariable equations).

The final solution I discuss—modifying the proposal densities—is much easier than reparameterizing the model. One reason that a model may not converge rapidly or mix well when there are strong posterior correlations between the parameters is that the proposal densities do not closely match the shape of the posterior density, and so the algorithm produces a large number of rejected candidates. Finding a multivariate proposal density with correlations that match those in the set of parameters that are highly correlated will generally lead to more rapid convergence and better mixing, because having a similar shape for the proposal and posterior allows the proposals to have greater density where they should: at regions where the posterior is more dense. Ultimately, altering the proposal densities is an equivalent strategy to reparameterization: Under reparameterization, the proposals remain constant, while the posterior is modified to more closely match the shape of the proposals; under proposal modification, the posterior remains constant, while the proposals are changed to more closely match the shape of the posterior. I personally prefer the latter approach, because it is simpler and does not require additional steps at the end to transform the samples back to the original parameterization.

Finally, the choice of proposal density may affect convergence and mixing even when strong posterior correlations are not present. The general rule is that, the less similar the proposal density is to the posterior density, the worse the convergence and mixing problems. In my own experience, using random walk metropolis algorithms (often with some Gibbs sampling steps) to estimate basic models that are commonly used in the social sciences, changing the proposal density is usually not necessary when strong posterior correlations between parameters are not evident. When it is necessary to change the proposal, it is usually not because of the fundamental *shape* of the proposal but rather the *scale,* in terms of its width or variance. This problem—having too narrow or too wide of a proposal density—is usually quite easy to diagnose, because the acceptance rate of the algorithm will either be too small or too large.

6.3 Recognizing poor performance

In the previous section, I described some common problems that produce non-convergence and poor mixing and discussed some relatively simple approaches to improving performance. But, how do we diagnose when convergence and mixing problems are present?

Since the original development of MCMC methods, a number of methods have been proposed to evaluate the convergence (and mixing) of MCMC algorithms. I will discuss several that appear to be most useful. It is important to note at the outset, however, that there is no *definitive* way of assessing convergence and mixing for problems that involve analytically intractable densities, and thus, a combination of methods should be employed to satisfy a researcher that convergence has been obtained. As with any statistical enterprise, MCMC estimation is to a large extent an art that is helped with experience.

6.3.1 Trace plots

The first, and probably most common, method of assessing convergence and mixing is the use of the trace plot. Trace plots were introduced earlier, and as discussed, they are simply plots of the sampled values from an algorithm at each iteration, with the x axis referencing the iteration of the algorithm and the y axis referencing the sampled value (parameter or data point). With a trace plot, a lack of convergence is evidenced by trending in the sampled values such that the algorithm never levels-off to a stable, stationary state.

As an example, I constructed an MH algorithm for sampling the slope parameters m_1 and m_2 and the intercept parameter b from a planar density applied to the free speech and political participation items described in Chapter 2. Figure 6.1 shows a trace plot of the first 1000 samples for the m_2

parameter (the slope parameter for the free speech item). The algorithm does not appear to have converged prior to the 400th iteration; instead, clear downward trending is present from the starting value of 0 down to approximately $-.012$. The algorithm *may* have converged somewhere around the 400th iteration (reference the dotted vertical line). Notice that the sampled values for the m_2 parameter do not evidence any clear, general trending from iteration 400 or so through iteration 1,000.

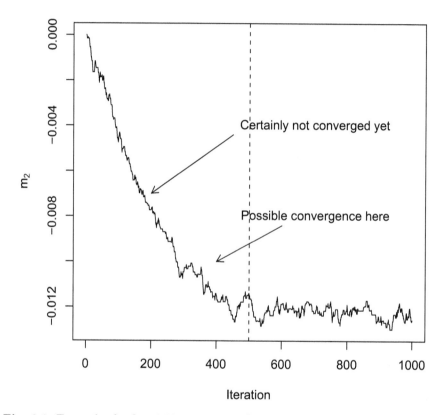

Fig. 6.1. Trace plot for first 1,000 iterations of an MH algorithm sampling parameters from planar density for GSS free speech and political participation data.

I say that the algorithm *may* have converged, because we do not have enough evidence to conclude that it has. Figure 6.2 is a trace plot of the first 4,000 iterations, with vertical lines referencing iterations 400-1,000 shown in the previous figure. From this view, especially given the upward trending in the last few hundred iterations, it is unclear whether the algorithm, in fact, had converged by iteration 400.

The figure also demonstrates that, even if the algorithm had converged by iteration 400 or so, it certainly had not thoroughly mixed through the

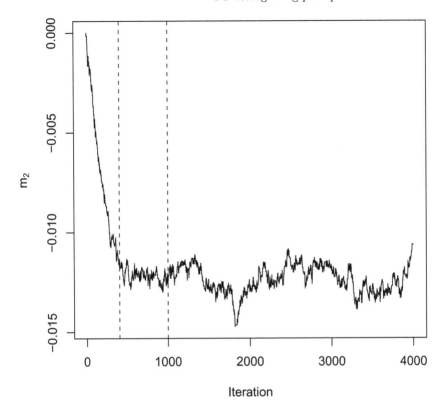

Fig. 6.2. Trace plot for first 4,000 iterations of an MH algorithm sampling parameters from planar density for GSS free speech and political participation data.

1000th iteration. That is, assume that the algorithm had converged. The 600 sampled values from iteration 401 to 1,000 are restricted to a fairly narrow range, compared with the range of values sampled over the additional 3,000 iterations. Specifically, the ratio of the ranges for the sampled values from iterations 401 to 4,000 to the sampled values from iterations 401 to 1,000 was 2.48. Similarly, the ratio of the standard deviations of the sampled values for iterations 401 to 4,000 versus 401 to 1,000 was 2.00. In other words, the density implied by the values for m_2 sampled from iterations 401 to 4000 is more than twice as broad as the density implied by the values for m_2 sampled from iterations 401 to 1,000. This result means that the algorithm certainly has not mixed thoroughly prior to iteration 1,000.

On the other hand, the means of the two samples differ by only about 1%, which suggests that perhaps the algorithm *had* at least converged to the appropriate region (and perhaps in distribution) by iteration 400. Figure 6.3 shows a trace plot of the algorithm across 50,000 iterations, with horizontal reference lines at the means for each of the three samples. The lines are quite close together, differing by only about 1%, which suggests the algorithm probably did converge early. Indeed, the means are so close that the mean for the entire sample of 50,000 iterations cannot be seen—it is identical to the mean of the first 600 iterations after the 400th. However, the standard deviations for the sample consisting of iterations 401-4,000 and the sample consisting of iterations 401-50,000 differ by about 28%, which that the algorithm had not mixed sufficiently over the first few thousand iterations.

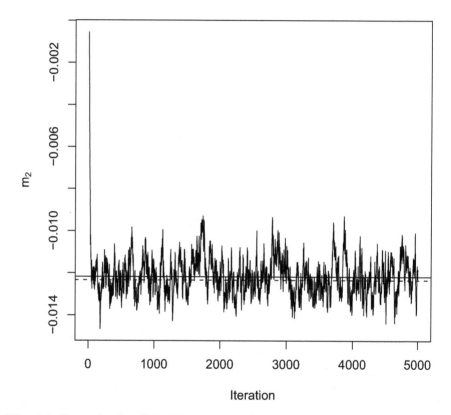

Fig. 6.3. Trace plot for all 50,000 iterations of an MH algorithm sampling parameters from planar density for GSS free speech and political participation data with means superimposed.

Trace plots need not be limited to examining a parameter itself, but rather, we may choose to monitor a sample statistic like the mean of a parameter (see also Robert and Casella 1999). Whereas the parameter itself should converge to a flat region and then wander around that region, a statistic like the mean of a parameter should, in the limit, converge to a flat line. If the starting values for a parameter are poor, it may take some time for the mean of a parameter to overcome the distortion/bias caused by the poorly sampled early values, but in the long run, the mean will eventually stabilize, provided the algorithm in fact has converged. Instead of examining a trace plot of the mean of the distribution, we may wish to consider a trace plot of means computed from different parts of the sample. For example, we could compute the mean for every "batch" of 1,000 iterations and plot them to determine whether these batch means evidence any trending. Figure 6.4 is a plot of both of these approaches. The solid line shows the mean of all sampled values up to the iteration shown on the x axis. The asterisks are the means of 1,000-item batches. The figure shows that the cumulative mean appeared to have converged by iteration 10,000, whereas the batch means suggest earlier convergence.

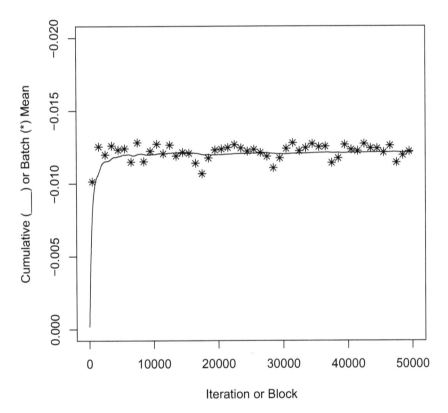

Fig. 6.4. Trace plot of cumulative and batch means for MH algorithm sampling parameters from planar density for GSS free speech and political participation data.

Figure 6.5 shows a plot of the cumulative standard deviation for iterations after the $10,000^{th}$ (after the cumulative mean had leveled off). The figure shows that the standard deviation levels off around iteration 25,000 (see vertical reference line).

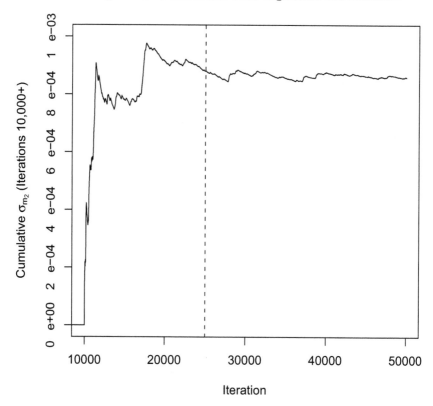

Fig. 6.5. Trace plot of cumulative standard deviation of m_2 from MH algorithm sampling parameters from planar density for GSS free speech and political participation data.

Taken together, these results suggest that we should probably discard the first 25,000 iterations of the algorithm as the "burn-in" period prior to convergence and base inference on the last 25,000 samples. Before we do so, however, we should also examine similar plots for the other parameters in the model.

Visual inspection of trace plots, although perhaps the most common way of assessing convergence and mixing, are notoriously problematic. For example, if we simply change the scale of the trace plot, the appearance of convergence and good mixing may be affected. One way the scale may be changed—assuming some default method for determining the range of the y axis is used—is if the starting values for the algorithm were extremely poor. In such a case, the algorithm may have appeared to converge because there may be a long, clearly observable trend up to a point, followed by a leveling-off, but the plot's scale may be so small that we cannot see whether there is still some shallower trending occurring. We may also be unable to see whether the algorithm is moving around rapidly beyond the leveling-off point, especially if we have run the algorithm for a large number of iterations and the scale in the x dimension is compressed.

More problematic than simple issues of scale, especially with multimodal posterior densities, is that the trace plot may suggest convergence, when in fact only one mode of the posterior has been explored. Furthermore, even if the posterior is unimodal, if the algorithm does not mix rapidly, it may have appeared to converge when in fact it has only converged in one part of the density (possibly a tail). It is important to note that this problem is not unique to the use of trace plots: There is no measure that can tell us definitively whether an algorithm has mixed thoroughly.

Nonetheless, even if satisfactory trace plots should not be the last criterion for declaring convergence and good mixing, they should probably be the first. A trace plot generally provides an immediate means for recognizing that an algorithm has not converged—or is not converging—and/or is not mixing well, and thus, it can help us decide to stop an algorithm, make a modification, and restart it much sooner than using other methods may.

6.3.2 Acceptance rates of MH algorithms

Beyond visual inspection of trace plots, several numerical methods and tests may be used in assessing MCMC performance. First, researchers using MCMC methods other than Gibbs sampling typically monitor the acceptance rate of the algorithm. In a Gibbs sampler, the acceptance rate is 1 and, hence, is noninformative. However, in an MH algorithm, rejection of candidates is possible, and hence, the rejection/acceptance rate should be monitored. Needless to say, an algorithm that *never* accepts a candidate cannot converge, nor will it mix well. At the other extreme, an algorithm that accepts *every* candidate is not necessarily performing any better. In fact, having an extremely high acceptance rate is a good indication that the algorithm is moving too slowly toward convergence, and, if it has converged, it is mixing very slowly. An acceptance rate of around 50% or slightly lower is ideal (see Johnson and Albert 1999). More generally, a rate somewhere between 25% and 75% is often acceptable.

Two factors determine the acceptance rate of an MH algorithm: (1) the size of the "jumps" from the sampled value at iteration j and the candidate value, and (2) the shape of the proposal density relative to that of the posterior density. The jump size is determined by the variance or width of the proposal density. Consider, for example, the posterior density for the parameter m_2 from the planar density obtained from the MH algorithm discussed in the previous section. The proposal density I used in the MH algorithm for this parameter (as well as the m_1 parameter) was a $U(-.0003, .0003)$ density. Overall, this proposal density (along with that for m_1) led to an acceptance rate of 37.5%. However, what if I had used a $U(-.003, .003)$ proposal density? Figure 6.6 shows the posterior density for m_2 (obtained from the last 25,000 iterations of the MH algorithm), as well as the two proposal densities.

The $U(-.0003, .0003)$ proposal that was used is quite narrow relative to the posterior density. The result, as we saw in the previous section, is that the algorithm takes very small steps in this dimension—it takes a large number of iterations before the algorithm mixes thoroughly. The $U(-.003, .003)$ proposal is much wider than the proposal density that was used, which means it may move from one end of the posterior density more quickly. However, as the figure shows, this proposal is substantially wider than the posterior for m_2, and thus, many candidates are likely to be rejected, especially when the current sampled value (θ^{j-1}) is in the tail of the distribution. The result is that the algorithm "sticks" in one place for long periods of time before moving.

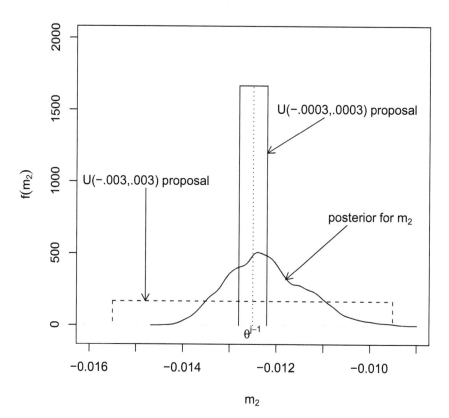

Fig. 6.6. Posterior density for m_2 parameter from planar density MH algorithm and two proposal densities: $U(-.0003, .0003)$ and $U(-.003, .003)$.

Figure 6.7 shows the first 1000 iterations of the algorithm when the broader proposal density is used. As the figure demonstrates, the algorithm quickly moved to the center of the posterior density, but then it very rarely moved. The acceptance rate confirms this numerically: The acceptance rate for the first 1,000 iterations was only 3.2%, but the acceptance rate for the first 18 iterations was 50% (the rate steadily declined after iteration 18). Thus, the broader proposal density produced even slower mixing, ultimately, than the narrower proposal.

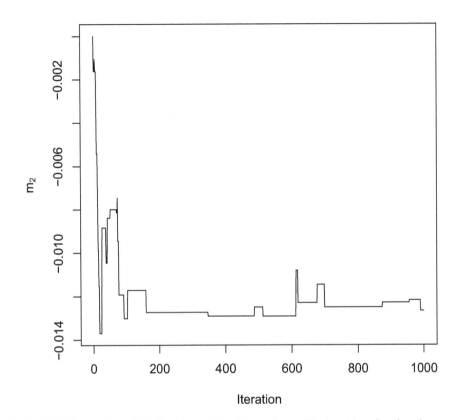

Fig. 6.7. Trace plot of the first 1,000 iterations of an MH algorithm for the planar density with a (relatively) broad $U(-.003, .003)$ proposal density.

The shape of the proposal density relative to that of the posterior density also influences the acceptance rate. In the planar density example, the proposal density was uniform, but the posterior is symmetric and bell-shaped (approximately normal). If we were to change the proposal density to a normal density with a width approximately equal to that of the $U(-.003, .003)$ density (see Figure 6.8), the acceptance rate would increase. In fact, I obtained an acceptance rate of 8.3% with this normal proposal, more than twice that obtained using the broad uniform proposal.

This acceptance rate is still quite low, despite the fact that the proposal shape for m_2 almost perfectly matches the shape of the marginal posterior for m_2. To increase the acceptance rate, we could consider using a normal proposal density with smaller variance. However, as shown in the previous

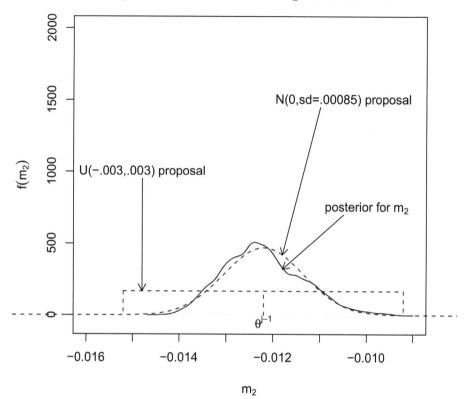

Fig. 6.8. Posterior density for m_2 parameter from planar density MH algorithm and two proposal densities: $U(-.003, .003)$ and $N(0, .00085)$.

section, using a substantially smaller uniform proposal, while increasing the acceptance rate, led to very slow mixing so that the algorithm needed to be run for 50,000 iterations to obtain an adequate sample from the posterior.

What we have not considered is the correlation between the parameters m_1 and m_2, which is another issue we should consider when selecting a proposal density. As we discussed in the previous section, a common source of poor mixing and/or slow convergence in MH algorithms is strong posterior correlation of the parameters. In this particular model, the posterior correlation of the parameters is greater than $-.9$, which suggests that uncorrelated proposal densities for the two slope parameters may be problematic.

Figure 6.9 is a two-dimensional trace plot of the two slope parameters from the original MH algorithm, with the contours of two proposal densities superimposed (at the center of the posterior): a bivariate normal with 0 correlation (as used previously) and a bivariate normal with $-.9$ correlation. As the figure shows, the proposal density with correlation 0 does not match the shape of the posterior very well, while the one with the strong negative correlation does.

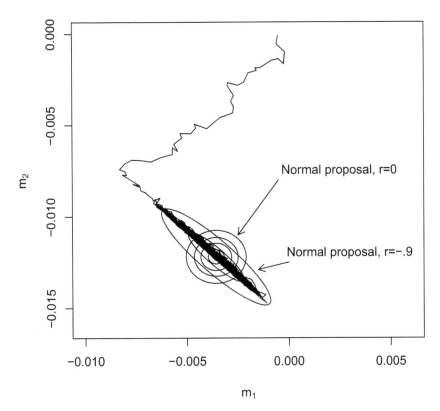

Fig. 6.9. Two-dimensional trace plot for initial run of MH algorithm sampling parameters from planar density for GSS free speech and political participation data: Two possible bivariate normal proposal densities are superimposed.

The fact that the 0-correlation proposal does not match the posterior very well suggests that this proposal will frequently propose poor candidates, leading to a high rejection rate, slow convergence, and poor mixing, as we have already observed.

I reran the MH algorithm, using the bivariate normal proposal with correlation $-.9$ (and variance equal to the variance of the parameters obtained from the original run of the MH algorithm). This algorithm had an acceptance rate of approximately 25%, converged quickly, and mixed much more rapidly than the algorithm using the other proposals. The acceptance rate is still somewhat low, and so we may consider reducing the scale of the proposal. In a final run of the algorithm, I used a bivariate normal proposal with correlation $-.9$ and standard deviations that that were half the size of those in the previous run. The acceptance rate for this run was 44%. Figure 6.10 shows a trace plot of the m_2 parameter from this run. As the figure suggests, the algorithm converged quickly and mixed rapidly. In fact, after discarding the first 1,000 samples, the variance of the sampled values of m_2 converged very rapidly, which suggests rapid and thorough mixing.

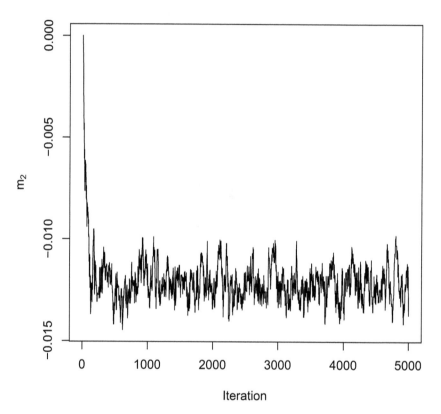

Fig. 6.10. Trace plot for 5000 iterations of an MH algorithm sampling parameters from planar density for GSS free speech and political participation data: Bivariate normal proposal density with correlation $-.9$.

6.3.3 Autocorrelation of parameters

MCMC algorithms, while producing samples from distributions, do not produce *independent* samples. Instead, MCMC algorithms produce samples that are autocorrelated—recall that the entire basis of MCMC sampling is that each sampled value depends (only) on the value sampled immediately prior (the Markov property). Slow mixing—as evidenced by acceptance rates that are too high or too low—tends to exacerbate autocorrelation.

The key problem with autocorrelation is that variance estimates will be incorrect; they will tend to be too small, just as standard errors are biased downward in a classical model that ignores dependence between observations. There are at least two simple ways adjustments can be made to compensate for autocorrelation. First, one can take every k^{th} sampled value, where k is the number of lags beyond which autocorrelation is not a problem. This approach is called "thinning the chain," and is computationally the easiest to perform (simply save every k^{th} sampled value). Second, one can use the "batch means" method. Under the batch means approach, rather than discarding $k-1$ out of every k sampled values, one computes the *means* of every block of k sampled values and treats the batch mean as the sampled value (see Figure 6.4, for example).

Under either approach, determining k—the number of lags beyond which the autocorrelation of sampled values is small enough to ignore—is relatively straightforward. As in time series analysis, we can compute the autocorrelation function at each lag (1+) and decide the number of iterations we need to skip in order to have a nonsignificant autocorrelation. The autocorrelation parameter for lag L is computed much the same as a standard correlation:

$$\text{ACF}_L = \left(\frac{T}{T-L}\right) \frac{\sum_{t=1}^{T-L}(x_t - \bar{x})(x_{t+L} - \bar{x})}{\sum_{t=1}^{T}(x_t - \bar{x})^2}. \tag{6.1}$$

In this computation, x_t refers to the sampled value of x at iteration t, T is the total number of sampled values, $\bar{x}$ is the mean of all the sampled values, and L is the lag. The fraction $T/(T-L)$ is an adjustment for the fact that the denominator contains more terms than the numerator, since the denominator is summed across all iterations, but the numerator cannot be.

Figure 6.11 is a plot of the autocorrelation function for the original MH algorithm (which used a pair of uniform proposal densities) and the final one using the bivariate normal proposal density with correlation $-.9$. Both plots show strong autocorrelation, but the bivariate normal proposal evidences less autocorrelation. Inference should be made after retaining only every 20th (or so) sample. Figure 6.12 shows the marginal posterior density for m_2 from this MH algorithm after discarding the first 2,000 samples and saving every 20th thereafter. The posterior mean for the parameter was $-.0122$, and the posterior standard deviation was $.00077$. These results are similar to those obtained from each of the previous algorithms, but with the better proposal, we were able to obtain them with a shorter run than the MH algorithms using the poorer proposal densities required.

6.3.4 "$\hat{R}$" and other calculations

One approach that is very useful for examining for convergence and thorough mixing of MCMC algorithms is running multiple instances of algorithms from highly dispersed starting values for the parameters and comparing the results.

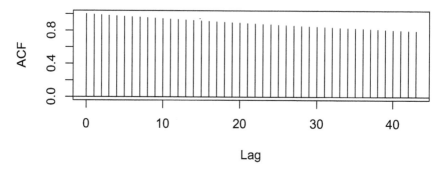

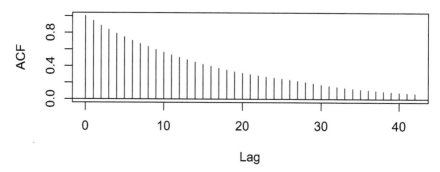

Fig. 6.11. Autocorrelation plots of parameter m_2 from MH algorithms for the planar density: Upper figure is for the MH algorithm with independent uniform proposals for m_1 and m_2; and lower figure is for the MH algorithm with a bivariate normal proposal with correlation $-.9$.

Historically, there has been considerable debate regarding whether one should run multiple instances of an algorithm and compare them, or whether one should run a single, but very long, instance to see whether the algorithm settles in one place for a long time but then eventually moves to another location (see Gelman 1996 for discussion). Under that approach, the chain can also be decomposed into segments, and the means of each segment can be compared numerically to determine whether there is any trending that suggests lack of convergence (e.g., by plotting the segment means or conducting time series regressions as we did in the previous section) and possibly poor mixing (e.g., by conducting ANOVA or dummy regression using the segment means, within-segment variance, and total variance—this strategy is akin to the calculation of R discussed below). In many problems, with the incredible increase in computing power over the last decade, there is often no reason not to do both: Run multiple, long chains.

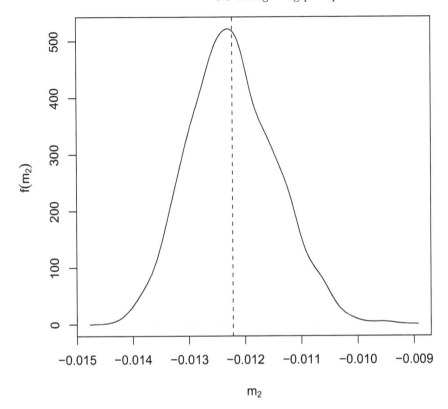

Fig. 6.12. Histogram of marginal posterior density for m_2 parameter: Dashed reference line is the posterior mean.

How do we determine starting values for multiple chains? One approach is to start all parameters at 0 for one chain (if such is sensible—e.g., for regression parameters, this approach may be reasonable; for a variance parameter, it may not be), use maximum likelihood estimates from a similar (or identical) model as starting values in another, and use wildly inappropriate starting values for the parameters for a third. If all three chains converge to the same location, it *may* indicate convergence.

What else can we do besides simply using different starting values? We can often do more than simply modify starting values in an MCMC algorithm. For example, we can modify the proposal densities (either their form or their width/variance) used in each algorithm. If we are updating parameters sequentially and not all simultaneously, we can switch the order of updating. In other words, we can play around with the fundamentals of the program conducting the simulation. Ultimately, the point is that, if the algorithms are converging and mixing well, they should all yield similar results.

How do we detect convergence from the results? Once a set of chains has been produced, we need to have some tools for evaluting the results. One way to compare multiple chains is to overlay all of them on a single trace plot. If the traces are indistinguishable, then the algorithm may have converged and mixed throughout the density of interest.

As an example, let's consider again the MH algorithm for the bivariate normal model for the free speech/political participation data. In the original MH model, we simulated μ_x and μ_y from their full conditional distributions (Gibbs sampling steps), but we simulated the variance parameters σ_x^2 and σ_y^2 as well as the correlation parameter ρ using MH steps with uniform proposal densities. I have rerun the MH algorithm three times, using different sets of starting values for the variance and correlation parameters. In the first run, I used $\sigma_x^2 = \sigma_y^2 = 1$ and $\rho = 0$ as starting values. In the second, I used $\sigma_x^2 = \sigma_y^2 = 10$ and $\rho = -.99$. In the third, I used $\sigma_x^2 = \sigma_y^2 = .01$ and $\rho = .99$. These starting values are highly dispersed: The starting values for ρ span the possible range for this parameter, and the starting values for the variance parameters span a large range of possible values, starting near the lowest possible value (0).

Figure 6.13 shows a trace plot of the sampled values of ρ for the first 600 iterations of the MH algorithm under each set of starting values. As the figure reveals, all three runs of the algorithm converge to a common region within little more than 400 iterations. Beyond 400 iterations, the simulation sequences become indistinguishable.

Figure 6.14 shows a two-dimensional trace plot of the sampled values of the variance parameters. This figure provides a picture consistent with that for ρ: Regardless of starting values for the variances, the algorithms converged rapidly to a common bivariate region for these parameters.

The acceptance rates for the three parameters, across the three algorithms, were quite stable at 55%, 64%, and 57% after the first 1,000 iterations (differing across runs by less than one percentage point), providing additional evidence that convergence had been reached relatively early, and that thorough mixing had occurred after the first 1,000 or so iterations.

Another approach involving multiple chains is to compare numerical results: Are means, variances, etc. similar across the different chains? They are almost certain to not be identical, but are they within the limits of MCMC sampling error?[1] In the current example, the means for ρ for the three runs were .4504, .4495, and .4490, with posterior standard deviations of .0215,

---

[1] MCMC algorithms produce samples from a distribution. Running an algorithm multiple times will produce different samples and, thus, different means, variances, and other statistics. The classical Central Limit Theorem says that these statistics will be normally distributed with a mean equal to the population mean and a standard deviation equal to the population standard deviation divided by the square root of the sample size. Thus, we can estimate MCMC error by computing the posterior standard deviation and dividing it by the square root of the MCMC sample size. The posterior mean *should* vary by a factor of this quantity. Specifically, 95% of MCMC runs should produce posterior means within ±1.96 standard errors.

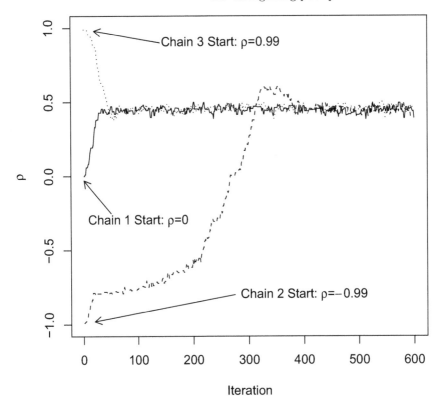

Fig. 6.13. Trace plot of first 600 sampled values of ρ from MH algorithms with three different starting values (GSS political participation and free speech data).

.0214, and .0209, respectively. Thus, the posterior means are all within MCMC sampling fluctuation of each other, providing some indication that the algorithm converged and mixed thoroughly.

A common aproach used to determine convergence and adequate mixing is the calculation of the "Scale reduction factor" $\hat{R}$ (often called the "Gelman-Rubin convergence diagnostic." This is *not* the ratio R from the MH algorithm!) (see Gelman 1996). When m chains are run, each of length n, we can compute the mean of a parameter θ for each chain ($\bar{\theta}_j$), the overall mean of the parameter if we combined all chains ($\bar{\theta}$), the within-chain variance [$(1/(m(n-1)))\sum_{i=1}^{m}\sum_{j=1}^{n}(\theta_{ij}-\bar{\theta}_i)^2$], and the between-chain variance [$n/(m-1)\sum_{i=1}^{m}(\bar{\theta}_i-\bar{\theta})^2$]. Gelman (1996) shows that the total variance of θ, then, is $(n-1)/n \times$ within variance $+ (1/n) \times$ between variance.

As the chains converge, the variance between the chains should decrease, implying that the within variance approaches the total variance. Thus, the scale reduction factor can be computed as: $\sqrt{\hat{R}} = \sqrt{\text{Total/Within}}$. This factor should be close to 1 when convergence has been reached. Continuing with

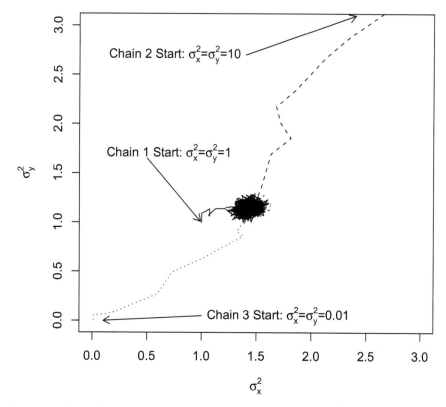

Fig. 6.14. Two-dimensional trace plot of sampled values of σ_x^2 and σ_y^2 from MH algorithms with three different starting values (GSS political participation and free speech data).

the bivariate normal model example, Figure 6.15 shows the $\hat{R}$ statistic for ρ, σ_x^2, and σ_y^2 computed across the first 500 iterations of the three MH algorithms. The plot shows that $\hat{R}$ rapidly declined to around 1 in the first 200 iterations. By 400 iterations, the value of $\hat{R}$ for all three parameters had leveled off at about 1. By iteration 500, the three values are indistinguishable and negligibly different from 1. These results are consistent with those presented in the trace plots: By iteration 600, all three algorithms had converged to a common location. Beyond iteration 600, through the end of the 10,000 iteration run, all three algorithms appeared to mix thoroughly.

The $\hat{R}$ statistic can be computed "on the fly," that is, during the course of the run of an algorithm updating three separate chains and can therefore help us determine when we have run the algorithm a sufficient number of iterations. However, this statistic has its limitations, just like any other. An $\hat{R}$ of approximately 1 does not *guarantee* that the algorithms have converged nor mixed thoroughly. It may be that our starting values were not sufficiently dispersed,

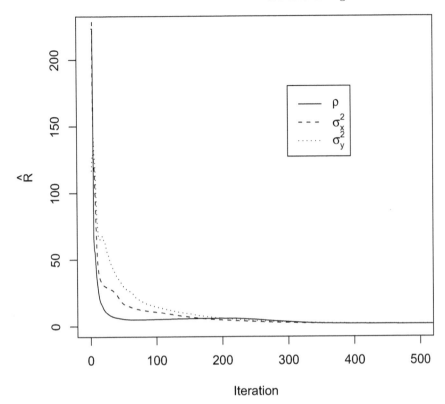

Fig. 6.15. Trace plot of the scale reduction factor $\hat{R}$ for ρ, σ_x^2, and σ_y^2 across the first 500 iterations of the MH algorithms.

and that all of our algorithms became stuck in the closest mode without exploring the entire posterior density. Nonetheless, this statistic, along with the additional evidence (stable and similar acceptance rates, trace plots, consistent means and variances of parameters, etc.) together provide consistent evidence that suggests our algorithms converged and mixed well.

6.4 Evaluating model fit

Once we have determined that the algorithm we used converged to the appropriate distribution and mixed well so that we have an adequate sample from the posterior distribution, our next step should be to determine whether the model fit the data well enough to justify drawing inference about the parameters. At this point, if we have estimated several different models, we can also begin to decide which is the best model.

In standard likelihood analyses we typically use a measure, such as R^2 or likelihood-ratio χ^2 statistics, to determine whether the model fits the data.

We can use such measures in a Bayesian setting as well, but the Bayesian approach offers a broader range of possibilities in addition to these, as we will discuss briefly here but more in depth in the remaining chapters of the book.

6.4.1 Residual analysis

One way we can evaluate model fit is to conduct residual analyses much as we would if we were conducting a classical analysis. The only difference between a Bayesian and a classical analysis of residuals is that, whereas the classical approach produces a point estimate for parameters, and thus a point estimate for the residual for each observation, the Bayesian approach produces a distribution of the parameters and thus a distribution of residuals for each observation in the data set. The distribution of residuals provides us with more information with which to assess the model, because we can examine the distribution of errors for each observation: We can construct "tests" to determine whether the distribution of errors for each case is "significantly" different from 0. Cases for which the distribution of errors is far from 0 indicate that the observation is not fit well by the model. Thus, we do not have to rely on a simple examination of how different a case's error is from the rest of the sample's errors—we can concentrate on each case itself. Furthermore, we can construct sample-level tests to determine the probability that some proportion of the errors exceeds some value. For example, in a sample of size $n = 100$, with an MCMC sample of 1,000 draws from the posterior distribution for the parameters, we could compute, iteration by iteration, the proportion of errors that exceed some value q, collect these proportions into a distribution of 1,000 proportions, and evaluate this distribution. A model that produces a relatively high average proportion of errors exceeding the criterion q may then be deemed a poorly fitting model.

Ultimately, Bayesian residual analysis provides greater flexibility in evaluating the fit of the model to the data than does a classical analysis. This fact will be even more evident when we discuss generalized linear models (GLMs). In GLMs, the classical approach is limited to using ad hoc tests of residuals that are based on ordinary least squares (OLS) regression residual analysis; however, these tests are not well suited to models in which the outcome is not measured at the interval level. The data-augmentation/latent data approach used by Bayesians, on the other hand, allows us to compute "latent residuals" that are continuously distributed, and thus allows us to follow the same format for residual analyses as OLS regression without stretching assumptions (see Johnson and Albert 1999 for an in-depth exposition of this topic in ordinal data models).

Because residual analyses are very similar, ultimately, to using posterior predictive simulation, and because they are primarily only useful in a regression-model setting, which we have yet to discuss, I do not discuss residual analysis further at this point. We will discuss this topic more in depth in the remaining chapters when we develop regression models.

6.4.2 Posterior predictive distributions

One of the best and most flexible approaches to examining model fit is the use of posterior predictive distributions. The posterior predictive distribution for a model is the distribution of future observations that could arise from the model under consideration. The posterior predictive distribution takes into account both (1) parametric uncertainty and (2) sampling uncertainty from the original model. Parametric uncertainty is captured via the posterior distribution for the parameters, a sample of which is the result of simulation using MCMC methods. Sampling uncertainty is captured via the specification of the sampling density for the data. Recall that the posterior density for the parameters is a product of the prior distribution for parameters and the likelihood function (sampling density for the data):

$$p(\theta \mid \text{data}) \propto p(\text{data} \mid \theta)p(\theta).$$

Once this posterior density is obtained, future observations should be expected to arise from the sampling distribution for the data in the original model; the parameters for this sampling distribution, however, are no longer weighted based on the prior from the original model, but rather they are weighted by the posterior distribution for the parameters. Formally, if we use y^{rep} to denote future observations, the probability density for future observations, given the observed sample data is:

$$p(y^{rep} \mid y) = \int p(y^{rep} \mid \theta)p(y \mid \theta)p(\theta)d\theta. \tag{6.2}$$

The latter two terms on the right side of this equation (not counting the $d\theta$) constitute the posterior distribution of the parameters. The first term on the right side is the probability density for a future observation that could be drawn from its sampling distribution, which, of course, is governed by the parameter θ.

   If a model fits the current data well—that is, we have adequately captured the data-generation process—future data simulated from the model should look much like the current data. Thus, we can simulate data from the posterior predictive distribution, compare it with the observed data, and, if the simulated data are similar to the observed data, we may conclude the model fits well. In order to determine whether the simulated and observed data are similar, we can conduct formal tests using Bayesian p-values. If we define $T(y)$ to be a function of the data (a test statistic) and $T(y^{rep})$ to be the same function applied to the replicated data, then we can compute a Bayesian p-value as:

$$p\text{-value} = p(T(y^{rep}) \geq T(y)|y). \tag{6.3}$$

In English, the p-value is the proportion of replicated future data sets whose function values $T(y^{rep})$ exceed that of the function $T(y)$ applied to the original data (Rubin 1984). For example, $T(y)$ could be $T(y) = \max(y)$, that is, the maximum observed y in the sample. If we generated 1,000 replicated data sets of size n, where n was the original sample size, and the maximum y^{rep} value exceeded the maximum observed y value in 3,500 of the replicated data sets, then the p-value would be .35. In that case, the replicated data appear consistent with the observed data.

The interpretation of tests based on the posterior predictive distribution is straightforward. Such tests represent the probability that a future observation would exceed the observed data, given the model. An extreme p-value, therefore, implies poor model fit. In addition to constructing tests that are solely functions of data, we can also compute "discrepancy statistics" that are functions of both data and parameters (see Gelman, Meng, and Stern 1996, and Rubin 1984).

There is no limit to the types and numbers of posterior predictive tests that can be performed to evaluate model fit. In general, posterior predictive tests allow for much greater flexibility in testing particular features of a model than classical tests provide, and I provide some specific examples in several chapters in the second part of the book. Lynch and Western (2004) provide some examples for models, the fits of which are not easily evaluable using classical methods.

Implementation of posterior predictive simulation is relatively simple, given an MCMC-generated sample of size J from the posterior distribution for the parameters in a model $(\theta_1 \ldots \theta_J)$, and can often be incorporated as part of the MCMC algorithm itself. For each value of θ simulated from the posterior, we generate a new observation from the sampling distribution for the data, using that parameter value, for every original observation in the sample.

As an example, consider the planar density and bivariate normal models for the free speech and political participation data. I have saved 500 samples from the posterior distribution for the parameters for both of these models (say $\theta_P^1 \ldots \theta_P^{500}$ and $\theta_{BVN}^1 \ldots \theta_{BVN}^{500}$), respectively. For each member of these parameter sets, I have generated a new sample of size $n = 1,377$ (the original sample size of the data) from the sampling density for the data. For the planar density model, this means sampling 500 samples of size $n = 1,377$ observations from the planar density; for the bivariate normal density, this means sampling 500 samples of size $n = 1,377$ observations from a bivariate normal distribution.

In these two models, the observations are exchangeable—there is no information to distinguish one observation from another. Thus, rather than examining the fit of the model for individual cases (as can be done in regression models), our posterior predictive tests must remain at the sample level.

I chose a variety of criteria by which to evaluate the fit of each model and, ultimately, to compare the two models, including the following: (1) the ratio of the median to the mean for both variables (political participation and free speech), (2) the number of observations in the lowest category of each variable [i.e., $(x, y) = (0, 0)$], (3) the number of observations in the highest category of each variable [i.e., $(x, y) = (5, 5)$], (4) the number of observations in the highest category of one variable but the lowest in the other [i.e., $(x, y) = (5, 0)$], and (5) vice versa [i.e., $(x, y) = (0, 5)$]. Given that the original data were discrete, the continuous values simulated from the bivariate normal and planar distributions were rounded to the nearest integer.[2] These particular measures were chosen to evaluate whether the models managed to capture the essential shape of the data. The ratio of the mean to the median gives us a sense of whether the models were able to capture the skew of the data, and the four measures of the number of observations at each corner of the data give us a sense of whether each model is actually replicating the shape of the data distribution.

Figure 6.16 shows the posterior predictive distributions for the ratio of the mean to the median for both variables (x and y) and for both models. The vertical reference line in each plot is the value of this ratio in the original data; the histograms are for the posterior predictive distributions. As the figure shows, neither model was successful at capturing the ratio of the mean to median (and hence the skew) for x (the political participation item). This value was 1.18 in the original sample. In the bivariate normal distribution model, the posterior predictive distribution for this measure was centered over 1 (as expected; there is no skew in a normal distribution). In the planar distribution model, the posterior predictive distribution is centered around 1.04, which is somewhat closer to the original sample's value than is the result for the normal distribution model.

For the y variable (the free speech item), the ratio in the sample was 1.02. The planar density overestimates the ratio, as evidenced by the posterior predictive distribution being centered around 1.13. However, the posterior predictive distribution for the bivariate normal distribution is consistent with the original sample's value. The Bayesian p-value for this test is .26: Only 26% of the posterior predictive samples have a mean/median ratio that is more extreme than the observed sample ratio.

Table 6.1 presents the results of all five tests. The results show that, although in the original data there were 361 observations in the (0,0) cell, the posterior predictive distributions for the two models predicted far fewer (95 and 27 for the bivariate normal and planar densities, respectively). Both Bayesian p-values are 0, which indicates that neither model fits the data well at this end of the distribution. At the other extreme end of the distribution (the 5,5 cell), the original data consisted of 5 observations. The posterior predictive distributions for the two models predicted .07 and 1.6 observations, with p-values of 0 and .01, respectively. Both models appear to underestimate

---

[2] This approach is not entirely satisfactory—as the results show, this approach reduces the number of observations in the most extreme cells, which have a smaller range of values that can be rounded to them. For example, values from 0 to .499 are rounded to 0, but values from .499 to 1.499 are rounded to 1.

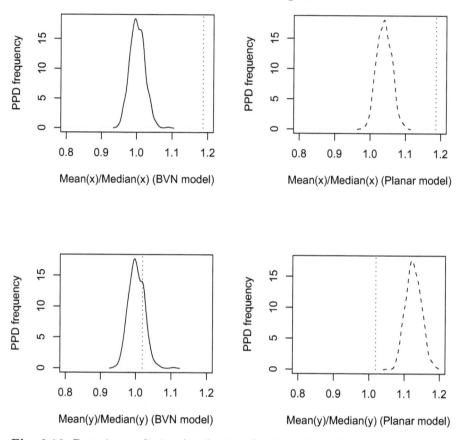

Fig. 6.16. Posterior predictive distributions for the ratio of the mean to the median in the bivariate normal distribution and planar distribution models: Vertical reference line is the observed value in the original data.

the number of observations in this cell, but the planar model underestimates less. The final two tests suggest that the bivariate normal distribution consistently underestimates the counts in the tails of the distribution, but the planar distribution does only slightly better.

We could conduct a similar test on each cell of the bivariate table, but as a simple summary, I computed the correlation between the observed and the posterior predictive distribution cell counts for both models. Figure 6.17 shows the distributions of these correlations. The mean correlation between observed and predictive cell counts for the planar distribution model was .32, which is a low to moderate correlation, while the mean correlation for the bivariate normal distribution model was .75.

Table 6.1. Posterior predictive tests for bivariate normal and planar distribution models.

		Bivariate Normal		Planar	
Test	Sample Value	μ_{PPD}	p-value	μ_{PPD}	p-value
Mean(x)/Median(x)	1.18	1.00	0.0	1.04	0.0
Mean(y)/Median(y)	1.02	0.99	0.26	1.13	0.
# of (0,0) Observations	361.0	94.7	0.0	26.5	0.0
# of (5,5) Observations	5.0	0.07	0.0	1.6	0.01
# of (5,0) Observations	11.0	0.17	0.0	20.3	0.03
# of (0,5) Observations	2.0	0.1	0.01	7.0	0.05

Note: Data are from the 2000 GSS special topic module on freedom (variables are expunpop and partpol).

Overall, the results of the posterior predictive simulation indicate that neither model fits these data particularly well. The normal distribution consistently underpredicts the number of observations in the tails of the distribution, and the planar distribution fails to match the overall shape of the data distribution. The results suggest that, of the two models, the bivariate normal should be preferred. However, this result is not particularly surprising. The planar density model involved three parameters and did not allow for a relationship between the two variables. The bivariate normal model, on the other hand, had five parameters, including one that captures the relationship between the two variables.

6.5 Formal comparison and combining models

6.5.1 Bayes factors

We are often interested in comparing two or more models to determine which is "best." Sometimes, choosing the best model may be our strategy for determining which of two competing theories or hypotheses provides a better explanation for the data at hand. Occasionally, the models we would like to compare are nested; that is, one model is a special case of another. In such cases, the classical approach using maximum likelihood methods provides a prescription for testing for "significant" differences between two models. More often, however, we need to compare models that are not nested. An informal,

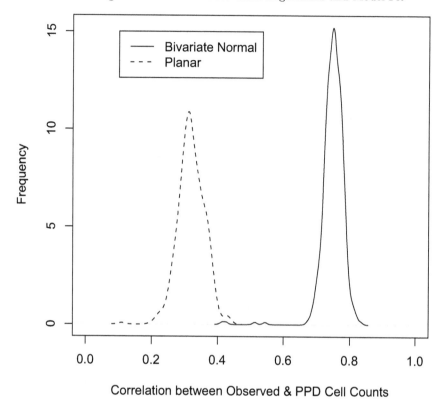

Fig. 6.17. Correlations between observed cell counts and posterior predictive distribution cell counts for the bivariate normal and planar distribution models.

yet flexible and multifaceted approach to comparing models is the use of posterior predictive simulation as described in the previous section. That is, we could establish a number of criteria (e.g., test statistics) along which to compare models and choose the model that bests meets the criteria. Indeed, ultimately, model comparison rests on comparing how well two models fit the same data, and residual analysis and posterior predictive simulation tell us how well a model fits the data.

The Bayesian approach to statistics also offers more formal means for comparing models. The use of Bayes factors is one tool for doing so (see Kass and Raftery 1995, and Raftery 1995, for more extensive discussion of model selection and the Bayes Factor in general, but also see Gelman and Rubin 1995).

Suppose we have two models M_1 and M_2 with parameters θ_1 and θ_2 that we would like to compare. Ultimately, what we would like to know is the posterior probability of each model, given the data we have observed—$P(M \mid \text{data})$. A comparison of the two models, given the posterior probabilities for each would then be straightforward:

$$\text{Posterior Odds} = \frac{p(M_1 \mid \text{data})}{p(M_2 \mid \text{data})}.$$

In this equation, a value for the posterior odds that is greater than 1 indicates that model 1 is favored; a value less than 1 indicates that model 2 is favored; and a value equal to 1 indicates that neither model is preferable.

The posterior probability for a model given the data can be computed using Bayes' rule: Both the numerator and the denominator of the posterior odds can be broken down so that $p(M, \text{data}) = p(\text{data} \mid M)p(M)$. [Or, expressed as a conditional: $p(M \mid \text{data}) \propto p(\text{data} \mid M)p(M)$.] The latter half of the resulting ratio—$p(M_1)/p(M_2)$—is called the "prior odds" for each model. Generally, we specify equal prior probabilities for the models, which means that this ratio is 1 and can be ignored.

The first part of the ratio—$p(\text{data}, M_1)/p(\text{data}, M_2)$—is the ratio of the marginal likelihoods for the data, once the parametric uncertainty in each model is integrated out [i.e., $p(y) = \int p(\text{data}, M)dM$] and is called the Bayes factor. Put another way, the marginal likelihood for the data is the integral of the posterior density over the parameters:

$$p(y \mid M_i) = \int_{\theta_i \in S_i} p(y \mid \theta_i, M_i)p(\theta_i \mid M_i)d\theta_i. \tag{6.4}$$

This integration is a significant limitation to the use of Bayes factors; the integration is difficult. The integration essentially produces the normalizing constant that we generally cannot easily compute and are able to avoid with MCMC estimation. Although Raftery (1995) shows an approximation to the integral (the Bayesian Information Criterion—BIC) that can be fairly easily computed using standard output from the maximum likelihood results in most software packages, it may not be easily computed from the results of an MCMC algorithm. Furthermore, the Bayes factor is quite sensitive to the choice of priors used for parameters in each model, and so it should be used with caution. I do not discuss the Bayes factor in this book for these reasons. Instead, I prefer the flexibility and ease of posterior predictive checks for selecting models, and I focus on them.

6.5.2 Bayesian model averaging

A fairly recent development in Bayesian statistics has been the emergence of Bayesian model averaging, seemingly as a response to (or extension of) the model selection approach encouraged by the use of Bayes factors. Whereas Bayes factors can be used to select the "best" model from a set of models, the model averaging approach essentially *combines* all models in a class of models to generate inference about a parameter. For example, in an OLS regression model with J predictor variables, the Bayes factor approach would be to select the best model (i.e., the best combination of predictors) and then use the results of that model for inference. Bayesian model averaging, on the other hand, averages over model uncertainty—the fact that we are ultimately uncertain *which* model is, in fact, best—by assigning prior weights to all models in a class of models and producing a marginal posterior distribution for the parameter that is basically a weighted combination of the posterior for the parameter under all models (Hoeting et al. 1999). Formally:

$$p(\theta \mid y) = \sum_{j=1}^{J} p(\theta \mid M_j, y) p(M_j \mid y). \tag{6.5}$$

The first term on the right-hand side of Equation 6.5 is the posterior distribution for the parameter under each specific model, and the second term is the posterior probability for each model itself. The posterior probability for each model is the numerator of the posterior odds presented in the previous section on Bayes factors; hence, it incorporates a prior for each model under consideration with its marginal likelihood, given the data. Thus, the posterior distribution for a parameter under BMA is ultimately just a weighted mixture of the posterior distribution for the parameter under all models.

Model averaging, although appealing, is difficult. First, it requires the construction of a huge number of prior distributions—one for each model in the class being examined. So, for example, in the OLS regression model mentioned above with J covariates, we would need 2^J priors. Of course, we could simply be agnostic and give equal weight to all models, but doing so may lead us, in the posterior, to favor models that are very similar to one another. Second, model averaging is potentially incredibly computationally intensive. With J covariates, the model space consists of 2^J models that must be estimated. Although there are ways to reduce the model space to a more manageable number of models (e.g., Occam's window; see Hoeting et al. 1999), doing so makes the model-averaged posterior distribution for the parameter inexact. An alternative is to use MCMC sampling to marginalize (average) over all of the models. However, this approach may be too computationally intensive.

I do not provide examples of BMA in this book, for a couple of reasons. First, this book is meant to be an introduction to Bayesian statistics and MCMC estimation, and BMA is a fairly complex process. As stated above, choosing appropriate priors for all models in a class can be quite difficult, and BMA is computationally incredibly intensive. Some of the models discussed in the second part of this book, for example, may take on the order of hours to run for a *single* model. Attempting to perform BMA with 2^J possible models may be unfeasible without substantial programming expertise and access to very powerful computer systems (e.g., like a Beowulf cluster). Second, and perhaps the more important reason I do not discuss BMA in this book, is that it seems in some ways contradictory to the basic approach to research taken by social scientists. That is, social science research typically begins with a theory and a set of hypotheses that guide us in the selection of variables and in the overall design of a model. The logic of BMA seems to run counter to this approach: BMA allows the data to tell us whether particular variables are important. Of course, we can incorporate our prior expectations for which variables/models are most important in a class via our prior specifications for the models, but if we do so, why not simply specify the model we are interested in testing in the first place! This strategy is akin to conducting BMA and assigning a prior probability of 0 for all models in the class of models we are evaluating except for the one that our theory leads us to believe is the appropriate one—and giving it a prior probability of 1.

6.6 Conclusions

In this chapter we have discussed (1) assessing the performance of MCMC algorithms and (2) assessing model fit. The assessment of MCMC algorithm performance is an important process, because, if the model has not converged and mixed well, the results cannot be used for making inference about model parameters. As we discussed, algorithm assessment requires a multifaceted approach, because no single approach constitutes a sufficient test for determining whether the routine has converged and mixed well. Indeed, developing better ways of assessing performance, as well as developing better performing algorithms for specific problems has been a key area of research in MCMC methods over the last decade. In this chapter, we have covered the most commonly used methods of assessing performance, and we have discussed several strategies for improving performance if it is found to be lacking.

Once we have determined that our MCMC algorithm sampled thoroughly from the posterior distribution of interest, our next step should be to assess whether the model in fact fits the data well. In this chapter, we discussed several methods for assessing model fit and comparing models, but the primary focus was on posterior predictive checks. I limited the in-depth discussion to this approach, because posterior predictive simulation is easy to perform, and it is a highly flexible approach to assessing how well the model fits any feature of the data we are concerned about.

Our coverage of these two topics has been relatively basic and limited largely to contrived examples. In the remaining chapters, we will employ a variety of strategies for assessing MCMC performance and evaluating model fit using common social science models and real social science data.

6.7 Exercises

1. How are residual analysis and posterior predictive simulation similar to one another?
2. How can posterior predictive simulation be considered a method to compare models and not simply a method to evaluate a single model?

3. Reconduct the bivariate normal distribution example from the last chapter, using an MH algorithm to estimate the parameters, but select extremely poor starting values for them. Run the algorithm five times with different sets of such poor starting values and compute the scale reduction factor R. Also construct trace plots. Does the R calculation lead you to a different conclusion concerning where to consider the burn-in to have ended than the trace plots?

4. Reconduct the final normal distribution example again with an MH algorithm. Use good starting values this time, but run the algorithm at least seven times using different widths for the proposal distribution for the means. Can you develop a rule (for this model) for determining the appropriate proposal density width/variance given a desired acceptance rate?

5. Generate 100 observations from a normal distribution with a mean of 5 and variance of 4, as in the example. Now square these values, assume they come from a normal distribution, and estimate the parameters for this normal distribution using either a Gibbs sampler or an MH algorithm. Next, use posterior predictive simulation to determine whether the model fits the data. Does it?

7

The Linear Regression Model

The first six chapters of this book have developed statistical modeling from a mathematical view of probability, introduced the Bayesian approach to data analysis, shown how to sample from Bayesian posterior distributions in order to make statistical inference, and demonstrated the basics for evaluating MCMC algorithm performance, evaluating model fit, and comparing models. So far, the models have been relatively simple; yet statistical modeling in social science research generally involves singling-out one or more variables as outcomes for which we would like to evaluate the influence of a set of theoretically important predictors and controls. In short, most social science data analysis involves some form of regression modeling. The remaining chapters of this book are geared to showing how to perform such analyses in a Bayesian framework. The basic models themselves should be quite familiar, and so the new content will be the Bayesian implementation of them. In the process of demonstrating how a Bayesian might approach these models, I will show some of the advantages of a Bayesian approach, including the ease of handling missing data, the ability to make statistical inference for functions of parameters in models, and the breadth of possible methods for evaluating model fit.

7.1 Development of the linear regression model

The linear regression model—often called the "ordinary least squares (OLS) Regression Model"—is the fundamental model of all social scientific research. Although over the last few decades it has been supplanted by more complicated models, especially generalized linear models and models that can handle serial correlation between errors (e.g., fixed and random effects models), the basic assumption that an outcome variable y (or a function thereof) can be expressed as a linear combination of predictor variables and some stochastic error is the foundation of virtually all parametric models in social science today.

Because the linear regression model is the first model that is discussed in most graduate programs, I do not spend much time developing the model and theory (see Fox 1997 or Neter et al. 1996 for detailed discussion of the linear model). Instead, I primarily focus on demonstrating several MCMC approaches that may be used to estimate the parameters of the model.

The OLS regression model is generally represented in one of two ways, one involving a direct specification of a distribution for the outcome variable y and the other involving a specification of a distribution for the error e. Under the classical—and typical social science—specification, we assume that y_i is equal to a linear combination of a set of predictors, $X_i^T \beta$ plus error e_i, and that the error term is normally distributed with a mean of 0 and some variance, σ_e^2. In matrix form for an entire sample:

$$Y = X\beta + e, \tag{7.1}$$

$$e \sim N(0, \sigma_e^2 I_n), \tag{7.2}$$

where I_n is an n-dimensional identity matrix. Often, this term is omitted in the specification, but the distribution for the *vector* is technically multivariate normal with a 0 mean vector and an $n \times n$ covariance matrix. The diagonal elements of this matrix are all equal (representing the homoscedasticity of the errors assumption), and the off-diagonal elements of this matrix are 0 (representing the independence of errors assumption).

The normality assumption for the error term is not necessary for OLS estimation, but it is necessary for maximum likelihood estimation and for classical statistical tests on the parameters (the t-tests). Under the maximum likelihood approach, a normal error assumption yields the following likelihood function:

$$L(\beta, \sigma_e^2 | X, Y) = \prod_{i=1}^{n} (2\pi\sigma_e^2)^{-1/2} \exp\left\{-\frac{1}{2\sigma_e^2}(y_i - X_i^T \beta)^2\right\} \tag{7.3}$$

$$= (2\pi\sigma_e^2)^{-n/2} \exp\left\{-\frac{1}{2\sigma_e^2}(Y - X\beta)^T(Y - X\beta)\right\}. \tag{7.4}$$

The maximum likelihood solution to find the best estimates of β and σ_e^2 ($\hat{\beta}$ and $\hat{\sigma}_e^2$, respectively) and their standard errors can be found by taking the first and second derivatives of the log of this likelihood function following the steps discussed in Chapter 2. After derivation, we find:

$$\hat{\beta} = (X^T X)^{-1}(X^T Y), \tag{7.5}$$

$$\hat{\sigma}_e^2 = \frac{1}{n} e^T e, \tag{7.6}$$

where e is the vector of errors obtained under $\hat{\beta}$. The estimated standard errors for the parameters can be found by square-rooting the diagonal elements of the asymptotic covariance matrix of the parameters, and the standard error for the error variance can be found as well[1]:

$$\mathrm{ACOV}(\hat{\beta}) = \hat{\sigma}_e^2 (X^T X)^{-1}, \tag{7.7}$$

$$\mathrm{SE}(\hat{\sigma}_e^2) = \left(\frac{2\hat{\sigma}_e^2}{n}\right)^{1/2}. \tag{7.8}$$

Rather than specifying a normal distribution on the error term, a Bayesian specification typically begins with a normality assumption on $y \mid x$ (often with the conditioning suppressed): $y_i \sim N(X_i^T \beta, \sigma_e^2)$. This specification yields the same likelihood function as the classical solution. What remains to make the model fully Bayesian is the specification of a prior for β and σ_e^2, and this is often done by specifying independent priors for each parameter. An improper uniform prior over the real line is often specified for the regression parameters, while the common reference prior for the normal distribution model (as discussed in Chapter 3)—$1/\sigma_e^2$—is often specified for the error variance parameter. This yields a posterior distribution that appears as:

$$P(\beta, \sigma_e^2 | X, Y) \propto (\sigma_e^2)^{-(n/2+1)} \exp\left\{-\frac{1}{2\sigma_e^2}(Y - X\beta)^T (Y - X\beta)\right\}, \tag{7.9}$$

after simplification. Note that this posterior differs from the likelihood function *only* in the leading exponent. The absolute value of the exponent for σ_e^2 is increased from $n/2$ to $n/2+1$, which is an asymptotically irrelevant modification of the likelihood function. This result once again highlights that, with large samples, the prior may matter very little in affecting posterior inference.

Given a posterior distribution, the goal of the Bayesian approach is to produce more than simply a point estimate for the parameter and its standard error, as we have discussed in the previous chapters. Thus, I now discuss several strategies for sampling from this posterior distribution. Although this model has been well studied, and the full conditionals are well known for the parameters, I will develop an MH algorithm along with two different Gibbs samplers.

---

[1] This standard error is almost never used, nor even reported in classical regression analysis, in part because normal theory tests based on it (e.g., t-tests like for the regression coefficients) are inappropriate. Variances are inverse gamma distributed and hence nonnegative. So, a typical t-test evaluating the statistical significance of a variance parameter is simply an unreasonable test. Unfortunately, in structural equation modeling, a setting in which standard errors of variance parameters are commonly reported, users often report the results of such t-tests and perpetuate the myth of testing the hypothesis that a variance is less than 0. This practice is especially common in modern latent growth modeling.

7.2 Sampling from the posterior distribution for the model parameters

7.2.1 Sampling with an MH algorithm

A variety of options exists for constructing an MH algorithm for the OLS regression model. Here, I develop a random walk metropolis algorithm in which each parameter is updated sequentially. The construction of an MH algorithm requires only that we be able to compute the unnormalized posterior density function (i.e., Equation 7.9); we do not need to derive any conditional distributions. Computing the unnormalized posterior density in this case is straightforward, and hence I skip directly to the R algorithm:

```
#R program for MH sampling of parameters in linear regression
#number of iterations
m=200000

#read in data, establish x and y matrices
x=as.matrix(read.table("c:\\ols_examp.dat")[1:2313,2:10])
y=as.matrix(read.table("c:\\ols_examp.dat")[1:2313,11])

#establish parameter vectors, proposal scales and acceptance rates
s2=matrix(1,m); b=matrix(0,m,9)
bscale=sqrt(diag(vcov(lm(y~x-1))))*.5
s2scale=sqrt(var(residuals(lm(y~x-1))*(2313-1)/(2313-9)))*.5
accrate=matrix(0,m,9); s2accrate=matrix(0,m)

#unnormalized posterior distribution function
post<-function(x,y,b,s2)
  {return((-1157.5*log(s2)+(-.5/s2)*(t(y- x%*%b)%*%(y- x%*%b))))}

#Begin MH Sampling
for(i in 2:m){
#temporarily set 'new' values of b
b[i,]=b[i-1,]

#update regression parameters
for(j in 1:9){
#generate candidate and assume it will be accepted...
b[i,j]=b[i-1,j]+rnorm(1,mean=0, sd=bscale[j]); acc=1
#...until it is evaluated for rejection
if((post(x,y,b[i,],s2[i-1]) - post(x,y,b[i-1,],s2[i-1]))
    <log(runif(1,min=0,max=1)))
  {b[i,j]=b[i-1,j]; acc=0}
accrate[i,j]=(accrate[i-1,j]*(i-1)+acc)/i
}

#update s2.  generate candidate and assume accepted
```

```
s2[i]=s2[i-1]+rnorm(1,mean=0, sd=s2scale); acc=1
#...until it is evaluated for rejection
if(s2[i]<0 ||
   (post(x,y,b[i,],s2[i]) - post(x,y,b[i,],s2[i-1]))
    <log(runif(1,min=0,max=1)))
  {s2[i]=s2[i-1]; acc=0}
s2accrate[i]=(s2accrate[i-1]*(i-1)+acc)/i

#write output to file and screen
write(c(b[i,],s2[i],accrate[i,],s2accrate[i]),
      file="c:\\ols_examp.out", append=T, ncol=20)
if(i%%10==0){print(c(i,b[i,1],s2[i],accrate[i,1],s2accrate[i]))}
}
```

The program is fairly straightforward, and the comments within it clarify what each section does, so only a few comments are in order. First, the proposal densities for all parameters are normal with a mean of 0 and some standard deviation. This standard deviation is determined in the second section using the ML estimated standard errors of the parameters multiplied by a fraction (.5) in order to produce a reasonable acceptance rate (here, about 35% for each parameter). If this model were not a standard model, I would have needed to establish some other method for obtaining the scale of the proposal densities, possibly through experimentation and/or approximation of the standard errors via ML estimation of similar models.

Second, I created a function to evaluate the log posterior density, as I have done in previous programs. The log posterior is used, again, to prevent possible underflow problems that arise from attempting to exponentiate large negative numbers. Using the log posterior necessitates comparing the ratio R—which is now a subtraction—with the log of a $U(0,1)$ random draw.

Third, the slope parameters in the program are updated sequentially, but at the beginning of each iteration, I set the current values of each parameter to the previous values first. I do this, because it allows me to send the posterior density function the current vector for the parameters without having to determine which sampled value of the parameter to send it (i.e., the current or previous, depending on which parameter is currently being updated, which have yet to be updated, and which have already been updated).

Fourth, the program writes all parameters and acceptance rates to a file at each iteration. Thus, it is really unnecessary to store all parameters in a vector of length 200,000. Instead, we could use two distinct variables for each parameter (e.g., currentb and previousb). I demonstrate this approach in programs in subsequent chapters.

7.2.2 Sampling the model parameters using Gibbs sampling

The MH algorithm presented in the previous section is quite long and cumbersome. Fortunately, the conditional posterior distributions for both the regression parameters and the error variance parameter are well known, and so Gibbs sampling provides a more efficient alternative.

The Full conditionals method

There are at least two general ways to develop a Gibbs sampler for the linear regression model. The first method involves determining the full conditionals for (1) the regression parameter vector and (2) the error variance parameter. The full conditional posterior distribution for the error variance parameter is straightforward to derive from Equation 7.9. With β known/fixed, the conditional posterior for σ^2 is:

$$p(\sigma^2|\beta, X, Y) \propto (\sigma^2)^{-(n/2+1)} \exp\left\{-\frac{e^T e}{2\sigma^2}\right\}, \tag{7.10}$$

where $e^T e$ is the sum of the square error terms under the given value for β. This conditional posterior is easily seen to be an inverse gamma distribution with parameters $\alpha = n/2$ and $\beta = e^T e/2$.

The conditional distribution for β is slightly more difficult to derive, because its derivation involves matrix algebra. However, the process is identical in concept to the approach we used in the univariate normal distribution example in Chapter 3. With σ^2 fixed, we can focus exclusively on the exponential:

$$\exp\left\{-\frac{1}{2\sigma^2}(Y - X\beta)^T(Y - X\beta)\right\}.$$

First, we can distribute the transpose in the first term in the numerator:

$$\exp\left\{-\frac{1}{2\sigma^2}(Y^T - \beta^T X^T)(Y - X\beta)\right\}$$

and then expand the multiplication:

$$\exp\left\{-\frac{1}{2\sigma^2}[Y^T Y - Y^T X\beta - \beta^T X^T Y + \beta^T X^T X\beta]\right\}.$$

The first term is constant with respect to β, and so it can be removed as a multiplicative proportionality constant as we have done before (e.g., in Chapter 4). The middle two terms are identical to one another—one is just a transposed version of the other, but both are 1×1; thus, one can be transposed, and the two may be grouped. After rearranging terms, we obtain:

$$\exp\left\{-\frac{1}{2\sigma^2}[\beta^T X^T X\beta - 2\beta^T X^T Y]\right\}.$$

If we now multiply the numerator and denominator through by $(X^T X)^{-1}$ appropriately,[2] we get:

$$\exp\left\{-\frac{1}{2\sigma^2(X^T X)^{-1}}[\beta^T \beta - 2\beta^T (X^T X)^{-1}(X^T Y)]\right\}.$$

At this point, we can complete the square in β, or we can simply recognize that doing so will yield a distribution for β that is normal with a mean equal to $(X^T X)^{-1}(X^T Y)$ and a variance of $\sigma_e^2(X^T X)^{-1}$.

With the conditionals derived, we can implement Gibbs sampling from the full conditionals by (1) establishing starting values for the parameters, (2) sampling β from its multivariate normal distribution with σ_e^2 fixed, and (3) sampling σ_e^2 from its inverse gamma distribution with β (and hence e) fixed. The following is an R program that implements this process:

```
#R program for Gibbs sampling from full conditionals in OLS example

#number of iterations
m=5000

#read only observations with complete information, n=2313
x=as.matrix(read.table("c:\\ols_examp.dat")[1:2313,2:10])
y=as.matrix(read.table("c:\\ols_examp.dat")[1:2313,11])

#establish parameter vectors and constant quantities
s2=matrix(1,m); b=matrix(0,m,9)
xtxi=solve(t(x)%*%x)
pars=coefficients(lm(y~x-1))

#Gibbs sampling begins
for(i in 2:m){
#simulate beta from its multivariate normal conditional
b[i,]=pars+t(rnorm(9,mean=0,sd=1))%*%chol(s2[i-1]*xtxi)

#simulate sigma from its inverse gamma distribution
s2[i]=1/rgamma(1,2313/2,.5*t(y-x%*%(b[i,]))%*%(y-x%*%(b[i,])))

#write output to file and screen
write(c(b[i,],s2[i]),file="c:\\ols_examp.out", append=T, ncol=10)
if(i%%50==0){print(c(i,b[i,1],s2[i]))}
}
```

This program is remarkably shorter than the MH algorithm and requires very little explanation. Before the Gibbs sampling begins, I compute the

---

[2] Technically, we cannot "divide" by $(X^T X)^{-1}$. Instead, we can multiply the numerator through by $(X^T X)(X^T X)^{-1}$ and just distribute the inverse term. Then, the inverse variance of the distribution for β is $(X^T X)/\sigma_e^2$. Inverting this quantity gives us the variance.

$(X^TX)^{-1}$ matrix and the OLS estimates $(X^TX)^{-1}(X^TY)$, both of which are used repeatedly and are unchanging. Once the Gibbs sampling loop begins, the entire vector of regression parameters is updated via a draw from the multivariate normal distribution with the appropriate covariance matrix (which is conditional on the previous value of σ_e^2). This is conducted as discussed in previous chapters: We multiply a vector of independent $N(0,1)$ random draws by the Cholesky decomposition of the variance/covariance matrix of the parameters.

Once the regression parameters have been updated, the error variance parameter is updated with a draw from the inverse gamma distribution. As discussed in previous chapters, R does not have an inverse gamma random number generator, and so a draw from the gamma distribution is obtained and then inverted.

The Composition method

A second, more efficient approach to Gibbs sampling in the linear regression model is to decompose the posterior distribution as the conditional distribution for the regression parameters, given the error variance parameter, multiplied by the marginal distribution for the error variance parameter:

$$p(\beta\,,\,\sigma_e^2|X,Y) = p(\beta|\sigma_e^2, X, Y)p(\sigma_e^2|X,Y).$$

This approach is the regression analog to the univariate normal distribution example discussed in Chapter 4. Under this decomposition, the marginal distribution for σ_e^2 is inverse gamma, and a sequence of draws from the appropriate inverse gamma distribution can be generated first. Then, given each sampled value of σ_e^2, the conditional distribution $p(\beta|\sigma_e^2)$ is normal. Thus, once the sequence of draws for σ_e^2 is obtained, one can simulate a sequence of draws for β from the appropriate normal distribution for each value of σ_e^2.

The conditional distribution for β is the same as in the previous Gibbs sampling approach: normal with mean equal to the least squares solution $(X^TX)^{-1}(X^TY)$ and variance $\sigma_e^2(X^TX)^{-1}$. Thus, given a fixed value for σ_e^2, we can simulate β directly from a normal distribution.

The marginal distribution for σ_e^2 can be derived by integrating the posterior density over the regression parameter vector [i.e., $p(\sigma^2) = \int p(\beta, \sigma^2)d\beta$] and is shown in Gelman et al. (1995) to be a scaled inverse-chi-square distribution with parameters $n - k$ and $(1/(n - k))(Y - X\hat{\beta})^T(Y - X\hat{\beta})$, where n is the sample size, k is the number of parameters in the β vector, and $\hat{\beta}$ is the least squares solution for β. The scaled inverse-chi-square distribution (with parameters v and s^2) is a special case of the inverse gamma distribution with parameters $\alpha = v/2$ and $\beta = (v/2)s^2$. Thus, we can draw σ_e^2 from its marginal distribution using an inverse gamma distribution with parameters $\alpha = (n - k)/2$ and $\beta = (1/2)e^Te$, where e is the vector of errors computed from the least squares solution.

Below is an R program that performs Gibbs sampling using this approach:

```
#R program for Gibbs sampling using composition method in OLS

#number of iterations
m=100000

x=as.matrix(read.table("c:\\ols_examp.dat")[1:2313,2:10])
y=as.matrix(read.table("c:\\ols_examp.dat")[1:2313,11:14])

#establish parameter vectors and constant quantities
s2=matrix(1,m); b=matrix(0,m,9)
xtxi=solve(t(x)%*%x)
pars=coefficients(lm(y[,1] ~ x-1))

#simulate sigma from its inverse gamma marginal
s2=1/rgamma(m,(2313-9)/2,.5*t(residuals(lm(y[,1] ~ x-1)))%*%
                        residuals(lm(y[,1] ~ x-1)))

#simulate beta vector from appropriate mvn
for(i in 1:m)
{
b[i,]=pars+t(rnorm(9,mean=0,sd=1))%*%chol(s2[i]*xtxi)

#write output to file and screen
write(c(b[i,],s2[i]),
        file="c:\\ols_examp.out", append=T, ncolumns=10)
if(i%%50==0){print(c(i,b[i,1],s2[i]))}
}
```

This algorithm differs very little from the previous Gibbs sampler, but it is faster and more efficient, because σ_e^2 is drawn all at once. Because every draw of σ_e^2 is directly from its marginal posterior distribution, there is no burn-in to discard.

One comment is in order concerning the two Gibbs samplers. They will both yield the same results, despite that one is sampling from the marginal distribution for σ_e^2, and the other is sampling from its conditional distribution (given β). This fact highlights a key feature of MCMC methods: They are a means of stochastic integration. Sampling values of σ^2 in proportion to their probability conditioning on β is equivalent to analytically integrating β out of the joint distribution for σ_e^2 and β to obtain the marginal distribution for σ_e^2. Regardless of the approach taken, although the conditional distribution for the regression vector is multivariate normal, the *marginal* distribution after integrating over σ_e^2 is multivariate t. This is precisely why I said in Chapter 2 that we often do not need to use the t and multivariate t distributions directly.

7.3 Example: Are people in the South "nicer" than others?

Conventional wisdom holds that Southern (US) culture is very different from Northeastern, Western, and even Midwestern culture. This is perhaps one reason why so many regression models in social science, when they include region as a control variable, include only an indicator variable for "South." Three important ways that the South is considered different from other regions in the US are (1) the pace of life is assumed to be slower than especially that of the Northeast and West, (2) people are assumed to be friendlier and more compassionate than persons from other regions, and (3) people are assumed to be poorer, less sophisticated, and perhaps even less intelligent than people from other regions.[3]

In 2002 and 2004, the General Social Survey (GSS) conducted a special topics module on "altruism," which allows us to examine item 2, the assumption that people in the South are more compassionate. For this example, I examine four outcome variables: (1) a summed scale of seven items that assesses individuals' feelings of empathy, (2) a single item measuring tolerance of others, (3) a summed scale of four items assessing selfless attitude, and (4) a summed scale of actual altruistic behavior.

I use age, sex, race, education, and family income as control variables. I measure region using a series of three dummy variables constructed from the region the respondent lived in at age 16 and the region the respondent currently lives in: continuous resident of the South, South in-migrant, South out-migrant.[4] I choose this measure, because, although the culture of the South may be indigenous to that region, individuals internalize culture over time. Thus, individuals who move into a region do not immediately adopt the cultural practices of the region, and individuals who move out of a region do not immediately shed their previous cultural identity.

The original sample size for the two years in which this topic module was used was $n = 2,712$. Sixteen persons (.6%) were missing on either age or education; they were deleted. An additional 257 persons (9.5%) were missing on income only, and an additional 127 persons (4.7%) were missing on an

---

[3] These assumptions probably stem largely from the agricultural history of the South, where/when time was measured by daylight, rather than by a clock, most workers were physical (agricultural) laborers lacking in formal education beyond elementary school, and the closed nature of rural communities produced "gemeinschaft-like" relations that made empathy and compassion more viable than in urban communities in which individuals were less similar to one another (i.e., where "gesellschaft-like" relations predominated) and thus less able to empathize with the plight of others. My goal here is not to develop a sociological theory of South/non-South differences. See Durkheim (1984) for the foundation of such sociological theory.

[4] Of course, this measure is not perfect. Individuals may have moved many times; this measure only captures residence at two points in time.

outcome variable and possibly income. For the initial analyses, I use individuals with complete information only (85.8% of the original sample, not including those missing on age or education). In subsequent analyses, I will show how to incorporate the missing data in a Bayesian framework. Table 7.1 presents descriptive statistics for the variables in the models.

Table 7.1. Descriptive statistics for variables in OLS regression example (2002 and 2004 GSS data, $n = 2,696$).

Variable	Mean(s.d.) or %	Range	% Missing	Cronbach's α
Predictors				
Age	46.3(17.3)	[16, 89]	0.0%	NA
Male	47.1%	[0, 1]	0.0%	NA
White	80.1%	[0, 1]	0.0%	NA
Yrs. Schooling	13.5(3.0)	[0, 20]	0.0%	NA
Income ($1,000s)	49.8(31.6)	[.5, 110]	11.2%	NA
Continuous South	28.0%	[0, 1]	0.0%	NA
South Out-Migrant	3.9%	[0, 1]	0.0%	NA
South In-Migrant	8.6%	[0, 1]	0.0%	NA
Outcomes				
Empathy	21.0(4.8)	[0, 28]	2.1%	.73
Tolerance	2.9(1.3)	[0, 5]	1.7%	NA
Selflessness	10.1(2.4)	[0, 16]	1.3%	.55
Altruistic Acts	13.3(6.5)	[0, 50]	2.6%	.71

7.3.1 Results and comparison of the algorithms

I ran each of these algorithms for at least 20,000 iterations. Figure 7.1 shows the scale reduction factor $\hat{R}$ discussed in Chapter 6 computed for each regression parameter from each of the three different MCMC algorithms. As the figure shows, the MH and Gibbs samplers converge very rapidly toward each other (and presumably on the posterior distribution).

Trace plots suggested that all three algorithms converged within 1,000 iterations. For example, Figure 7.2 shows trace plots for the error variance parameter for all three algorithms. As the plot shows, the three algorithms produce indistinguishable traces after only a few iterations.

Based on these similarities, which of these three algorithms is preferrable to the others? One of the Gibbs samplers is probably the best approach because of the efficiency of Gibbs sampling over MH sampling. However, the answer to this question is case-specific and depends on a couple of considerations. First,

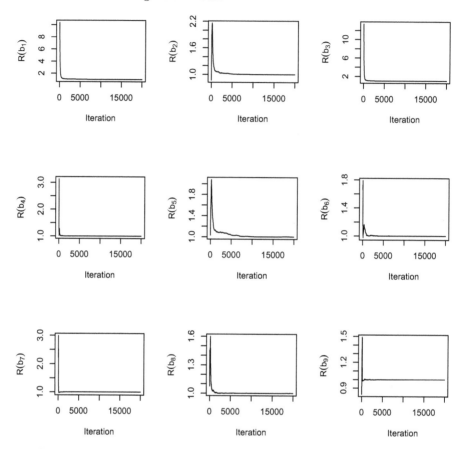

Fig. 7.1. Scale reduction factors by iteration for all regression parameters.

notice that as the programs became shorter and more efficient, they required more mathematical investment. The MH algorithm required us only to know the posterior density up to a normalizing constant. The full conditionals Gibbs sampling algorithm required us to derive the conditional distributions for both parameters. The composition method required us to find the full conditional distribution only for β, but it also required us to integrate the posterior density over β to obtain the marginal distribution for σ_e^2. Thus, when deciding which algorithm to use, a key consideration may be the difficulty of deriving the conditionals and/or marginal distributions. Second, if the data are such that it is difficult to obtain reasonable acceptance rates on all parameters using an MH algorithm, a Gibbs sampler may be preferred. In the example presented here, all three algorithms yielded comparable results, and so one of the Gibbs samplers is best, given its rapid convergence and mixing.

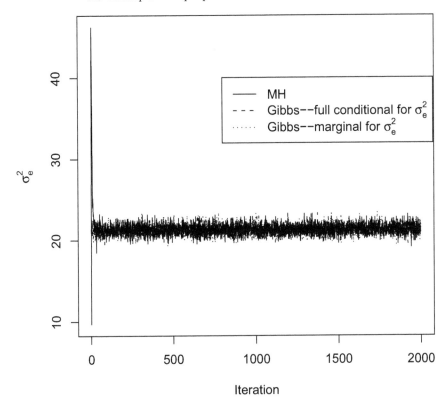

Fig. 7.2. Trace plot of error variance parameter in three different MCMC algorithms.

I report the results from the full-conditionals Gibbs sampler. After discarding the first half of the samples, and keeping every 10th iteration to reduce autocorrelation (which is not really necessary in this problem), and repeating this process for each of the four outcomes, I computed the posterior means and standard deviations of all parameters using 1,000 samples. These results are displayed in Table 7.2. The results are consistent with the hypothesis that Southerners are nicer than others. Individuals who resided in the South at age 16 and at the present wave of the study have higher levels of empathy, evidence greater tolerance, are more selfless, and commit more altruistic acts than persons from or in other regions. There is some evidence, based on the sign and magnitude of most of the coefficients, that, if the culture of the South is nicer than that of other regions, the influence of the regional culture takes some time to fade, but perhaps not to adopt. Both emigrants from the South and immigrants to the South have higher scores on almost all outcome measures, net of the control variables in the model.

Although I have reported the results with asterisks, as is common in classical statistical research, there is no need to do this in a Bayesian setting.

Instead, we could directly discuss the probabilities that say, immigrants to the South are nicer than persons who have never lived in the South. For example, the probability that immigrants have greater empathy than persons who have never lived in the South is .821. This probability was obtained simply by computing the proportion of sampled regression parameter values that exceed 0. Thus, although this parameter was not considered "significant" from a classical standpoint, the Bayesian approach suggests that immigrants are quite likely to be nicer (by this measure) than persons who have never lived in the South.

The bottom of the table reports interval estimates for the model R^2. Given that we have complete distributions for the regression parameters and error variance parameter, and not simply point estimates, we can compute the R^2 implied by each sample of the parameters, thereby obtaining a sample from the posterior distribution for the model R^2. Once this sample is sorted, we can then select the 2.5th and 97.5th percentile values as the end points for a 95% interval estimate.

Table 7.2. Results of linear regression of measures of "niceness" on three measures of region.

Variable	Empathy	Tolerance	Selflessness	Altruistic Acts
		Outcome		
Intercept	19.62(.57)***	3.16(.15)***	8.71(.30)***	9.17(.76)***
Age	0.018(.006)**	−0.008(.002)***	0.01(.003)***	−0.03(.01)***
Male	−2.42(.19)***	−0.35(.05)***	−0.87(.10)***	0.32(.26)
White	0.55(.26)*	0.09(.07)#	0.17(.13)#	0.01(.33)
Yrs. Schooling	0.06(.04)*	0.004(.01)	0.07(.02)***	0.32(.05)***
Income ($1,000s)	0.003(.003)	0.0006(.0009)	0.001(.002)	0.02(.005)***
Continuous South	0.65(.21)**	0.22(.06)***	0.25(.11)*	0.41(.30)#
South Out-Migrant	0.39(.50)	0.11(.14)	−0.33(.25)#	0.01(.70)
South In-Migrant	0.34(.35)	0.24(.10)**	0.17(.17)	−0.01(.45)
$\sqrt{\sigma_e^2}$	4.61	1.22	2.31	6.23
R^2	.07[.066,.072]	.03[.029,.036]	.05[.047,.054]	.055[.051,.057]

Note: The Bayesian estimates are posterior means. The Bayesian p-values are based on one-sided tail probabilities that the parameter exceeds 0 truncated to the classical cut-points of #$p < .1$, *$p < .05$, **$p < .01$, ***$p < .001$. The R^2 reported are based on the posterior mean estimates for the parameters; a 95% interval estimate is also reported.

7.3.2 Model evaluation

Although I modeled the tolerance outcome variable as if it were a continuous measure, in fact it is a single ordinal item with five categories. Thus, we should evaluate the fit of the model and verify that it fits the data. The R^2 presented in the table is quite low (3%), which suggests poor fit, but R^2 reveals only one aspect of how well the model fits the data in this problem. Some remaining questions include: (1) How well does the model fit various aspects of the data? and (2) Are there particularly poorly fitted cases that contribute to the model's poor fit? As discussed in earlier chapters, a Bayesian approach allows us many more options to address these questions than the classical approach, and it allows us to take into account both sampling and parametric uncertainty in doing so.

In order to begin to address these questions, I used posterior predictive simulation. For each person in the sample, I generated 1,000 posterior predictive cases with the same covariate structure, using every sampled value of β and σ_e^2. This approach requires two steps:

1. Compute $\hat{y}_i^j = x_i^T \beta^j$, $\forall$ individuals, i, and all sampled values of the regression coefficients β^j.
2. Simulate a predictive score $y_i^j = \hat{y}_i^j + N(0, \sigma_e^{2(j)})$, for each case.

If you visualize the original data set, with 2,313 rows representing the original sample members with complete data and 10 columns representing the 9 predictors plus the outcome variable, these predictive cases can be viewed as expanding the column space of the data array by an additional 1,000 columns. For any row, i, each new column (j) represents a future observation with outcome y^j as a function of the jth sampled value of β and σ_e^2, and the covariate profile of the ith person. Thus, each new complete column can be considered a replicated *sample*, whereas the new 1,000 elements of each row can be considered replications of individual i under different parameter values. This means we can examine how well a model fits various features of the original sample (like the ratio of the mean of y to its median) by examining the column-wise collection of these values in repeated samples. Plus, we can examine how well a model fits particular cases by examining the row-wise distributions for each observation in the sample.

For this particular example, I considered three posterior predictive distribution features of the first type—sample level features. First, I examined the extent to which the *distribution* of replicated values of y matched the *distribution* of the original y. The top plot in Figure 7.3 shows this result. In general, the distribution of replicated data *appears* to match that of the observed data fairly well. Second, I computed the ratio of the mean of y to its median. The second plot in the figure shows that the distribution of the ratio of the mean to the median in the replicated samples is centered over 1 (as it should be, given that the error distribution is assumed normal), while the observed ratio was .95. As the plot shows, the Bayesian p-value associated with a test of this statistic (the mean/median ratio) would be 0 (or 1), which indicates very poor fit of the model to the data. Third I computed the range of y from each posterior predictive sample. The third plot in the figure reinforces that the model has poor fit. This plot shows the distribution of the range of values in the replicated data with a vertical reference line for the range in the observed data. Again, the posterior predictive distribution does not overlap the observed value, which indicates poor fit.

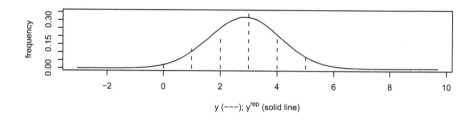

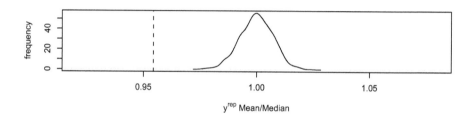

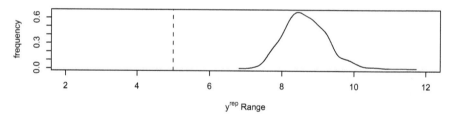

Fig. 7.3. Posterior predictive distributions: (1) The distribution of all replicated samples and the distribution of the original data; (2) the distribution of the ratio of the sample mean of y to the median, with the observed ratio superimposed; and (3) the distribution of the ranges of predicted values with the observed range superimposed.

In addition to these tests of the overall fit of the model, as I said above, we can examine how well a model fits any particular case by examining the row-wise collection of new observations and comparing it with the observed value of y for each individual. One way to identify potential outliers is to compute the proportion of future observations for individual i that would have a higher (or lower) value on the response variable. Observed cases in which the posterior predictive distribution is extreme (either a high or low proportion of posterior predictive cases exceed the observed value) indicate the model tends to poorly fit the outcome for that case. For instance, person 1,452 had an observed value of 5 for the outcome variable, but .8% of the posterior predictive cases for this individual had a predicted value of y that exceeded this value (and 99.2% of the posterior predictive cases were smaller than this value), which suggests that this case is not fit well by the model. Similarly, person 1,997 had the largest proportion of future observations with a predicted tolerance level exceeding her observed tolerance (100.0%). She was a 31-year-old nonwhite female with 12 years of schooling and a family income of \$4,500 who is a continuous resident of the South. Her expected tolerance was much higher than what was observed. Figure 7.4 shows these two extreme cases. As the figure shows, the posterior predictive distributions for these two persons are not centered over the true values of y for them, which indicates poor fit of these cases.

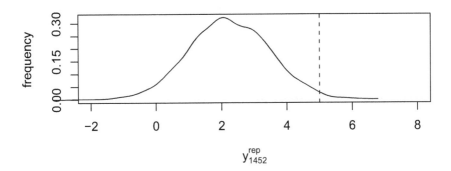

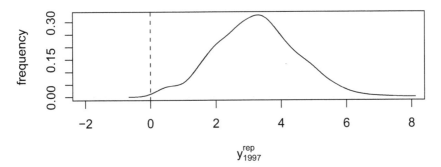

Fig. 7.4. Posterior predictive distributions (solid lines) and observed values (dashed vertical lines) for persons 1,452 and 1,997.

To determine whether such persons are outliers or whether the model simply is not fitting particular covariates well, we can examine collections of possible outliers and determine whether they share similar characteristics. For example, in these data, although there is only one person (1,452) whose tolerance is substantially underpredicted, there are 31 observations for whom the proportion of replicated outcomes exceeding the observed outcome is at least 99%. If these individuals are substantially similar to one another on one or more covariates, then the implication would be that the model does not fit those covariates well. Figure 7.5 shows the sample distribution of age, education, and income with the distribution of these variables for the 31 potential outlying cases superimposed. The figure shows quite clearly that these individuals do not appear to differ from the overall sample on these three characteristics. Thus, it is reasonable to conclude that these cases are probably simply outliers, at least in the context of the current model. We should probably consider including additional covariates that may help explain their low tolerance levels.

All in all, the posterior predictive checks suggest that the OLS regression model does not fit the tolerance item well, and so perhaps an alternative model should be considered for this item. Specifically, we may consider treating this outcome as an ordinal measure and model it using a generalized linear model as discussed in the next chapter. If we were to estimate a new model, we could apply similar tests and decide which model fits better either formally or informally. For example, formally, we could begin with a test of the proportion of values of R^2 for the new model exceeded the maximum value of R^2 for the first model. This proportion would be a measure of the probability that the new model fit the data better than the original model and would therefore serve as a basis for deciding which model to prefer. Note that this type of comparison does not require that the models be nested, because, from a Bayesian perspective, any two probability distributions can be compared if it makes sense to compare them.

7.4 Incorporating missing data

In the previous sections I discussed the results of models in which the cases with missing data were simply listwise deleted, leaving us with 85.8% of the original sample (14.2% missing). Conventional wisdom in the social sciences claims that this amount of missing data is unacceptable, and so some alternative to listwise deletion of observations with missing data should be considered. The Bayesian paradigm using MCMC simulation offers some relatively simple, yet appropriate methods for handling missing data.

7.4.1 Types of missingness

Before determining how to handle missing data, we should decide whether the missing data mechanism—that is, the process that generated the missing

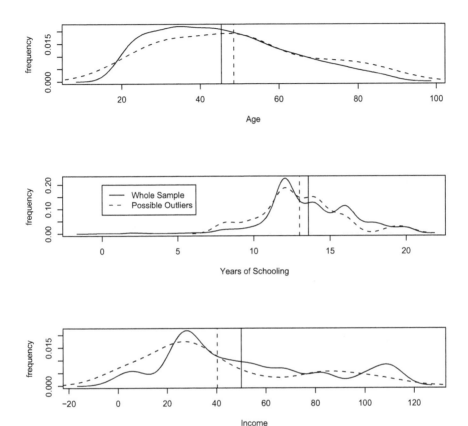

Fig. 7.5. Distribution of age, education, and income for entire sample and for 31 potential outliers identified from posterior predictive simulation (reference lines at means).

data—is ignorable or nonignorable. Little and Rubin (1987) developed a now classic schema for understanding the implications of missing data:

- Data missing on Y are *observed at random (OAR)* if missingness on Y is not a function of X. Phrased another way, if X determines missingness on Y, the data are not OAR.
- Data missing on Y are *missing at random (MAR)* if missingness on Y is not a function of Y. Phrased another way, if Y determines missingness on Y, the data are not MAR.
- Data are *missing completely at random (MCAR)* if missingness on Y is unrelated to X or Y. In other words MCAR = OAR + MAR.

If the data are MCAR or at least MAR, then the missing data mechanism is considered "ignorable." Otherwise, the missing data mechanism is considered "nonignorable."

To make these ideas concrete, suppose we are examining the effect of education on income. If missingness on income is a function of education (e.g., highly educated individuals do not report their incomes), then the data are not OAR. If missingness on income is a function of income (e.g., persons with high income do not report their income), on the other hand, then the missing data are not MAR, and the missing data mechanism is nonignorable.

Why are missing data that are MAR but not OAR ignorable? When missing data are not OAR, the fundamental pattern between the predictors and the outcome is not altered. Instead, the result is much the same as simply having a sample in which some values of x are not represented. Figure 7.6 illustrates. I simulated two sets of 10,000 $N(0, 1)$ observations. The first set I considered to be the X variable; the second set I considered to be error (e). I then constructed a vector $Y = 5 + 3X + 10e$, which implies that Y has a linear relationship with X as regression modeling assumes. The upper left figure shows a subset of these 10,000 observations along with the regression line through the points. Based on the simulation parameters, the regression coefficients should be 5 and 3, and the R^2 for this model should be $R^2 = 1 - [var(10e)/(var(5+3X+10e)] = 1 - (100/109) = .083$. This particular sample yielded 4.98 and 3.06 for the coefficients, with an R^2 of .081.

The upper right plot shows a subset of the data for which cases with values of $x < 0$ have been eliminated from the data, meaning the y data are not OAR. As the figure shows, the new regresssion line is almost identical to the original (indeed, it cannot be distinguished from the original line), with coefficients equal to 4.99 and 3.07. The R^2 was substantially less, however, at .032, reflecting the added uncertainty that results from the loss of information on the left half of the distribution. The lower left plot, in contrast, shows the results when observations with values of $y < 5$ are eliminated, meaning that the data are not MAR. In this case, the regression coefficients are substantially affected (at 13.1 and 1.3; $R^2 = .04$). The bias occurs because the distribution for y has been systematically truncated, distorting the relationship between x and y.

There are a number of ways in which we may encounter missing data in social science research, not all of which produce missing data that is nonignorable. For example, in a panel study, some individuals may not be followed up by design. Similarly, some individuals may be lost-at-follow-up because they moved between waves of the study for reasons unrelated to the outcome variable of interest. In these cases, the missing data mechanism is ignorable, and listwise deletion of the observations with missing data introduces no biases whatsoever. In most cases, however, it is unclear whether the missing data mechanism is ignorable. Item nonresponse—a common source of missingness in social surveys—may be random, or it may be attributable to the fact that the respondent would have selected a value of the response variable that would

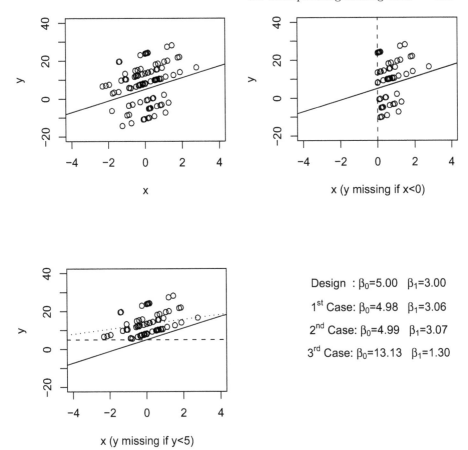

Fig. 7.6. Examples of types of missingness: No missing, missing are not OAR, and missing are not MAR.

have been extreme and potentially undesirable. For instance, consider a highly prejudiced white male respondent answering questions regarding prejudicial attitudes asked by a black female interviewer. In cases like this one, in which the missing response is due to the value of the response, the missing data mechanism is nonignorable.

How do we determine whether the missing data mechanism is ignorable? Although it is common practice in social science literature to report whether various x variables predict missingness on another x or y, formally this approach only tells us whether the data are OAR. There is no definitive way to determine whether data are MAR, because, of course, the data we need to make this determination are missing. Thus, ultimately, we must rely on some sort of prior, out-of-sample, knowledge to decide whether the missing data mechanism is ignorable or nonignorable. For example, in the GSS data, there were 302 persons missing on income. Suppose income had been our outcome variable, and we estimated a probit model with education predicting missingness on the income item. The result of that analysis (not presented here) showed that education was strongly related to missingness on income, such that more educated persons were less likely to be missing on income (conversely, less educated persons are more likely to be missing on income). This result simply tells us that income is not OAR. *However*, if we have prior (out-of-sample) information indicating that more educated individuals tend to have higher incomes, then we might infer that the missing data on income is not MAR: Lower income predicts missingness on income.

If we decide that the missing data mechanism is ignorable, then the only cost of listwise deletion—that is, deletion of an entire case when one or more variable is missing—is the reduction in sample size and the corresponding inefficiency in estimating standard errors (or posterior standard deviations) of parameters. Indeed, if we attempt to perform some sort of imputation in this setting, we are more likely to produce biases or underestimate uncertainty in the parameters (see Allison 2003).

If, on the other hand, the missing data mechanism is nonignorable, listwise deletion will produce biased parameter estimates, but so will most forms of simple imputation or modeling strategies that fail to accurately capture the process that generates the missing data. For example, so-called "full-information maximum likelihood" (FIML) estimation (sometimes also called "direct maximum likelihood estimation"), estimation based on the EM algorithm, multiple imputation methods, and other popular contemporary methods *do not resolve the nonignorability of the missing data mechanism.* Instead, in their typical application, these approaches simply assume the missing data follow the same distribution (or pattern) as the observed data. Therefore, these methods are ultimately of little use when the missing data are not MAR, despite their growth in popularity.

7.4.2 A generic Bayesian approach when data are MAR: The "niceness" example revisited

The Bayesian paradigm (coupled with MCMC methods) offers a simple approach to handling missing data when the missing data mechanism is ignorable, one that is generally easier to implement than (1) switching software or estimators when the package you are using does not have a missing data method (e.g., switching from one structural equation modeling package to another that can handle missing data) or (2) performing multistep procedures to compute parameters and adjust standard errors for missing data models (e.g., using a secondary package to adjust standard errors when performing multiple imputation).

As an example demonstrating the ease with which the Gibbs sampler can handle missing data, I return to the first outcome (empathy) in the previous example. Recall that the original sample size was 2,696, but that a number of persons were missing on either income or one of the outcome variables, leaving us with 2,313 persons with complete information. We will continue to ignore persons missing on income for the moment, but suppose we wished to include persons missing on the empathy item. There were 34 such persons in the sample. Focusing on this outcome only allows us to incorporate individuals who were missing on the other outcomes, and so our sample size is 2,394.

Let Y be the observed outcome data, and let Z be the missing outcome data. In the OLS regression model without missing data, the posterior distribution we sought included the regression parameter vector β and the error variance parameter σ_e^2. However, when we have missing data, the missing data can also be treated as unknown, and hence, the posterior distribution may involve Z as well. Thus (suppressing dependence on X), our posterior becomes:

$$p(\beta, \sigma_e^2, Z|Y) \propto p(Y|\beta, \sigma_e^2, Z)p(\beta, \sigma_e^2, Z).$$

The latter term in this posterior is a joint prior probability for the missing data, the regression parameters, and the error variance, and it can be decomposed as:

$$p(\beta, \sigma_e^2, Z) \propto p(Z|\beta, \sigma_e^2)p(\beta, \sigma_e^2).$$

Furthermore, just as the observed cases are assumed to be independent, we may also assume that the observed and missing cases are independent, and so the first term in the posterior reduces to $p(Y|\beta, \sigma_e^2)$. The full posterior distribution, then, is:

$$p(\beta, \sigma_e^2, Z|Y) \propto p(Y|\beta, \sigma_e^2)p(Z|\beta, \sigma_e^2)p(\beta, \sigma_e^2),$$

where the latter term is simply the joint prior for the regression parameters and error variance. Let's assume the same reference prior as we did in the example with complete data $(1/\sigma_e^2)$.

A Gibbs sampler for sampling from this posterior distribution simply involves sequentially sampling from the conditional posterior distributions for β, σ_e^2, and Z. The conditional posterior distribution for $\beta|Z, \sigma_e^2, Y$ is straightforward, given values for Z. Indeed, assume we have values for Z, so that $Y^* = [Y, Z]$ is a set of complete data. In that case:

$$(\beta| Y^*, \sigma_e^2) \sim N((X^TX)^{-1}(X^TY^*), \sigma_e^2(X^TX)^{-1}),$$

which is a result identical to that we obtained previously, only now we have incorporated the missing data.

Similarly, given Y^*, the conditional posterior for the error variance is:

$$(\sigma_e^2 \,|\, Y^*, \beta) \sim IG(\alpha = n^*/2, \beta = e^{*T}e^*/2),$$

where n^* is the sample size, and $e^{*T}e^*$ is the error sum of squares, after including the missing data ($e^* = Y^* - X\beta$).

What remains is the specification of the conditional posterior for the missing data Z, so that we can form Y^*. Given that Y and Z are independent, that each of the Z are independent, and given that we have assumed the same model for Z as for Y (that the missing data mechanism is ignorable; the data are MAR), we have no information regarding the posterior distribution for each Z beyond what is known about β and σ_e^2 from the observed data Y. Therefore, the posterior distribution for each Z is simply normal with a mean of $X_i^T\beta$ and variance σ_e^2.

All in all, then, incorporating the missing data involves the addition of only a couple of lines of programming code to our original (full conditional) Gibbs sampler. Below is some replacement code for the "meat" of the Gibbs sampler. The original variable, y, is the outcome vector with missing data coded 999. First, ystar is set equal to the value for y, but for each person with missing data, y is replaced with a normal random variable with a mean of $X_i^T\beta$ and a variance of σ_e^2, using current values of those parameters.

The only two additional changes include: (1) Given that the outcome vector changes at each iteration due to the simulation of the missing data, the mean for the conditional posterior for β must be computed at every iteration (i.e., this is the line: b[i,]<-coefficients(lm(ystar x-1))...); and (2) The second parameter of the inverse gamma distribution for σ_e^2 uses the complete data after y^* has been updated.

. . .

```
for(i in 2:m){
#simulate missing data
ystar=y
ystar[y==999]=rnorm(length(ystar[y==999]),
            mean=x[y==999,]%*%(b[i-1,]), sd=sqrt(s2[i-1]))

#simulate beta from its multivariate normal conditional
b[i,]<-coefficients(lm(ystar ~ x-1))+
        t(rnorm(9,mean=0,sd=1))%*%chol(s2[i-1]*xtxi)

#simulate sigma from its inverse gamma distribution
s2[i]<-1/rgamma(1,length(y)/2,
            .5*t(ystar-x%*%(b[i,]))%*%(ystar-x%*%(b[i,])))
. . .
```

I reran the Gibbs sampler with these modifications and obtained virtually identical results to those obtained from listwise deletion. In fact, a classical regression of the original parameter means and posterior standard deviations on the parameter means and standard deviations obtained using the modified algorithm yielded an intercept of .02 (s.e. = .02) and slope of .997 (s.e. = .002) (R^2 = .999) suggesting nearly one-to-one correspondence between sets of estimates. This result is not surprising, given that we only had 34 observations for whom missing data were present, and we assumed that missing cases were similar to observed cases (i.e., they followed the same model).

Returning to the current example, let's now also include the observations missing on income. In the original data, 302 persons were missing on income. If we include individuals who are missing on income and missing on the empathy outcome variable, we have the complete sample of 2,696. Incorporating missingness on income is perhaps even more straightforward than incorporating missingness on the outcome, because income is an exogenous variable in the model. Thus, a simple approach to handling missingness on income is to assume that the missing income data are MAR. Under this assumption, we can simply add a step to the Gibbs sampler in which the missing values of income are replaced with simulated values. With no conditional model for income, and under the MAR assumption, it is reasonable to simulate values for income based on the distribution of income among observed cases. If we assume that income is normally distributed (which may not necessarily be a good assumption), then we can simulate values of income for those missing on this variable using the mean and standard deviation of income among those observed on income. This means we only need to make the following changes to the Gibbs sampler:

```
...
for(i in 2:m){

xstar=x
xstar[x[,6]==999,6]=rnorm(length(xstar[x[,6]==999,6]),
                mean=mean(x[x[,6]!=999,6]),sd=sd(x[x[,6]!=999,6]))

ystar=y
ystar[y==999]=rnorm(length(ystar[y==999]),
                mean=x[y==999,]%*%(b[i-1,]), sd=sqrt(s2[i-1]))

#simulate beta from its multivariate normal conditional
b[i,]=coefficients(lm(y ~ x-1)) +
   t(rnorm(9,mean=0,sd=1))%*%chol(s2[i-1]*solve(t(xstar)%*%xstar))

...
```

Notice that this change mirrors the change we made to incorporate missing data on y. The key difference is that the missing values for y were replaced by a simulated value using the regression-predicted value as the mean and the error variance as the variance, whereas the missing values for income were simulated using simply the mean and variance of the observed values of income. Notice also that we now must compute $(X^T X)^{-1}$ at every iteration, because the X matrix changes each time the missing X are simulated.

The parameter estimates obtained under this approach do not differ substantially from those obtained using listwise deletion nor using the previous change to include the missing data on the outcome variable, with the exception of the effect of being a South out-migrant (see Exercises). However, the posterior standard deviations are smaller, as a result of the increased sample size, coupled with the assumption that the missing follow the same model as the nonmissing (i.e., they are MAR).

Table 7.3. Results of regression of empathy on region with and without missing data: Missing data assumed to be MAR.

Variable	Model (What Missing Is Incorporated?)			
	No Missing	Y only	Y & X (Mean)	Y & X (Regression)
Intercept	19.58(.58)	19.56(.58)	19.42(.54)	19.43(.55)
Age	0.018(.006)	0.018(.006)	0.020(.005)	0.02(.005)
Male	−2.43(.20)	−2.44(.19)	−2.43(.18)	−2.43(.19)
White	0.52(.25)	0.52(.25)	0.60(.24)	0.60(.24)
Yrs. Schooling	0.07(.04)	0.07(.04)	0.07(.03)	0.06(.04)
Income ($1,000s)	0.004(.003)	0.004(.003)	0.003(.003)	0.003(.003)
Continuous South	0.69(.23)	0.69(.22)	0.75(.21)	0.76(.21)
South Out-Migrant	0.19(.50)	0.18(.50)	0.38(.49)	0.39(.48)
South In-Migrant	0.29(.35)	0.27(.35)	0.25(.33)	0.25(.33)
$\sqrt{\sigma_e^2}$	4.62(.07)	4.63(.07)	4.65(.06)	4.65(.06)
n	2,360	2,394	2,696	2,696

Note: The first column shows the results when only cases with complete information are used. The second column shows the results when persons missing on Y are included in the analysis (see text). The third column presents the results when missing income values are replaced stochastically using simulated values from a normal distribution with a mean and variance equal to those for the observed cases. The fourth column presents the results when missing income values are replaced stochastically with predicted values and the error variance from a regression model predicting income for observed cases using all other predictor variables.

Table 7.3 shows the parameter estimates and posterior standard deviations for the various models. The final column in the table shows the results of one additional approach to handling missing data on the income item: regression-based simulation. Under the previous approach, we simply simulated missing income from a distribution that was common to all observations, regardless of the values of the covariates for the missing cases. An alternative approach is to estimate the regression of income on all other predictors and simulate a value of income from a normal distribution with a mean equal to the regression-based predicted score for income and a variance equal to the residual variance.[5] I leave the modification of the Gibbs sampler to handle this approach as an exercise. This set of results is virtually identical to those obtained using the previous approach for handling missingness on income.

Overall, the results reveal more similarities than differences between parameter estimates, but the latter two approaches show a substantial reduction in the posterior standard deviations of the parameters. The reason is that the sample size is increased by retaining observations that would have been deleted due to having missing data. Is this reduction in the standard error legitimate; that is, should we see smaller posterior standard deviations despite the fact that our models recognize the uncertainty the missing data present? Yes—in fact, the posterior standard deviations are reduced proportional to the gain in the square root of the sample size obtained by incorporating the observations with missing data, just as the Central Limit Theorem suggests. However, it is important to recognize that, if we had taken the common approach of simply imputing a single *fixed* value for the missing data (either using regression imputation or mean imputation), the uncertainty presented by the missing data would have been ignored, and the posterior standard deviations would have been even smaller (and inappropriately so).

Does the fact that the parameter estimates are consistent across these models reassure us of the robustness of the results to missing data? The answer to this question is "absolutely not," although it is tempting to believe that such consistency of results demonstrates robustness. Each of the approaches that we have taken has assumed that the missing data are MAR (but possibly not OAR). So long as that assumption is maintained in our missing data strategy, the results will be consistently similar.

In order to obtain different results, we would need to make adjustments to the model that compensate for possible violations of the MAR assumption. Of course, in that case, we have no way to know whether the results we obtain at that point are realistic or not: That determination rests on our prior knowledge regarding the missing data generation mechanism. In brief, there is no free lunch when it comes to violations of the MAR assumption. If the data are not MAR, we cannot know from the data at hand how to obtain unbiased parameter estimates.

7.5 Conclusions

In this chapter, we demonstrated the Bayesian approach to the multiple regression model using a Metropolis-Hastings sampling algorithm and two Gibbs samplers. In this process, I used several of the techniques discussed in the previous chapter for assessing how well the algorithms performed, as well as for

---

[5] Allison (2003) argues that y should also be included in imputing the missing values of x, but I have used only other x variables in this example.

assessing how well the models fit the data. Finally, I showed how Gibbs sampling can be adapted easily to handle missing data that are MAR. In the next chapter, we will consider some basic generalized linear models that are useful when the outcome variable is not continuous.

7.6 Exercises

1. Derive the maximum likelihood estimate for the regression vector (β) in the linear regression model (i.e., Equation 7.5).
2. Develop an MH algorithm for the linear regression model that samples all regression parameters simultaneously. How difficult is it to find a proposal density that yields a reasonable acceptance rate? What are some possible strategies for finding a good proposal density?
3. How can we work with the original posterior density (not the logged version) without worrying about overflow/underflow problems. Hint: Consider computing the ratio case by case. Write the R code and test it.
4. Develop a Gibbs sampler that handles missingness on income via regression-based simulation of income on all other covariates.
5. We discovered, under the various missing data approaches that assumed the data to be MAR, that the only coefficients that changed substantially were some of the region coefficients. Why did they change?
6. Using your own data, treat the outcome variable as missing for every tenth case and rerun the Gibbs sampler that handles missingness on the outcome. Repeat the process with every fifth case treated as missing. Finally, repeat the process with every other case missing (50% missing). What happens to the posterior means and standard deviations of the parameters?

8

Generalized Linear Models

In the last chapter, we discussed the linear regression model. A requirement for using that model is that the outcome variable must be continuous and normally distributed. In social science research, having a continuous outcome variable is rare. More often, we tend to have dichotomous, ordinal, or nominal outcomes. In these cases, the linear regression model discussed in the previous chapter is inappropriate for several reasons. First, heteroscedasticity and nonnormal errors are guaranteed when the outcome is not continuous, nullifying the justification for statistical tests on the parameters (see Long 1997). Second, the linear model will often predict values that are impossible. For example, although the tolerance item in the last chapter had a range of 5, nothing in the model prevents predicted values from falling outside the [0,5] interval.[1] Third, the functional form specified by the linear model will often be incorrect. For example, we should doubt that increases in a covariate will yield the same returns on the dependent variable at the extremes as would be obtained toward the middle. Although we did not explore this issue in the previous chapter, it seems clear that the effect of education on tolerance, say, would be greatest in the middle of the education distribution than at either end. Adding a few years of education beyond a college degree or adding a few years but maintaining a grade level below 8 will probably not be as influential as transitioning from 11 to 12 years of education or from 12 to 16 years in influencing an individual's tolerance.

Generalized linear models (GLMs) provide a way to handle these problems. Recall that the basic OLS regression model can be expressed as:

$$\mu_i = X_i^T \beta,$$

---

[1] As it turns out, no combination of covariates will actually produce predicted values outside the allowable range, but this is because the model fits poorly—the covariates as specified do not have much influence on the outcome.

where $\mu_i = E(y_i)$. Observe that there is no error term in this specification: This is because the *expected* value of y_i is simply the linear predictor. Generalized linear models can be expressed as:

$$F(\mu_i) = X_i^T \beta,$$
$$\mu_i = E(y_i).$$

That is, some function F of the expected value of y_i is equal to the linear predictor with which we are already familiar. This function is called a "link" function, because it links the nonlinear/noncontinuous variable y_i with the linear predictor $X_i^T \beta$. The most common GLMs used in the social sciences and their link functions can be found in Table 8.1. As the table shows, when the link function is simply $F(\mu) = \mu$, we have the linear regression model; when the link function is $F(\mu) = \ln(\mu/(1 - \mu))$, we have the logistic regression model; and so on.

Table 8.1. Link functions and corrresponding generalized linear models (individual subscripts omitted).

Link Function ($F(\mu)$ is ?)	Model
μ	Linear Regression
$\ln\left(\frac{\mu}{1-\mu}\right)$	Logistic Regresssion
$\Phi^{-1}(\mu)$	Probit Regression
$\ln(\mu)$	Poisson Regression
$\ln(-\ln(1-\mu))$	Complementary Log–Log Regression

An alternative way of expressing the link function is in terms of a transformation of $X_i^T \beta$, rather than a transformation of μ_i. In that case, we could write the logistic regression model, for example, as:

$$\mu_i = G(X_i^T \beta) \equiv \frac{e^{X_i^T \beta}}{1 + e^{X_i^T \beta}},$$

where $G = F^{-1}$. In the dichotomous logit and probit models, $E(y_i) = p(y_i = 1)$, and so the model can be written in terms of probabilities:

$$p(y_i = 1) = G(X_i^T \beta).$$

In this notation, G is the link function.

For a logistic regression model, G is the cumulative standard logistic distribution function, whereas for a probit model, G is the cumulative standard normal distribution function.

8.1 The dichotomous probit model

One of the first generalized linear regression models to achieve popularity in the social sciences was the logistic regression model for dichotomous outcome variables (Hosmer and Lemeshow 1989). Dichotomous outcomes are prevalent in social science research, but prior to the 1980s, the computing power required to estimate the parameters of generalized linear regression models exceeded capacity. As a result, many social science researchers estimated parameters using OLS regression, which, as we discussed above, is an undesirable approach for several reasons. With the development of the iteratively reweighted least squares algorithm, coupled with an increase in computing power, the use of logistic regression rapidly replaced OLS regression as the preferred method for handling dichotomous outcomes. The logistic regression model obtained popularity primarily because of the relative ease of interpretation of the model parameters, as I show below. Nonetheless, in this chapter, my examples involve only the dichotomous probit model and its extension to the ordinal probit models.

The choice of the probit model over the logistic regression model or other models (e.g., the complementary log-log model) is largely for convenience: As we will see, the probit model, from a probability standpoint is often easier to work with, because it involves use of the normal distribution. Nonetheless, the extensions to logistic and complementary log-log models are straightforward. For a classical approach to these models, I recommend Long (1997) and Powers and Xie (2000). For an in-depth Bayesian exposition to dichotomous and ordinal outcome models, I recommend Johnson and Albert (1999).

8.1.1 Model development and parameter interpretation

If our outcome variable in a regression model is dichotomous (0,1), then an appropriate likelihood function for the data is based on the binomial or Bernoulli distribution. The likelihood function can be expressed as:

$$L(P|y) \propto \prod_{i=1}^{n} p_i^{y_i} (1 - p_i)^{1-y_i}, \tag{8.1}$$

where y_i is the observed dichotomous outcome for person i. For a person with a "1" on the outcome, the contribution to the likelihood reduces to the first term; for a person with a 0, the contribution to the likelihood reduces to the second term.

As written, this likelihood function has no regression parameters, but we would like to link p_i—the probability of a "1" response—to the linear combination $X_i^T \beta$. As discussed at the beginning of the chapter, this is problematic because an identity link [i.e., $p_i = X_i^T \beta$] can predict illegitimate values for p_i. Cumulative distribution functions constitutes a class of functions that can map the predictor from the entire real line onto the interval $[0, 1]$, because cdfs are naturally constrained to produce values that fall in this range (refer to Chapter 2). In the probit model case, we allow $p_i = \Phi(X_i^T \beta)$, where $\Phi(.)$ is the cumulative normal distribution function (i.e., $\int_{-\infty}^{X_i^T \beta} N(0, 1)$). Regardless of the value of $X_i^T \beta$, p_i will fall in the acceptable range. To obtain a logistic regression model, one would simply need to set $p_i = e^{X_i^T \beta}/(1 + e^{X_i^T \beta})$ (the cumulative logistic distribution function).

Another way to think about dichotomous probit and logistic regression models—one that is useful for setting up a Gibbs sampler—is in terms of latent variables. We could express the probit or logistic regression model as a linear model for a continuously distributed unobserved trait or propensity score, y_i^* as:

$$y_i^* = X_i^T \beta + e_i \qquad (8.2)$$

using the link:

$$y_i = \begin{cases} 1 & \text{iff} \quad y_i^* > 0 \\ 0 & \text{iff} \quad y_i^* \le 0. \end{cases} \qquad (8.3)$$

From this perspective, although y_i^* is continuous, crude measurement limits our observation to the dichotomous individual response y_i. If the individual's propensity is great enough (i.e., it falls above the threshold of 0), we observe a 1 on y; otherwise, we observe a 0.

Given this setup, we need to rearrange the model somewhat to allow estimation of the regression parameters of interest. We can combine Equations 8.2 and 8.3 such that:

$$\text{If } y_i = \begin{cases} 1, & e_i > -X_i^T \beta \\ 0, & e_i < -X_i^T \beta. \end{cases} \qquad (8.4)$$

If we assume a standard normal distribution for e, then we obtain the probit model:

$$p(y_i = 1) = p(e_i > -X_i^T \beta) = p(e_i < X_i^T \beta) = \int_{-\infty}^{X_i^T \beta} N(0, 1). \qquad (8.5)$$

Observe that this is the same expression we placed into the likelihood function above in Equation 8.1. If we assume a logistic distribution for the error instead of a normal distribution, then we obtain the logistic regression model discussed above.

To make the probit model fully Bayesian, we need to specify priors on the regression parameters in the model. For that purpose, we could use improper uniform priors over the real line, as we did in the previous chapter, we could use very vague normal priors [e.g., $\beta \sim N(0, 10000)$], or we could use something called "conditional means priors." Under this approach, we would specify prior expected probabilities for several combinations of covariates, invert these probabilities into the regression coefficient scale, and combine this information with the likelihood function to obtain the posterior (see Johnson and Albert 1999 for examples). In the examples, I simply use uniform priors so that comparisons can be made with estimates obtained via maximum likelihood estimation.

With priors established, and $\Phi(X_i^T\beta)$ substituted for p_i, the posterior distribution is:

$$p(\beta|Y, X) \propto \prod_{i=1}^{n} \Phi(X_i^T\beta)^{y_i}(1 - \Phi(X_i^T\beta))^{1-y_i}. \tag{8.6}$$

The interpretation of the parameters in this model—and all GLMs—is not as easy as the interpretation of parameters in the OLS regression model (see Liao 1994). Because the link function is nonlinear (an integral of a nonlinear function), the model itself is nonlinear in the probabilities, even though the predictor is linear. This nonlinearity complicates interpretation, because the effects of each variable is no longer independent of the effects of other variables. The probit model is linear, however, in z (standard normal) units. That is, given that $X\beta$ implies a particular upper limit for the integral of the standard normal distribution, each β can be viewed in terms of its expected effect on the z score for a one-unit increase in its corresponding covariate. The logistic regression model, on the other hand, is linear in log-odds units. Recall that odds are computed as the ratio of $\frac{p}{1-p}$. The logistic link function, then, is a log-odds function. The coefficients from the model can be interpreted in terms of their linear effect on the log-odds, but this is not much help. Instead, if we exponentiate the model, we obtain:

$$\exp\left(\ln\left(\frac{p_i}{1 - p_i}\right)\right) = \exp\left(X_i^T\beta\right) = e^{\beta_0}e^{\beta_1 x_{i1}}\ldots e^{\beta_k x_{ik}}. \tag{8.7}$$

This result says that the odds are equal to the multiple of the exponentiated coefficients. Suppose we had an exponentiated coefficient of 2 for sex (measured as a dummy variable in which male = 1). This exponentiated coefficient would imply that the odds for a male responding "1" on the outcome variable are twice as great as the odds for a female responding "1," net of the other variables in the model. This ease of interpretation has made the logistic regression model popular in the social sciences. The limitations, however, include (1) that this interpretation tells us nothing about absolute risk, only relative risk; and (2) the odds ratios are commonly interpreted as if they were ratios of probabilities.[2] In fact, there is not one-to-one correspondence between absolute risk measured by a ratio of probabilities and relative risk measured by a ratio of odds. For example, if groups A and B have absolute risks of .1 and .01, respectively, the odds ratio representing the relative risk for group A versus B is the same as if the probabilities were .99 and .9: The odds ratio is 11, but certainly the absolute risks are substantially different. The ratio of *probabilities* conveys this information about the absolute risk. The ratio of probabilities is 10 under the first set of probabilities and is 1.1 under the second, which indicates a substantially larger difference in the absolute probabilities for the first pair than for the second pair.

For both the logistic and the probit models, model probabilities can be obtained by (1) evaluating the linear predictor, and (2) applying the link function to obtain p.

8.1.2 Sampling from the posterior distribution for the model parameters

With the posterior distribution established in Equation 8.6, MCMC sampling relies either on using this posterior as written for an MH algorithm or on deriving the conditional distribution for β for Gibbs sampling. Developing an MH algorithm for this model is straightforward using the pnorm function in R (or its equivalent in other languages), and I leave doing so as an exercise (see Exercises).

As written in Equation 8.6, the posterior cannot be simplified further, making the construction of a Gibbs sampler appear to be a daunting process. However, as I mentioned above, the latent variable approach makes the process of Gibbs sampling simple. The unknown quantities in the model are the vector β and the vector Y^*. We know from the initial specification that $Y^* \sim N(X\beta, 1)$, subject to the constraint that each $y_i^* > 0$ iff $y_i = 1$ and $y_i^* < 0$ iff $y_i = 0$. Together, these specifications imply that $y_i^* | y_i, X_i, \beta \sim TN(X_i^T \beta, 1)$, where TN is the *truncated normal* distribution. The point of truncation is 0, and the side of the distribution that is truncated is determined by y_i: For individuals with $y = 0$, the distribution is truncated above 0; for individuals with $y = 1$, the distribution is truncated below 0 (see Albert and Chib 1993).

What is the distribution for β? Because the vector Y^* is normally distributed, given Y^*, the conditional distribution for β is the same as for the OLS regression model (with $\sigma^2 = 1$): $\beta | X, Y^* \sim N\left((X^T X)^{-1}(X^T Y^*), (X^T X)^{-1}\right)$.

Thus, a Gibbs sampler can be specified in four steps:

1. Establish starting values for β.
2. Simulate $Y^* | X, Y, \beta \sim TN(X\beta, 1)$.

---

[2] Researchers commonly say that an odds ratio of 2 implies that one group is "twice as likely" as another to have a "1" on the outcome, but this language implies that the odds ratio is a ratio of two probabilities, and it is not.

3. Simulate $\beta|X, Y^*, Y \sim N\left((X^T X)^{-1}(X^T Y^*), (X^T X)^{-1}\right)$.
4. Return to step 2 (repeat).

An R program for implementing this Gibbs sampler is as follows:

```
#R program for dichotomous probit model
#read the data
x=as.matrix(read.table("c:\\bookdead.dat")[,3:9])
y=as.matrix(read.table("c:\\bookdead.dat")[,10])

#create variables, set values, and write out starting values
b=matrix(0,7); vb=solve(t(x)%*%x); ch<-chol(vb)

write(c(i,t(b)), file="c:\\dprob_gibbs.out", append=T, ncol=8)

#begin MCMC simulation
for(i in 2:5000){

#simulate latent data from truncated normal distributions
u=as.matrix(runif(length(y),min=0,max=1))
xb=as.matrix(x%*%b)

ystar=qnorm(y*u + u*(-1)^y*pnorm(0,mean=xb,sd=x[,1]) +
            y*pnorm(0,mean=xb,sd=1), mean=xb, sd=x[,1])

#simulate beta vector from appropriate mvn distribution
b<-vb%*%(t(x)%*%ystar) + t((rnorm(7,mean=0,sd=1))%*%ch)

write(c(i,t(b))), file="c:\\dprob_gibbs.out", append=T, ncolumns=8)
if(i%%10==0){print(c(i,t(b))),digits=2)}
}
```

This program is similar to the Gibbs samplers for the OLS regression model in the previous chapter, with four key differences. First, there is no simulation of σ_e^2 in this program, because this parameter is fixed at 1 in the probit model (i.e., the error is assumed to be standard normal). Second, latent data (ystar) are simulated to replace the observed dichotomous y. Third, the regression parameter vector mean changes at every iteration. This change is attributable to the fact that the latent data, ystar, change at every iteration, and thus $(X^T X)^{-1}(X^T Y^*)$ changes. Fourth, because I am saving the results to a file, I do not need to double-subscript b (the regression parameter vector) to reflect the iteration of the algorithm. Instead, the current value of the vector, after it is sampled, is written to the file.

I have written this program to be quite compact—with many statements I have used separately in previous programs now being combined into a single line—but only one section of this program requires some discussion: the simulation of the latent data from truncated normal distributions.

8.1.3 Simulating from truncated normal distributions

Simulation from truncated normal distributions can be quite simple but inefficient, or it can be very fast but mathematically challenging. In this and the following sections, I discuss three ways to perform such simulation: a naive but simple way, a rejection sampling approach, and an inversion sampling approach. Ultimately, I use the inversion sampling approach, but I have often used the naive approach. I describe the rejection sampling approach largely to motivate thinking about sampling from uncommon distributions in a more practical setting than in previous chapters.

The naive approach

A "naive" way of simulating from truncated normal distributions, as Robert and Casella (1999) call it, is to repeatedly simulate draws from a full normal distribution with the specified mean until a draw is obtained in the appropriate part of the distribution. This approach is very simple to implement but has one serious drawback: It is extremely inefficient. If an individual is an outlier, that is, his/her $X_i^T\beta$ is large (small) but s/he reported a 0 (1), most of the mass of the normal distribution from which we would be simulating possible values will be centered well away from the region from which the latent score must be drawn. This fact implies that it may take hundreds or even thousands of simulated scores before obtaining just one that falls in the right region. For a general example, see Figure 8.1. The figure shows a complete normal distribution with a mean of 1.645 and a standard deviation of 1. If a person with $X_i^T\beta = 1.645$ happened to respond "0" on the outcome variable, his/her latent score would need to be simulated to the left of the point of truncation (0), which is 1.645 standard deviations away from the mean. It is well known that only 5% of the mass of a normal density lies to the left of 1.645 standard deviations from the mean, and so it would take an expected 20 draws before we would sample this person's latent score at that particular iteration of the algorithm (5 out of every 100 draws should come from that region). Simulating an expected 20 draws to obtain one valid value is highly inefficient, considering that we may need to draw from a tail region for many cases (e.g., if the model does not fit the data well and/or has many outliers), and we need to do this for thousands of iterations. If one has chosen particularly poor starting values for the parameters, an algorithm may not even begin to simulate parameters, because it may find itself stuck indefinitely attempting to simulate latent scores at the first iteration!

In all fairness, this naive sampling scheme often works well and may be fast enough despite its inefficiency if one has access to very powerful computing. However, it may not be satisfactory. Fortunately, alternative approaches to simulating values from truncated normal distributions can be constructed.

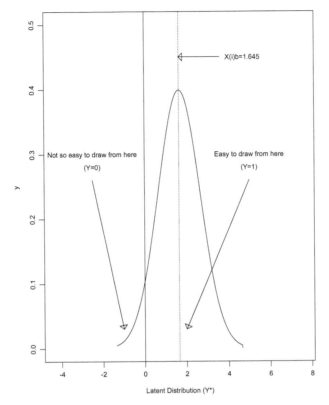

Fig. 8.1. Depiction of simulation from a truncated normal distribution.

A rejection sampling strategy

Recall from Chapter 4 that rejection sampling involves sampling a value (z) from a known density (g) that—when multiplied by a constant m—envelops the unknown but desired density f (mathematically: $m \times g(z) > f(z)$, $\forall z$) and evaluating whether the value will be accepted. We can apply this strategy to the truncated normal distribution.

Figure 8.2 provides a larger depiction of the region of the truncated normal distribution (from Figure 8.1) from which sampling may be desired. The first step in constructing a rejection sampling routine is to evaluate the height of the normal density at the point of truncation. This is easily done within R as: h=dnorm(0,mean=?,sd=1), where the mean (?) is set to the expected predicted score $(X_i^T \beta)$ for the person for whom the sampling is to be performed. We then sample a point z from a uniform density on the interval $[-2, 0]$, giving us a point in the x dimension to evaluate. Next we draw a $U(0, 1)$ random variable u and multiply it by the height of the normal density, which, as the figure shows, is also the height of our scaled uniform proposal density. This gives us a point in the y dimension, at $x = z$, to evaluate. If $u \times h < f(z)$, where $f(z)$ is the height of the normal density at z, then we accept the draw as coming from the normal density. In other words, if the sampled value u falls below the normal curve, we accept it; otherwise we reject it and try again.

Since 5% of the mass of a $N(1.645, 1)$ density falls below 0, and the mass of our uniform proposal density is $[f(0) = .103] \times (-2) = .206$, this rejection scheme will have an acceptance rate of approximately 25%: one out of four draws will be accepted. This represents a five-fold improvement over the naive sampling approach and may produce a remarkable increase in the speed of the algorithm. However, this sampling routine can be improved, and there is one issue to consider. First, it could be improved by using a triangular proposal density rather than a uniform (rectangular) density. Since the normal distribution is monotonic beyond 1 standard deviation from the mean, if we establish a set point for our left "end" of the normal distributions tail we can construct a triangular proposal and sample from it using the inversion method. I will not elaborate on this approach here, because there is an even faster way to generate draws from the tail region with a 100% acceptance rate that we will discuss in the next section (but see Exercises).

Second, with the construction of a bounded uniform proposal density, we have truncated the tail of the already truncated normal distribution: We will not draw samples from beyond $x = -2$. For all practical purposes, this is not much of a problem, because there is only a mass of .0001 we are excluding from a normal with mean 1.645 by imposing this boundary (the area under the normal curve up to -3.645 standard deviations from the mean). Nonetheless, the boundary can be expanded as far as one likes, but doing so will reduce the acceptance rate of the rejection sampling strategy because the mass of the proposal rectangle will expand faster than the area under the normal density. Thus, we must balance two considerations, including (1) how large the mean must be before we decide to bypass the naive sampling approach and turn to the rejection sampling approach, (2) how much error we will allow in the rejection sampling routine. Those two considerations can be balanced by deciding a limit on the error, and then finding a mean for the normal distribution at which the acceptance rates of the naive sampler and the rejection sampler coincide. For example, we know that, at a mean of 1.645, the naive sampler will only have an acceptance rate of 5% when sampling from the tail. However, as we just discused, the rejection sampler will have an acceptance rate of about 25% (actually less if we discount the error region we are not sampling from). At a mean of 0, the naive sampler will have an acceptance rate of 50%, and the rejection sampler will have an acceptance rate of 59.8%, which indicates we would always be better off using the rejection sampler! But, the error is quite large in these cases—with a mean of 0 and a proposal width of 2, we would be missing approximately 5% of the left-hand side of the distribution under the rejection sampler. Thus, if we decide to reduce our limit on the error by using a uniform density with a width of three units, the acceptance rates of the rejection sampler and the naive sampler intersect (with the rejection samplers rate being better) for distributions with a mean around .6.

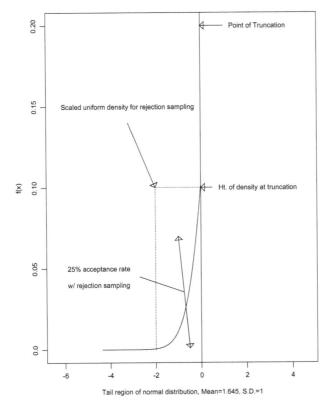

Fig. 8.2. Depiction of rejection sampling from the tail region of a truncated normal distribution.

A better strategy: Inversion sampling

For sampling from univariate truncated normal distributions, there is no inherent reason to use the rejection sampling approach we just discussed for simulating. The inversion method, when the truncated region of the normal distribution is renormalized, is much faster and has an acceptance rate of 100%. We discussed the inversion method of sampling in Chapter 4. The inversion method involves (1) drawing a $U(0,1)$ random variable that represents the *area* under the distribution of interest, and (2) using the inverse-distribution function to find the value x from the distribution that yields that area below it. For example, if we were attempting to draw samples from a standard normal distribution and we drew a .5 from the uniform distribution, the inversion method would produce $x = 0$ as our sample from the $N(0, 1)$ distribution. If we drew a .025 from the uniform distribution, the inversion method would produce $x = -1.96$, etc.

The inversion method can be adapted to sample from truncated normal distributions. I will first show how to simulate from the left-hand side of the distribution. In the first step, we must "renormalize" the truncated region; that is, we must multiply the density by a constant so that the area of the truncated region integrates to 1. This renormalization step involves simply determining the area of the normal distribution that falls in the truncated region and hence just involves using the distribution function $\Phi_{\mu,\sigma}(T) = \int_{-\infty}^{T} N(\mu, \sigma)$, with a given mean μ, standard deviation σ, and truncation point T. For the probit model, we have already stated the mean is the expected value for the given observation/case, the standard deviation is 1, and the truncation point is $x = 0$. Thus, in R we use: A=pnorm(0,xb,1), where 0 is the truncation point, xb is the mean, and 1 is the standard deviation. Our constant for renormalizing is then $1/A$.

In the next step, we draw a $U(0, 1)$ random variable u, just as in the original inversion routine. Finally, we multiply u by A, and we then apply the inverse-normal distribution function to this draw to obtain the draw from the truncated region. Why do we multiply u by A? In the original inversion approach, we let $u = \Phi(x)$, where u is our uniform draw and x is our sampled value of interest. In order to find x, we take $\Phi^{-1}(u) = \Phi^{-1}(\Phi(x)) = x$. In the truncated distribution, however, our area is determined by the integral from $-\infty$ to T. Φ must then be rescaled to produce an area no bigger than A, and so we use: $u = (1/A)\Phi(x)$. To solve for x, we move A to the left side of this equation: $uA = \Phi(x)$. Since u can be no bigger than 1, uA can be no bigger than A. So, $\Phi(x)$ will be limited between 0 and A and hence Φ^{-1} will be limited to the interval $[-\infty, T]$.

Sampling from the right-hand side of the normal distribution is only slightly more tedious. We can do this in one of two ways: (1) use the fact that the normal distribution is symmetric and reverse the sign of the mean and then reverse the sign of x once it is computed using Φ^{-1}, or (2) keep the mean as is and simply add the appropriate constant before applying Φ^{-1} to keep x from falling below the truncation point. I discuss the latter approach here, because it is easier to understand, and because it is easier to use in the ordinal probit model to be discussed later.

As before, when sampling from the right-hand side of a truncated normal distribution, we first need to renormalize the area to the right of the truncation point. Given that the area under the normal curve totals 1, this can be computed easily as: $B = 1 - \Phi(T)$. Now, in this case, we need x to be bounded between T and ∞. We know from before that uA provides the area for which $x = T$, and so, we need Φ to yield a minimum value of uA. We also need Φ to yield a maximum value of 1. For Φ to yield A at a minimum, we therefore need $\Phi^{-1}(A + C)$, where C must range from 0 to $1 - A$ (or B) to ensure that x falls in the appropriate region. Thus, we let $C = uB$, and we have $x = \Phi^{-1}(A + uB)$ as our solution. When u is 0, the function returns T; when $u = 1$, the function returns ∞, because $A + B = 1$.

Another way to perform inversion sampling, rather than renormalizing the appropriate area (left or right side of the distribution), is to set the minimum and maximum values of the uniform random number function to the appropriate values. For example, if we are sampling from the left side of a normal distribution, we could set the minimum value for the uniform density to $\Phi(-\infty) = 0$ and the maximum to $\Phi(0)$ for the normal density with mean xb and standard deviation 1 [e.g., in R, we would use: u=runif(1,min=0,max=pnorm(0,mean=xb,sd=1)]. This approach is mathematically equivalent to the previous one. In the first one, we leave the uniform density as $U(0,1)$ but multiply it to rescale its maximum value; in the second, we simply resize the uniform density. Under either approach, we would need to apply the inverse normal distribution function (qnorm in R) to u to obtain our latent y^*. Both approaches involve the same number of "steps," but one approach may be easier to implement than another, depending on the programming language being used.

Returning to the Gibbs sampler presented earlier, the truncated normal sampling code was:

```
u=as.matrix(runif(length(y),min=0,max=1))
xb=as.matrix(x%*%b)

ystar=qnorm(y*u + u*(-1)^y*pnorm(0,mean=xb,sd=1) +
            y*pnorm(0,mean=xb,sd=1), mean=xb, sd=1)
```

The first line simply generates an n-length vector of $U(0,1)$ random numbers. The second line generates an n-length vector of predicted values/expected means. The remaining code performs all the truncated normal simulation steps discussed above, but simultaneously handles (1) all cases in one step, relying on R's ability to handle operations to entire vectors at once, and (2) simulation for $y = 0$ and $y = 1$. Feature (1) is straightforward: y, u, and xb are all vectors, and so ystar also is a vector. The second feature is a little more difficult to see. Suppose, for an individual, $y = 0$. In that case, the first argument within the qnorm function reduces to:

```
u*pnorm(0,mean=xb,sd=1)
```

This is the appropriate argument for cases in which $y = 0$, as shown above. In the event $y = 1$, the first argument reduces to:

```
u - u*pnorm(0,mean=xb,sd=1) + pnorm(0,mean=xb,sd=1)
```

Rearranging terms and factoring u reveals that this is, indeed, the correct argument for cases in which $y = 1$.

An alternative argument, based on the second strategy listed above— adjusting the minimum and maximum arguments to the uniform random draw—can be implemented as:

```
ystar=qnorm(mean=xb,sd=1,
runif(length(y),
     min=(y*pnorm(0,xb,1)), max=(pnorm(0,xb,1)^(1-y))))
```

Notice here that when $y = 0$, the `min=0` and the `max=pnorm(0,xb,1)`; when $y = 1$, `min=pnorm(0,xb,1)` and `max=1`. (Also notice that I have shuffled around the arguments to the `qnorm` function—the order of arguments is irrelevant to R for most functions).

8.1.4 Dichotomous probit model example: Black–white differences in mortality

Racial differences in mortality—especially black-white differences—are an important concern for mortality demographers and health researchers. It is well known that blacks have higher levels of mortality than whites. A common goal in the literature has been to try to understand why this health advantage for whites exists (see Markides and Black 1996). Interestingly, this white advantage, however, does not exist across the entire age range. Instead, at advanced ages (usually over 75 years of age), a crossover is observed such black mortality rates fall below those of whites. Although a relatively large demographic literature has emerged over the last few decades suggesting possible explanations for the crossover (e.g., see Elo and Preston 1994; Lynch, Brown and Harmsen 2003; Preston et al. 1996), very few studies have attempted to quantify uncertainty in the age at which the crossover occurs, largely because the crossover age is a quantity for which the standard error is difficult to derive using classical methods. The example of the dichotomous probit model (and ordinal probit model) I use here seeks to quantify this uncertainty.

A standard approach to modeling racial differences in mortality is to use dichotomous probit or logistic regression models, often in a discrete-time format, when individual-level longitudinal data are used. In a discrete-time specification, each person contributes more than one observation to the final dataset—one record for every year observed (Allison 1984; Hosmer and Lemeshow 1999; Yamaguchi 1991). I construct such a data set here, using data from the National Health and Nutrition Examination Survey (NHANES) and its follow-ups, the National Epidemiologic Follow-up Surveys (NHEFS). The NHANES was a cross-sectional survey designed to assess the nation's health using a sample of roughly 34,000 individuals ages 24-77 beginning in 1971. Of these, roughly 7,000 sample members were administered a physical exam by a physician, as well as a health care supplemental survey measuring self-rated health, and were then followed-up on at least three occasions: in 1982, 1987, and 1992. Using individuals who (1) survived to 1975 (the last year of the baseline study), (2) were at least 40 years of age in 1975, (3) had no missing data on variables used in the analyses, and (4) were either white or black, I created an analytic sample of 3,201 persons, of which 685 died during the observation period. The resulting person-year file consisted of 55,173 records, with an average person-year contribution of 14.43 years by those who died (18 person-years were contributed by those who survived through 1992).

The predictor variables used in the analyses include age, sex, race (black or white), southern residence at baseline, years of schooling, and an interaction between age and race. Age is the only time-varying covariate: It is incremented up until the point of censoring (if the respondent survived the observation period) or until death for each person-year record contributed by an individual.

The outcome variable is an indicator for whether the individual died in a particular year. For individuals who survived the observation period, this variable takes a 0 for every person-year record contributed by the individual (18 records). For individuals who died during the observation period, this variable takes a 0 for every person-year record contributed until the year of death and takes a 1 for the person-year record for the year in which the respondent died. Thus, out of 55,173 person-records, only 685 records have a value of 1 on this variable, representing 1.2% of all records. Table 8.2 presents descriptive statistics for the original 3201 individuals in the baseline sample.

Table 8.2. Descriptive statistics for NHANES/NHEFS data used in dichotomous probit model example (baseline $n = 3,201$).

Variable	Mean(s.d.) or %	Range
Predictors		
Age	55.9(9.1)	[40,77]
Female	56.6%	[0 or 1]
Black	10.8%	[0 or 1]
Yrs. Schooling	11.0(3.3)	[0,17]
South (in '71)	31.7%	[0 or 1]
Died	21.4%	[0 or 1]

Why use a Bayesian approach to this model when we could simply use a standard maximum likelihood approach? There are several reasons. First, we could incorporate prior information, although I have simply chosen not to here. Second, as we have discussed in previous chapters, the Bayesian approach offers a broader array of model diagnostics, especially in a GLM setting, than traditional approaches to estimation. Under a traditional maximum likelihood (ML) approach, we may obtain two measures of model fit—a pseudo-R^2 and a model chi-square—and residual diagnostic tests that are derived from OLS regression residual diagnostic tests. We can obtain these same measures of model fit here (distributions of them, actually) using the Bayesian approach, but we can also obtain better residual diagnostic tests that do not rest on assumptions that the dichotomous data cannot meet (see Johnson and Albert 1999 for more discussion).

Assessing model fit is important in a discrete time setting. Something that is often overlooked in discrete time analyses is that the dilution of the original data via construction of a person-year file reduces the "success" proportion in the outcome variable. For example, here, 21% of the respondents died over the observation period (685/3201), yet deaths represent only 1.2% of the records in the person-year data. Logit and probit models tend to fare best when the "success" proportion is close to .5, and thus we should carefully consider model fit when using discrete time models.[3]

A third reason for taking a Bayesian approach is that, although the black-white crossover is an important phenomenon to mortality demographers attempting to understand racial heterogeneity and inequality, the ML approach offers no simple approach to testing hypotheses about it. The Bayesian approach, on the other hand, does. The crossover age can be computed by setting the regression equations equal for blacks and whites and solving for age to find the point of intersection. With only age, race, and an interaction between them in the model, the model is:

$$y^* = b_0 + b_1 \text{Age} + b_2 \text{Black} + b_3 \text{Age} \times \text{Black}. \qquad (8.8)$$

For blacks, Black $= 1$, and so the right-hand side reduces to $(b_0 + b_2) + (b_1 + b_3)$Age. For whites, Black $= 0$, and so the right-hand side reduces to $b_0 + b_1$Age. Setting these equal, we find:

$$b_2 + b_3 \text{Age} = 0, \qquad (8.9)$$

and so the age at which the crossover occurs is $-b_2/b_3$. This estimate can be found with the ML approach to estimation, but there is no simple way to quantify our uncertainty in it using the estimated standard errors of the contributing parameters—the product of normally distributed random variables has no known distribution, and so the standard error of a product of normal variables is not defined. In the Bayesian setting, however, we can construct this crossover age for every sampled value of the contributing parameters produced by the Gibbs sampler and thereby obtain a distribution for this quantity. Doing so allows us to answer important questions like: What is the probability that the crossover age lies outside reasonable bounds on the life span?

I ran the Gibbs sampler presented in Section 8.1.2 several times, using different starting values for the parameters for each run. Figure 8.3 shows a trace plot of the intercept parameter, along with a plot of the autocorrelation

---

[3] One issue that is problematic when the success proportion is extreme (either high or low) is that a model that simply predicts success or failure for every observation will tend to predict the observed outcome very well. In this particular example, a model that simply predicts that no one died would seem to explain 98.8% of the observed responses! See Hosmer and Lemeshow for more discussion of this issue.

function (ACF). The trace plot (and R statistic) shows rapid convergence, but the ACF plot shows a high level of autocorrelation. Ultimately, I ran the final algorithm for 25,000 iterations, eliminated the first 1,000 as the burn-in, and thinned the chain to every 24th sampled value to reduce autocorrelation. This process left me with 1,000 posterior samples for the regression coefficients. The latter plot shows the ACF after thinning the chain.

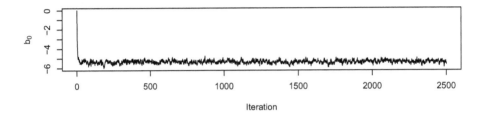

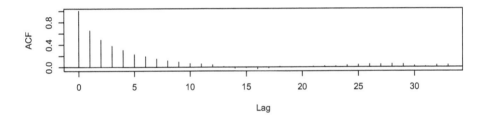

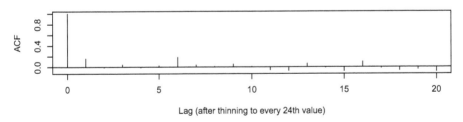

Fig. 8.3. Trace plot and autocorrelation function (ACF) plot for intercept parameter in dichotomous probit model example (upper plots show samples thinned to every 10th sample; lower plot shows the ACF after thinning to every 24th post-burn-in sample).

Figure 8.4 shows sampled latent propensities (y^*) for four person-records. The first, second, and third graphs show the distributions for three person-years in which the respondent died. The first is the latent propensity distribution for an 84-year-old black male not from the South with 11 years of schooling. The second is the latent propensity distribution for a 62-year-old white male not from the South with 16 years of schooling. The third is the distribution of latent propensities for an 87-year-old white female not from the South with 17 years of education. Finally, the fourth is the distribution for a 93-year-old black southern male with no formal education. This person-record represents a case in which the respondent did not die, and thus, although the first three distributions are to the right of 0, the fourth distribution is to the left of 0. Notice that the distributions for the first and third cases are very similar, while the distribution for the second case is quite different. The reason for the dissimilarity is that the second case is for a person who was substantially younger than the others—62 years of age—and the age-dependence of mortality is strong. Thus, the latent trait distribution tends to be clustered close to 0.

These latent distributions can be used in multiple ways to assess model fit. First, I retained the variance of the complete sample of Y^* at each iteration. Because we know that the error distribution is $N(0,1)$, we can construct a distribution for R^2 as[4]:

$$R^2 = 1 - \frac{\text{var}(N(0,1))}{\text{var}(Y^*)}. \tag{8.10}$$

The results of performing this calculation for each of the 1,000 retained values for $\text{var}(Y^*)$ produced a mean estimated R^2 of .192 and a 95% interval estimate of $[.17, .22]$. These results suggest the model fits the data rather well by social science standards.

In addition to this type of global test of model fit, we can also conduct residual analyses. How do we calculate a residual in a dichotomous probit model? For each individual in the sample, we only observe a 0 or 1 for the outcome variable. However, the predicted scores are in z units (or in log-odds units if we are using logistic regression). Thus, the standard approaches to residual analysis that have been well studied for linear regression model are generally poorly suited to studying residuals in GLMs.

The Bayesian approach offers a solution to this dilemma. With the use of latent data (Y^*), we can construct latent residuals $(e^* = Y^* - X\beta)$ and use whatever linear regression-based residual diagnostics we prefer. These latent residuals can be computed for every sampled value of β and Y^*; in which case we will have a distribution of latent residuals for each individual, or they can be computed using the mean of the Y^* for each observation and the mean of β.

---

[4] There are numerous methods for computing pseudo-R^2 measures in GLMs; this is simply one approach. See Long and Freese 2003

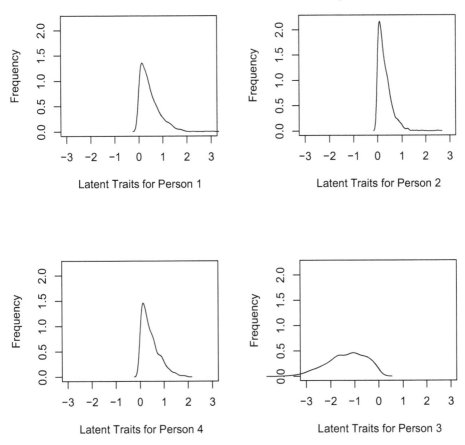

Fig. 8.4. Sampled latent health scores for four sample members from the probit model example.

Figure 8.5 shows the distributions of latent scores obtained during the run of the Gibbs sampler as well as the latent distributions of predicted scores computed from the results of the Gibbs sampler. Figure 8.6 shows the distribution of latent residuals—computed as the difference between these distributions—for the four cases discussed above. Of the four latent residual distributions, only one overlaps 0, which suggests adequate fit of the case. The other cases have residuals that are large and positive, which indicates that their latent propensities are substantially larger than the model predicts, as shown in Figure 8.5. In other words, the model predicts that these individuals should *not* have died, but in fact they did, which leads to values for Y^* that are positive (but predicted values that are negative).

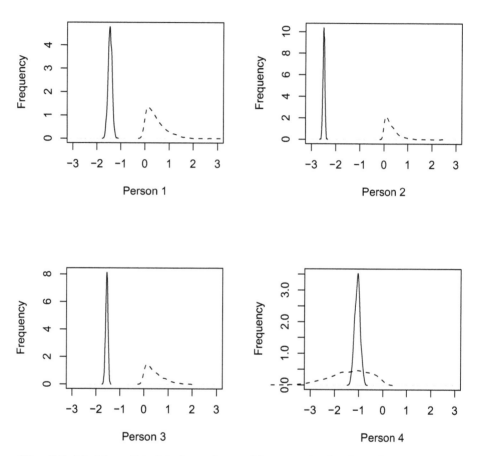

Fig. 8.5. Model-predicted traits and actual latent traits for four observations in probit model (solid line = model-predicted latent traits from sample values of β; dashed line = latent traits simulated from the Gibbs sampler).

I selected these cases for this particular reason: As I discussed above, in a model with a proportion of "successes" that is substantially far from .5, a model that predicts that all cases are either successes or failures will appear, on its face, to fit the data well. In this particular model, we have very few deaths, and so the model tends to predict that no one dies. In order to be convinced that the model fits well, we might consider investigating the latent

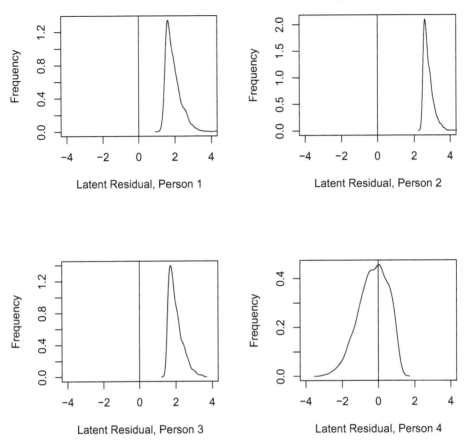

Fig. 8.6. Latent residuals for four observations in probit model (reference line at 0).

error distribution for all cases or construct summary measures of them. For this particular model, doing so suggested adequate overall fit of the model.

Table 8.3 shows the parameter estimates derived from the Gibbs sampler. The results show that age has a strong, positive effect on mortality risk, as does sex, with females evidencing substantially lower mortality risk than males. Region of residence and years of schooling have effects that are in the expected direction, but the effects would not be "significant" by classical standards. Under the Bayesian interpretation, the probability that these parameters are greater than (or less than, in the case of education) 0 is not less than .05.

From the sampled values for the race parameter and the age-by-race interaction, we can construct a distribution for the crossover age. This distribution is decidedly non-normal with a number of extreme values. The minimum and

Table 8.3. Gibbs sampling results for dichotomous probit model predicting mortality.

Variable	Parameter
Intercept	$-5.37(.15)^{***}$
Age	$0.047(.002)^{***}$
Female	$-0.24(.03)^{***}$
Black	$0.81(.36)^{*}$
Yrs. Schooling	$-0.003(.005)$
South (in '71)	$0.03(.04)$
Age $\times$ Black	$-0.0099(.005)^{*}$

Note: The Bayesian estimates are posterior means. The p-values are based on one-sided tail probabilities that the parameter exceeds 0 truncated to the classical cut-points of $\#p < .1$, $^{*}p < .05$, $^{**}p < .01$, $^{**}p < .001$.

maximum values for the crossover age, for example, were $-13,226.38$ and 393.33, respectively. These extreme values are a product of the fact that we have uncertainty in both of the contributing parameters. Figure 8.7 shows the bivariate distribution for these contributing parameters, with horizontal and vertical reference lines at 0 dividing the distribution into four "cases." In Case 1, the main effect parameter is negative, and the interaction effect parameter is positive. This combination produces crossover ages that are positive. However, under this scenario blacks begin life advantaged over whites and slowly see this advantage erode. In Case 2, the main and interaction effect parameters are both positive, which produces crossover ages that are negative. Throughout the observed life span, the black-white gap expands. In Case 3, the main and interaction effect parameters are both negative, producing crossover ages that also occur outside the life span (negative). In these cases, blacks evidence lower mortality than whites throughout life with the gap expanding across age. Finally, in Case 4, the main effect is positive and the interaction effect is negative, producing crossover ages that are positive and generally consistent with expectation. That is, the white advantage erodes across age.

As the figure shows, the vast majority of the sampled parameter values—97.3% of them—fall under scenario 4. Overall, 1.6% of the sample parameter values fall under scenario 1, while 1.1% of the sample parameter values fall under scenario 2, and none fall under scenario 3. Thus, from a Bayesian view, there is a large probability that a crossover exists, and that the age pattern of mortality is consistent with theory—that is, blacks are disadvantaged in early life, but the white advantage decreases across age. In contrast, there is 0 probability that blacks actually experience a large and growing advantage in mortality across age (cases 3), and very low probabilities that whites experience a growing advantage across age (case 2) or that blacks begin life with an advantage that declines across age (case 1).

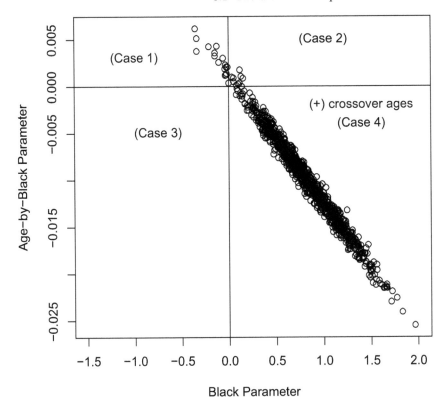

Fig. 8.7. Distribution of black and age-by-black parameters (Cases 2 and 3 = both values are positive or negative, respectively; Cases 1 and 4 = values are of opposite signs. Case 4 is the typically-seen/expected pattern).

We can consider the crossover in more detail by summarizing its distribution, rather than considering the contributing parameters. Figure 8.8 shows a trace plot as well as a histogram of the distribution for crossover ages between 0 years of age and 200 years of age. The trace plot shows a seemingly stationary distribution of crossover ages, with periodically very high or very low sampled values. The histogram shows several summary statistics for the crossover, including the mean age based on *all* sampled values of the crossover age, the median crossover age based on all sampled values, the mean age based on only values falling between ages 0 and 200, and the typical maximum likelihood-estimated crossover age. This latter age is found by taking the maximum likelihood estimates for the contributing parameters, substituting them into Equation 8.9, and solving for age.

In general, the various measures of the crossover age vary substantially. The posterior mean when all sampled values for the crossover age are considered is 69.04, but the posterior mean when only those values falling in the interval [0,200] are considered was 84.1. The median age, when all values are

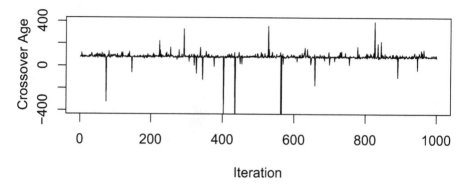

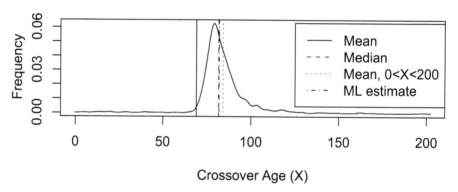

Fig. 8.8. Distribution of black-white crossover ages for ages > 0 and < 200 (various summary measures superimposed as reference lines).

considered, was 81.6, which is very close to the maximum likelihood estimate of 81.9. The posterior mean estimates, both with and without the constraints on the age range are more extreme than the median and maximum likelihood estimates. This extremeness is attributable to the influence the extreme positive and negative values exert on the mean, bringing us to the question posed at the beginning of the section: What is the probability that the crossover falls outside the human "life span," making it an irrelevant quantity/issue? Obviously, 0 is the lower bound on the life span. Thus far, the oldest living human lived to age 122, and so 122 may be a reasonable upper bound. Based on our results, the probability that the crossover age falls in this range is .966.

The probability that the crossover age is negative is .011; the probability that the crossover age is greater than 122 is .023. These results suggest that the crossover most likely occurs during the life span.

As an alternative to using 122 as the upper boundary, we may consider life expectancy at birth to be a more reasonable upper bound, given that it represents (in theory) an age around which most deaths cluster in a population.[5] Life expectancy at birth is approximately 78. The probability that the crossover occurs before this age (but after age 0!) is: .258, a relatively small probability. However, research has argued that the crossover is an artifact of within-population heterogeneity in mortality rates (Lynch, Brown, and Harmsen 2003), and thus, we may *not* expect the crossover to occur until after half the population has died. Approximately half of individuals born today can expect to live to age 80, and so we may consider the probability that the crossover age falls between 80 and 100, the age at which only approximately 1-2% of the population remains alive. Thus, if the crossover occurs after this age, it has little substantive importance. The probability that the crossover age falls between 80 and 100 is .506.

In addition to these specific probabilities, we may consider constructing probability intervals for the crossover age. A 95% probability interval for the crossover age is [57.1,120.2], and a 90% interval is [72.1,108.0]. All of these results taken together provide a much more detailed summary of the crossover age than the maximum likelihood approach can offer. Substantively, from these results, we might conclude that the crossover exists and that it occurs within the normal life span of individuals within a population.[6]

8.2 The ordinal probit model

The dichotomous probit model is easily generalizable in the event our outcome variable is ordinal rather than dichotomous. In the event the outcome variable is ordinal with numerous categories (e.g., more than five), we may consider an OLS regression model. However, by definition ordinal variables have rankable outcome categories with unequal spacing between categories, which makes OLS regression theoretically inappropriate. For example, in health research, a four-category self-rated health measure—with categories Excellent, Good, Fair, and Poor—is a commonly used outcome variable. Although the order of the categories reflects an unmistakable progression from best health to worst

---

[5] Technically, it is the expected value for the age of death distribution, but in most modern societies, deaths increasingly cluster around this point.

[6] In all fairness, a key reason the crossover is assumed not to exist is that it is an artifact of age misreporting among older persons (see Elo and Preston 1994). Age misreporting is less problematic in a longitudinal study in which most individuals are observed at a younger age than we typically expect to find such misreporting. Nonetheless, we cannot easily control for such measurement error with the model we have used.

health, the interval between, say, Excellent and Good is not necessarily comparable with the interval between Fair and Poor. Thus, OLS regression, which requires an interval level outcome, is an inappropriate model. Nonetheless, as the number of categories increases—and thus the interval width between any two categories shrinks—the difference between interval widths may become negligible and potentialize the legitimate use of OLS regression. We will consider this possibility in the example.

8.2.1 Model development and parameter interpretation

Whereas the likelihood function for the dichotomous probit model relied on the binomial distribution, the likelihood function for the ordinal probit model relies on the multinomial distribution. As we discussed in Chapter 2, the multinomial distribution is simply an extension of the binomial distribution for the case in which there are multiple p parameters being modeled rather than simply one. Thus, the likelihood function for the ordinal probit model is:

$$L(P|Y) \propto \prod_{i=1}^{n} \left(\prod_{j=1}^{J} p_{ij}^{I(y_i=j)} \right). \tag{8.11}$$

This representation may at first appear confusing, but it is a straightforward extension of the binomial likelihood function in Equation 8.1. First, in the ordinal probit case, p is replaced by P to represent the fact that we are now dealing with more than simply the probability of an individual falling in one category versus its complement (e.g., Healthy versus Not): Now we have multiple possible categories (e.g., Excellent health, Good health, Fair health, Poor health). Second, we have two product symbols. The first constructs the joint sampling density for all individuals in the sample, just as the product in the binomial likelihood. The second is an extension to handle the fact that we now have J outcome categories rather than two. In the binomial likelihood function, a given individual's contribution is $p_i^{y_i}(1 - p_i)^{1-y_i}$, where p_i represents the probability the individual registers a "1" (versus a 0) on the outcome. An individual who registers a "1" ends up only contributing the former term, whereas an individual who registers a "0" ends up only contributing the latter term. In the multinomial version, the individual's contribution is $p_{i1}^{I(y_i=1)} p_{i2}^{I(y_i=2)} \dots p_{iJ}^{I(y_i=J)}$, where $I(y_i = j)$ is an indicator function indicating that the individual's response is in category j. Thus, the individual only ultimately contributes one term to the likelihood (all others drop, because the indicator function takes a value of 0).

How do we incorporate the regression parameters (and X) into this model? As before, the p_{ij} correspond to integrals of the standard normal distribution. Consider the latent variable approach discussed above. If we assume once again that a latent variable y_i^* underlies our observed ordinal measure, then we can expand the link equation presented earlier (see Equation 8.3) to:

$$
y_i = \begin{cases} 1 & \text{iff} & -\infty = \tau_1 \le y_i^* < \tau_2 \\ 2 & \text{iff} & \tau_2 \le y_i^* < \tau_3 \\ \vdots \\ k & \text{iff} & \tau_k \le y_i^* < \tau_{k+1} = \infty. \end{cases} \tag{8.12}
$$

Figure 8.9 presents a graphic depiction of the process outlined in the equation. The latent distribution (y^*) is divided by thresholds (τ), with individuals' observed values of y determined by the location of their y^* and the placement of the thresholds. For example, an individual whose value of y^* is small enough to fall between τ_1 and τ_2 will respond "1" to the measured item.[7]

As before, the link equation, given a distributional specification for the error term, implies an integral over the error distribution, but now the integral is bounded by thresholds that divide the latent y^* into the observed ordinal "bins":

$$
p(y_i = j) = P(\tau_{j-1} - X_i^T \beta < e_i < \tau_j - X_i^T \beta) = \int_{\tau_{j-1} - X_i^T \beta}^{\tau_j - X_i^T \beta} N(0, 1). \tag{8.13}
$$

This result allows us to write the likelihood more succinctly as:

$$
L(\beta, \tau | y) \propto \prod_{i=1}^{n} \int_{\tau_{y_i-1} - X_i^T \beta}^{\tau_{y_i} - X_i^T \beta} N(0, 1) \equiv \prod_{i=1}^{n} \Phi(\tau_{y_i} - X_i^T \beta) - \Phi(\tau_{y_i-1} - X_i^T \beta). \tag{8.14}
$$

To make the model fully Bayesian, we simply need to specify priors for the regression parameters and thresholds. Once again, I opt to use improper uniform priors for all parameters, and so the posterior distribution is proportional to the likelihood.

The interpretation of parameters from this model poses the same difficulties as described in the previous section. The metric for the coefficients in the ordinal probit model, just as in the dichotomous probit model, is the z scale, and thus the interpretation of the effect of the parameters is in terms of shifting the z score for an individual up or down β units for each unit increase in the corresponding variable. Alternative interpretations in terms of determining the probability an individual falls in a particular category—or in a particular category or higher—can be derived (see Johnson and Albert 1999), although interest generally centers simply on the sign, relative magnitude, and statistical significance of the coefficient.

As with the dichotomous logistic regression model, an ordinal logistic regression model coefficient can be exponentiated to reflect the change in the

---

[7] Although many texts begin their threshold subscripts at 0, I begin the threshold numbering at 1 for ease of translation into R, which does not allow 0 subscripts.

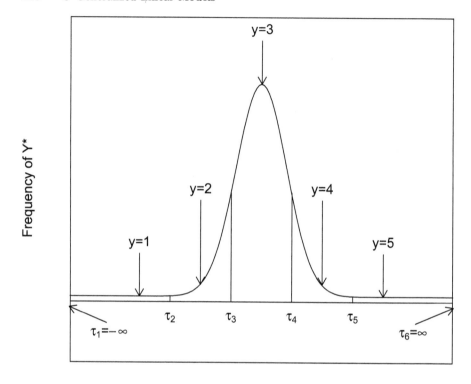

Latent Distribution (Y*)

Fig. 8.9. Depiction of latent distribution for Y^* and Y with thresholds superimposed.

relative odds for being in one category versus the next lower category associated with a one-unit increase in the covariate corresponding to the exponentiated coefficient (see Long 1997). Because this odds ratio applies to each category relative to the one immediately below it, the model is sometimes called a "proportional odds model."

8.2.2 Sampling from the posterior distribution for the parameters

For an ordinal probit model, the algorithm for the dichotomous probit model only needs (1) to be extended to handle estimation of the thresholds that bound the categories and (2) to be adapted to simulate from doubly truncated normal distributions. Recall from the posterior density shown above that the parameters of the model include not only the regression coefficients, but also the category thresholds that "slice up" the latent distribution into the observed ordinal bins. In the dichotomous probit model, we fixed the sole threshold at 0. This constraint is necessary for the intercept to be identified; if the threshold is allowed to vary, the intercept can simply change without affecting the likelihood. In the ordinal probit model, we need to constrain one threshold parameter, but we can estimate the remainder of them (but see Johnson and Albert, 1999, who discuss using a proper prior on the thresholds to allow estimation of all of them). Thus, our Gibbs sampling algorithm must be extended to include simulating the thresholds from their conditional posterior distribution. Assuming uniform priors for the thresholds, the conditional distribution for threshold j is a uniform distribution on the interval between the maximum latent propensity (Y^*) drawn for an individual in category $j-1$ and the minimum latent propensity drawn for an individual in category j. Thus, the algorithm is extended as:

1. Establish starting values for all parameters. Now the parameter vector also includes thresholds, which need some reasonable starting values. A simple approach to obtaining starting values for threshold j is to use the inverse normal cumulative distribution function (CDF) for the proportion of observations in category j or below.
2. Sample latent propensities (Y^*) from truncated normal distributions. Whereas with the dichotomous probit in which the propensities were sampled from above 0 if the response was a 1 and below 0 if the response was a 0, the truncation points in the ordinal probit model are the thresholds that bound the ordinal category in which the response falls.
3. Sample threshold $j(\forall j)$ from uniform densities on the interval $[\max(y : y \in j-1), \min(y : y \in j)]$.
4. Sample regression coefficients from their conditional distribution: $\beta \sim (X'X)^{-1}(X'Y^*)$.
5. Repeat until enough draws are obtained.

Notice that the only two differences between this algorithm and the one for the dichotomous probit model are (1) the inclusion of the step in which the thresholds are sampled, and (2) the sampling of the latent propensities from doubly truncated normal distributions implied by the introduction of additional thresholds.

Sampling from doubly-truncated normal distributions using the inversion method requires relatively little change from the inversion method discussed in the previous section. In the polytomous case, we need to renormalize the area *between* thresholds rather than simply computing the area from $-\infty$ to 0 or from 0 to ∞. Thus, determining the bounded area requires two calls to the function that computes Φ. To sample from a particular category k the appropriate renormalized density is:

$$z_{[\tau_k, \tau_{k+1}]} \sim \Phi^{-1}\left[u\left(\Phi(\tau_{k+1}) - \Phi(\tau_k)\right) + \Phi(\tau_k)\right], \tag{8.15}$$

where $z_{[\tau_k, \tau_{k+1}]}$ is the latent draw from category k, τ_{k+1} is the upper threshold for category k, and u is a random draw from the $U(0, 1)$ distribution. Since u can range from 0 to 1, z will range from τ_k to τ_{k+1}.

An even easier method for simulating from doubly truncated normal distributions in R is to set the minimum and maximum values for the uniform draw equal to the current values of the normal integrals implied by the current value of the thresholds. For example, if $\tau_2 = 0$ and $\tau_3 = 1$, the respondent's value of $X_i^T \beta = 0$, and his/her value of $y = 2$—meaning that the observed response falls in the category bounded by τ_2 and τ_3, the minimum and maximum for the uniform draw would be .5 and .84, respectively. These are the values of the cumulative distribution function at 0 and 1, and so the uniform draw representing the cumulative area under the density at which we want a value z is between .5 and .84.

Below is the R program that implements the ordered probit model for a five-category ordinal outcome:

```
#R program for ordinal probit model
x=as.matrix(read.table("c:\\bookheal.dat")[,1:7])
y=as.matrix(read.table("c:\\bookheal.dat")[,8])

t=matrix(0,6)
t[1]=-Inf; t[2]=0; t[6]=Inf
t[3]=qnorm(sum(y<=2)/nrow(y),-qnorm(sum(y==1)/nrow(y),0,1),1)
t[4]=qnorm(sum(y<=3)/nrow(y),-qnorm(sum(y==1)/nrow(y),0,1),1)
t[5]=qnorm(sum(y<=4)/nrow(y),-qnorm(sum(y==1)/nrow(y),0,1),1)

b=matrix(0,7); vb=solve(t(x)%*%x); ch=chol(vb)

write(c(1,0,0,0,0,0,0,0,0,0,0),file="c:\\oprob_gibbs.out",
      append=T, ncolumns=11)

for(i in 2:100000){
#simulate latent data from truncated normal distributions
xb=as.matrix(x%*%b)
ystar=qnorm(runif(nrow(y),min=pnorm(t[y],xb,1),
                  max=pnorm(t[y+1],xb,1)),mean=xb,1)

#simulate thresholds
for(k in 3:5){t[k]=runif(1,min=max(ystar[y==k-1]),
                         max=min(ystar[y==k]))}

#simulate beta vector from appropriate mvn
b=vb%*%(t(x)%*%ystar) + t((rnorm(7,mean=0,sd=1))%*%ch)

write(c(i,t(b),t[3],t[4],t[5]), file="c:\\oprob_gibbs.out2",
      append=T, ncolumns=11)

if(i%%10==0){print(c(i,t(b),t[3],t[4],t[5]),digits=2)}
}
```

The program follows the same general structure as the one for the dichotomous probit model. First, the data are read from the file, variables are defined and initiated, and the starting values for all parameters are written to the output file. Notice that there are six thresholds defined. The first and last are set to $+\infty$ and $-\infty$, respectively, and the second threshold is set to 0 to identify the model. The remaining three thresholds are initialized based on the proportion of the sample falling in each category of the outcome. The mean argument to the qnorm function is -qnorm(sum(y==1)/nrow(y),0,1) because the normal distribution must be shifted so that the proportion of cases falling below the second threshold of 0 is equal to the proportion of individuals who fall in the first category of the outcome variable.

After all variables are initialized, the Gibbs sampler begins. First, given the current values of the regression parameters and thresholds, latent data are simulated to replace the observed ordinal outcome. As we did in the dichotomous probit model program, we make use of R's ability to handle entire vectors simultaneously, and so the latent data simulation is performed in one step. Notice that I use the second method for simulating from the doubly truncated normal distribution: The minimum and maximum values for the latent data for an individual are determined by applying the qnorm function to the thresholds that bound the observed response.

Once the latent data have been simulated, the three free thresholds are simulated from uniform distributions on the interval between the largest latent value simulated for the category below the threshold and the smallest latent value simulated for the category above the threshold. Finally, given a complete set of latent data, the regression parameters are simulated as before.

8.2.3 Ordinal probit model example: Black–white differences in health

For an example of the ordinal probit model, I extend the example in the previous section using self-rated health as the outcome measure. Additionally, rather than using a person-year file, I use only the 1992 wave of the study. I ran the Gibbs sampler above several times for 100,000 iterations each time using different starting values for the threshold parameters. Although there was no need to run the Gibbs sampler for so many iterations, the algorithm is extremely fast, and thus there is little cost to doing so. The results of the three runs suggested that the regression parameters converged quickly, but the threshold parameters converged slowly. Figure 8.10 shows trace plots of the three estimated threshold parameters from the first run of the algorithm in which the thresholds were initialized at values that were higher than they should be. As the figure indicates, the threshold parameters did not converge until after 20,000 or so iterations. Slow convergence—and mixing—of threshold parameters occurs when the sample size is large enough that the minimum simulated latent score for one category and the maximum simulated score for the prior category are similar, so that the conditional uniform density for the threshold is narrow. A solution to this dilemma is to use Cowles' algorithm (1996). In Cowles' algorithm, the Gibbs sampling step for sampling the thresholds is replaced with an MH step. I do not present an example here using this alternative, primarily because the speed of the Gibbs sampler in R nullifies the need to seek out a more efficient alternative (but see Chapter 10).

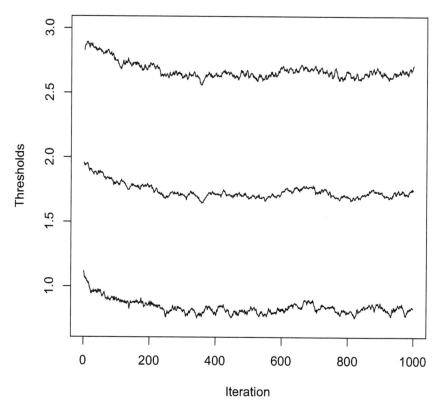

Fig. 8.10. Trace plot for threshold parameters in ordinal probit model.

Figure 8.11 replicates the results of Figure 8.4 in showing the distributions of latent scores for several cases. Specifically, the figure shows the latent distributions for five sample members, each of whom had a different observed response to the health item. In order to better illustrate the process of drawing latent scores from doubly truncated normal distributions, the figure shows all five latent trait distributions together. The far-left distribution is the latent distribution for an individual who responded "1" to the item; the second distribution is for an individual who responded "2" on the observed item; and so on. Although the heights of the densities are not consistent because the widths of the densities vary due to placement of the thresholds, the five distributions appear to be "slices" of an overall latent trait distribution. It is important to note that each individual's distribution appears to overlap the adjacent distributions. The distributions overlap because the thresholds are updated at every iteration—when a threshold is low, the acceptable range for the latent traits in the categories split by the threshold is affected.

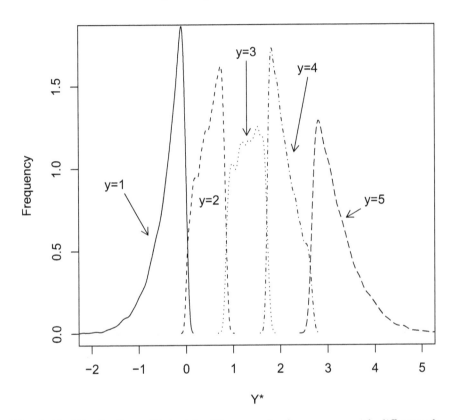

Fig. 8.11. Distributions of latent health scores for five persons with different observed values of y.

Table 8.4 shows the results of the ordinal probit model algorithm, along with maximum likelihood results. With the exception of the intercept and the thresholds, the maximum likelihood and Bayesian (posterior mean) estimates are virtually identical. Men have better health, and nonwhites have poorer health. Persons who have been hospitalized have worse health, as do persons with more physical conditions. Age, and doctor visits do not have a significant effect on health, but the body mass index has a marginally significant effect, even after controlling for the physical health measures.

The difference between the maximum likelihood and Bayesian estimates for the intercept and thresholds reflects different parameterizations of the model. STATA (the package used to obtain the maximum likelihood estimates) fixes the intercept for the model to 0 but estimates all thresholds. In contrast, we allowed the intercept to be estimated but constrained the second threshold to be equal to 0. The only difference in these parameterizations is in the location of the latent distribution: For our parameterization, the latent distribution is shifted to the right relative to the latent distribution for STATA's parameterization. Notice that subtracting our intercept from each of the thresholds (and the intercept itself) yields roughly the same estimates for the thresholds obtained by STATA. The only striking difference, ultimately, between the STATA results and the Gibbs sampling results is in the psuedo-R^2. Although the Gibbs sampler estimate ranges between .105 and .182, with a mean of .144, the STATA estimate is substantially smaller at .049. The reason for this seemingly large discrepancy is that there are many different methods for calculating pseudo-r-square, and the method I used differs from STATA's.[8]

Table 8.4. Maximum likelihood and Gibbs sampling results for ordinal probit model example.

Variable	MLE (STATA)	Gibbs Sampler Estimates
Intercept	0 (fixed)	1.86(.15)***
Age	−0.02(.002)***	−0.02(.002)***
Female	−0.001(.03)	−0.001(.04)
Black	−0.91(.33)**	−0.90(.33)**
Years of Schooling	0.09(.01)***	0.09(.01)***
South	−0.13(.04)**	−0.13(.04)***
Age-by-Black	0.008(.005)	0.008(.005)#
τ_1	−∞ (fixed)	−∞ (fixed)
τ_2	−1.85(.15)	0 (fixed)
τ_3	−1.04(.15)	0.83(.03)
τ_4	−0.15(.15)	1.72(.03)
τ_5	0.79(.15)	2.65(.03)
τ_6	∞ (fixed)	−∞ (fixed)
Pseudo-R^2	0.049	.14[.11, .18]

Note: The Bayesian estimates are posterior means. The p-values are based on one-sided tail probabilities that the parameter exceeds 0 truncated to the classical cut-points of #$p < .1$, *$p < .05$, **$p < .01$.

The approach used here to produce a pseudo-R^2 is the same approach as described earlier for the dichotomous probit model. In OLS regression, one approach to computing R^2 is to subtract the ratio of the error variance to the

---

[8] STATA uses $r^2 = 1 - LL/L0$, where $L0$ is the maximum likelihood function value for a model with only an intercept and LL is the value for the full model.

total variance for the outcome variable—the proportion of the total variance that is error variance, in other words—from 1. The only difference, therefore, between the OLS approach and the one used in the dichotomous and ordinal probit models is that the variance of the *latent* data are used, rather than the variance of the observed outcome variable as is used in OLS. The net result is that the distribution for R^2 will tend to be slightly wider in the probit models than in the OLS model, reflecting the additional uncertainty introduced by the crude measurement of the latent data.

One issue that I discussed earlier in the chapter is whether, with an ordinal outcome variable, it is necessary to use some sort of GLM as opposed to simply using OLS regression. Although it is true that the differences between OLS and GLM results tend to decrease as the number of outcome categories increases, the actual number of categories needed in the outcome may change from model to model. Thus, if we are really interested in deciding whether to use a GLM or OLS regression, we may choose to estimate both models and decide whether they produce a substantially different fit. The classical approach offers little in the way of formal comparison between nonnested models; the Bayesian approach, on the other hand, offers unlimited ability to make formal comparisons. One such comparison that can be made is to compare the distributions for R^2 from the OLS model to the pseudo-R^2 distribution for the ordinal probit model. Figure 8.12 shows the distributions of R^2 for both the ordinal probit model and an OLS model. As the figure shows, it appears that the models fit more-or-less equally well, with the ordinal probit fitting perhaps only slightly better. The mean R^2 for the probit and OLS models were .144 and .138, respectively. From a Bayesian view, these distributions can be formally compared. The probability that the ordinal probit model fits better than the OLS model is $p(R^2_{\text{probit}} > R^2_{\text{OLS}})$, which can be computed as the proportion of R^2 values in the ordinal probit distribution for R^2 that exceed the maximum R^2 value in the OLS distribution for R^2. This value is 0. The probability that the OLS model fits worse than the probit model is .00025. Thus, the results suggest that the two models are indistinguishable.

Can comparisons be made across coefficients in the two models? Unfortunately, no: Given that the probit model assumes that the error variance is 1, while the error variance parameter is estimated in the OLS regression model, the coefficients cannot be directly compared across models. Bayesians have no trouble making comparisons across probability distributions, but we should always determine whether our comparisons make sense. In comparing the probit and OLS models, the coefficients are in different scales, and so the coefficients cannot be directly compared.[9]

The results of the ordinal probit model can be used to produce a distribution of a health crossover age, just as we did in the dichotomous probit model,

---

[9] Interestingly, however, in this particular example, the error variance parameter is close to 1 in the OLS regression model, and so the coefficients and standard errors are remarkably similar.

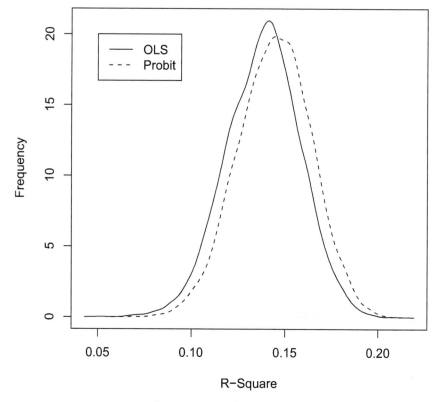

Fig. 8.12. Distributions of R^2 and pseudo-R^2 from OLS and probit models, respectively.

using the distributions for the "black" parameter and the age-by-black interaction parameter. Table 8.5 provides a number of summaries for the health crossover age. The central age (mean or median) for the health crossover is substantially higher than the mortality crossover age. In fact, the various summary measures suggest that there is a low probability that a health crossover occurs during the normal human life span. Taken together, the results of the dichotomous probit and ordinal probit models indicate that, although mortality rates for blacks fall below those for whites in later life, blacks have poorer health at all ages. A stronger approach to reaching this conclusion would require a model that simultaneously considers health and mortality—a multivariate model. Multivariate models are the subject of Chapter 10.

8.3 Conclusions

In this chapter we have covered two commonly used generalized linear models—the dichotomous probit model and the ordinal probit model. For

Table 8.5. Various summary measures for the black-white health crossover age.

Description of Summary Measure	Summary (Age)
Maximum Likelihood estimate of crossover age	113.8
Posterior Mean (all values)	157.7
Posterior Median (all values included)	112.2
Posterior Mean (of values 0-200)	117.1
95% Interval	[-236.0, 680.0]
90% Interval	[75.7, 370.6]
$p(0 < Age < 200)$	.831
$p(0 < Age < 120)$	.535
$p(0 < Age < 78)$	.003
$p(80 < Age < 100)$	.264

each model, we discussed a single Gibbs sampler. A key difference between these samplers and that for the linear regression model in the last chapter is the need to sample latent data from truncated normal distributions. Thus, we discussed three strategies for performing such simulation.

We also spent considerable time in this chapter demonstrating how to make use of the Gibbs sampler to generate samples from distributions of quantities not directly included in the model (e.g., the crossover age), as well as how to perform basic residual analyses in the probit model. We will continue discussing the benefits of the Bayesian approach in the remaining two chapters, but in the next chapter—which covers hierarchical modeling—we will primarily focus on the ease with which the Bayesian approach can incorporate hierarchical structure to the data and model.

8.4 Exercises

1. Develop an MH algorithm for the dichotomous probit model.
2. Develop a rejection sampler for simulating from a truncated normal distribution using a triangular density, rather than a uniform density, as discussed in Section 8.1.3.
3. Starting with the Gibbs sampler shown earlier for the dichotomous probit model, modify it to make it a hybridized Gibbs-MH algorithm. That is, continue to sample the latent data at each iteration (a Gibbs sampling step), but update the parameters using MH steps.
4. Write an algorithm to estimate the parameters in the dichotomous probit model using the binomial likelihood function-with link function. The likelihood function will contain normal integrals. Compare results between this algorithm and the Gibbs sampler. Are there any differences in the speed of convergence? Are the parameter estimates and standard errors comparable?

5. Construct an MH algorithm to estimate the parameters in the ordinal probit model.

6. There are several alternative methods for calculating pseudo-R^2 values in GLMs. One such approach in a dichotomous probit model is to construct a two-by-two table of observed and predicted outcomes, where individuals with $X\beta > 0$ assigned to have a predicted score of "1" (otherwise they receive a predicted score of "0"). The R^2 is then simply the proportion of correctly classified individuals. Under a Bayesian approach, we would obtain multiple values for β and, hence, multiple possible R^2 values. Perform this process and compare the result with what is obtained using the method I described in the chapter. How does the distribution of the outcome variable influence the difference between these two types of R^2s?

7. Develop a strategy for handling missing data in the probit model (dichotomous or ordinal). Assume the data are MAR.

9

Introduction to Hierarchical Models

One of the important features of a Bayesian approach is the relative ease with which hierarchical models can be constructed and estimated using Gibbs sampling. In fact, one of the key reasons for the recent growth in the use of Bayesian methods in the social sciences is that the use of hierarchical models has also increased dramatically in the last two decades.

Hierarchical models serve two purposes. One purpose is methodological; the other is substantive. Methodologically, when units of analysis are drawn from clusters within a population (communities, neighborhoods, city blocks, etc.), they can no longer be considered independent. Individuals who come from the same cluster will be more similar to each other than they will be to individuals from other clusters. Therefore, unobserved variables may induce statistical dependence between observations within clusters that may be uncaptured by covariates within the model, violating a key assumption of maximum likelihood estimation as it is typically conducted when independence of errors is assumed. Recall that a likelihood function, when observations are independent, is simply the product of the density functions for each observation taken over all the observations. However, when independence does not hold, we cannot construct the likelihood as simply. Thus, one reason for constructing hierarchical models is to compensate for the biases—largely in the standard errors—that are introduced when the independence assumption is violated. See Ezell, Land, and Cohen (2003) for a thorough review of the approaches that have been used to correct standard errors in hazard modeling applications with repeated events, one class of models in which repeated measurement yields hierarchical clustering.

In addition to the methodological need for hierarchical models, substantively we may believe that there are differences in how predictors in a regression model influence an outcome of interest across clusters, and we may wish to model these differences. In other words, the influence of predictors may be *context-dependent*, a notion that is extremely important and relevant to a social scientific—especially sociological—understanding of the world. For example, the emergence of hierarchical modeling in education research occurred because there is a natural nesting of students within classes (and classes within schools, schools within communities, and so on), and grades, test performance, etc. may be dependent on teacher quality, making students in one class different from those in another class. In other words, student performance may be dependent on the teacher—the environmental context of classes.

In this chapter, I discuss simple hierarchical models in general as well as hierarchical linear regression models. I conclude the chapter with a brief discussion of terminological issues that make hierarchical modeling seem mysterious and complicated. I recommend Gelman et al. (1995) for an in-depth exposition of the Bayesian approach to a variety of hierarchical models, both the simple hierarchical models discussed in the next section as well as hierarchical regression models discussed later in the chapter. I recommend Raudenbush and Bryk (2002) and Snijders and Bosker (1999) for thorough coverage of the classical approach to hierarchical linear regression models.

9.1 Hierarchical models in general

Hierarchical models are models in which there is some sort of hierarchical structure to the parameters and potentially to the covariates if the model is a regression model. I begin by discussing the simpler case in which the model of interest is not a regression model with covariates, but rather is simply hierarchical in the parameters.

Recall that Bayes' Theorem is often expressed as:

$$\underbrace{p(\theta \mid \text{data})}_{\text{posterior}} \propto \underbrace{p(\text{data} \mid \theta)}_{\text{likelihood}} \times \underbrace{p(\theta)}_{\text{prior}}$$

This equation itself reveals a simple hierarchical structure in the parameters, because it says that a posterior distribution for a parameter is equal to a conditional distribution for data under the parameter (first level) multiplied by the marginal (prior) probability for the parameter (a second, higher, level). Put another way, the posterior distribution is the prior distribution weighted by the observed information.

This hierarchical structure of the parameters need not stop at one higher level; instead, the conditioning structure in theory can continue *ad infinitum*. For instance, suppose we have a model that contains an added layer of hierarchy. Suppose we have J observations within each of G groups: $y_{11}, \ldots, y_{J1}, y_{12}, \ldots, y_{J2}, \ldots, y_{1G}, \ldots, y_{JG}$, and we assume that the data are distributed within groups according to some distribution Q with parameter θ, but that each group has its own parameter (θ_g). Thus:

$$y_{ig} \sim Q(\theta_g).$$

Suppose we assume further that these parameters θ_g arise from a common distribution W with parameter γ (this parameter is called a "hyperparameter"). So:

$$\theta_g \sim W(\gamma).$$

Finally, assume γ has some vague distribution like a uniform:

$$\gamma \sim U(-100, 100).$$

A posterior distribution for all unknown parameters would then be (after substituting the densities Q and W into the conditional structure below):

$$p(\gamma, \theta|y) \propto p(y \mid \theta, \gamma)p(\theta \mid \gamma)p(\gamma).$$

To see how this hierarchical structure "works," notice that the last two terms here $[p(\theta \mid \gamma)p(\gamma)]$, when multiplied together, yield a joint distribution for γ and θ $[p(\theta, \gamma)]$. Thus, we are left with a marginal joint distribution for the two parameters, which is then multiplied by a sampling density for the data $[p(y \mid \theta, \gamma)]$. Bayes' theorem tells us that the multiple of this marginal joint density for the parameters and the sampling density for the data, given the parameters, yields a posterior density for all of the parameters.

Ultimately we might not be interested much in the posterior distributions for the group level parameters (θ_g), but rather in the posterior distribution for the hyperparameter γ that structures the distribution of the group level parameters. In other words, we may be interested only in the marginal distribution for γ:

$$p(\gamma|y) \propto \int p(y|\theta, \gamma)p(\theta|\gamma)p(\gamma)d\theta.$$

As we have discussed throughout the last several chapters, this integration is performed stochastically via MCMC methods as we sample from the conditional posterior distributions for each parameter.

This result demonstrates the simplicity with which a Bayesian approach can handle hierarchical structure in data or parameters. We could very easily, if desired, add subsequent layers to the structure, and we can also break each layer of the structure into regression components.

9.1.1 The voting example redux

In Chapter 3, I illustrated Bayes' Theorem with a voting example from 2004 pre-election polls. In that example, we considered the posterior probability that Kerry would win the election in Ohio using the most recent poll as the current data and data from three previous polls as prior information. We assumed a binomial likelihood function/sampling density for the current polling data (x) given the proportion of voters who would vote for Kerry (K), and we used a beta distribution as the prior for K, with the number of votes for Kerry and Bush in the previous polls being represented by the parameters α and β, respectively. To summarize, our posterior density was:

$$p(K|\alpha, \beta, X) \propto \underbrace{K^{556}(1-K)^{511}}_{\substack{\text{current data} \\ \text{(likelihood)}}} \underbrace{K^{941}(1-K)^{1007}}_{\substack{\text{previous poll data} \\ \text{(prior)}}}.$$

In the original example I noted that, although the four polls we used appeared to show some trending, complete data from all available polls from various polling organizations did not suggest any trending, justifying our combination of the previous pollng data into a single prior distribution for α and β. As an alternative approach, without trending, the polls could be considered as separate samples drawn from the same population, each one providing conditionally independent information regarding the parameters α and β. In that case, we could consider that each poll's results were the result of a unique, poll-specific parameter K_i, with the K_i being random realizations from the beta distribution with *hyperparameters* α and β. This approach recasts the voting example as a hierarchical model with the following structure:

$$p(\alpha, \beta, K|X) \propto \underbrace{p(X|K)}_{\text{likelihood}} \underbrace{p(K|\alpha, \beta)}_{\text{prior}} \underbrace{p(\alpha, \beta)}_{\text{hyperprior}}.$$

Here, and throughout the remainder of the chapter, I suppress notation in the conditional distributions when a particular quantity does not directly depend on a higher level parameter. For example, the likelihood function here ultimately depends on the hyperparameters α and β; however, it only depends on these parameters through the prior for K, and so, I do not spell out the complete likelihood as $p(X|K, \alpha, \beta)$.

The likelihood portion of the model is the product of the sampling densities for the four polls:

$$p(X|K) \propto \prod_{i=1}^{4} K_i^{x_i}(1-K_i)^{n_i-x_i}.$$

The prior densities for each K $(K_1 \ldots K_4)$ are beta densities; their product is the full prior density:

$$p(K|\alpha, \beta) \propto \prod_{i=1}^{4} \left(\frac{\Gamma(\alpha+\beta)}{\Gamma(\alpha)\Gamma(\beta)} \right) K_i^{\alpha-1}(1-K_i)^{\beta-1}.$$

Finally, we must establish hyperpriors for the hyperparameters α and β. However, before we consider the form of the hyperprior, let's consider the full expression for the posterior density:

$$p(\alpha, \beta, K | x) \propto$$

$$\left(\prod_{i=1}^{4} K_i^{x_i} (1 - K_i)^{n_i - x_i} \right) \left(\prod_{i=1}^{4} \left(\frac{\Gamma(\alpha+\beta)}{\Gamma(\alpha)\Gamma(\beta)} \right) K_i^{\alpha-1} (1 - K_i)^{\beta-1} \right) p(\alpha, \beta).$$

We can simplify this posterior distribution by combining like products as follows:

$$p(\alpha, \beta, K | x) \propto$$

$$\left(\frac{\Gamma(\alpha+\beta)}{\Gamma(\alpha)\Gamma(\beta)} \right)^4 \left(\prod_{i=1}^{4} K_i^{x_i+\alpha-1} (1 - K_i)^{n_i - x_i + \beta - 1} \right) p(\alpha, \beta). \tag{9.1}$$

The key difference between the current approach and as it was presented in the original example in Chapter 3 is that the current data were assumed to be simply the most recent polling data, and the previous three polls were combined and assumed to be fixed quantities representing the values of α and β. Under the current approach, in contrast, the previous polling data— rather than being treated as fixed prior information—are also considered to arise from a random process governed by the hyperparameters α and β. When these parameters were assumed to be fixed, the posterior density only involved the single parameter K. Now, however, the full posterior involves each K_i in addition to α and β. Before, the leading expression involving the gamma function $[\Gamma(\alpha+\beta)/(\Gamma(\alpha)\Gamma(\beta))]$ could be dropped as a normalizing constant, because α and β were, in fact, constant. However, under the hierarchical approach they are now considered random variables, and terms involving them cannot simply be dropped. Indeed, although the individual K parameters are still of interest, interest centers primarily on α and β, which are thought to be the population parameters governing the proportion of voters who would vote for Kerry and which drive each individual poll result.

A Gibbs sampling strategy, then, should involve sampling the α, β, and each K from their conditional posterior distributions. The conditional posterior distributions for each K, after eliminating terms in the posterior in Equation 9.1 that do not involve them, are easily seen to be beta distributions with parameters $A = x_i + \alpha$ and $B = n_i - x_i + \beta$:

$$p(K_i | \alpha, \beta, x_i) \propto K_i^{x_i+\alpha-1} (1 - K_i)^{n_i - x_i + \beta - 1}.$$

The conditional posterior distributions for α and β are not as simple. Consider the posterior for α. If we eliminate terms not involving α, the posterior for α is:

$$\left(\frac{\Gamma(\alpha+\beta)}{\Gamma(\alpha)\Gamma(\beta)} \right)^4 \prod_{i=1}^{4} K_i^{x_i+\alpha-1} p(\alpha, \beta).$$

This posterior can be simplified considerably if we use a "trick" to allow the combination of the exponents. If we take the log and exponentiate simultaneously, we obtain:

$$\left(\frac{\Gamma(\alpha+\beta)}{\Gamma(\alpha)\Gamma(\beta)}\right)^4 \exp\left\{\ln\left(\prod_{i=1}^4 K_i^{x_i+\alpha-1}\right)\right\} p(\alpha,\beta).$$

The exponents can be brought down in front of the logarithm, the product of the logs become sums, and we obtain:

$$\left(\frac{\Gamma(\alpha+\beta)}{\Gamma(\alpha)\Gamma(\beta)}\right)^4 \exp\left\{\sum_{i=1}^4 (x_i+\alpha-1)\ln K_i\right\} p(\alpha,\beta).$$

At this point, we can expand the summation, distribute the three terms in front of the logarithms, and group like terms. We can also again remove terms that do not involve α. We are left with:

$$p(\alpha|\beta,K,x) \propto \left(\frac{\Gamma(\alpha+\beta)}{\Gamma(\alpha)\Gamma(\beta)}\right)^4 \exp\left\{\alpha\left(\sum_{i=1}^4 \ln K_i\right)\right\} p(\alpha,\beta).$$

A similar strategy reveals that the posterior density for β is:

$$p(\beta|\alpha,K,x) \propto \left(\frac{\Gamma(\alpha+\beta)}{\Gamma(\alpha)\Gamma(\beta)}\right)^4 \exp\left\{\beta\left(\sum_{i=1}^4 \ln(1-K_i)\right)\right\} p(\alpha,\beta).$$

What remains is the specification of the prior density $p(\alpha,\beta)$. Ideally, we may like a prior that is relatively noninformative. However, in this particular example, we must be careful, because these conditional posterior densities are not of known forms and, with too vague of a prior, will not be proper.

Recall that the hyperparameters α and β of the beta distribution can be viewed as prior successes and failures, respectively, and are therefore constrained to be nonnegative. In the example in Chapter 3, we fixed these parameters at constants to represent the successes/failures from the first three surveys in Ohio. Now, in contrast, we want to specify distributions for them. An appropriate distribution that would constrain these parameters to be nonnegative is the gamma distribution, which itself has two parameters, say C and D. If we assume that α and β have independent prior distributions, then $p(\alpha,\beta) = p(\alpha)p(\beta)$, and we can assign each a gamma distribution prior:

$$p(\alpha) \propto \alpha^{C_\alpha-1} \exp\left(-D_\alpha\alpha\right)$$
$$p(\beta) \propto \beta^{C_\beta-1} \exp\left(-D_\beta\beta\right).$$

This hyperprior yields the following conditional posterior for α:

$$p(\alpha|\beta,K,x,C_\alpha,D_\alpha) \propto \left(\frac{\Gamma(\alpha+\beta)}{\Gamma(\alpha)\Gamma(\beta)}\right)^4 \alpha^{C_\alpha-1} \exp\left\{\alpha\left(\sum_{i=1}^4 \ln K_i - D_\alpha\right)\right\}.$$

A comparable result can be obtained for β. All that remains is to specify values for C and D in each hyperprior.

Given parameters C and D, the mean of a gamma distribution is equal to C/D, and the variance is equal to C/D^2. We may choose to set these parameters at values that reflect our prior knowledge. Numerous previous polls throughout the country had showed the race to be virtually a dead heat, and so, we may choose comparable values of C and D for both prior distributions. The typical poll conducted throughout the fall by different polling organizations consisted of about 500 or so potential voters, roughly half of which were expected to vote for Kerry. So, we may choose values of C and D such that $C/D = 250$. We can capture prior uncertainty in this estimate by specifying the variance to be large. For example, if we choose a standard deviation to be equal to 100, then $C/D^2 = 10,000$, and so $C = 6.25$ and $D = .025$. To evaluate the influence of the hyperparameter specification, I varied these parameters and conducted several runs of the Gibbs sampler, as discussed below.

Below is a hybrid Gibbs sampler/MH algorithm for simulating the parameters of the model. Although the K parameters, conditional on the data and values for α and β, can be drawn directly from beta distributions, the α and β hyperparameters are not known forms and must therefore be simulated using MH steps:

```
#MCMC algorithm for hierarchical beta-binomial model

a=matrix(10,100000);b=matrix(10,100000); acca=0; accb=0
y=matrix(c(556,346,312,284),4); n=matrix(c(1067,685,637,628),4)
k=matrix((y)/n,m,4,byrow=T)

apost<-function(f,g,k){
  post=4*(lgamma(f+g)-lgamma(f)-lgamma(g)) + f * sum(log(k))
  post=post+(6.25-1)*log(f)-(f*.025)
  return(post)
}
bpost<-function(f,g,k){
  post=4*(lgamma(f+g)-lgamma(f)-lgamma(g)) + g * sum(log(1-k))
  post=post+(6.25-1)*log(g)-(g*.025)
  return(post)
}

for(i in 2:100000){
#draw a
a[i]=a[i-1]+rnorm(1,0,20)
if(a[i]>0){
  acca=acca+1
  newpost=apost(a[i],b[i-1],k[i-1,])
  oldpost=apost(a[i-1],b[i-1],k[i-1,])
  if(log(runif(1,min=0,max=1))>(newpost-oldpost))
```

```
   {a[i]=a[i-1]; acca=acca-1}
   }
 if(a[i]<0){a[i]=a[i-1]}

 #draw b
 b[i]=b[i-1]+rnorm(1,0,20)
 if(b[i]>0){
  accb=accb+1
  newpost=bpost(a[i],b[i],k[i-1,])
  oldpost=bpost(a[i],b[i-1],k[i-1,])
  if(log(runif(1,min=0,max=1))>(newpost-oldpost))
   {b[i]=b[i-1]; accb=accb-1}
  }
 if(b[i]<0){b[i]=b[i-1]}

 #draw k from beta distributions
 k[i,]=rbeta(4,(y+a[i]),(n-y+b[i]))

 if(i%%10==0){print(c(i,a[i],b[i],acca/i,accb/i))}
 }
```

This program is fairly straightforward. First, matrices are established for the α and β parameters, and acceptance rate variables are also constructed for monitoring the MH steps used to simulate them. Next, the data, including votes for Kerry (y), poll sizes (n), and proportions favoring Kerry (k), are established. The next two program blocks are functions that evaluate the conditional log-posterior densities for α and β, respectively, given values of these parameters, the previous value for the observed sample proportions, and a prior distribution (the second line of each function is the hyperprior).

The program then proceeds to simulate 100,000 draws from the posterior for all the parameters. The α and β parameters are drawn using MH steps. Candidates are generated from normal proposals with a standard deviation set to produce an approximate acceptance rate of 50%. Once a candidate is generated, the log-posterior is evaluated at the candidate values for these parameters and the previous values. I have structured these blocks so that the candidate parameter is assumed to be accepted and is evaluated for rejection. If the candidate is less than 0, or the log of the uniform draw exceeds the ratio of the log-posterior at the current versus previous values, the current value of the parameter is reset to the previous value, and the acceptance tally is reduced by one. Once values of these parameters have been drawn, each K_i parameter is drawn from the appropriate beta distribution.

The key parameters of interest in the model include the individual survey proportions $(K_1 \ldots K_4)$ and the population proportion implied by the α and β parameters, which is equal to $\alpha/(\alpha+\beta)$. Table 9.1 shows posterior summaries of these parameters under a variety of specifications for C and D in the hyperpriors for α and β. The first four columns of the table show the gamma distribution hyperprior specifications for the α and β parameters of the prior distribution. These values for the hyperpriors were chosen to examine how sensitive the posterior inferences are to prior specification.

The first two columns show the mean and standard deviation of the gamma hyperprior distribution for α, respectively; the third and fourth columns show the mean and standard deviation of the hyperprior for β. Recall from above that the mean of the gamma distribution for α can be considered as previous votes for Kerry, and the variance/standard deviation of this distribution can be viewed as a measure of our uncertainty in this number of previous votes. Similarly, the mean of the gamma distribution for β can be considered as previous votes for Bush, and its standard deviation reflects our uncertainty in this number. Thus, the first specification implies that previous polls have shown an equal—and small—number of votes for both candidates, and the relatively large standard deviation of each (10) suggests that we are not very certain of these numbers.

Thus, the first row shows the posterior inference when the prior information is fairly weak. That is, this hyperprior specification implies that we have prior information equivalent to 10 previous votes for Kerry and 10 for Bush, with a fairly large standard deviation reflecting considerable uncertainty about these numbers of votes. In contrast, the final hyperprior specification implies that we have prior information equivalent to 2,500 votes for Kerry and 500 votes for Bush, and that our confidence in these numbers is relatively strong (standard deviation of only 50, compared with the number of prior votes).

The bottom two rows of the table show the results under two alternative approaches to the hierarchical approach discussed here. The first row at the bottom shows the results obtained if the four polls are analyzed independently; the second shows the results obtained if the data from all polls are pooled and given a noninformative prior distribution—an equivalent approach to treating the most recent polling data as the current data and the earlier three polls as prior information (see Chapter 3).

Overall, all the hyperprior specifications lead to similar posterior inference for the prior distribution mean $\alpha/(\alpha + \beta)$ and for each of the polls, with the exception of the most informative specification which shows heavy favoritism for Kerry (2,500 prior votes versus 500). Under that specification, the posterior mean for the second level beta prior distribution is pulled strongly away from the mean implied by the polling data and toward the prior.

A couple of comments are warranted regarding these results. First, notice that pooling the data led to a posterior mean of .497 for Kerry's proportion of the vote, and that a similar proportion was obtained using $\alpha/(\alpha+\beta)$ in the hierarchical model, except for the final one with the strongest and most unbalanced hyperprior. However, although the posterior means are comparable, the posterior standard deviation for this proportion tended to be much larger under the hierarchical approach. The reason for this result is that, under the hierarchical approach, the distribution for $\alpha/(\alpha+\beta)$ captures the range of the survey specific K_i parameters, each of which contains its own variability. Under the pooled-data approach, on the other hand, three of the K_i are assumed

Table 9.1. Results of hierarchical model for voting example under different gamma hyperprior specifications.

Gamma Priors					Posterior Inferences			
α		β						
$\frac{C}{D}$	$\sqrt{\frac{C}{D^2}}$	$\frac{C}{D}$	$\sqrt{\frac{C}{D^2}}$	$\frac{\alpha}{\alpha+\beta}$	K_1	K_2	K_3	K_4
10	10	10	10	.493(.048)	.520(.015)	.505(.019)	.490(.019)	.454(.019)
100	100	100	100	.493(.021)	.516(.014)	.502(.017)	.491(.018)	.463(.018)
250	100	250	100	.494(.015)	.513(.014)	.501(.016)	.491(.016)	.470(.017)
250	100	100	100	.494(.016)	.514(.014)	.501(.016)	.491(.017)	.469(.017)
2500	50	500	50	.586(.008)	.572(.010)	.574(.010)	.572(.010)	.567(.010)
Separate Models				NA	.521(.015)	.505(.019)	.490(.020)	.452(.020)
Pooled Data				.497(.009)	NA	NA	NA	NA

Note: The hyperpriors are gamma distributions for both α and β. The hyperparameters C and D in each gamma distribution were set to produce the means and standard deviations shown (C/D and $\sqrt{C/D^2}$, respectively). The posterior quantities are the posterior mean of the beta prior distribution, $\alpha/(\alpha+\beta)$, and the posterior means for each of the sample proportions (posterior standard deviations are in parentheses).

be known, fixed quantities, reducing variability in the overall mean. Second, notice that it is generally the case that the variability for each K_i parameter is smaller than that obtained under the separate-models approach. The reason for this result is that, by combining all samples into a single, hierarchical model, each K_i distribution "borrows strength" from the common linkage of all the polls provided by the hyperparameters α and β.

9.2 Hierarchical linear regression models

The example in the previous section shows a basic hierarchical model in which the model parameters, but not the data, were structured hierarchically—all of the data were measured at the same level (individual polls). It is common in social science research, however, to have hierarchical structure to the data, that is, to have variables collected at different levels. In these cases, social scientists often turn to hierarchical models to capture variation at different levels of analysis. Because these models involve variables measured at different levels, they are sometimes called "multilevel models." Most commonly, individuals are nested within physical or geographic units, or time-specific measures are nested within individuals. As a few examples of the former type of nesting, consider students within classrooms or individuals within neighborhoods. As an example of the latter type of nesting, consider a panel study in which individuals are measured repeatedly across time. In such a case, the "group" is the individual, and the time-specific measures are nested within the individual. The examples here will follow this latter format—time-specific measures nested within individuals—although the underlying concepts of hierarchy are identical.

I discuss several types of such hierarchical regression models, beginning with an example that evaluates the extent to which Internet usage influences income using a two-wave panel study.[1] These data are from the 2000 and 2001 Current Population Survey Computer Use and Internet Supplement. This supplement measured, among other variables, individual use of computers and the Internet in 2000 and again in 2001 and allows us to examine the relationship between Internet usage and wages across a brief, but important, period of time when availability of broadband Internet connectivity was exploding. Wages in these examples have been transformed to 1982 dollars and are recoded into log-dollars per hour for additional analyses not presented here.

At the end of the chapter, I turn to an example that examines factors that influence health trajectories for individuals across age using a four-wave study (the National Health Epidemiologic Follow-up Surveys) discussed in previous chapters.

9.2.1 Random effects: The random intercept model

Generally, the goal of hierarchical modeling is to determine the extent to which factors measured at different levels influence an outcome using a typical regression modeling framework. OLS regression, however, is inappropriate, because of the lack of independence of errors for observations within groups. Thus, an alternative model must be developed to compensate for this lack of independence.

The foundation for the hierarchical regression model is the simple random effects model. Assume, as an example, that we observe a collection of individuals twice over a two-year period and ask their income at each point in time. It is most likely the case that each individual's income changes only slightly over the time period, and so, we could model the data such that each individual receives his/her own intercept (or mean). In equation form:

$$y_{it} = \alpha_i + e_{it},$$

with $\alpha_i \sim N(\alpha, \tau^2)$ and $e_{it} \sim N(0, \sigma^2)$. This specification shows that the outcome of interest (income; y) is considered a function of "variables" measured at two different levels: α_i is an individual (group) level variable, and e_{it} is a time-specific (individual) random error term.

An alternative, but equivalent, way to specify this model is to use probability notation. This approach clarifies the hierarchical nature of the model:

---

[1] I thank Bart Bonikowski and Paul DiMaggio for allowing me to use their Internet/income data in the examples.

$$y_{it} \sim N(\alpha_i, \sigma^2)$$
$$\alpha_i \sim N(\alpha, \tau^2)$$
$$\alpha \sim N(m, s^2)$$
$$\tau^2 \sim IG(a, b)$$
$$\sigma^2 \sim IG(c, d).$$

This specification says that an individual's time-specific income is a random normal variable with a mean equal to an individual-specific mean and some variance. The second equation shows that the individual-specific means themselves come from a (normal) distribution with a mean equal to some population mean and some variance. Finally, the last three equations specify hyperprior distributions for the population grand mean α, the population variance (around the mean) τ^2, and the error variance σ^2. The hyperprior distribution for the population mean is specified here to be normal, with parameters m and s^2; Without prior knowledge, these parameters should be specified to make the hyperprior vague (e.g., say $m = 0$ and $s^2 = 10,000$). The hyperprior distributions for the population variance and the error variance are inverse gamma distributions, with parameters a and b and c and d, respectively. Once again, without prior information, these parameters should be fixed to make the hyperprior vague.

In addition to being a simple random effects model, this model is sometimes called a "random intercept model," because the model can be viewed as a regression model with each α_i considered a group-specific intercept term arising from a (normal) probability distribution (at this point, with no covariates included).

To implement a Gibbs sampler for this model, we first need to construct the posterior distribution. The posterior distribution for this model is straightforward to derive following the hierarchical modeling structure using conditional distributions presented at the beginning of the chapter. The parameters of interest in the posterior distribution are the individual α_i, the population mean α, its variance τ^2, and the residual variance σ^2, and so our posterior density is:

$$p(\alpha, \tau^2, \alpha_i, \sigma^2 | Y) \propto p(Y | \alpha_i, \sigma^2) p(\alpha_i | \alpha, \tau^2) p(\alpha | m, s^2) p(\tau^2 | c, d) p(\sigma^2 | a, b).$$

To complete the specification of the posterior distribution, we simply need to replace each term with its actual distribution. As discussed above, the data are assumed to be normally distributed, and so the likelihood term is:

$$p(Y | \alpha_i, \sigma^2) \propto \prod_{i=1}^{n} \prod_{t=1}^{2} \frac{1}{\sqrt{\sigma^2}} \exp\left\{ -\frac{(y_{it} - \alpha_i)^2}{2\sigma^2} \right\}.$$

The distribution for each α_i is also normal and is:

$$p(\alpha_i|\alpha, \tau^2) \propto \prod_{i=1}^{n} \frac{1}{\sqrt{\tau^2}} \exp\left\{-\frac{(\alpha_i - \alpha)^2}{2\tau^2}\right\}.$$

The remaining terms are hyperprior distributions for the population mean (α), population random effects variance (τ^2), and residual variance (σ^2). As mentioned above, α is assumed to come from a normal distribution with parameters m and s^2, and the two variance parameters are assumed to come from inverse gamma distributions with parameters a and b and c and d, respectively. This implies the following joint hyperprior distribution:

$$p(\alpha|m, s^2)p(\tau^2|a, b)p(\sigma^2|c, d) \propto$$

$$\frac{1}{\sqrt{s^2}} \exp\left\{-\frac{(\alpha - m)^2}{2s^2}\right\} \times \frac{1}{(\tau^2)^{a+1}} \exp\left\{-b/(\tau^2)\right\} \times \frac{1}{(\sigma^2)^{c+1}} \exp\left\{-d/(\sigma^2)\right\}.$$

The full posterior, then, is simply the product of these three terms—the likelihood, prior, and hyperprior distributions. Although the posterior distribution can be simplified considerably by carrying out the multiplication of exponentials and combining like terms, it is simpler to derive the conditionals for the Gibbs sampler by leaving the posterior written as is. For the Gibbs sampler, we need the conditional distributions for each of the parameters; deriving them from the posterior is a simple but tedious matter of selecting only the terms that contain the parameter of interest, discarding all other multiplicative terms as proportionality constants, and simplifying/rearranging what's left to determine the resulting distribution. If we begin with the parameter α, the relevant terms in the posterior are:

$$p(\alpha|.) \propto p(\alpha_i|\alpha, \tau^2)p(\alpha)$$

$$\propto \left(\prod_{i=1}^{n} \frac{1}{\sqrt{\tau^2}} \exp\left\{-\frac{(\alpha_i - \alpha)^2}{2\tau^2}\right\}\right) \frac{1}{\sqrt{s^2}} \exp\left\{-\frac{(\alpha - m)^2}{2s^2}\right\}.$$

From this expression, the leading fractions involving the variances can be removed as normalizing constants (they do not depend on α), and the exponential expressions can be combined to obtain:

$$p(\alpha|.) \propto \exp\left\{\left(-\frac{1}{2}\right)\left(\frac{\tau^2(\alpha - m)^2 + s^2 \sum_{i=1}^{n}(\alpha_i - \alpha)^2}{\tau^2 s^2}\right)\right\}.$$

Next, we can expand the numerator of the exponential, extract terms not involving α as constants, and we have:

$$p(\alpha|.) \propto \exp\left\{\left(-\frac{1}{2}\right)\left(\frac{\tau^2\alpha^2 - 2\tau^2\alpha m - 2s^2\alpha \sum \alpha_i + ns^2\alpha^2}{\tau^2 s^2}\right)\right\}.$$

Rearranging terms, we obtain:

$$p(\alpha|.) \propto \exp\left\{\left(-\frac{1}{2}\right)\left(\frac{(\tau^2 + ns^2)\alpha^2 - 2\alpha(\tau^2 m + s^2 \sum \alpha_i)}{\tau^2 s^2}\right)\right\}.$$

As we did in Chapter 3, we can complete the square in α, and we find that the conditional posterior for α is:

$$p(\alpha|.) \propto N\left(\frac{\tau^2 m + s^2 \sum \alpha_i}{\tau^2 + ns^2}\,,\,\frac{\tau^2 s^2}{\tau^2 + ns^2}\right) \tag{9.2}$$

The conditional posterior distribution for each α_i is even easier to obtain. Once again, we begin with terms involving only α_i. We should realize, however, that, for each individual i, the only relevant terms in the product are those involving that particular individual. Thus, the conditional posterior for person i ($\forall i$) is:

$$p(\alpha_i|.) \propto p(Y|\alpha_i, \sigma^2)p(\alpha_i|\alpha, \tau^2)$$

$$\propto \left(\prod_{t=1}^{2} \frac{1}{\sqrt{\sigma^2}} \exp\left\{-\frac{(y_{it} - \alpha_i)^2}{2\sigma^2}\right\}\right)\left(\frac{1}{\sqrt{\tau^2}} \exp\left\{-\frac{(\alpha_i - \alpha)^2}{2\tau^2}\right\}\right).$$

We can follow the same steps as for α, and we obtain:

$$p(\alpha_i|.) \propto \exp\left\{\left(-\frac{1}{2}\right)\left(\frac{(2\tau^2 + \sigma^2)\alpha_i^2 - 2\alpha_i(\tau^2 \sum y_{it} + \sigma^2\alpha)}{\tau^2\sigma^2}\right)\right\}.$$

If we complete the square in α_i, we find that:

$$p(\alpha_i|.) \propto N\left(\frac{\tau^2 \sum y_{it} + \sigma^2\alpha}{2\tau^2 + \sigma^2}\,,\,\frac{\tau^2\sigma^2}{2\tau^2 + \sigma^2}\right). \tag{9.3}$$

The variance parameters σ^2 and τ^2 can be derived following the same strategy. The conditional posterior for σ^2 is:

$$p(\sigma^2|.) \propto p(Y|\alpha_i, \sigma^2)p(\sigma^2|a, b).$$

After substitution we obtain:

$$p(\sigma^2|.) \propto \left(\prod_{i=1}^{n}\prod_{t=1}^{2} \frac{1}{\sqrt{\sigma^2}} \exp\left\{-\frac{(y_{it} - \alpha_i)^2)}{2\sigma^2}\right\}\right)\frac{1}{(\sigma^2)^{c+1}} \exp\left\{-\frac{d}{\sigma^2}\right\},$$

and after some simplification, we get:

$$p(\sigma^2|.) \propto \left(\sigma^2\right)^{-(n+c+1)} \exp\left\{\frac{-\left(\sum_{i=1}^{n}\sum_{t=1}^{2}(y_{it}-\alpha_i)^2 + 2d\right)}{2\sigma^2}\right\}.$$

This result shows that the conditional posterior for σ^2 is an inverse gamma distribution:

$$p(\sigma^2|.) \propto IG\left(n+c, \ \frac{\sum_{i=1}^{n}\sum_{t=1}^{2}(y_{it}-\alpha_i)^2 + 2d}{2}\right). \qquad (9.4)$$

The conditional posterior for τ can be derived similarly. The posterior is:

$$p(\tau^2|.) \propto p(\alpha_i|\alpha, \tau^2)p(\tau^2)$$

$$\propto \left(\prod_{i=1}^{n}\frac{1}{\sqrt{\tau^2}}\exp\left\{-\frac{(\alpha_i-\alpha)^2}{2\tau^2}\right\}\right)\frac{1}{(\tau^2)^{a+1}}\exp\left\{-\frac{b}{\tau^2}\right\}.$$

After simplification, we obtain:

$$p(\tau^2|.) \propto IG\left(n/2+a+1, \ \frac{\sum_{i=1}^{n}(\alpha_i-\alpha)^2 + 2b}{2}\right) \qquad (9.5)$$

(see Exercises).

Given a complete set of conditional posterior distributions, we can implement a Gibbs sampler for the model by sequentially drawing from these conditionals. Below is an R program that conducts the Gibbs sampling:

```
#R program for simple random effects model
#read data
y=as.matrix(read.table("c:\\internet_examp.dat")[,3:4])

m=0; s2=10000; a=c=.001; b=d=.001; tau2=1; sigma2=1; malpha=0
n=nrow(y)

for(i in 1:20000){

#draw alpha_i
alpha= rnorm(n,
mean=(((tau2*(y[,1]+y[,2]))+sigma2*malpha)/(2*tau2+sigma2)),
sd=sqrt((tau2*sigma2)/(2*tau2+sigma2)))

#draw malpha
malpha=rnorm(1,
mean=(tau2*m+s2*sum(alpha))/((tau2+n*s2)),
sd=sqrt((tau2*s2)/((tau2+n*s2))))

#draw tau2
tau2=rgamma(1, shape=(n/2+a), rate=(sum((alpha-malpha)^2)+2*b)/2)
```

```
tau2=1/tau2

#draw sigma2
sigma2=rgamma(1, shape=n+c, rate=(sum((y-alpha)^2) +2*d)/2)
sigma2=1/sigma2

#write results to file
if(i%%10==0 | i==1)
  {print(c(i,alpha[1],malpha,tau2,sigma2))
   write(c(i,alpha[1],malpha,tau2,sigma2),
         file="c:\\bart2.out",append=T,ncol=5)}
}
```

As with previous programs, the first block reads in the data and establishes starting (and fixed) values for the parameters. The hyperparameters associated with the hyperpriors for α, τ^2, and σ^2 are fixed to 0, 10,000, .001, .001, .001, and .001, respectively, in order to ensure that the hyperparameters have little influence on the results (see Exercises). The starting values for the population/grand mean (α) as well as for τ^2 and σ^2 are arbitrarily set to benign values.

Subsequent sections of the program constitute nothing more than iteratively sampling from the conditional posterior distributions derived above.

Although this R program is relatively short, the derivation of the conditional distributions was a tedious process. Fortunately, however, a software package exists that allows us to simulate values from the posterior distributions for the parameters of this model more directly: WinBugs. WinBugs is a freely available software package that simplifies Gibbs sampling for a variety of models. The syntax for WinBugs is substantially similar to that of R, but many of the conditional posterior distribution derivations are done for us by WinBugs, reducing the need to derive the conditional posterior distributions manually. For example, a WinBugs program for the same example involves nothing more than specifying the likelihood, prior, and hyperprior distributions and parameter as follows:

```
#Winbugs program for simple random effects model
model
{
  for(i in 1:9249)
    {
    for(j in 1:2)
      {
       y[i,j]~dnorm(alpha[i],sigma2inv)
      }
    alpha[i]~dnorm(malpha,tau2inv)
    }
  malpha~dnorm(0,1.0E-4)

  tau2inv~dgamma(.01,.01)
```

```
tau2<-1/sqrt(tau2inv)

sigma2inv~dgamma(.01,.01)
sigma2<-1/sqrt(sigma2inv)
}
```

The syntax in this program is similar to that of R with a few exceptions. First, the tilde is used to simulate from distributions. Second, "$< -$" is used to assign values to variables.[2] Third, the parameterization of the normal distribution in WinBugs involves a precision parameter rather than a variance parameter. The precision is simply the inverse of the variance, and so, we can recover the variance parameter simply by inverting the draw from the gamma distribution for the precision parameters.

The key results from the R program, the equivalent WinBugs program, and the equivalent maximum likelihood results obtained from STATA (versions 8 and 9 were used throughout) using the xtreg procedure are presented in Table 9.2. As the results show, all three approaches yielded virtually the same results and therefore lead to the same conclusions. The Bayesian results, however, whether from R or WinBugs, yield more information by default than the STATA results, because the Bayesian approach yields distributions for all parameters/quantities of interest, including the variance parameters.

Table 9.2. Results of hierarchical model for two-wave panel of income and Internet use data.

Variable	R	WinBugs	STATA xtreg
Population Mean (α)	2.103(.005)	2.103(.005)	NA
Intercept	NA	NA	2.103(.005)
$\sqrt{\tau^2}$	0.434(.004)	0.434(.004)	0.434
$\sqrt{\sigma^2}$	0.311(.002)	0.311(.002)	0.311
$\tau^2/(\tau^2 + \sigma^2)$	0.661(.006)	0.660(.006)	0.660

Note: Posterior means (and posterior standard deviations) are reported for R and WinBugs algorithms. Generalized least squares estimates (and standard errors) are reported for STATA.

Overall, these results indicate that mean log wages are 2.103 log-dollars per hour with a standard deviation of .434 log-dollars. Within individuals, the standard deviation of wages was .311 log-dollars, and the ratio of the between-individual to total variance is about 66%. This result suggests that much of the variation we observe in log-wages—as we might expect—is due

---

[2] This syntax can also be used in R, but I have generally not done so throughout the text.

to differences between individuals and not within individuals across the two-year period. As a side note, the total variance in hourly wages is equal to $\tau^2 + \sigma^2$. Because we obtain estimates for both of these variances—the "between-individual" and "within-individual" variances—hieararchical models like this one are sometimes called "variance components" models.

The next step in our hierarchical modeling approach is to allow variation in the group level parameters to be functions of group level variables and to let the individual level (here, time-specific level) random error term to be a function of individual level variables. First, for example, we could include group level characteristics in our model by decomposing the random intercept into a regression on group level variables. For example, suppose we now wish to determine whether sex influences respondents' wages. In that case, we can specify the model as:

$$y_{it} \sim N(\alpha_i + \alpha_{(1)}\text{sex}_i, \, \sigma^2)$$
$$\alpha_i \sim N(\alpha_{(0)}, \tau^2)$$
$$\alpha_{(0)} \sim N(m0, s0)$$
$$\sigma^2 \sim IG(a, b)$$
$$\alpha_{(1)} \sim N(m1, s1)$$
$$\tau^2 \sim IG(c, d).$$

Essentially the only substantial difference between this and the previous model is that the individual-specific intercept has now been decomposed into a population intercept and an effect of sex. A WinBugs program for this model is simple to specify from these distributions:

```
model
{
 for(i in 1:9249)
   {
    for(t in 1:2)
      {
       y[i,t]~dnorm(alpha[i],sigma2inv)
      }
    alpha[i]~dnorm(mu[i],tau2inv)
    mu[i]<-alpha0+alpha1*sex[i]
   }
 alpha0~dnorm(0,1.0E-4)
 alpha1~dnorm(0,1.0E-4)

 sigma2inv~dgamma(.01,.01)
 sigma2<-1/sqrt(sigma2inv)

 tau2inv~dgamma(.01,.01)
 tau2<-1/sqrt(tau2inv)
}
```

In this program, I have specified independent (univariate) normal distribution priors for the population mean and the parameter representing the influence of sex. The fact that I have specified independent priors, however, does not imply that the two parameters are necessarily uncorrelated in the posterior. In fact, the two parameters are highly negatively correlated, as Figure 9.1 shows.

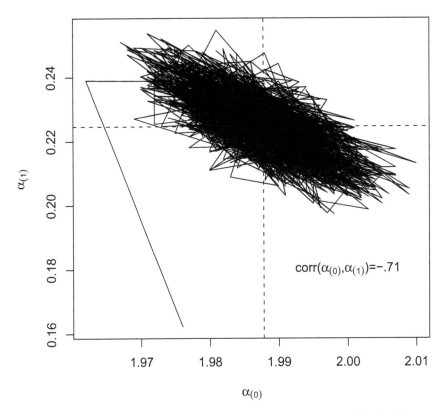

Fig. 9.1. Two-dimensional trace plot of $\alpha_{(0)}$ and $\alpha_{(1)}$ parameters (dashed lines at posterior means for each parameter).

The posterior mean for the adjusted population mean ($\alpha_{(0)}$) was 1.99 (s.d. = .007), and the mean for the influence of sex ($\alpha_{(1)}$) was .225 (s.d. = .0098), indicating that males have higher log wages. The only additional change between this and the previous model is the magnitude of τ^2. Recall that τ^2 reflects unexplained between-individual variation in the random intercept for log-wages. With the inclusion of sex as an explantory variable differentiating individuals' wages, τ^2 has been reduced. Its posterior mean is now .419 (s.d. of .004), which is a reduction of 3.5% over the mean value obtained under the previous model. This reduction can be viewed as an R^2 term; put another way, sex differences account for 3.5% of the between-individual variance in wages.

Additional time-invariant variables can be easily included to further account for between-individual variation in wages. But what if we would like to consider the influence of time-varying covariates? For example, suppose we are interested in examining the extent to which Internet usage at a given point in time influences wages at the same point in time. Our data include time-specific measures of Internet usage, measured at the same points in time that wages are measured. There are two ways we can accomplish this goal. First, we can allow such covariates to influence the time-specific outcomes directly:

$$y_{it} \sim N(\alpha_i + \alpha_{(1)}\text{sex}_i + \alpha_{(2)}\text{Internet}_{it},\ \sigma^2)$$
$$\alpha_i \sim N(\alpha_{(0)}, \tau^2)$$
$$\alpha_{(0)} \sim N(m0, s0)$$
$$\alpha_{(1)} \sim N(m1, s1)$$
$$\alpha_{(2)} \sim N(m2, s2)$$
$$\sigma^2 \sim IG(a, b)$$
$$\tau^2 \sim IG(c, d)$$

In this model, time-specific wages are considered a function of individual random intercepts and time-specific Internet usage indicators, and the random intercepts are considered a function of a grand mean and an indicator for sex.[3] A WinBugs program to implement this model is as follows:

```
model
{
  for(i in 1:9249)
    {
    for(t in 1:2)
      {
      y[i,t]~dnorm(mu[i,t],sigma2inv)
      mu[i,t]<-(alpha[i]+alpha1*sex[i])+alpha2*internet[i,t]
      }
    alpha[i]~dnorm(alpha0,tau2inv)
    }
  alpha0~dnorm(0,1.0E-4)
  alpha1~dnorm(0,1.0E-4)
  alpha2~dnorm(0,1.0E-4)

  sigma2inv~dgamma(.01,.01)
  sigma2<-1/sqrt(sigma2inv)
```

---

[3] An equivalent way of specifying this model is: $y_{it} \sim N(\alpha_i + \alpha_{(2)}\text{Internet}_{it},\ \sigma^2)$, with $\alpha_i \sim N(\alpha_0 + \alpha_{(1)}\text{sex}_i,\ \tau^2)$.

```
tau2inv~dgamma(.01,.01)
tau2<-1/sqrt(tau2inv)
}
```

This program is only slightly more complicated than the previous programs. The only substantial differences are that (1) we have included the new parameter $(\alpha_{(2)})$ within the double loop (i, t), and (2) we have incorporated a prior distribution for it. The results of this model suggest that Internet usage does, in fact, influence income. The posterior mean for the influence of Internet usage is .18 (s.d. $= .0075$), and the intercept $(\alpha_{(0)})$ falls to 1.86 (s.d. $=$ .009).

9.2.2 Random effects: The random coefficient model

As written, the last model in the previous section forces the effect of Internet usage to be constant across time: There was only a single parameter representing the effect of Internet usage on wages. This constraint may introduce error into the model if, in fact, the influence of Internet usage on wages varies across time. Thus, a second way we can include this time-varying variable is to allow the influence of Internet usage to vary across time. This model is:

$$y_{it} \sim N(\alpha_i + \alpha_{(1)}\text{sex}_i + \alpha_{(2t)}\text{Internet}_{it}, \sigma^2)$$
$$\alpha_i \sim N(\alpha_{(0)}, \tau^2)$$
$$\alpha_{(0)} \sim N(m0, s0)$$
$$\alpha_{(1)} \sim N(m1, s1)$$
$$\alpha_{(21)} \sim N(m2, s2)$$
$$\alpha_{(22)} \sim N(m3, s3)$$
$$\sigma^2 \sim IG(a, b)$$
$$\tau^2 \sim IG(c, d)$$

The alterations of the WinBugs program to accommodate this new parameter are very slight: The `alpha2` parameter must be subscripted appropriately (i.e., `alpha2[t]`), and an additional hyperprior distribution must be incorporated. By some terminologies, we can now call the model a *random coefficient model*, because a *slope*—and not simply an intercept—is now considered a function of other variables.[4]

---

[4] It may be easier to recognize that allowing `alpha2` to vary across time implies that `alpha2` is now a slope, and not simply an intercept, if we consider that our current representation is equivalent to specifying α_2 to be a function of a dummy variable reflecting time of measurement: $\alpha_2 = \beta_0 + \beta_1 I(t = 2)$, where β_1 is a regression slope.

The results of this model do not vary substantially from those obtained when the effect of Internet usage was treated as constant. However, the influence of Internet usage at time 1 was found to be .167 (s.d. = .009), while the effect of Internet usage at time 2 was .188 (s.d. = .008). A distribution for a new variable representing the difference between these parameters was constructed in order to determine whether this difference is greater than 0; 99.9% of the mass of the resulting distribution was above 0 (posterior mean of .02; s.d. = .006), which indicates that Internet usage indeed influenced wages to a greater extent at the second wave of the study than at the first wave.

From a substantive perspective, this result seems to be more consistent with the view that Internet usage influences income than the view that wages influence Internet usage. That is, Internet availability has become less dependent on income over time as the hardware for accessing the Internet (i.e., computers and modems), as well as Internet service, has become cheaper. If wages influenced Internet usage, on the other hand, we might expect the influence of wages on Internet use to decrease rather than increase over the period of observation. Thus, the result we obtained may be explained such that Internet usage builds social capital, allowing individuals to find or acquire better, higher paying jobs.

One could still argue, however, that higher paying jobs have become increasingly dependent on Internet usage/access, and that a polarization of the labor market is occurring. Thus, higher paid workers have increasingly come to use the Internet, while lower paid jobs continue to not require Internet access/use.

The relationship between Internet usage and income may not just vary across time; it may vary across individuals. For example, individuals in low-income, low-skill occupations may get less of a return to their income from using the Internet. In contrast, individuals in high-skilled occupations may get a large return to their income from using the Internet. In order to examine this possibility, we can alter the model so that the $\alpha_{(2)}$ parameter varies by individual (i) rather than by time (t). Thus, the model becomes:

$$y_{it} \sim N(\alpha_i + \alpha_{(1)}\text{sex}_i + \alpha_{(2i)}\text{Internet}_{it},\ \sigma^2)$$
$$\alpha_i \sim N(\alpha_{(0)}, \tau^2)$$
$$\alpha_{(2i)} \sim N(\alpha_{(20)}, \tau_2^2)$$
$$\alpha_{(0)} \sim N(m0, s0)$$
$$\alpha_{(1)} \sim N(m1, s1)$$
$$\alpha_{(20)} \sim N(m2, s2)$$
$$\sigma^2 \sim IG(a, b)$$
$$\tau^2 \sim IG(c, d)$$
$$\tau_2^2 \sim IG(e, f)$$

This model is easily implemented in WinBugs with only minor changes to our previous programs:

```
model
{
 for(i in 1:9249)
  {
    for(t in 1:2)
     {
       y[i,t]~dnorm(mu[i,t],sigma2inv)
       mu[i,t]<-alpha[i]+alpha1*sex[i]+alpha2[i]*internet[i,t]
     }
    alpha[i]~dnorm(alpha0,tau2inv)
    alpha2[i]~dnorm(alpha20,tau20inv)
   }
  alpha0~dnorm(0,1.0E-4)
  alpha1~dnorm(0,1.0E-4)
  alpha20~dnorm(0,1.0E-4)

  sigma2inv~dgamma(.01,.01)
  sigma2<-1/sqrt(sigma2inv)

  tau2inv~dgamma(.01,.01)
  tau2<-1/sqrt(tau2inv)

  tau20inv~dgamma(.01,.01)
  tau20<-1/sqrt(tau20inv)
}
```

The results of this model suggest that there is considerable variation in the relationship between Internet usage and income across individuals. The estimated mean effect of Internet usage ($\alpha_{(2i)}$) was .205, and the estimated standard deviation for this effect (τ_2) was .224. This result yields (under the assumption that the random effect $\alpha_{(2)}$ is normally distributed) a 95% probability interval for the influence of Internet usage of [-.234, .644], which indicates that Internet usage may be, in some cases, harmful to wages (playing games at the office, lowering productivity?!).

What factors determine the influence of Internet usage on wages? In other words, why do some people appear to benefit from using the Internet, whereas others do not? We have previously decomposed the individual-specific random intercepts into an adjusted intercept and an effect of respondent's sex. When we begin to allow regression parameters (like the the one capturing the influence of Internet usage) to vary across individuals, we can also decompose it into a regression on higher level factors. For example, suppose we assumed that sex not only influenced the random intercept for wages, but also that it influences the extent to which Internet usage affects income. We can easily incorporate this idea into our model as follows. I switch notation slightly to avoid confusion:

$$y_{it} \sim N(\alpha_i + \beta_i \text{Internet}_{it}, \sigma^2)$$
$$\alpha_i \sim N(\alpha_{(0)} + \alpha_{(1)} \text{sex}_i, \tau_\alpha^2)$$
$$\beta_i \sim N(\beta_{(0)} + \beta_{(1)} \text{sex}_i, \tau_\beta^2)$$
$$\alpha_{(0)} \sim N(m1, s1)$$
$$\alpha_{(1)} \sim N(m2, s2)$$
$$\beta_{(0)} \sim N(m3, s3)$$
$$\beta_{(1)} \sim N(m4, s4)$$
$$\tau_\alpha^2 \sim IG(a, b)$$
$$\tau_\beta^2 \sim IG(c, d)$$
$$\sigma^2 \sim IG(e, f)$$

This model clarifies the hierarchical structuring of the data and parameters. Each individual's income is a function of his/her own intercept and slope, and these individual-level intercepts and slopes are determined, in part, by sex—a characteristic that differentiates individuals. The model consists of seven vague hyperprior distributions, one for each of the parameters that are not themselves endogenous within the model.

This model is sometimes called a multilevel or hierarchical model with cross-level interactions. The cross-level interactions, although not immediately apparent in the above specification, can be observed if we revert to the equation-based, more classical representation of the model. Under that approach:

$$y_{it} = \alpha_i + \beta_i \text{Internet}_{it} + e_{it}$$
$$\alpha_i = \alpha_{(0)} + \alpha_{(1)} \text{sex}_i + u_i$$
$$\beta_i = \beta_{(0)} + \beta_{(1)} \text{sex}_i + v_i,$$

with appropriate specifications for the variances of the errors at each level. If we then substitute the expressions for α_i and β_i into the first equation, we obtain:

$$y_{it} =$$
$$\alpha_{(0)} + \alpha_{(1)} \text{sex}_i + u_i + \beta_{(0)} \text{Internet}_{it} + \beta_{(1)} \text{sex}_i \times \text{Internet}_{it} + v_i \text{Internet}_{it} + e_{it}.$$

In this representation, we have a grand mean ($\alpha_{(0)}$) and an individual adjustment to it (u_i), a main effect of sex ($\alpha_{(1)}$), a time-constant main effect of Internet usage (β_0) and an individual adjustment to it (v_i), an interaction effect between sex and Internet usage ($\beta_{(1)}$), and an error term (e_{it}). The interaction term is considered a cross-level interaction, because sex is measured at the individual level (the "group" in this context), whereas Internet usage is measured at the within-individual level. Historically, prior to the widespread use of hierarchical modeling, this model was estimated simply using OLS regression with the relevant interaction. However, as we have discussed, and as this equation shows, the OLS approach is not optimal, because it absorbs the various random quantities (i.e., u_i, $v_i$internet$_{it}$, and e_{it}) into a single error term for each individual. These error terms are assumed to be independent across time-specific observations, but, as the single subscripting for u_i and v_i suggest, they are not truly independent.

Returning to the Bayesian specification, the model can be implemented very easily in WinBugs with the following code:

```
model
{
 for(i in 1:9249)
   {
    for(t in 1:2)
      {
       y[i,t]~dnorm(mu[i,t],sigma2inv)
       mu[i,t]<-alpha[i]+beta[i]*internet[i,t]
      }
   alpha[i]~dnorm(ma[i],tauinv.alpha)
   beta[i]~dnorm(mb[i],tauinv.beta)
   ma[i]<-alpha0 + alpha1*sex[i]
   mb[i]<-beta0 + beta1*sex[i]
   }
 alpha0~dnorm(0,1.0E-4)
 alpha1~dnorm(0,1.0E-4)
 beta0~dnorm(0,1.0E-4)
 beta1~dnorm(0,1.0E-4)

 sigma2inv~dgamma(.01,.01)
 sigma2<-1/sqrt(sigma2inv)

 tauinv.alpha~dgamma(.01,.01)
 tau.alpha<-1/sqrt(tauinv.alpha)

 tauinv.beta~dgamma(.01,.01)
 tau.beta<-1/sqrt(tauinv.beta)
}
```

The key results of this model are not only that men make higher wages than women ($\alpha_{(0)} = 1.86$; $\alpha_{(1)} = .20$), but also that Internet usage has substantially higher returns for men than for women ($\beta_{(0)} = .18$; $\beta_{(1)} = .05$). In fact, based on these point estimates, the return to income of Internet usage for men is 28% greater than it is for women. A 95% interval estimate of this percentage is [11%, 48%].

9.2.3 Growth models

Often, we may wish to include time as one of our variables affecting an outcome. For example, in the previous model, we allowed the effect of Internet usage on wages to vary across individuals, but we could also consider that wages grow at differential rates for individuals. Similarly, we found earlier that the influence of Internet usage on wages varied across time. We may therefore consider specifying a model in which wages are expected to grow at differential rates for individuals, with Internet usage influencing the rate of growth. This type of model is often called a "growth model," or "latent growth model," because we are modeling the time-specific outcomes as realizations of an underlying growth process that unfolds across age/time at the individual level. Such a model may look like:

$$y_{it} \sim N(\alpha_i + \beta_i t_{it}, \sigma^2)$$
$$\alpha_i \sim N(\alpha_{(0)} + \alpha_{(1)}\text{sex}_i + \alpha_{(2)}\text{Internet}_i, \tau_\alpha^2)$$
$$\beta_i \sim N(\beta_{(0)} + \beta_{(1)}\text{sex}_i + \beta_{(2)}\text{internet}_i, \tau_\beta^2)$$
$$\alpha_{(0)} \sim N(m1, s1)$$
$$\alpha_{(1)} \sim N(m2, s2)$$
$$\alpha_{(2)} \sim N(m3, s3)$$
$$\beta_{(0)} \sim N(m4, s4)$$
$$\beta_{(1)} \sim N(m5, s5)$$
$$\beta_{(2)} \sim N(m6, s6)$$
$$\tau_\alpha^2 \sim IG(a, b)$$
$$\tau_\beta^2 \sim IG(c, d)$$
$$\sigma^2 \sim IG(e, f).$$

Although this model has a lengthy specification, it is has a fairly straightforward interpretation. Individual wages are expected to start and grow at individual-specific levels and rates (α_i and β_i, respectively). An individual's specific level and rate is then seen as depending on his/her sex and Internet usage. The remaining lines of the model specification are simply hyperpriors for the various parameters.

A couple of notes are in order regarding the growth model presented above. First, I have included Internet usage measured only at the first point in time. The reason for this is that the model is underidentified if we attempt to estimate it with Internet usage treated as a time-varying covariate influencing individual-specific effects of time (see Exercises). Second, given that this model only consists of two waves of data, the model is only measuring the extent to which sex and Internet usage influence change in wages over a single time interval, making the model nothing more than a slightly different parameterization of a change score regression model. Third, because of the limited number of waves, some additional constraints must be enforced. One is that the error variance σ^2 must be constrained to be time invariant. Often, growth models allow this parameter to vary across time (see Bollen and Curran 2006), but here we simply cannot allow that, given our limitation of having only two time-specific measures per person. The results of this model can be found in Table 9.3.

Table 9.3. Results of "growth" model for two-wave panel of income and Internet use data.

Parameter Meaning	Parameter	Posterior Mean(s.d.)
Adjusted intercept for time-1 wages	α_0	1.74(.016)
Influence of sex on wages	α_1	0.259(.015)
Influence of Internet on wages	α_2	0.296(.016)
Adjusted intercept for change in wages	β_0	0.033(.009)
Influence of sex on change in wages	β_1	−0.013(.009)
Influence of Internet on change in wages	β_2	0.006(.009)
Residual variance in wages	σ^2	0.308(.002)
Residual variance in time-1 wages	τ_α^2	0.383(.004)
Residual variance in change in wages	τ_β^2	0.061(.006)

Note: Posterior means (and posterior standard deviations) are reported.

These results indicate that sex and Internet usage each influence baseline wages, with men earning more than women (see $\alpha_{(1)}$) and Internet users earning more than nonusers (see α_2). Indeed, the Internet effect is roughly 20% larger than the sex effect. The results also indicate that wages grew slightly across the one-year time period (see $\beta_{(0)}$). Wages grew less for men (see $\beta_{(1)}$), but more for Internet users (see $\beta_{(2)}$), although this effect was slight at best (observe the posterior standard deviation for $\beta_{(2)}$ compared with its mean). These results may also be written in equation form to clarify their interpretation:

$$E(\text{wages}_{it}) = \alpha_i + \beta_i$$
$$E(\alpha_i) = 1.74 + .259\text{male}_i + .296\text{Internet}_{i1}$$
$$E(\beta_i) = .033 - .013\text{male}_i + .006\text{internet}_{i1}.$$

For a fuller, more detailed example involving more time points of measurement, I examine health trajectories of individuals across a 20-year span. My assumption is that health tends to decline across the life course of individuals, and that baseline health and the rate of decline in health are a function of age, sex, race, area and type of residence, and education. My primary interest is in examining how socioeconomic status (measured by education) influences the health differential across time. One hypothesis in the literature—the cumulative advantage hypothesis—argues that the health gap between high and low SES groups widens across age as a function of the cumulative disadvantage that low SES generates across the life course (see Lynch 2003). At young ages, risk factors like smoking and lack of health care access matter little, because most young adults are quite healthy. However, across age, exposure to risk factors accumulates and produces a larger health differential. An alternate hypothesis is the age-as-leveler hypothesis. This hypothesis argues that the health gap narrows across age because age overwhelms all risk factors—the biological effect of aging supercedes any socially based risk factor (see House et al. 1994). Often a selective mortality argument is also advanced to support this hypothesis: that the observed health gap at a particular age is ultimately a between-individual measure, and only the health of survivors is observed. Thus, those with the poorest health have been eliminated from the observed population, and the gap is simply a comparison of a robust subset of lower SES individuals with higher SES individuals. In other words, there are different populations being compared at young and older ages (see Lynch 2003 for extensive discussion).

A life course perspective suggests that we should examine trajectories of health for individuals, and that selective mortality should be "controlled out." One way to do this is to allow decedents to be included in the model, rather than to exclude them, as cross-sectional analyses must do (because only survivors can be observed in a cross-section). A Bayesian growth model can easily handle the unbalanced data that result from mortality, and health trajectories can even be estimated for individuals for whom we only observe a single measure. Their trajectories become a compromise between their observed measures and those of persons with similar covariate profiles who do survive. Ultimately, this approach underestimates the rate of decline in health, because surviving low-SES individuals drive the estimate of the mean growth rate, and surely decedents have/had steeper—but unobserved—rates of health decline. However, this argument implies that the finding with regard to the cumulative advantage hypothesis are conservative.

For this example, I again use the data from the National Health and Nutrition Examination Survey (NHANES) and its follow-ups, the National Health Epidemiologic Follow-up Surveys (NHEFS) (see Chapter 8 for a description). After eliminating individuals who were missing on one or another variable in the analyses and individuals whose final status in 1992 was unknown, the analytic sample consisted of 6,403 persons.

In this example, I include only individuals who were between 30 and 34 years of age at baseline, because age presents a problem in these analyses: The variable "age" represents both age and cohort. Research has shown that a common pattern for the health gap between individuals with low versus high SES across age is divergent until midlife and then convergent after (see House et al. 1994). This pattern is a function of two things: selective mortality and cohort change in the importance of education in affecting health (see Lynch

2003). Thus, for the sake of simplicity in this example, I restrict the analyses to the 608 individuals who fall in this age range, eliminating cohort effects.

I include age (mean = 32.0, s.d. = 1.4), sex (male = 1, 41.6%), race (non-white = 1, 12.3%), region (south = 1, 28.1%), urban residence (urban = 1, 23.2%), and education (in years, mean = 12.6, s.d. = 2.6, minimum = 0, maximum = 17) as second-level covariates that may influence the random intercept and slope factors. The outcome measure is self-rated health measured on a 5-point Likert scale ranging from excellent health (5) to poor health (1). Health measured on a 5-point scale is known to be a reliable and valid indicator of health (especially at younger ages), and the data are fairly symmetric, with a slight skew toward excellent health. I expect that individuals random intercepts are relatively high, and that in general, health declines between 30 and 55—the age range covered by the study. Furthermore, I expect that education differentiates health at baseline, with higher educated individuals having better health than lower educated ones. Finally, if the cumulative advantage hypothesis is true at least prior to age 55, education serves to reduce the rate of decline in health. This hypothesis implies that the growth rate in health is negative in general, but that education's influence on the growth rate is positive.

Below is the WinBugs program specifying the growth model:

```
model
{
 for(i in 1:608)
   {
    for(t in 1:pyrs[i])
      {
       h[i,t]~dnorm(mu[i,t],sigma2inv)
       mu[i,t]<-alpha[i]+beta[i]*yr[i,t]
      }
    alpha[i]~dnorm(ma[i],tauinv.alpha)
    beta[i]~dnorm(mb[i],tauinv.beta)
    ma[i]<-alpha0 + alpha1*age[i] + alpha2*male[i] + alpha3*nonw[i] +
          alpha4*south[i] + alpha5*urban[i] + alpha6*educ[i]
    mb[i]<-beta0             + beta2*male[i]  + beta3*nonw[i]  +
          beta4*south[i]  + beta5*urban[i]  + beta6*educ[i]
   }
 alpha0~dnorm(0,1.0E-4)
 alpha1~dnorm(0,1.0E-4)
 alpha2~dnorm(0,1.0E-4)
 alpha3~dnorm(0,1.0E-4)
 alpha4~dnorm(0,1.0E-4)
 alpha5~dnorm(0,1.0E-4)
 alpha6~dnorm(0,1.0E-4)
 beta0~dnorm(0,1.0E-4)
 beta2~dnorm(0,1.0E-4)
 beta3~dnorm(0,1.0E-4)
 beta4~dnorm(0,1.0E-4)
```

```
beta5~dnorm(0,1.0E-4)
beta6~dnorm(0,1.0E-4)

sigma2inv~dgamma(.01,.01)
sigma2<-1/sqrt(sigma2inv)

tauinv.alpha~dgamma(.01,.01)
tau.alpha<-1/sqrt(tauinv.alpha)

tauinv.beta~dgamma(.01,.01)
tau.beta<-1/sqrt(tauinv.beta)
}
```

This program, although longer than our previous growth model program because of the inclusion of additional level 2 covariates, is only slightly different from it. In order for WinBugs to handle unbalanced data—that is, data collected at different times and on different numbers of occasions for different respondents—I include a variable called pyrs, which tells the program at how many occasions the respondent was interviewed, and time of measurement is treated as a time-specific, individual-level variable. Individuals who die— or are lost—before the first follow-up (after baseline) contribute only a single person-year record and single measure of time. Persons who die—or are lost— before the second follow-up contribute two person-year records, etc. In these data, there are 16 persons who contribute one person-year record, 7 persons who contribute two records, 6 who contribute three, and 579 who contribute the maximum of four. These data provide some initial indication that there is some education-based selective mortality: The mean for education among persons who contribute 4 person-records is 12.7, whereas the mean for those who contribute fewer records is 10.9. In other words, the less-educated die earlier than the more-educated.

The remainder of the model is virtually identical to the one presented earlier, only with more covariates and therefore more hyperprior distributions. One note is in order: I do not include the effect of respondent's age on growth. The reason for this is that for age to influence the growth rate, either (1) the underlying latent health trajectories must be assumed to be nonlinear or (2) there are cohort differences in growth rates (see Mehta and West 2000).

I ran the program for 10,000 iterations and retained the last 1,000 samples for inference. Figure 9.2 shows 200 sampled values for the random intercepts and random slopes for four individuals. Person 1 only survived through the first wave of the study; person 17 survived through two waves; person 24 survived through three waves; and person 35 survived through all four waves. As the figure shows, the scatter of points is widest for person 1, reflecting the lack of certainty about this individual's true random intercept and slope values due to the existence of only one observed measure for his health. As the number of time points observed increases, the variance in the random intercept and slope for each individual decreases. For example, in the bottom right plot, the random intercept and slope scatter is centered very narrowly over approximately $(3, -.08)$, which indicates that we are fairly certain that this individual's latent trajectory starts around 3 health units at baseline and declines about .08 units per year.

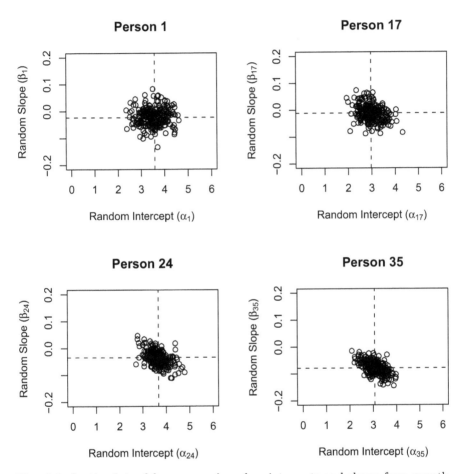

Fig. 9.2. Scatterplots of four persons' random intercepts and slopes from growth curve model of health (posterior means superimposed as horizontal and vertical dashed lines).

Table 9.4 presents the posterior means and standard deviations for the model parameters. The columns in the table report the influence of each covariate on the random intercept and random slope. The intercept for the random intercept term was 4.52. Older persons (recall the age range was only 30-34) reported worse health than younger persons at baseline $(-.06)$. Men reported better health at baseline than women (.05), and persons from the South reported worse health (−.05), but these effects were not substantially different from 0, based on posterior probabilities that the parameters were greater than (or less than) 0, truncated to the p-value ranges used by classical statistics (i.e., $p < .05$). Nonwhites and persons living in urban areas reported worse health than whites and persons living in other areas. Finally, education had a strong, positive effect on baseline health.

Almost none of the covariates influenced the random slope. The intercept for the random slope was negative, implying that the tendency was for health to decline slightly across the 20-year period. Males and nonwhites had a slightly steeper decline in health, although these effects would not be statistically significant by classical standards. Persons from the South and from urban areas had shallower declines in health than persons from other areas, although, again, these effects would not be statistically significant by classical standards. Finally, education had the expected positive effect (.001, $p < .1$), indicating that health trajectories do diverge across age (for the range from age 30 to age 55), such that persons with more education experience a shallower decline in health across age than persons with less education. Indeed, although the coefficient's magnitude appears small, the results indicate that a person with 17 years of schooling (the maximum) would experience a rate of health decline only 43% as great as a person with 0 years of schooling and only 76% as great as a person with 12 years of schooling.

Table 9.4. Results of growth curve model of health across time.

Variable	Random Intercept	Random Slope
Intercept	4.52(.70)***	−0.03(.01)**
Age	−0.06(.02)**	
Male	0.05(.08)	−0.006(.005)
Nonwhite	−0.54(.11)***	−0.006(.008)
South	−0.05(.08)	0.003(.005)
Urban	−0.23(.08)***	0.003(.005)
Education	0.11(.01)***	0.001(.0009)#
Variance	0.37(.03)	0.001(.0001)
Within-ind. Variance	0.42(.02)	

Note: The Bayesian estimates are posterior means. The p-values are the probabilities that the parameter exceeds 0 (either positively or negatively), truncated to the classical cutpoints of $\#p < .1$, $*p < .05$, $**p < .01$, $***p < .001$.

The results can be used in two ways to predict health trajectories. First, we may directly use the simulated latent intercepts and slopes for individuals *in the sample* (as shown in Figure 9.2). For example, we could use the posterior means for these simulated intercepts and slopes to construct an expected trajectory: $y_{it} = \mu_{\alpha_i} + \mu_{\beta_i} \times t$. Second, we may use the posterior distributions for the model parameters—the covariate effects—to compute predicted latent intercepts and slopes for persons with particular covariate profiles. This approach allows us to predict trajectories for individuals *out of the sample*, in addition to those in the sample. Person 1 shown in Figure 9.2 was a 31-year-old nonwhite male living in a non-southern, urban area with 11 years of schooling. Based on the posterior means for the effects of the covariates, this individual would have a predicted intercept of 3.22 for his health trajectory and a predicted slope of $-.022$.

Figure 9.3 shows these two types of predicted trajectories for the four individuals shown in the previous figure, along with their observed health measures. The solid line in each graph shows the predicted trajectory based on the posterior means of the simulated, individual-specific random intercepts and slopes (i.e., the simulated values from Figure 9.2). The dashed line in each graph shows the model predicted trajectory based on the posterior means of the parameters applied to each individual's covariate profile.

There is a substantial difference between these two trajectories, as well as between either trajectory and the observed health measures. This variation reflects the different types of (error) variance captured by the model. The discrepancies between the solid-line trajectories and the observed health measures are captured by the within-individual error variance parameter σ^2. In brief, we do not expect each individual's health measure to fall exactly on the solid line, because a number of unobserved factors may "bump" an individual off of his/her expected, latent health trajectory at any point in time. Instead, what the model has attempted to capture is the best fitting line for the observed health measures. This error may be reduced by including time-specific measures into the model as we did in the previous section in the model in which we included Internet usage as a time-varying covariate.

The discrepancies between the solid and dashed-line trajectories, on the other hand, reflect the extent of between-individual variation captured (or not!) by the covariates in the model. Put another way, if the covariates *perfectly* explained all differences between individuals' health trajectories, the solid and dashed lines would perfectly coincide. The fact that these lines are not overlapping suggests that our covariates do a poor job differentiating individuals in the sample. This conclusion is foretold by the lack of strong results in Table 9.4, especially with respect to the general lack of effect of covariates on the latent growth rate. Indeed, if we consider the estimated rate of decline in health for each individual in Figure 9.3, all four individuals are expected to have similar, shallow rates of health decline that obviously do not match the observed health declines (or those predicted by the simulated individual-specific random effects). In contrast, the estimated intercepts for these trajectories show greater variability, reflecting the stronger effects of the covariates in predicting baseline health. In an additional model (not shown), I re-estimated this growth model with no covariates to obtain estimates of the variance of the mean latent intercept and slope. An R^2 for the effects of the covariates on the estimated latent intercept was found by computing $1 - \tau^2_{\alpha,\text{cov}}/\tau^2_{\alpha,\text{nocov}}$, using the posterior means for these variance parameters from the two models. A similar calculation was performed for the variance of the latent slope (τ^2_β). The results indicated that the covariates reduced the between-individual variance in the latent intercept by 29% (i.e., $R^2 = .29$), but the covariates reduced the between-individual variance in the latent slope by only 10%. These results confirm that our covariates have little effect on the latent slope, and therefore, it is no surprise that our two types of predicted trajectories differ substantially.

As a final note on growth modeling, the use of growth models has been rapidly expanding in psychology and sociology over the last decade, in part because the growing availability of longitudinal (panel) data has enabled the investigation of life course processes for which growth modeling is well suited. Additionally, growth models have become increasingly popular, because they can be estimated via a variety of software packages, including HLM and various structural equation modeling packages (see Willett and Sayer 1994; see also McArdle and Epstein 1987, Meredith and Tisak 1990 and Rogosa and Willett 1985). The HLM approach closely resembles the modeling strategy developed in this section. The structural equation modeling approach, on the other hand, is in some ways more intuitive, although it is mathematically equivalent to the Bayesian and HLM approaches.[5] However, that approach typically requires balanced data—that is, data that have been collected at the same time and at all times for all individuals in the sample. This latter requirement can be relaxed by assuming that individuals who are missing at one or more occasions are missing at random and estimating the model using a full information maximum likelihood (FIML) estimator. The former restriction, however, is not easily relaxed. However, estimating the model using a Bayesian approach or using other hierarchical modeling packages offer a straightforward way to handling unbalanced data. For more details on latent growth modeling within a structural equation modeling framework, I highly recommend Bollen and Curran (2006).

9.3 A note on fixed versus random effects models and other terminology

One issue that makes understanding hierarchical models difficult is the terminology that different disciplines and statistical paradigms use to describe various features of the models. In this section, I hope to clarify some of the terminology, although there is certain to be some disagreement regarding my

---

[5] In fact, for each growth model example presented here, I estimated the equivalent model using a structural equation approach. The results were nearly identical.

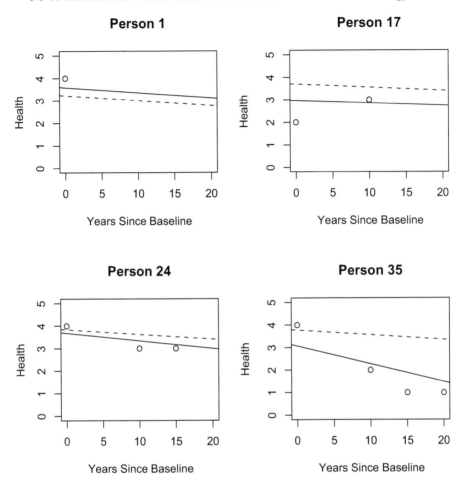

Fig. 9.3. Predicted trajectories and observed health for four persons: The solid lines are the predicted trajectories based on the posterior means of the random intercepts and slopes from Figure 9.2; and the dashed lines are the predicted trajectories based on the individuals' covariate profiles and posterior means of the parameters in Table 9.4

use of terms. To be sure, many of the terms used in discussions of hierarchical modeling have not had static definitions over time, adding to the confusion.

First, the terms "fixed effects" and "random effects" are frequently tossed about in discussions of hierarchical modeling. From a Bayesian perspective, controversy over these terms is often much ado about nothing, because from a Bayesian view (1) parameters are seen as random quantities arising from proper probability distributions, making all effects "random"; and (2) fixed effects models generally contain "random" effects, making the distinction between fixed and random effects models somewhat dubious. Consider the OLS regression model $Y = X\beta + e$, which is often considered to be a fixed effects regression model. In this model, X is considered a *fixed* variable matrix, and β is considered a fixed regression parameter vector—i.e., "fixed effects." From a classical statistical standpoint, the only random quantity in this model is the vector e, which is generally portrayed as random by the expression $e \sim N(0, \sigma_e^2 I_n)$. In other words, in the classical representation, e is a random effect because it comes from a *specified* probability distribution. The β vector, on the other hand, is considered fixed—these parameters are what they are in the population and do not stem from a probability distribution. From a Bayesian view, however, β *may* be considered as a vector of random effects, because we can produce a posterior probability distribution for the vector. The only difference between the Bayesian approach to this model and the classical approach is that the classical approach implicitly assumes uniform prior distributions on β, whereas a Bayesian approach makes this assumption explicit in the formulation of the prior. Whether we consider β fixed or random, nonetheless, one could argue that the model is a random effects model with some fixed effects (β) if the priors are left unspecified.

Next, consider the basic random effects model considered in this chapter in which individuals have their "own" intercepts or means:

$$y_{it} \sim N(\alpha_i, \sigma^2),$$

with $\alpha_i \sim N(\alpha_0, \tau^2)$. From a Bayesian perspective, this model is considered a random effects model, because the α_i are treated as arising from a normal distribution with parameters α_0 and τ^2. A classical statistician, on the other hand, might introduce a dummy variable for each observation, coupled with a β for each dummy variable, and call this model a fixed effects model, because the β vector could be considered a fixed parameter vector. In other words, the classical statistician may specify the model as an OLS regression model, $Y = X\beta + e$, again with X being a matrix of dummy variables, β being a vector of effects of these dummy variables, and $e \sim N(0, \sigma_e^2)$ being considered the only random quantity. The data structure in this specification would be a person-year matrix, with each individual contributing t rows, with X having dummy variables for each person-record corresponding to each person. From a Bayesian view, this is a random effects model, but from a classical view, this is still a fixed effects model. The Bayesian, however, recognizes that, again, the only difference between these models is the explicit statement that each α_i (intercept/mean) has a proper prior distribution; the classical statistician again implicitly assumes uniform priors distributions on these "fixed" effects.

The next step in our modeling process in this chapter was to incorporate additional individual-level (level 2) variables via essentially the decomposition of the intercept term into a regression on individual-level factors. Specifically, we allowed individuals' α_i to be a function of their sex. One representation of this model is:

$$y_{it} \sim N(\alpha_i, \sigma^2)$$
$$\alpha_i \sim N(\alpha_{(0)} + \alpha_{(1)}\text{sex}_i, \tau^2),$$

along with appropriate (vague) hyperpriors for the hyperparameters $\alpha_{(0)}$, $\alpha_{(1)}$, σ^2, and τ^2. Alternatively, but equivalently, the model may be specified as we did earlier:

$$y_{it} \sim N(\alpha_i + \alpha_{(1)}\text{sex}_i, \sigma^2)$$
$$\alpha_i \sim N(\alpha_0, \tau^2),$$

again with appropriate priors for $\alpha_{(0)}$, $\alpha_{(1)}$, σ^2, and τ^2. A Bayesian then would call this a random intercept model. The classical statistician, on the other hand, would write this model as:

$$y_{it} = \alpha_i + \alpha_1\text{sex}_i + e_{it}$$
$$e_{it} \sim N(0, \sigma^2)$$
$$\alpha_i = \alpha_0 + u_i$$
$$u_{it} \sim N(0, \tau^2).$$

After substituting the third equation into the first, we would obtain:

$$y_{it} = \alpha_0 + u_i + \alpha_1\text{sex}_i + e_{it}.$$

Under this representation, the classical statistician would claim that α_0 and α_1 are fixed effects, and that the only random effects are u_i and e_{it}. If u_i is considered a component of α_0, then the model *could* be called a random intercept model with fixed effects. Once again, however, the Bayesian would argue that the explicit assignment of proper priors for α_0 and α_1 makes the model a random effects model: The classical approach is implicitly assuming uniform priors on these parameters.

In subsequent steps of our modeling building process, we included Internet usage as a time-varying (level 1) variable, and we eventually allowed the influence of Internet usage on wages to vary across individuals and we allowed the individual-specific influence of Internet usage to be a function of individuals' sex:

$$y_{it} \sim N(\alpha_i + \beta_i\text{Internet}_{it}, \sigma^2)$$
$$\alpha_i \sim N(\alpha_0 + \alpha_1\text{sex}_i, \tau_\alpha^2)$$
$$\beta_i \sim N(\beta_0 + \beta_1\text{sex}_i, \tau_\beta^2),$$

once again with appropriate hyperprior distributions for the higher level hyperparameters. Using Bayesian terminology, this model is a "random coefficients" model, because the regression coefficient β_i is allowed to vary across individuals. The classical approach, however, would find

$$y_{it} = \alpha_0 + \alpha_1 \text{sex}_i + u_i + \beta_0 \text{Internet}_{it} + \beta_1 \text{sex}_i \text{Internet}_{it} + v_i \text{Internet}_{it} + e_{it}$$

after subsitution and might call the model a fixed effects model with random intercepts, random coefficients, and cross-level interactions.

To make a long story short, all of these models are considered hierarchical models because there is a hierarchical structure to the parameters. They may also be called multilevel models because the variables in the models are measured at different levels (time-specific measures and individual-level measures). Additionally, all the models contain random effects and may therefore be called random effects models, despite the fact that the classical statistician may prefer to include the term "fixed effects" in describing them. When the regression parameters—and not simply the intercepts—are allowed to vary across individuals, they may be called "random coefficient models." When time is included as a variable and its influence—a random coefficient—is allowed to vary across individuals, the model may be called a "(latent) growth (curve) model." Finally, all of these models are sometimes called "mixed models," because they generally include both fixed and random effects when the terms "fixed" and "random" are applied to distinguish between effects that have implicit versus explicit prior distributions.

9.4 Conclusions

In this chapter, we have covered considerable ground. We began by discussing how we can use the conditional probability rule to produce hierarchical structure in the parameters and obtain a posterior distribution for all parameters in a simple model without covariates. We then discussed how hierarchical regression models can easily be constructed to capture hierarchical structure in both the parameters and the data with variables measured at different levels. Finally, we showed how the general hierarchical linear regression model can be specialized to examine growth in the outcome over time by including time in the model as a covariate. As the chapter demonstrated, the Bayesian approach is naturally suited to hierarchical modeling. Indeed, the Bayesian approach handles hierarchicality so easily that virtually no text on Bayesian statistics omits hierarchical modeling, and I can find no Bayesian text that *only* covers hierarchical modeling. For further reading on Bayesian hierarchical modeling, as I said at the beginning of the chapter, I recommend Gelman et al. (1995). I also recommend Gill (2002) for an introductory exposition, and I suggest Spiegelhalter et al. (1996) for an illustrative example of growth modeling.

9.5 Exercises

1. Show the steps in the derivation of the conditional posterior distribution for τ in Equation 9.5.
2. Explain why the values chosen to complete the hyperprior specification in Section 9.2.1 are noninformative.
3. Explain in your own words why the first growth model presented in Section 9.2.3 cannot allow Internet usage to be a time-varying variable in the model as it is specified.
4. Using your own data, write an R routine to estimate a growth model. Then write a WinBugs routine to estimate the same model. Are the results similar?

Introduction to Multivariate Regression Models

In the social sciences, we commonly use multiple outcome variables in answering a research question rather than a single outcome variable. In these cases, we may prefer to construct "multivariate models" rather than a series of univariate models like those presented in the previous three chapters. Typically, when social scientists refer to multivariate models, they mean simply that they are estimating a model with more than one variable; however, for a statistician, the term "multivariate model" generally implies that a model has more than one outcome/response variable. A variety of different types of multivariate response models exists; in this chapter, we will consider only two of them: the multivariate linear regression model and the multivariate probit model. My goal in this chapter is not to provide an exhaustive account of multivariate models, a task that would require an entire book. Instead, my goal is to present the basic ideas of multivariate modeling.

There are two primary reasons for constructing a multivariate model in place of a set of univariate ones: (1) to eliminate biases or improve efficiency over using a set of univariate models, and (2) to facilitate the use of model parameters from a joint model in making inference for unestimated parameters/quantities. We will consider the first reason first in reconsidering the ordinary least squares (OLS) regression models for "niceness" from Chapter 7. Then we will consider the latter reason in an example for the multivariate probit model.

10.1 Multivariate linear regression

10.1.1 Model development

The most basic type of multivariate regression model is the extension of the OLS regression model to handle an M-length vector of responses Y for each individual in a sample, rather than a single response outcome (i.e., $M = 1$). For example, reconsidering the example from Chapter 7 in which we evaluated whether Southerners are "nicer" than persons who have always lived in other regions of the country, we could have treated the four outcomes—empathy, selflessness, tolerance, and altruistic acts—as a vector of responses for each individual rather than as separate responses. The result would have been a single model, rather than four separate ones. In that case, the X variables would have been the same for each equation, but each X would have been allowed to have a different effect on each outcome. This model can be expressed just as the OLS regression model:

$$Y = X\beta + e,$$

but the dimensions of the model matrices are expanded to handle the additional responses. In this representation, Y and e are now $n \times M$, rather than $n \times 1$, with the additional columns representing the additional dimensions of response. X is still $n \times k$, but now β is expanded to be $k \times M$ to allow each X to have a distinct influence on each outcome. Thus, the expanded matrix representation appears as:

$$
\underbrace{\begin{bmatrix} y_{11} & \cdots & y_{1M} \\ \vdots & \ddots & \vdots \\ y_{n1} & \cdots & y_{nM} \end{bmatrix}}_{n \times M} = \underbrace{\begin{bmatrix} x_{11} & \cdots & x_{1k} \\ \vdots & \ddots & \vdots \\ x_{n1} & \cdots & x_{nk} \end{bmatrix}}_{n \times k} \underbrace{\begin{bmatrix} \beta_{11} & \cdots & \beta_{1M} \\ \vdots & \ddots & \vdots \\ \beta_{k1} & \cdots & \beta_{kM} \end{bmatrix}}_{k \times M} + \underbrace{\begin{bmatrix} e_{11} & \cdots & e_{1M} \\ \vdots & \ddots & \vdots \\ e_{n1} & \cdots & e_{nM} \end{bmatrix}}_{n \times M},
$$

(10.1)

When the errors from each regression equation are unrelated, i.e., $(e^T e)_{ij} = 0, \forall i \neq j$, the model is equivalent to running independent univariate OLS regression models. In that case, the OLS solution of $\hat{\beta} = (X^T X)^{-1}(X^T Y)$ is still the optimal classical solution—only the dimensionality of the solution has changed—and, under uniform priors, this solution is still the posterior mean for β. That is, $p(\beta|X, Y) \sim N(\hat{\beta}_{\text{OLS}}, \sigma_e^2(X^T X)^{-1})$, where σ_e^2 is a diagonal matrix of error variances.

However, when errors are correlated across equations, the univariate and multivariate approaches are *not necessarily* equivalent. It can be shown that, when the cross-equation errors are correlated, the independent OLS solutions will not be the same as the multivariate solution if (1) the covariate vectors are not identical across equations; that is, if the X vectors differ across equations, or (2) if cross-equation constraints are imposed. For example, suppose we allowed education to influence the empathy outcome but not the other three outcomes. Alternatively, suppose we forced education's influence on empathy and altruistic acts to be the same, or we fixed its effect to be some constant. In these cases, this model is called the "seemingly-unrelated regression model" in econometrics (see Zellner 1962), and the OLS solution will no longer be "best"—it will be less efficient than the multivariate solution.

To obtain the multivariate solution, we begin with construction of a multivariate likelihood function. Whereas with the univariate linear regression model the likelihood function involved the use of a univariate normal sampling density for the observations (error term), the multivariate regression model requires us to use the multivariate normal distribution for the observations (error terms). The multivariate normal likelihood function, when $Y \sim MVN(X\beta, \Sigma)$ is:

$$L(\beta, \Sigma | X, Y) \propto \prod_{i=1}^{n} |\Sigma|^{-(1/2)} \exp\left\{-\frac{1}{2} e_i^T \Sigma^{-1} e_i\right\}, \qquad (10.2)$$

where e_i is the $M \times 1$ vector of errors for the ith individual.

To make the analysis fully Bayesian, it is common to assume independent priors on β and Σ, and to use improper uniform $(U(-\infty, \infty))$ priors on the elements of β and a noninformative prior for Σ. A common noninformative prior for Σ is the Jeffreys prior: $p(\Sigma) \propto |\Sigma|^{-(M+1)/2}$. With these priors, the posterior is simply:

$$p(\beta, \Sigma | X, Y) \propto |\Sigma|^{-(M+n+1/2)} \exp\left\{-\frac{1}{2} tr(S\Sigma^{-1})\right\}, \qquad (10.3)$$

where $S = \sum_{i=1}^{n} e_i e_i^T$ is the $M \times M$ matrix of the sums of cross-products of errors, and $tr(S\Sigma^{-1})$ is simply an equivalent expression to $\sum e_i^T \Sigma^{-1} e_i$.

Written this way, deriving the conditional distribution for Σ $(p(\Sigma|\beta, X, Y))$ is straightforward: It is recognizable as inverse Wishart, with scale matrix S and n degrees of freedom.[1]

Deriving the conditional posterior distribution for β is not as simple. However, Zellner (1962) and others (e.g., Gelman et al. 1995; Judge et al. 1985) have shown that the multivariate regression model from Equation 10.1 can be rewritten as a univariate regression, where the columns of Y and e can be "stacked" (this is called the "vec()" operator in matrix algebra) so that Y is $Mn \times 1$, rather than $n \times M$, as is e. β can also be stacked to be $Mk \times 1$, and the X matrix can be be constructed as a block-diagonal matrix to yield the following alternative specification for the multivariate model:

---

[1] As with other normal-inverse gamma and multivariate normal-inverse Wishart setups, we can derive the marginal distribution for the covariance matrix; however, it is just as easy under Gibbs sampling to use the conditional posterior distribution for the matrix.

$$
\begin{bmatrix} y_{11} \\ \vdots \\ y_{n1} \\ y_{12} \\ \vdots \\ y_{n2} \\ \vdots \\ y_{1m} \\ \vdots \\ y_{nm} \end{bmatrix}
=
\begin{bmatrix} X_1 & 0 & \dots & 0 \\ 0 & X_2 & \dots & 0 \\ \vdots & \vdots & \ddots & \vdots \\ 0 & 0 & \dots & X_M \end{bmatrix}
\begin{bmatrix} \beta_{11} \\ \vdots \\ \beta_{k1} \\ \beta_{12} \\ \vdots \\ \beta_{k2} \\ \vdots \\ \beta_{1m} \\ \vdots \\ \beta_{km} \end{bmatrix}
+
\begin{bmatrix} e_{11} \\ \vdots \\ e_{n1} \\ e_{12} \\ \vdots \\ e_{n2} \\ \vdots \\ e_{1m} \\ \vdots \\ e_{nm} \end{bmatrix}.
\tag{10.4}
$$

In this representation, X_m is the mth repetition of the $n \times k$ matrix X. However, it is not necessary for $X_i \equiv X_j$—i.e., X_i and X_j may contain different numbers of variables—but if the same X matrix is used in all equations, programming can be made relatively simple, as we will see. The solution for the regression coefficients is:

$$
\hat{\beta} = (X^T \Omega^{-1} X)^{-1}(X^T \Omega^{-1} Y),
\tag{10.5}
$$

which is simply the generalized least squares (GLS) estimator. The standard error is then $(X^T \Omega^{-1} X)^{-1}$. The GLS solution for $\hat{\beta}$ is the same as the expected value for β in a Bayesian analysis with the noninformative priors we have selected, and so the conditional posterior distribution for the regression coefficients is:

$$
f(\beta | \Sigma, X, Y) \sim MVN((X^T \Omega^{-1} X)^{-1}(X^T \Omega^{-1} Y) , (X^T \Omega^{-1} X)^{-1}).
\tag{10.6}
$$

In this distribution, $\Omega = \Sigma \otimes I_n$ (and $\Omega^{-1} = \Sigma^{-1} \otimes I_n$), where $\otimes$ indicates Kronecker multiplication, and I_n is the n-dimensional identity matrix. The Kronecker product of matrices A and B is defined as:

$$
A \otimes B =
\begin{bmatrix} A_{11}B & A_{12}B & \dots & A_{1J}B \\ A_{21}B & A_{22}B & \dots & A_{2J}B \\ \vdots & \vdots & \ddots & \vdots \\ A_{I1}B & A_{I2}B & \dots & A_{IJ}B \end{bmatrix}
\tag{10.7}
$$

That is, each element of the first matrix is replaced with the multiple of that element by the entire second matrix. Thus, if matrix A is $I \times J$, and matrix B is $R \times C$, the result of the Kronecker product $A \otimes B$ will be $IR \times JC$.

Mathematically, the multivariate regression solution for the regression coefficients seems straightforward, and a Gibbs sampler seems to be an easy repetition of two steps: (1) Simulate the regression parameters from their conditional posterior distribution defined in Equation 10.3, and (2) simulate

Σ from the appropriate inverse Wishart distribution, using the error cross-product matrix S that can be obtained after step (1).

Unfortunately, it is not so easy to implement this Gibbs sampler with typical social science data because of the size of the Ω matrix. Simulating the regression parameters when the sample size is small is simple. However, when the sample size is large, the Ω matrix becomes unwieldy. For example, in the OLS regression example from Chapter 7, the sample size is $n = 2,313$ (with the cases with missing data listwise deleted), and the dimensionality of the outcome is $M = 4$. Thus, the Ω matrix is the Kronecker product of a 4×4 matrix with a $2,313 \times 2,313$ matrix—a $9,252 \times 9,252$ matrix. This matrix has more than 85 million elements, which is computationally impossible to handle directly. First, the memory requirements for a matrix of this size may exceed the capacity of the computer and/or software (this matrix would require some 680 Mb of memory). Second, even if we could construct a matrix of this size, performing repeated computations with this matrix would be extremely costly, in terms of the time it would take to run the Gibbs sampler. So, how can we proceed?

Judge et al (1985:468) show that the GLS solution for the β vector can be written as:

$$
\begin{bmatrix} \beta_1 \\ \beta_2 \\ \vdots \\ \beta_M \end{bmatrix} = \begin{bmatrix} \sigma^{11}(X_1^T X_1) & \sigma^{12}(X_1^T X_2) & \cdots & \sigma^{1M}(X_1^T X_M) \\ \sigma^{21}(X_2^T X_1) & \sigma^{22}(X_2^T X_2) & \cdots & \sigma^{2M}(X_2^T X_M) \\ \vdots & \vdots & \ddots & \vdots \\ \sigma^{M1}(X_M^T X_1) & \sigma^{M2}(X_M^T X_2) & \cdots & \sigma^{MM}(X_M^T X_M) \end{bmatrix}^{-1} \begin{bmatrix} \sum_{i=1}^M \sigma^{1i}(X_1^T Y_i) \\ \sum_{i=1}^M \sigma^{2i}(X_2^T Y_i) \\ \vdots \\ \sum_{i=1}^M \sigma^{Mi}(X_M^T Y_i) \end{bmatrix},
$$
(10.8)

where M is the dimension of the outcome, so that each β is a vector; σ^{ij} is the (i, j)th element of Σ^{-1}; X_m is the X matrix for the mth equation; and Y_i is the $n \times 1$ vector for outcome i.

If $X_i \equiv X_j, \forall i \neq j$—that is, the same regressors are used in all equations–the first matrix can be reduced to $\Sigma^{-1} \otimes (X^T X)$. Although this expression involves the use of a Kronecker product, the matrices involved are not overwhelmingly large. Σ^{-1} is $M \times M$, and $X^T X$ is $k \times k$, and so the Kronecker product is just $Mk \times Mk$. In the OLS regression example, this would be $(4)(9) \times (4)(9)$, which is a very manageable matrix size. The latter term in Equation 10.8 can also be written slightly differently to simplify computation. If we compute $X^T Y$ using the original $n \times M$ specification for Y and post-multiply it by Σ^{-1}, we end up with a $k \times M$ matrix to which we can apply the vec() operator to convert it to a $km \times 1$ column vector. This approach yields the latter term in the equation.

10.1.2 Implementing the algorithm

Below is an R program implementing Gibbs sampling for simulating the parameters from the model. The example is the same example as in Chapter 7 (with missing data deleted):

```
#R program for multivariate regression
x<-as.matrix(read.table("c:\\mvn_examp.dat")[,2:10])
y<-as.matrix(read.table("c:\\mvn_examp.dat")[,11:14])

d=4;k=9
b<-matrix(0,(d*k)); s<-diag(d)

for(i in 2:1000){
#draw b from mvn
vb=solve(solve(s)%x%(t(x)%*%x))
mn=vb%*%(as.vector(t(x)%*%y%*%t(solve(s))))

b=mn+t(rnorm((d*k),0,1)%*%chol(vb))

#draw s from inverse wishart
e=matrix((as.vector(y)-(diag(d)%x%x%*%b)),nrow(y),d)
v=t(e)%*%e

s=riwish(nrow(y)-1,v)

print(c(b[1],b[10],b[19],b[28],s[1,1],s[2,2],s[3,3],s[4,4]))
write(c(t(b),t(s)),file="c:\\mvn2.out",ncolumns=52,append=T)
}
```

The program first reads the data into two matrices x and y and assigns the number of dimensions of the outcome (d=4) and covariate vector (k=9). It then creates a vector for the regression coefficients and a matrix for the error covariance and assigns starting values for each—all regression coefficients are assumed to be 0; the error covariance matrix is set to an identity.

The Gibbs sampler begins first with the construction of the variance matrix for the parameters (vb), which is also the first part of the regression vector mean. The remainder of the regression vector mean is then computed (mn), and then the regression vector is drawn from its multivariate normal conditional distribution. Once the regression vector is drawn, the *matrix* of errors—as in the original model specification in Equation 10.1—is computed, and the cross-product matrix of the errors is computed (v). This matrix is used as the scale matrix S in the inverse Wishart distribution for drawing the error covariance matrix Σ.

Table 10.1 shows the results of the multivariate regression model. If you compare these results with those of Table 7.2 in Chapter 7, you will see that the results are substantially similar. Indeed, only a few coefficients and posterior standard deviations change at all, and those that do change do not change substantially. That is, if one considers the implied posterior distributions for the parameters, their overlap overshadows their slight differences.

As I stated above, when the X matrix is the same for all equations as it is in this example, there is nothing gained—beyond elegance—by using a multivariate model rather than a series of univariate OLS regressions. However, if

Table 10.1. Results of multivariate regression of measures of "niceness" on three measures of region.

| | Outcome | | | |
Variable	Empathy	Tolerance	Selflessness	Altruistic Acts
Intercept	19.64(.57)***	3.16(.15)***	8.72(.29)***	9.16(.79)***
Age	0.018(.006)**	−0.008(.002)***	0.01(.003)***	−0.03(.01)***
Male	−2.41(.19)***	−0.35(.05)***	−0.87(.10)***	0.31(.26)
White	0.53(.25)*	0.09(.07)#	0.17(.13)#	0.001(.33)
Yrs. Schooling	0.06(.03)*	0.004(.01)	0.07(.02)***	0.32(.05)***
Income ($1,000s)	0.003(.003)	0.0006(.0009)	0.001(.002)	0.02(.004)***
Continuous South	0.65(.22)**	0.23(.06)***	0.25(.11)*	0.40(.31)#
South Out-Migrant	0.41(.50)	0.11(.13)	−0.34(.25)#	0.001(.68)
South In-Migrant	0.34(.35)	0.23(.09)**	0.16(.17)	−0.03(.46)
$\sqrt{\sigma_e^2}$	4.61	1.22	2.31	6.24

Note: The Bayesian estimates are posterior means. The Bayesian p-values are based on one-sided tail probabilities that the parameter exceeds 0 truncated to the classical cut-points of #$p < .1$, *$p < .05$, **$p < .01$, ***$p < .001$.

we were to exclude a variable from one (or more) equations, the multivariate approach will differ from the univariate approach. The reason is that the error covariance structure enables information from X variables in one equation to bear on the equation(s) in which that particular X is missing. In that case, the multivariate approach is more efficient.

It may be a rare situation in which we choose to allow the X matrices to vary across equations, but there are additional reasons to use multivariate models. First, we may have interrelationships between endogenous variables in our models—that is, we may choose to allow a y variable from one equation have a regression effect on a y in another equation. In econometrics, these are called "simultaneous equation models." In sociology and other social sciences, such modeling is often called "path analysis." More general models, which allow for measurement error and the estimation of relationships between latent constructs—called structural equation models—can also be estimated within a Bayesian framework. Discussing such models here is beyond the scope of this chapter and book, but see the conclusion for suggestions for further reading.

A second reason for estimating a multivariate model rather than a series of univariate models is if interest centers not on the model parameters themselves but instead on functions of the model parameters. I present such examples in the next sections in the context of multivariate probit models.

10.2 Multivariate probit models

As we discussed at the beginning of Chapter 8, it is rare in social science to have continuous outcomes. Sometimes, we may be interested in estimating models that have either multiple ordinal outcomes or a mixture of ordinal and continuous outcomes. On other occasions, we may be interested in a model that has a single, but nominal-level, outcome. In the former cases, we simply need an extension of the multivariate regression model discussed in the previous section combined with a generalization that allows us to work with non-continuous outcomes, as discussed in Chapter 8—called a multivariate probit model. In the latter case, we need a similar, but more constrained, model in which the outcome variable is converted into a series of dichotomous outcomes that are treated as mutually exclusive in the model—called a multinomial probit model. Algorithms to estimate these two different models differ primarily in this mutual-exclusivity criterion.

A model with multiple ordinal outcomes (including possibly multiple dichotomous outcomes) is relatively straightforward to construct and estimate. We can use an algorithm similar to that for the multivariate linear model with only three alterations. First, we must include a Gibbs sampling step in which we sample latent data underlying the observed ordinal responses, just as we did in the generalized linear model (GLM) extension of the OLS regression model. However, the latent data now must be sampled from truncated multivariate normal distributions rather than from truncated univariate normal distributions, and such truncated multivariate normal simulation is not nearly as simple as truncated univariate normal simulation. Second, the error covariance matrix can technically no longer be simulated from an inverse Wishart distribution. In order to identify the multivariate probit model, we must constrain the variances of the latent variables to be 1. This constraint makes simulating from the inverse Wishart distribution difficult or impossible; instead, we may use a Metropolis step to simulate the free parameters of the error correlation matrix. Third, as in the ordinal probit model in Chapter 8, when there are more than two outcome categories for a particular variable, the model will include free thresholds that must be estimated. In the following sections, I present two examples. The first example shows the basic approach to handling multivariate ordinal data. The second example shows how we can expand the model to handle "missing" data and use the results to construct distributions of quantities not directly estimated within the model that are a function of parameters from the multivariate equations.

10.2.1 Model development

Before we address the issues raised in the previous section, let's consider the general multivariate probit model (see also Chib and Greenberg 1998). In the examples, I will limit the outcome to two dimensions, but there is no inherent need to do so. As a generic example, suppose we want to determine whether political views and party affiliations have changed over time (see DiMaggio, Evans, and Bryson 1996, who tackle a similar question of interest). The GSS has asked at least two relevant questions since 1972. One asks whether respondents view themselves as liberal or conservative, while the other asks respondents whether they consider themselves to be Democrats or Republicans. Both items are measured with 7-point Likert scale items and are therefore ordinal. For the purposes of this example, I have collapsed the variables into two three-category variables. Political orientation is measured as liberal, moderate, or conservative, and political affiliation is measured as Democrat, Independent,[2] or Republican. Thus, the two-dimensional outcome, rather than being bivariate normal, can be viewed as a three-by-three contingency table. Table 10.2 shows the distribution of these data.

As the table suggests, there appears to be some sort of relationship between political orientation and party affiliation. Overall, 44% of the sample falls in the diagonal cells, and another 44% falls just off the diagonal. A chi-square test confirms that the two variables are associated ($\chi^2 = 3{,}094$, 4 df), and the Pearson correlation between the two variables is .28, a low-to-moderate positive correlation.[3]

Table 10.2. Political orientation and party affiliation.

Political Orientation

Party Affiliation	Liberal	Moderate	Conservative	Total
Democrat	5,133(14%)	5,697(15%)	3,357(9%)	14,187(38%)
Independent	3,608(10%)	5,460(15%)	3,805(10%)	12,873(35%)
Republican	1,337(4%)	3,159(9%)	5,472(15%)	9,968(27%)
Total	10,078(27%)	14,316(39%)	12,634(34%)	$n = 37{,}028$

Note: The data are from the 1972-2004 General Social Surveys. All years are covered, except 1979, 1981-2, 1992, 1995, 1997, 1999, 2001, and 2003. Percentages are of total sample and may not sum to 100 due to rounding.

Just as we assumed a binomial likelihood function for the observed data in the dichotomous probit model and a multinomial likelihood function for the observed data in the ordinal probit model in Chapter 8, we can assume a multinomial likelihood function for the observed multivariate data. Thus, the likelihood function for the data is:

---

[2] This category includes individuals with leanings one way or the other who define themselves as independents.

[3] The Pearson correlation is known to be an incorrect measure of association between ordinal variables. Instead, the polychoric correlation should be used. The polychoric correlation is a precursor to a multivariate probit model—it is the correlation between the "errors" in the multivariate probit model if there are no predictors. See the exercises. Also see Olsson 1979, Olsson, Drasgow, and Dorans 1982, and Poon and Lee 1987.

$$L(p|Y) \propto \prod_{i=1}^{n} \left(\prod_{r=1}^{R} \prod_{c=1}^{C} p_{irc}^{y_{irc}} \right), \tag{10.9}$$

where y_{irc} is 1 if the ith individual's response falls in the $(r,c)^{\text{th}}$ cell of the contingency table and is 0 otherwise. More generally, if there are K outcome variables $Y(1) \ldots Y(K)$, each of which is ordinal with $c(k)$ categories, the likelihood function is:

$$L(P|Y) \propto \prod_{i=1}^{n} \left(\prod_{a(1)=1}^{c(1)} \prod_{a(2)=1}^{c(2)} \cdots \prod_{a(k)=1}^{c(K)} p_{i,a(1)a(2)\ldots a(K)}^{y_{i,a(1)a(2)\ldots a(K)}} \right), \tag{10.10}$$

where $y_{i,a(1)\ldots a(K)} = 1$ if the ith individual's response falls in the $a(1) \ldots a(K)^{\text{th}}$ cell of the multinomial (and is 0 otherwise). The parenthetical "subscripting" is used to represent the dimensions of the outcome as well as parameters that vary by outcome/equation. In our current example, $K = 2$, and so $c(1) = 3$ is the number of categories in the political orientation variable, $c(2) = 3$ is the number of categories in the party affiliation variable, and $a(1)$ and $a(2)$ are index variables. In this example, $a(1)$ indexes the three outcomes of the political orientation variable, and $a(2)$ indexes the three outcomes of the party affiliation variable. Thus, each individual's contribution to the likelihood function is the product over the nine cells of the outcome contingency table with the respondent's $y_{i,a(1)a(2)}$ outcome being an indicator for whether the respondent's response falls in the $a(1)a(2)^{th}$ cell. So, Equation 10.9 (or Equation 10.10) can be expanded as:

$$L(p|Y) \propto \prod_{i=1}^{n} \left(p_{i,11}^{y_{i,11}} \cdot p_{i,12}^{y_{i,12}} \cdot p_{i,13}^{y_{i,13}} \cdot p_{i,21}^{y_{i,21}} \cdot p_{i,22}^{y_{i,22}} \cdot p_{i,23}^{y_{i,23}} \cdot p_{i,31}^{y_{i,31}} \cdot p_{i,32}^{y_{i,32}} \cdot p_{i,33}^{y_{i,33}} \right).$$

$$\tag{10.11}$$

Notice that each individual ultimately only contributes one component to the likelihood function—the $p_{i,a(1)a(2)}$ for which $y_{i,a(1)a(2)} = 1$. The $p_{i,a(1)a(2)}$ are the cell probabilities, which depend on an individual's covariate profile. The cell probabilities in the dichotomous and ordinal probit models in Chapter 8 were integrals of the univariate normal distribution, and the probabilities were linked to the covariates via the "link" function. For example, $p(y_i = 1) = \Phi(X_i^T \beta, 1)$ in the dichotomous probit model and $p(y_i = k) = \Phi(X_i^T \beta, 1, \tau_k, \tau_{k+1})$ in the ordinal probit model, where τ_k and τ_{k+1} are the thresholds that bound the latent continuous propensity to place the individual in category k of the observed ordinal outcome. We can take a similar latent variable approach in the multivariate probit model; in the multivariate probit model, the integrals are multivariate, such that:

$$p(y_{i,a(1)a(2)\ldots a(K)} = 1) = \Phi_K \left(X_i^T \beta, \Sigma, \tau_L, \tau_U \right). \tag{10.12}$$

Here, $p(y_{i,a(1)a(2)...a(K)} = 1)$ is the probability the ith individual's response falls in the $a(1)a(2)...a(K)^{\text{th}}$ cell of the multinomial, $\Phi_K()$ is the integral of the K-dimensional multivariate normal pdf, $X_i^T\beta$ is the predicted multivariate $(K \times 1)$ z score for the ith individual, Σ is the error covariance matrix (diagonal elements are constrained to 1; off-diagonal elements are estimated), and τ_L and τ_U are K-length *vectors* of thresholds that bound the latent continuous response (z) in multiple dimensions. That is, $\tau(1)_{a(1)}$ is the lower threshold, and $\tau(1)_{a(1)+1}$ is the upper threshold, in the first dimension of the outcome bounding a response observed to be in category $a(1)$. In our current example, the political orientation and party affiliation variables each have four thresholds, bounding the three possible outcome categories in each dimension. $\tau(1)_1 = -\infty$, $\tau(1)_2 = 0$, $\tau(1)_3$ is estimated, and $\tau(1)_4 = \infty$. The same result is true for the vector $\tau(2)$. Thus, the probability that an individual falls in the (2,3) cell of the multinomial in this example is the integral of the bivariate normal with mean $M = X_i^T\beta$ (a $K \times 1$ vector of means for the ith individual) and covariance matrix Σ:

$$p(y_i = (2,3)) = \Phi_2(M, \Sigma, \tau(1)_2, \tau(1)_3; \tau(2)_3, \tau(2)_4).$$

Figure 10.1 presents a graphic depiction of this integral. The contours represent the bivariate normal distribution for the latent propensities Z (or Y^*) thought to underlie the multivariate ordinal response. The vertical and horizontal dotted lines are the thresholds that partition the latent distribution into the observed 3×3 contingency table of ordinal responses, and the dark-outlined region of the contour plot is the probability that an individual falls in cell (2,3) of the observed contingency table—it is the integral of the bivariate normal distribution between lower and upper thresholds of the cell in the two dimensions.

Multivariate normal integration is difficult and costly (see Drezner 1992 and Schervish 1984, for example). Thus, instead, we can bring the latent data (Z) into the modeling strategy just as we developed an alternative representation for the dichotomous and ordinal probit model in Chapter 8. In the univariate probit models discussed in Chapter 8, the latent traits were simulated from truncated normal distributions based on the observed outcome. In the multivariate probit model, the latent traits are simulated from truncated multivariate normal distributions. Once these latent data are simulated, the remainder of an MCMC algorithm for simulating the multivariate probit parameters is virtually identical to the one we developed for the multivariate regression model in the previous sections, only requiring an additional step to simulate the free thresholds that categorize the continuous latent data into the observed ordinal bins:

1. Select starting values for β and Σ, with $\Sigma_{ii} = 1, \forall i$.

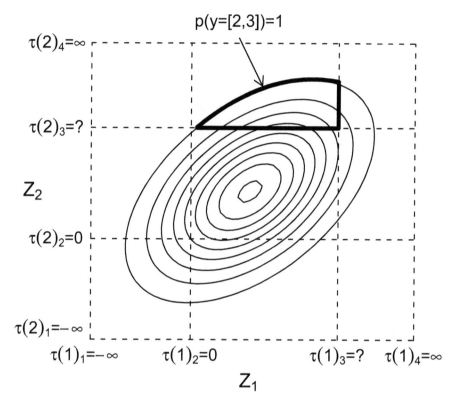

Fig. 10.1. Depiction of a bivariate outcome space for continuous latent variables Z_1 and Z_2: The observed variables Y_1 and Y_2 are formed by the imposition of the vectors of thresholds in each dimension; and the darkened area is the probability that an individual's response falls in the $[2,3]$ cell, conditional on the distribution for Z.

2. Simulate $Z|Y, X, \beta, \Sigma, \tau \sim TMVN(X\beta, \Sigma)$.

3. Simulate $\tau(k)_c|Z(k) \sim U(\max Z(k)_c, \min Z(k)_{c+1}), \forall k, c$.

4. Simulate $\beta|Z, X, \Sigma \sim MVN((X^T \Omega^{-1} X)^{-1}(X^T \Omega^{-1} Z) , (X^T \Omega^{-1} X)^{-1})$.

5. Simulate $\Sigma|Z,\beta,X \sim IW(S,n)$, where $S = \sum_{i=1}^{n}(Z - X_i\beta)(Z - X_i\beta)^T$, subject to the constraint the $\Sigma_{ii} = 1, \forall i$.

6. Return to Step 2.

The first step, finding starting values, is straightforward. I generally start all regression parameters at 0 and the error covariance matrix Σ as an identity matrix. The fourth step—simulation of the regression coefficients—requires very little discussion. Once the latent data Z replace the observed ordinal data Y and an appropriate Σ matrix is available, the conditional distribution for the regression parameters is identical to that of the multivariate regression model presented in the previous section. The second, third, and fifth steps, on the other hand, require some discussion.

10.2.2 Step 2: Simulating draws from truncated multivariate normal distributions

Simulating draws from truncated multivariate normal distributions is substantially more complicated than simulating draws from truncated univariate normal distributions. One method for simulating such draws is the naive approach we discussed in Chapter 8: We simulate from untruncated normal distributions until we obtain a draw from the appropriate region. For example, using the current example, if we wished to simulate a latent score for a person with an observed $y = (2,3)$ response, we would simulate from the entire bivariate normal distribution exemplified in Figure 10.1 until we obtained a draw that fell in the dark-outlined region. It is easy to see that this naive approach is extremely inefficient, and becomes increasingly so as the dimensionality of the problem increases and as the number of categories in the ordinal variables increases. Basically, anything that reduces the ratio of the area under the multivariate normal curve in one cell relative to the total area under the multivariate normal curve reduces the naive approach's efficiency.

We have already discussed how to simulate from truncated univariate normal distributions, and so, if we can break simulation from our truncated multivariate normal distribution into a series of truncated univariate normal distribution simulations, it seems our problem is solved. One way that we can break the multivariate simulation problem into a series of univariate ones is to decompose the joint density function $f(x_1, x_2, \ldots, x_{K-1}, x_K)$ into the product of conditional distributions (as we did to construct hierarchical models in Chapter 9) using the conditional probability rule that $f(A, B) = f(A|B)f(B)$. We can carry this decomposition out beyond two variables as:

$$f(x_1, x_2, \ldots, x_K) = f(x_K|x_{K-1}, \ldots, x_1) \ldots f(x_3|x_1, x_2)f(x_2|x_1)f(x_1).$$
$$(10.13)$$

That this decomposition is correct can be seen by starting from the right end and recognizing that the first marginal times the first conditional leads to a joint distribution for two variables. This joint distribution is then a new marginal distribution, which, when multiplied by the next conditional distribution, yields a joint distribution for three variables, and so on:

$$f(x_1, x_2, \ldots, x_K) = \ldots f(x_4|x_1, x_2, x_3) \; f(x_3|x_1, x_2) \; f(x_2|x_1) \; f(x_1)$$

$$\underbrace{}$$
$$f(x_1, x_2)$$

$$f(x_1, x_2, x_3)$$

$$f(x_1, x_2, x_3, x_4)$$

$$\vdots$$

Thus, we can first draw x_1 from its appropriate univariate normal distribution. Then, conditional on this draw, we can draw x_2 from $f(x_2|x_1)$. Then, conditional on these draws, we can draw x_3 from $f(x_3|x_1, x_2)$, and so on. Earlier, we discussed that the conditional distribution for one variable (e.g., x_2) from a *standard* bivariate normal distribution given the other (e.g., x_1) is univariate normal with a mean of ρx_1 and variance $1 - \rho^2$. More generally, it is known that the conditional distribution for a single variable in a multivariate normal distribution is itself normal. If $Z \sim MVN(\mu, \Sigma)$, then $(Z_a|\mu_{(-a)} = M) \sim N(\mu^*, \Sigma^*)$, where:

$$\mu^* = \mu_a + \Sigma_{a.} \Sigma_{(-a)}^{-1} \left(\mu_{(-a)} - M \right) \tag{10.14}$$

$$\Sigma^* = \Sigma_{aa} - \Sigma_{a.} \Sigma_{(-a)}^{-1} \Sigma_{.a}. \tag{10.15}$$

In these expressions, $\Sigma_{(-a)}$ is the multivariate covariance matrix obtained by omitting row and column a, $\Sigma_{a.}$ is the ath row of Σ (similarly, $\Sigma_{.a}$ is the ath column of Σ), and M is the current value of the normal draws for the other (i.e., $-a$) dimensions.

Thus, sampling from a multivariate normal distribution involves simply sampling the first variable from its univariate marginal distribution; then sampling the second variable from its univariate conditional distribution, which depends only on the first variable, then sampling the third variable from its univariate conditional distribution, which depends only on the first and second variables; and so on. Below is an R subroutine that samples 10,000 draws from a five-dimensional normal distribution with mean vector $\mu^T = [1\,2\,3\,4\,5]$ and covariance matrix with all covariances equal to .5 and the variances $\sigma_{ii}^2 = [5\,4\,3\,2\,1]$. The sampling begins with the last element (x_5) and samples from the appropriate conditional distribution moving backward to x_1.

Thus, as the fourth element is being sampled from its conditional distribution, the relevant covariance matrix is the 2×2 matrix for variables x_4 and x_5. As the third element is being sampled, the relevant covariance matrix is the 3×3 covariance matrix for variables x_3, x_4, and x_5, etc.:

```
d=5
x<-matrix(NA,10000,d)

mu=matrix(c(1,2,3,4,5),d)
sig=matrix(.5,d,d)
sig[1,1]=5; sig[2,2]=4; sig[3,3]=3; sig[4,4]=2; sig[5,5]=1

for(i in 1:10000)
  {
  #simulate 5th element
  x[i,d]=rnorm(1,mu[d],sqrt(sig[d,d]))

  #simulate 4th, 3rd...
  for(j in d:2)
    {
    m=mu[j-1] +
      sig[(j-1),(j:d)]%*%solve(sig[j:d,j:d])%*%(x[i,j:d]-mu[j:d])
    s=sig[j-1,j-1] -
      sig[(j-1),(j:d)]%*%(solve(sig[j:d,j:d]))%*%sig[(j:d),(j-1)]

    x[i,j-1]=rnorm(1,m,sqrt(s))
    }
  print(c(i,x[i,]))
  }
```

The resulting mean vector of the 10,000 draws was:

$$\bar{x}^T = [1.00\ 1.97\ 3.04\ 4.00\ 5.00],$$

and the covariance matrix was:

$$\begin{bmatrix} 4.99 & & & & \\ .47 & 4.01 & & & \\ .44 & .51 & 3.00 & & \\ .48 & .47 & .53 & 2.01 & \\ .47 & .48 & .52 & .51 & 1.01 \end{bmatrix}.$$

Based on these results, it seems that a strategy for sampling from truncated multivariate normal distributions might simply involve applying this approach but ensuring that, for each univariate draw, we enforce the univariate truncation requirements as we did in Chapter 8. Below is a simple R program for performing such simulation on a truncated standard bivariate normal distribution with corrrelation/covariance .5, with the point of truncation being 0 in both dimensions so that draws must come from above 0 in each dimension. The program simulates 2,000 draws from this distribution, using both naive simulation and using the conditional decomposition approach:

```
covmat=diag(2)
covmat[1,2]=covmat[2,1]=.5
z=matrix(0,2000,2)
q=matrix(0,2000,2)
count=0

for(i in 1:2000)
  {
  #naive simulation
  z[i,]=0
  while(z[i,1]<=0 | z[i,2]<=0)
    {count=count+1
     z[i,]=rnorm(2,0,1)%*%(chol(covmat))
    }

  #conditional simulation based on decomposition
  q[i,1]=qnorm(runif(1,min=.5,max=1),0,1)
  mm=covmat[1,2]*q[i,1]
  ss=1-.5^2
  q[i,2]=qnorm(runif(1,min=pnorm(0,mm,sqrt(ss)),max=1),mm,sqrt(ss))
  }
```

Figure 10.2 shows some results of the naive and conditional/decomposition approach. The upper plots show the contours of the $BVN(0, 1, \rho = .5)$ distribution, with the two sets of simulated values superimposed. The upper left plot shows the results of the naive simulation approach—which required 5,854 draws to obtain 2,000 samples in the appropriate region—and the upper right plot shows the results of the conditional decomposition approach. Although both methods *appear* to sample thoroughly throughout the desired region, the conditional approach appears not to have sampled as thoroughly from the x_1 dimension as from the x_2 dimension (notice that the contours are more visible close to the x_1 axis under the conditional approach). This conclusion is substantiated in the bottom figures, as the histograms for x_1 are not even approximately identical. The histograms show that the sampled values for x_1 obtained using the conditional approach seem to be overly clustered close to 0. This result is not an artifact of simulating only a few thousand samples. I reconducted the simulation, drawing 200,000 samples using both the naive and the conditional/decomposition approaches. The mean for x_1 of that simulation was .90 under the naive simulation approach but .80 under the conditional approach, and the variance of x_1 was .40 under the naive approach and .36 under the conditional approach. The results for x_2 were not as different. The mean for x_2 was .90 and .87 under the naive and conditional approaches (respectively), and the variances were .40 and .39, respectively.

Why does this conditional decomposition approach appear to work for x_2, but not for x_1? The answer is that the marginal distribution for x_1 ultimately

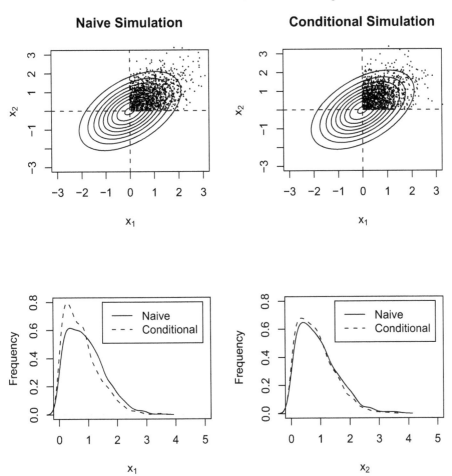

Fig. 10.2. Comparison of truncated bivariate normal simulation using naive simulation and conditional/decomposition simulation: Upper plots show the true contours (solid lines) of the bivariate normal distribution with sampled values superimposed (dots); and lower plots show histograms of the values sampled from the two dimensions under the two alternative sampling approaches.

depends on the marginal distribution for x_2, and so our first draw—for x_1—is *using the wrong marginal distribution*. Figure 10.3 clarifies the problem. If we simply simulate from a truncated univariate normal distribution for x_1 subject only to its truncation constraints, we end up simulating from the entire right side of the bivariate distribution. However, given that x_2 is also truncated, the lower right "wedge" should be omitted from the mass of the marginal for x_1. Leaving this mass in the marginal for x_1 yields too much mass close to 0, which leads to the oversampling of values close to 0 and, consequently, a mean and variance that are too small for x_1.

Once we have obtained a value for x_1—which at least is in the right region (above 0)—the draw for $x_2|x_1$ ($\sim TN(\rho x_1, 1 - \rho^2)$) is from the approximately correct distribution. The result is that the marginal distribution for x_2 ends up being close to the correct distribution, only slightly off due to the oversampling of certain values of x_1.

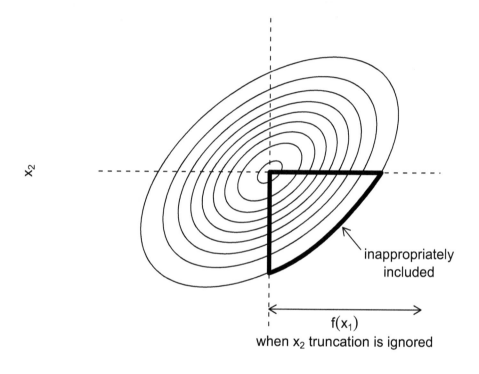

Fig. 10.3. Truncated bivariate normal distribution: Marginal distribution for x_1 when truncation of x_2 is ignored.

If the draw from $x_2|x_1$ is close to correct, it seems that we could then use this draw to draw a new x_1; that is, we could then draw $x_1|x_2 \sim TN(\rho x_2, 1 - \rho^2)$, to obtain a better draw for x_1. Then, we could use this new, better draw for x_1 to produce a better draw for x_2. Indeed, we can do this, and what we have now done is to complete a pair of iterations of a Gibbs sampler for the truncated multivariate normal distribution! Recall that Gibbs sampling involves iteratively sampling from the conditional distributions for one random variable, given all others. Thus, simulation from a K-dimensional normal distribution would involve:

1.	Simulate	$x_1 \vert x_2, x_3, x_4, \ldots, x_{K-1}, x_K.$
2.	Simulate	$x_2 \vert x_1, x_3, x_4, \ldots, x_{K-1}, x_K.$
3.	Simulate	$x_3 \vert x_1, x_2, x_4, \ldots, x_{K-1}, x_K.$

$$\vdots \qquad\qquad \vdots$$

$K-1$.	Simulate	$x_{K-1} \vert x_1, x_2, x_3, \ldots, x_{K-2}, x_K.$
K.	Simulate	$x_K \vert x_1, x_2, x_3, \ldots, x_{K-2}, x_{K-1}.$

If we follow this Gibbs sampling strategy, simulating each variable from its conditional distribution subject to its univariate truncation constraints, the Gibbs sampler will produce a sample from the truncated multivariate normal distribution within a few iterations. To perform the Gibbs sampling, each conditional distribution can be derived using Equations 10.14 and 10.15.

Figure 10.4 shows the results of 2,000 samples if we follow this Gibbs sampling strategy for only *two* iterations per sample.[4] As the histograms show, the distributions for both x_1 and x_2 now closely match those obtained from the less efficient naive sampling approach. The means for x_1 and x_2 under this approach were .89 and .90, respectively—both close to the means of .90 and .90 obtained via naive sampling—and the variances were .40 and .40, respectively—both almost indistinguishable from the variances of .40 and .40 obtained via naive sampling (see Robert 1995 who presents a more detailed and theoretical discussion of this approach).

In conclusion, although simulating from truncated multivariate normal distributions is more complex than simulating from truncated univariate normal distributions, we can perform such simulation using a Gibbs sampler with few iterations, suggesting that we can simulate our latent data in a multivariate probit model algorithm fairly efficiently—a Gibbs-sampler-within-a-Gibbs-sampler approach!

10.2.3 Step 3: Simulation of thresholds in the multivariate probit model

As we discussed in Chapter 8, the conditional distributions for the free thresholds are straightforward to derive: The conditionals in the univariate probit model are simply uniform on the interval between the largest latent score simulated for a person in the category below the threshold of interest and the smallest latent score simulated for a person in the category above the threshold of interest. The thresholds in the multivariate probit are equally easy to derive. For the sake of simplicity of notation, let's assume a bivariate probit model with uniform prior distributon for all parameters. The latent variable representation of the posterior distribution then is:

---

[4] The last three lines of the algorithm, in which mm and ss and q[i,?] are derived, are repeated twice: q[i,1] is drawn; then q[i,2] is drawn again.

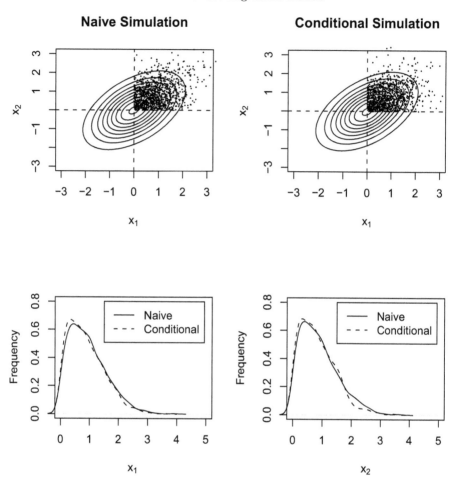

Fig. 10.4. Comparison of truncated bivariate normal distribution simulation using naive simulation and two iterations of Gibbs sampling: Upper plots show the true contours (solid lines) of the bivariate normal distribution with sampled values superimposed (dots); and lower plots show histograms of the values sampled from the two dimensions under the two alternative approaches to sampling.

$$p(\tau, \beta, \Sigma, Z | X, Y) \propto$$
$$\prod_{i=1}^{n} \left(\sum_{r=1}^{R} \sum_{c=1}^{C} \phi_2(Z_i - X_i^T \beta, \ \Sigma) I(\tau_r < z_{i1} < \tau_{r+1}) I(\tau_c < z_{i2} < \tau_{c+1}) \right),$$

where Z_i is the two-dimensional latent variable for individual i, with z_{i1} and z_{i2} representing the specific elements, $\phi_2(a, b)$ is the bivariate normal density function with mean a and covariance matrix b, τ_r is the rth threshold in the first dimension, and τ_c is the cth threshold in the second dimension. This posterior can be expanded as in Equation 10.11, but as in that example, each individual only contributes a single term to the posterior, namely the component for which the indicator functions both take a value of 1.

If we are considering a particular threshold, say τ_k, all terms in the posterior that do not involve τ_k can be removed as proportionality constants. Thus, the $\phi()$ components, and all other indicator functions that do not include τ_k, can be eliminated, leaving us with a string of products of indicators like:

$$p(\tau_k|\theta) \propto I(\tau_{k-1} < Z_{k-1} < \tau_k) \times I(\tau_k < Z_k < \tau_{k+1}),$$

where the first indicator function is repeated for all $Z : \tau_{k-1} < Z < \tau_k$, and the second indicator function is repeated for all $Z : \tau_k < Z < \tau_{k+1}$. We know that all of the indicator functions are "true," and so, we can ultimately drop the indicator function itself. If $\tau_k > Z_{k-1} \,\forall Z_{k-1}$, then $\tau_k > \max(Z_{k-1})$. Similarly, if $\tau_k < Z_k \,\forall Z_k$, then $\tau_k < \min(Z_k)$. The shape of the distribution over this interval is proportional to a constant and is therefore uniform. Thus, in the multivariate probit model, the distributions for the free thresholds are uniform just as they were in the univariate probit model. Furthermore, the conditional distributions for the thresholds in one dimension do not depend on the thresholds in the other dimension, suggesting that we can draw the thresholds one at a time from independent uniform distributions within and across equations.

Although this finding leads to a simple approach to simulating the thresholds, there is a substantial drawback to implementing it. When there are large numbers of individuals in each category, the difference between the maximum latent score in one category and the minimum latent score in the next tends to be small and leads to very slow movement of the thresholds in the Gibbs sampler. In the current example, we have a sample size of well over 30,000 individuals, which is guaranteed to produce slow convergence and mixing of the thresholds. In the probit models discussed in Chapter 8, slow convergence and mixing of the thresholds was not particularly problematic, because the sample size was relatively small and the dimensionality of the outcome was one, and we could rapidly run tens of thousands of iterations of the Gibbs sampler. In a multivariate probit model with a large sample size, on the other hand, it may simply be too costly to run the algorithm for an extended number of iterations. For example, I ran the algorithm for the multivariate probit model for 100,000 iterations sampling the threshold parameters from uniform distributions. The algorithm took 10 hours to run, and worse, the threshold parameters did not converge and therefore certainly did not thoroughly mix. Worse still, because of the slow movement of the thresholds, autocorrelation function plots showed unacceptably high autocorrelations even up to 25-30 lags. Clearly, we need an alternative approach to sampling the thresholds in the multivariate probit model—at least when the sample size is so large.

In the current example, we have two free thresholds (one in each dimension) that must be estimated. Figure 10.5 shows trace plots of the threshold parameters for three runs of the Gibbs sampler for the multivariate probit model (to be discussed in the next section), as well as autocorrelation function plots for the threshold parameter in the first equation/dimension of the outcome (τ_{13}). The first two plots in the first column of the 3-by-3 figure shows the trace plots for the two threshold parameters from a 10,000 iteration run of the Gibbs sampler, with every tenth sample saved. From the figures, it is not clear that the threshold parameters' samples have mixed well, nor is it clear whether the algorithm has even converged. The bottom plot in the column is the autocorrrelation function plot for τ_{13}. Even after thinning the Gibbs samples to every tenth sample, the threshold parameter shows extremely high autocorrelation. The second column of the figure shows the results of extending the algorithm another 90,000 iterations (still saving every tenth). Once again, it is not clear that the algorithm has mixed well nor converged. Furthermore, the autocorrelation plot at the bottom of the column shows extremely high autocorrelation. The third column, in contrast, shows the results for the thresholds when Cowles' (1996) algorithm is used to sample them. This algorithm was run for 6,000 iterations, with the samples thinned to every fifth iteration. The upper two plots show rapid convergence and thorough mixing. Furthermore, the autocorrelation function plot shows little autocorrrelation beyond one lag.

What is Cowles' algorithm? Cowles' algorithm is a Metropolis–Hastings (MH) step that replaces the Gibbs sampling step for simulating the thresholds from uniform distributions (Cowles 1996). Rather than simulating the thresholds from narrow uniform distributions, Cowles' algorithm generates candidate thresholds over the entire interval between adjacent thresholds and then uses the standard MH accept/reject criterion for determining whether to accept the candidate. The result is that the thresholds, even though all candidates are not accepted, make larger "jumps" when they move, leading to more rapid convergence, faster mixing, and less autocorrelation between successive samples of the thresholds. I describe Cowles' algorithm for one dimension—i.e., one vector of thresholds—but the algorithm is extendable to multivariate models, as I show in Section 10.2.5.

Consider a vector of thresholds, τ for a one-dimensional ordinal variable with K categories:

$$\tau = [(\tau_1 = -\infty) \quad (\tau_2 = 0) \quad \ldots \quad (\tau_{K-1}) \quad (\tau_K) \quad (\tau_{K+1} = \infty)].$$

Cowles' algorithm begins by simulating candidate parameters for each free element of τ from normal distributions centered over the current value of each τ truncated at the current values of the thresholds below and above the threshold being simulated:

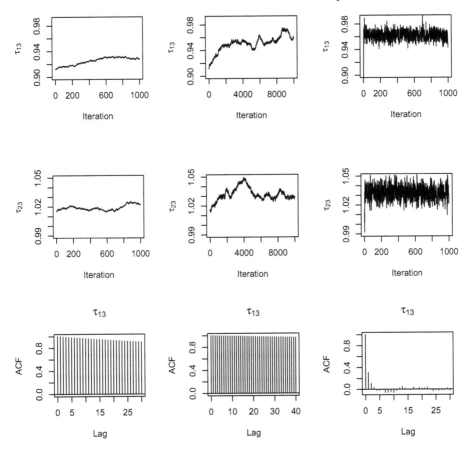

Fig. 10.5. Gibbs sampling versus Cowles' algorithm for sampling threshold parameters.

$$
\begin{aligned}
\tau_3^c &\sim N(\tau_3\,,\,\sigma^2,\,\tau_2 = 0,\,\tau_4) \\
\tau_4^c &\sim N(\tau_4\,,\,\sigma^2,\,\tau_3^c,\,\tau_5) \\
\tau_5^c &\sim N(\tau_5\,,\,\sigma^2,\,\tau_4^c,\,\tau_6) \\
&\;\;\vdots \\
\tau_{K-1}^c &\sim N(\tau_{K-1}\,,\,\sigma^2,\,\tau_{K-2}^c,\,\tau_K) \\
\tau_K^c &\sim N(\tau_K\,,\,\sigma^2,\,\tau_{K-1}^c,\,\tau_{K+1} = \infty).
\end{aligned}
$$

Here, $N(a, b, c, d)$ is the truncated normal distribution with mean a, variance b, and lower and upper truncation points of c and d, respectively. Thus, the generation of candidate values for the vector τ is sequential, with the lower truncation point for τ_k being determined by the *candidate* threshold below (i.e., τ_{k-1}^c), and the upper truncation point being determined by the current value of the threshold above.

In our current political orientation/party affiliation example, only one threshold is freely estimated in each dimension, and so, $\tau_{13}^c \sim N(\tau_{13}, \sigma, \tau_{12} = 0, \tau_{14} = \infty)$ and $\tau_{23}^c \sim N(\tau_{23}, \sigma, \tau_{22} = 0, \tau_{24} = \infty)$.

Once a set of candidates is generated, the next step in the MH algorithm is to compute the ratio R. In this case, given the truncation of the normal proposal densities, the proposals are asymmetric, and hence, the full ratio must be computed. Given that the posterior distributions for the threshold parameters are independent across equations, $p(\tau|\beta, \Sigma, Z, Y, X) \propto p(\tau|\beta, X, Y)$, and so:

$$R = \frac{f(\tau^c|\beta, X, Y)g(\tau|\tau^c)}{f(\tau|\beta, X, Y)g(\tau^c|\tau)},$$

where $f(a|b)$ is the posterior density evaluated at τ (or τ^c) and $g(c|d)$ is the value of the proposal density at c when the proposal is centered over d. The posterior for the thresholds is:

$$p(\tau|\beta, X, Y) \propto \prod_{i=1}^{n} \Phi(X_i^T \beta, \tau_{y_i}, \tau_{y_i+1}),$$

where $\Phi(a, b, c)$ is the integral of the normal density function with mean a and variance 1 between thresholds b and c. Thus, the first half of the ratio R is:

$$\prod_{i=1}^{n} \frac{\Phi(\beta^T X_i, \tau_{y_i}^c, \tau_{y_i+1}^c)}{\Phi(\beta^T X_i, \tau_{y_i}, \tau_{y_i+1}),}.$$

The latter half of the ratio corrects for the asymmetry in the proposals and is:

$$\prod_{j=3}^{K} \frac{\Phi(\tau_j, \sigma, \tau_{j-1}^c, \tau_{j+1})}{\Phi(\tau_j^c, \sigma, \tau_{j-1}, \tau_{j+1}^c)},$$

where in this case $\Phi(a, b, c, d)$ is the integral of the normal distribution with mean a and standard deviation b between the thresholds c and d. The standard deviation b is chosen to produce an acceptance rate around 50%.

The product of these components constitutes the full ratio R. Once this ratio is computed, we follow the usual MH steps: We compare this ratio to a $u \sim U(0, 1)$ random draw, and we accept τ^c if $R > u$.

In the example at hand, we have a two-dimensional outcome, each dimension of which only requires simulation of one threshold. As discussed in greater detail in Section 10.2.5, I perform a separate MH step for each dimension of the outcome.

10.2.4 Step 5: Simulating the error covariance matrix

Drawing samples of covariance matrices is straightforward, only involving simulation from an appropriate inverse Wishart distribution. Simulation of covariance matrices subject to constraints, on the other hand, is not so simple. In the multivariate regression model, no constraints were placed on the error covariance matrix. However, in the multivariate probit model, we must impose constraints to identify the model. Specifically, the typical constraint imposed is that the diagonal elements of the error covariance matrix are all 1.[5] This set of constraints makes the error covariance matrix a correlation matrix, and correlation matrices have no standard/known distribution.

Simulation of the error covariance/correlation matrix in a multivariate probit model, then, requires some alternative to simulating the matrix from an inverse Wishart distribution. One alternative is to use an MH algorithm to update the free elements of the error covariance matrix within a larger Gibbs sampler for the other parameters of the algorithm (Chib and Greenberg 1998). A second alternative is to (1) simulate the approximate error covariance matrix, $\tilde{\Sigma}$, from an inverse Wishart distribution, and (2) convert $\tilde{\Sigma}$ into a correlation matrix by computing:

$$\Sigma = (\text{diag}(\Sigma)^{-1/2})\tilde{\Sigma}(\text{diag}(\Sigma)^{-1/2}).$$

This set of matrix multiplications simply divides each element ($\tilde{\sigma}_{ij}$) of the original matrix by the square root of the $\tilde{\sigma}_{ii}$ and $\tilde{\sigma}_{jj}$ (see Imai and van Dyk 2005 for example, within the context of the multinomial probit model). In other words, each element is divided by the standard deviations of the relevant variables, yielding correlations off the main diagonal and ones along the diagonal. This approach *is not exact,* but in my experience, I find it generally leads to acceptable inference when (1) the sample size is large; and (2) the error correlations are small—both of which are often true with social science data. In fact, when the sample is large (say, above 1,000), sampling from an inverse Wishart distribution and then converting the draw to a correlation matrix generally produces comparable posterior means for the correlations but larger posterior standard deviations for them compared with using an MH algorithm to sample directly from the posterior distribution for the correlations. The reason is that sampling the entire matrix allows the diagonal elements to vary, and often, the sample variances will be less than one. Multiplying the off-diagonal elements by the inverse standard deviations of the relevant diagonal elements thus tends to produce a broader distribution for the correlation than using an MH algorithm to sample directly from the distribution for each correlation. All in all, then, this approach may yield more conservative inference than using MH sampling.

---

[5] Technically, there can only be $d(d-1)/2$ free elements of the covariance matrix, where d is the number of dimensions of the outcome.

If we decide to use an MH algorithm to sample the correlations, such can be done fairly easily. In a multivariate probit with d outcomes, we will have $d(d-1)/2$ free correlations to estimate. We can sequentially update these parameters, rather than updating them simultaneously, by drawing candidate values for each correlation from normal distributions centered over the previous value of the parameter, with some variance chosen to produce an acceptance rate of around 50%. Below are some example MH steps for sequentially drawing the correlations from a model with a three-dimensional outcome:

```
   .
   .
   .

for(j in 1:3)
  {
    cs=s
    like=-.5*(n+3+1)*log(det(s))-.5*sum(diag(v%*%solve(s)))
    if(j==1){cs[2,1]=cs[1,2]=cs[2,1]+rnorm(1,mean=0,sd=.007)}
    if(j==2){cs[3,1]=cs[1,3]=cs[3,1]+rnorm(1,mean=0,sd=.007)}
    if(j==3){cs[3,2]=cs[2,3]=cs[3,2]+rnorm(1,mean=0,sd=.007)}

    if((j==1 & abs(cs[2,1])<1) |
       (j==2 & abs(cs[3,1])<1) |
       (j==3 & abs(cs[3,2])<1))
     {
       clike=-.5*(n+3+1)*log(det(cs))-.5*sum(diag(v%*%solve(cs)))
       if((clike-like)>log(runif(1,0,1)))
         {s[i,,]=cs; acc[j]=acc[j]+1}
     }
  }
   .
   .
   .
```

This set of steps is intended to be placed somewhere within a larger algorithm for the multivariate probit model, where the variable v has been computed and is the matrix of sums of cross-products of errors and s is the error covariance matrix from the previous iteration, with diagonal elements permanently fixed at 1. The j loop loops over the three free elements of the covariance/correlation matrix. First, the log-posterior density is computed up to a proportionality constant. Then, a candidate is drawn for an element of the covariance matrix (cs[a,b]). If this candidate falls in the interval $[-1, 1]$—the allowable range for a correlation—then the log-posterior is computed using the candidate and the log-ratio R is computed (which is a subtraction in log scale) and compared with the log of a $U(0, 1)$ random draw, u. If the ratio exceeds $\log(u)$, then the correlation matrix is updated using the candidate. Otherwise, the matrix s[] remains as is.

10.2.5 Implementing the algorithm

We have already discussed the steps involved in the Gibbs sampler for the multivariate probit model, and in the previous sections, we have discussed various issues that must be handled in the algorithm that differentiate it from the algorithm we discussed for the multivariate linear regression model. All that remains is to integrate these. Below is the complete R algorithm for the current party affiliation/political orientation example:

```
#R program for multivariate probit model

x=as.matrix(read.table("c:\\mvnprob.dat1")[,1:7])
z=as.matrix(read.table("c:\\mvnprob.dat1")[,8:9])

#create variables and starting values
zstar=matrix(0,nrow(z),2)
d=2;k=7
b<-matrix(0,(d*k))
s=cs=diag(d)

tz=matrix(0,d,4)
tz[,1]=-Inf; tz[,2]=0; tz[,4]=Inf
tz[1,3]=qnorm(sum(z[,1]<=2)/nrow(z),
            mean=-qnorm(sum(z[,1]==1)/nrow(z),mean=0,sd=1),
            sd=1)
tz[2,3]=qnorm(sum(z[,2]<=2)/nrow(z),
            mean=-qnorm(sum(z[,2]==1)/nrow(z),mean=0,sd=1),
            sd=1)
ctz=tz

acc1=acc2=acctot=0;

write(c(0,t(b),t(s),tz[1,3],tz[2,3]),
      file="c:\\mvprob.res",ncolumns=(d*k+k*k +3),append=T)

#begin Gibbs sampling
for(i in 2:6000){

#draw latent data: one-iteration gibbs sampler for tmvn simulation
bb=matrix(b,k,2)
m=x%*%bb

for(j in 1:d)
{
 mm=m[,j]   + t(s[j,-j])%*%solve(s[-j,-j])%*%(zstar[,-j]-m[,-j])
 ss=s[j,j] - t(s[j,-j])%*%solve(s[-j,-j])%*%s[j,-j]

 zstar[,j]=qnorm(runif(nrow(z),
                 min=pnorm(tz[j,z[,j]],mm,sqrt(ss)),
```

```
                        max=pnorm(tz[j,(z[,j]+1)],mm,sqrt(ss))),
                mean=mm,sd=sqrt(ss))
}

#draw thresholds using Cowles' algorithm

ctz[1,3]=qnorm(runif(1,min=pnorm(0,mean=tz[1,3],sd=.01),max=1),
              mean=tz[1,3],sd=.01)
r=as.matrix((pnorm(ctz[1,z[,1]+1]-m[,1],0,1)
            -pnorm(ctz[1,z[,1]]-m[,1],0,1))
             /
            (pnorm(tz[1,z[,1]+1]-m[,1],0,1)
            -pnorm(tz[1,z[,1]]-m[,1],0,1)))
r= t(log(r))%*%matrix(1,nrow(z))
   +log((1-pnorm(-tz[1,3]/.01,0,1))/(1-pnorm(-ctz[1,3]/.01,0,1)))

if(r>log(runif(1,0,1))){tz[1,3]=ctz[1,3]; acc1=acc1+1}

ctz[2,3]=qnorm(runif(1,min=pnorm(0,mean=tz[2,3],sd=.01),max=1),
              mean=tz[2,3],sd=.01)
r=as.matrix((pnorm(ctz[2,z[,2]+1]-m[,2],0,1)
            -pnorm(ctz[2,z[,2]]-m[,2],0,1))
             /
            (pnorm(tz[2,z[,2]+1]-m[,2],0,1)
            -pnorm(tz[2,z[,2]]-m[,2],0,1)))

r=t(log(r))%*%matrix(1,nrow(z))
   +log((1-pnorm(-tz[2,3]/.01,0,1))/(1-pnorm(-ctz[2,3]/.01,0,1)))

if(r>log(runif(1,0,1))){tz[2,3]=ctz[2,3]; acc2=acc2+1}

#draw b from mvn
vb=solve(solve(s)%x%(t(x)%*%x))
mn=vb%*%(as.vector(t(x)%*%zstar%*%t(solve(s))))
b=mn+t(rnorm((d*k),0,1)%*%chol(vb))

#use metropolis-hastings sampling to draw sigma
e=matrix((as.vector(zstar)-(diag(d)%x%x%*%b)),nrow(z),d)
v=t(e)%*%e

like=-.5*((d+nrow(z)+1)*log(det(s)) + sum(diag(v%*%solve(s))))
cs[1,2]=cs[2,1]=s[1,2]+rnorm(1,mean=0,sd=.01)

if(abs(cs[1,2])<1)
 {
  cslike=-.5*((d+nrow(z)+1)*log(det(cs)) + sum(diag(v%*%solve(cs))))
  if((cslike-like)>log(runif(1,0,1)))
   {
    s[1,2]=s[2,1]=cs[1,2]; acctot=acctot+1
```

```
      }
    }

  if(i%%10==0){print(i)}
  if(i%%5==0){write(c(i,t(b),t(s),tz[1,3],tz[2,3]),
             file="c:\\mvprob.res",ncolumns=(d*k+k*k+3),append=T)}
  }
```

This algorithm is certainly the longest algorithm in the book thus far, but it is not inherently difficult to follow if it is considered in parts. As with other algorithms in the book, we first read the covariates and outcome variables into two matrices (x and z, respectively). Next, we establish matrices and starting values for the various parameters in the algorithm. Here, I created a variable to store the latent variables in (zstar), started each regression coefficient at 0, and started the error covariance matrix as an identity matrix. I created two matrices for the error covariance matrix—s and cs. One (cs) is a storage variable for candidate parameters, and the other (s) holds the previous value. Next, I created two sets of threshold parameters—one for the candidates, and one for the previous values, just as with the covariance matrix—and I initialized them as in Chapter 8 based on the proportion of respondents in each category of the original variable z. Finally, I created three acceptance rate variables in which to monitor the parameters being updated with MH steps.

Once the Gibbs sampler begins, the latent data are simulated using the Gibbs sampling approach described in Section 10.2.2. The only difference between the algorithm as written here versus in Section 10.2.2 is that it appears that I am only performing one iteration of the Gibbs sampler to obtain a draw for each zstar. In fact, this algorithm *does* only iterate the Gibbs sampler one time: It samples each latent trait (for each person) conditional on the values of the latent variable in the other dimensions. Whereas we needed to perform at least two iterations to produce a legitimate draw from the truncated multivariate normal distribution in Section 10.2.2, here, I rely on the value of the latent variable stored from the *previous* iteration of the overall Gibbs sampler for the model. As the overall Gibbs sampler for the model converges, so should the simulations from the truncated multivariate normal distribution within.

After these latent vectors are drawn, the two free thresholds are updated using Cowles' algorithm, as described in Section 10.2.3. This section of the program is repeated: The first instance is for the threshold in the latent distribution for the first dimension/equation; the second is for the the threshold in the latent distribution for the second dimension/equation. Next, the regression parameters are updated as in the original multivariate regression model at the beginning of this chapter. Finally, the free element in the error covariance matrix—the error correlation between the two dimensions of the outcome—is simulated using an MH step as described in the previous section.

The algorithm took approximately 45 minutes to run 6,000 iterations on my (average) desktop computer. Although this length of time is long compared with the time taken by the other algorithms presented in the book, it is considerably shorter than it would take if we had not used Cowles' algorithm to sample the thresholds, and it is considerably shorter than it would have taken a few years ago when processor speeds were much slower. Additionally, using R under another platform (e.g., UNIX), and/or using an alternative programming language (e.g., C in UNIX), would drastically improve speed.

Table 10.3 presents the results—after thinning the samples to every fifth value and dropping the first 200 samples as burn-in—and compares them to the results obtained from SAS's `proc logistic descending` procedure (STATA results are equivalent to the SAS results) using independent univariate ordinal probit models.

Table 10.3. Multivariate probit regression model of political orientation and party affiliation on covariates (GSS data, $n = 37,028$).

Variable	Multivariate Probit Model Bayesian Posterior Means		Univariate Probit Models Classical MLE	
	Dem. vs. Rep.	Lib. vs. Cons.	Dem. vs. Rep.	Lib. vs. Cons.
Intercept1	$-1.55(.07)^{***}$	$-0.35(.07)^{***}$	$-2.52(.07)^{***}$	$-1.37(.07)^{***}$
Intercept2	NA	NA	$-1.57(.07)^{***}$	$-0.34(.07)^{***}$
Year	$0.0097(.0007)^{***}$	$0.004(.0007)^{***}$	$0.0097(.0007)^{***}$	$0.004(.0007)^{***}$
Age	$-0.002(.0003)^{***}$	$0.007(.0003)^{***}$	$-0.002(.0004)^{***}$	$0.007(.0003)^{***}$
Male	$0.094(.012)^{***}$	$0.08(.01)^{***}$	$0.095(.012)^{***}$	$0.08(.01)^{***}$
White	$0.798(.018)^{***}$	$0.27(.016)^{***}$	$0.801(.017)^{***}$	$0.26(.02)^{***}$
South	$-0.014(.012)$	$0.15(.01)^{***}$	$-0.014(.013)$	$0.15(.01)^{***}$
Educ	$0.029(.002)^{***}$	$-0.001(.002)$	$0.029(.002)^{***}$	$-0.002(.002)$
τ_1	$-\infty$	$-\infty$	$-\infty$	$-\infty$
τ_2	0.0	0.0	NA	NA
τ_3	$0..96(.007)^{***}$	$1.03(.007)^{***}$	NA	NA
τ_4	$+\infty$	$+\infty$	$+\infty$	$+\infty$
ρ_e	$.327(.006)^{***}$			

Note: The Bayesian p-values are based on one-sided tail probabilities that the parameter exceeds 0 truncated to the classical cut-points of $^*p < .05$, $^{**}p < .01$, $^{***}p < .001$. For the MLEs, the p-values are based on the usual t-test.

The Bayesian results for the effect of year indicate that individuals have become more likely to consider themselves Republicans, and have become more conservative, over time. Older persons are more likely to be Democrats but are also more conservative than younger persons. Males and whites are more likely to be both conservative and Republican. There is no obvious regional difference in party affiliation, but Southerners are more likely to be conservative. Interestingly, years of schooling has a positive influence on the tendency to be Republican but does not affect political orientation.

The results of separate classical univariate probit models differ very little from the Bayesian results, with a couple of exceptions. First, as estimated by SAS, the univariate probit models have two intercepts and no estimated thresholds. This is a slightly different parameterization of the model than STATA's, which estimates no model intercept but multiple thresholds (see

Chapter 8), and it is clearly a different parameterization than our model with one intercept and one estimated threshold. However, if we consider our intercept as SAS's "Intercept 2", we can subtract the estimated threshold from this intercept to obtain SAS's "Intercept 1." Given that these threshold parameters are nuissance parameters, the parameterization of the model with respect to them has no substantive implications.

Second, the multivariate probit model results include an additional parameter, ρ_e, that was not estimated (obviously) in the univariate probit models. Our result for this parameter indicates that the errors are moderately and positively correlated ($\rho = .33$), meaning that unobserved factors that influence party affiliation tend to be positively correlated with unobserved factors that influence political orientation.

If the results of the multivariate probit model are generally indistinct from those of the separate univariate probit models estimated via maximum likelihood by extant software packages, then what is the advantage of the multivariate approach specifically and the Bayesian approach more generally? As we discussed at the beginning of the chapter, the main advantages to adopting a multivariate modeling strategy include (1) the elegance of using a single model, rather than multiple models; and (2) the gain in efficiency if the covariate vectors differ across equations. Additionally, if interest centers on making inference regarding *functions* of parameters rather than on the parameters themselves, a multivariate Bayesian approach can provide more information more simply than a classical approach.

In assessing this latter claim, using the current example, suppose our interest lay in understanding change in the concurrence of party affiliation and political orientation over time, and not on change in each independently. For instance, suppose our question is whether there has been a shift over time in the propensity for individuals to self-identify as conservative Republicans. This question requires us to examine the influence of time on a bivariate propensity—a two-dimensional integral in this model. Refer again to Figure 10.1—this probabiilty is the area above the third threshold in each dimension. This integral depends on the error correlation between equations as well as the model parameters applied to a set of specified covariate values. A set of univariate models lacks the error correlation and therefore cannot help us address this question. A classically estimated bivariate probit model, on the other hand, can help us obtain a point estimate of the probability a hypothetical individual (with a given set of covariate values) will self-identify as a conservative Republican. However, producing an interval estimate of this probability is not straightforward, because it would involve using some combination of the standard errors of the model parameters across the equations, plus incorporating the standard error of the error correlation, plus considering how these standard errors translate through the bivariate normal integral.

Under the Bayesian approach, we can easily produce a posterior distribution for the probability of self-identifying as a conservative Republican by using posterior predictive simulation. Throughout the book, we have used and discussed posterior predictive simulation as a tool for evaluating how well a model fits the data at hand; this is still true. However, posterior predictive simulation can also be used to make inference beyond that which can be made directly from the estimated model parameters. Specifically, we can make inference about change over time in the probability an individual with given characteristics will self-identify as a conservative Republican. The R program below shows how we can accomplish this:

```
g=as.matrix(read.table("c:\\mvprob1.out")[201:1200,])
summ=matrix(0,31,4)

#loop across all years
for(m in 1:31)
 {
   x=matrix(c(1,m+73,30,1,1,1,12),7)
   cellsum=matrix(0,1000)

   #loop over 1000 post-burnin samples of parameters
   for(i in 1:1000)
    {
     s=matrix(c(1,g[i,17],g[i,17],1),2,2)
     b=matrix(g[i,2:15],7,2)
     t1=g[i,20]; t2=g[i,21]
     xb=t(b)%*%x

     #generate 1000 ppd samples to compute probabilities
     #this step is equivalent to integration over desired cell
     for(j in 1:1000)
      {
        zz=xb+t(rnorm(2,0,1)%*%chol(s))
        if(zz[1]>t1 & zz[2]>t2){cellsum[i]=cellsum[i]+1}
      }
     if(i%%5==0){print(c(m,i))}
    }

   summ[m,1]=mean(cellsum/1000)
   summ[m,2]=sd(cellsum/1000)
   summ[m,3]=sort(cellsum)[25]
   summ[m,4]=sort(cellsum)[975]
 }
```

The R program first reads in the 1,000 post-burn-in parameter samples from the multivariate probit output file and creates a matrix to store summary statistics about the posterior predictive distributions for 31 individuals. The first loop (over m) is across the years of observation (1974 to 2004, a 31-year period). The vector x is then defined so that the posterior predictive simulation will be for a 30-year-old white male from the south with 12 years of education, for each year from 1974 through 2004.

Once the error correlation matrix (s), regression parameter matrix (b), and thresholds (t1 and t2) have been defined, a predicted score (xb) is computed. Next, 1,000 samples from a bivariate normal distribution with this predicted mean and given error covariance matrix are generated, and a tally of the number of these samples that fall above the appropriate threshold in each dimension is kept (cellsum). This step is equivalent to computing the integral of the bivariate normal distribution with the given mean and covariance over its upper right tail.

Once we have computed this tally for the current sample of the model parameters, we repeat the process for all 1,000 post-burn-in values of the parameters. The end result of this process is that, for each year, we obtain summaries of the distribution for the probability of self-identifying as a conservative Republican.

Figure 10.6 is a plot of the 95% probability intervals for being a conservative Republican from 1974 to 2004. As the figure shows, this probability has increased substantially over the 31-year period. In 1974, the probability a 30-year-old white Southern male with a high-school diploma would consider himself a conservative Republican was about .136 (95% interval of [.11, .16]). By 2004, this probability had increased to .197 (95% interval of [.17, .22]), which is a 45% increase in the probability.

In this example, I have shown how to answer only one question using posterior predictive simulation from the multivariate model results. Nonetheless, it should be clear that the approach is flexible and can be used for making any number of additional inferences. In the next section, I provide a more detailed and realistic use of the Bayesian approach to making inference to parameters not directly estimated in a multivariate setting.

10.3 A multivariate probit model for generating distributions of multistate life tables

The life table is a basic tool of demography that has been used for centuries. The basic measure produced by a life table—life expectancy—is the expected number of years of life remaining for individuals at given ages and is produced using age-specific probabilities (or rates) of mortality in a specific year (see Preston, Heuveline, and Guillot 2001; Schoen 1988). In the early 1970s, researchers began using hazard regression models (e.g., the discrete time probit model discussed in Chapter 8) to produce smoothed (parametric and predicted) mortality probabilities for life table estimation (see Cox 1972; Menken et al. 1981). Using hazard models allowed researchers to produce life tables for specific subpopulations, because estimated age-specific mortality rates for a subpopulation could be obtained from the hazard model by (1) applying the estimated model parameters to a given covariate profile (e.g., a specific value for age, sex, race, etc.) to obtain a predicted score and (2) transforming this value into a probability by inverting the link function used in the hazard

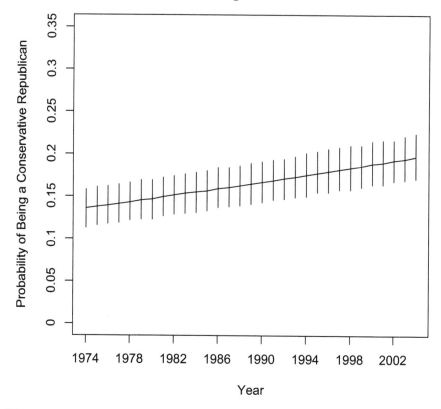

Fig. 10.6. Posterior predictive distributions for the probability a 30-year-old white male from the South self-identifies as a conservative Republican across time.

model. Once a complete set of age-specific estimated mortality probabilities is produced—by incrementing age and repeating the calculations, as we did in the previous section with the year variable—basic life table calculations can then be applied to produce a life table.

The multistate life table is an important extension of the basic life table that allows one to decompose total life expectancy into estimates of life remaining to be lived in different states (see Schoen 1988). For example, an important current measure derived from multistate life tables is healthy life expectancy (HLE), which is the number of remaining years that can be expected to be lived healthy (or some similar health-based state). Its complement, unhealthy life expectancy (ULE), is the number of remaining years that can be expected to be lived unhealthy, and the sum of HLE and ULE is total life expectancy (TLE) (e.g., see Crimmins, Saito, and Ingegneri 1997).

Whereas the basic life table requires age-specific mortality probabilities as input, the multistate life table requires age-specific transition probability *matrices* as input, where these matrices contain the probabilities of transitioning between the various states being considered. Figure 10.7 shows the "state

space" for a simple three-state model in which individuals can be healthy
(state 1), unhealthy (state 2), or dead (state 3), and the allowable transitions
are from the healthy state to healthy, unhealthy, or dead states, and from the
unhealthy state to either the healthy, unhealthy, or dead states. Thus, there
are six required transition probabilities (at each age).

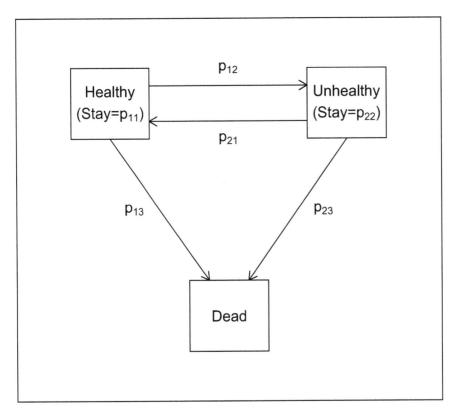

Fig. 10.7. Representation of state space for a three state model.

Figure 10.8 shows that the necessary age-specific transition probabilities
may be estimated with a bivariate dichotomous probit model, with healthy
versus unhealthy being one outcome variable, and alive versus dead being the
other. In order to actually capture transition probabilities, we need two-wave
panel data, so that we may know both the state in which individuals begin a
time interval and the state in which individuals end the interval. If we have
such data, then age and the starting state can be included as covariates, along
with any other variables desired.

Age-specific transition probabilities can then be produced from the model
parameters by computing the linear combination of parameters and desired
covariate values. To obtain the complete age range, this linear combination

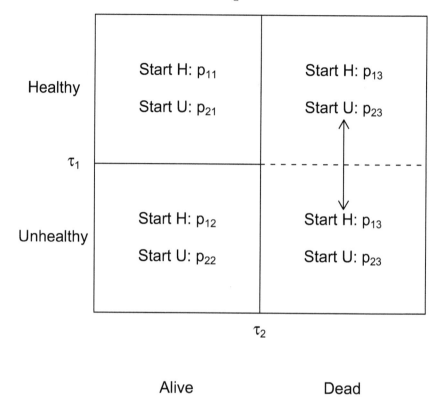

	Alive	Dead

Fig. 10.8. Two-dimensional outcome for capturing a three-state state space.

should be repeated, incrementing age from the youngest to oldest ages. To obtain all transition probabilities, the covariate value for the starting state (i.e., healthy vs. unhealthy) must be set to each of its possible values. The transition probabilities can then be obtained as in the univariate hazard model discussed above by inverting the link function applied to the predicted values. However, in the multistate case, the link function is multivariate, and so the transition probabilities are obtained via bivariate integration. I illustrate this process in the example.

The process of using a multivariate model with covariates to produce transition probabilities for input into multistate life table calculations is not new (see Land, Guralnik, and Blazer 1994). However, the classical approach to estimation using maximum likelihood methods does not allow a straightforward method for constructing interval estimates of the state expectancies (HLE, ULE, and TLE) in these tables (but see Laditka and Wolf 1998 for a method to do so via simulation). It is unclear how the estimated standard errors for the parameters translate into standard errors for state expectancies, as we discussed regarding the party affiliation/political orientation example in the previous section. Thus, to date, most researchers using multistate life tables produced from hazard model results have simply reported point estimates for life table quantities. Yet, given that the data used for model estimation typically come from samples, and are not population data, we need to be able to quantify at a minimum the uncertainty inherent in using sample data to make inference to populations. The Bayesian approach offers a straightforward way of doing so (see Lynch and Brown 2005 for a more in-depth discussion than what is presented below for single decrement, multiple decrement, and multistate life tables using Gibbs samplers and MH algorithms).

10.3.1 Model specification and simulation

The data for this example are from the 1987 and 1992 NHEFS. As described earlier, the NHEFS is a series of at least four surveys, begun in 1971 and continuing in 1982, 1987, and 1992. The original sample size was 14,407 persons. After elminating persons who died or dropped out of the survey by 1987, restricting the age range to persons 45 years of age or older in 1987, and eliminating individuals who were missing on one or more variables of interest, I obtained a sample of $n = 3,495$ persons. I include age in 1987, sex, race, region of residence, marital status (both measured in 1987), education, and self-rated health in 1987 and 1992 in the analyses. Self-rated health is dichotomized as "Excellent" or "Good" health versus "Fair" or "Poor" health in both 1987 and 1992, and the 1987 measure is included as a covariate. Age is measured in five-year intervals (i.e., 45-49 = 0, 50-54 = 1, ..., 85+ = 8). Sex, race, region, and marital status are measured as dummy variables (male = 1, nonwhite = 1, South = 1, married = 1), and education is measured as years of schooling.

A bivariate probit model for predicting health status (unhealthy vs. healthy) and survival status (dead vs. alive) in 1992 is constructed, with health status in 1987, and an interaction between age and health status in 1987, included as predictors, along with sex, race, region, marital status, and education. The bivariate probit model for predicting health and survival status in 1992 does not differ substantially from the bivariate probit model discussed in the previous section, and so I do not repeat the general model here (refer to the previous section).

One feature of the model, however, does differ and requires some discussion. Given the outcome space shown in Figure 10.8, it is clear that we can observe health status among *survivors* but not among *decedents*. For individuals who died between the 1987 and 1992 waves, health status in 1992 is not observed, because the respondent, of course, could not be interviewed in 1992. This dilemma constitutes a missing data problem of sorts and is easily handled via Gibbs sampling. The only change in the model—and really, in the Gibbs sampler—is that latent data for the health outcome for decedents must be simulated without the truncation constraint. Below is the R program for the model after making this adjustment:

```
#read data
x=as.matrix(read.table("c:\\mvnprob.dat2")[,1:9])
z=as.matrix(read.table("c:\\mvnprob.dat2")[,10:11])

#estabish variables
zstar=matrix(0,nrow(z),2)

b<-matrix(0,18)
s<-diag(d); cs<-diag(d)

acctot=0

#define thresholds--note 'trick' for t3 and t4
tz=matrix(0,d,4);ctz=matrix(0,d,4)
tz[1]=-Inf; tz[2]=0; tz[3]=tz[4]=Inf

write(c(0,t(b),t(s)),file="c:\\mshaz.out", ncolumns=23,append=T)

#begin Gibbs sampler
for(i in 2:10000){

#draw latent data
bb=matrix(b,9,2)
m=x%*%bb

#mini mvn gibbs sampler--KEY PART
mm=m[,2] + s[1,2]*(zstar[,1]-m[,1])
ss=1-s[1,2]^2

zstar[,2]=qnorm(runif(nrow(z),
min=pnorm(tz[z[,2]+1],mm,sqrt(ss)),
max=pnorm(tz[z[,2]+2],mm,sqrt(ss))),mean=mm,sd=sqrt(ss))

mm=m[,1] + s[1,2]*(zstar[,2]-m[,2])
ss=1-s[1,2]^2

zstar[,1]=qnorm(runif(nrow(z),
min=pnorm(tz[z[,1]-z[,2]+1],mm,sqrt(ss)),
max=pnorm(tz[z[,1]+z[,2]+2],mm,sqrt(ss))),mean=mm,sd=sqrt(ss))

#draw b from mvn
vb=solve(solve(s)%x%(t(x)%*%x))
mn=vb%*%(as.vector(t(x)%*%zstar%*%t(solve(s))))
b=mn+t(rnorm(18,0,1)%*%chol(vb))

#simulate s using MH sampling
e=matrix((as.vector(zstar)-(diag(2)%x%x%*%b)),nrow(z),2)
v=t(e)%*%e
```

```
like=-.5*(2+nrow(z)+1)*log(det(s))-.5*sum(diag(v%*%solve(s)))
cs[1,2]=cs[2,1]=s[1,2]+rnorm(1,mean=0,sd=.03)

if(abs(cs[1,2])<1)
{
  cslike=-.5*(2+nrow(z)+1)*log(det(cs))-.5*sum(diag(v%*%solve(cs)))
  if((cslike-like)>log(runif(1,0,1)))
    {s[1,2]=s[2,1]=cs[1,2]; acctot=acctot+1}
}

if(i%%10==0){print(c(i,b[1],b[1+k],s[1,2],acctot/i),digits=5)}
if(i%%5==0)
  {write(c(i,t(b),t(s)),file="c:\\mshaz.out",ncolumns=23,append=T)}
}
```

This algorithm is remarkably similar to the longer algorithm presented in the previous section with only a few exceptions. First, there is no estimation of thresholds. Given that both dimensions of the outcome are dichotomous, there are only three thresholds in each dimension, and these are fixed at $-\infty$, 0, and ∞ in each dimension to identify the model. Second, I have added a fourth threshold in each dimension; these thresholds are set equal to ∞—like the third threshold in each dimension—and are used as a computing convenience.

Third, and most importantly, the simulation of the latent data imposes slightly different truncation requirements (see the lines after the KEY PART comment). The outcome variables are coded so that the mortality outcome takes a 1 or 0 value, and the health outcome takes a 1 or 0 value for survivors and a 1 for decedents. With this coding, simulation of the latent data underlying the observed dichotomous outcomes is as follows:

Observed outcome	Latent health trait	Latent mortality trait
alive and healthy	below 0	below 0
alive and unhealthy	above 0	below 0
dead	no truncation	above 0

The specifc snippets of code that perform the last simulation are:

```
...min=pnorm(tz[z[,1]-z[,2]+1]...
   max=pnorm(tz[z[,1]+z[,2]+2]...
```

For individuals who die, the first snippet reduces to tz[1], and the second reduces to tz[4]. Thus, the latent trait for health is simulated from $-\infty$ to ∞. For persons who remain alive and are healthy in 1992, in contrast, these snippets reduce to t[1] and t[2] ($-\infty$ to 0). Finally, for persons who remain alive but are unhealthy in 1992, these snippets reduce to t[2] and t[3] (0 to ∞).

It is important to realize that, although these are minor changes to the model/program, handling this missing data could not be easily done without a multivariate model. If we were using separate univariate probit models for health and mortality, decedents would be treated as missing observations and would, by default, be listwise deleted by most software packages. Even if a univariate model were employed that used a FIML estimator or some other method to compensate for the missing outcome data, it would be less efficient than the multivariate approach, which can use the error correlation between equations, as well as the covariate effects in the mortality dimension, to inform inference regarding the missing data.

10.3.2 Life table generation and other posterior inferences

As the program indicates, I ran this Gibbs sampler for 10,000 iterations, saving every fifth sample. All parameters converged very rapidly and mixed very thoroughly, and I retained the last 1,000 samples for posterior inference. Table 10.4 shows the posterior means and posterior standard deviations for model parameters. Age and poor health in 1987 had expected positive effects on both poor health and mortality. Also, as expected, males, nonwhites, and Southerners had generally poorer health and greater mortality risk than females, whites, and nonsoutherners, while education and marriage had protective effects.

Table 10.4. Results of multivariate probit regression of health and mortality on covariates.

	Outcome	
Variable	Poor Health	Mortality
Intercept	$-0.65(.15)$***	$-2.50(.18)$***
Age	$0.069(.02)$***	$0.34(.02)$***
Unhealthy in '87	$1.44(.12)$***	$0.77(.16)$***
Age×Unhealthy in '87	$-0.03(.03)$	$-0.04(.03)$#
Male	$0.13(.06)$*	$0.38(.07)$***
Nonwhite	$0.35(.09)$***	$0.05(.10)$
South	$0.04(.06)$	$0.09(.07)$#
Married	$-0.20(.07)$**	$-0.16(.07)$*
Yrs. Schooling	$-0.05(.01)$***	$-0.02(.01)$*
σ_{12}	$-0.10(.17)$	

Note: The Bayesian estimates are posterior means. The Bayesian p-values are based on one-sided tail probabilities that the parameter exceeds 0 truncated to the classical cut-points of #$p < .1$, *$p < .05$, **$p < .01$.

While these parameters themselves may be of interest, we can also use them to construct multistate life tables for specific subpopulations. In the previous section's example, we considered the probability an individual would self-identify as a conservative Republican. This probability was computed by (1) producing a predicted value based on an established set of covariates and each sample of model parameters, (2) using posterior predictive simulation to simulate observations with the given characteristics, and (3) tallying the number of simulated individuals who fell in the appropriate cell of the contingency table, based on their scores and the values of the thresholds that divide the continuous latent variable into the ordinal ones. In the example, the proportion of individuals that fell above the third threshold in both dimensions was the probability of being a conservative Republican. In the current example, we need to follow a similar procedure, but with a few differences.

First, we must compute more than one proportion—we need a number of probabilities to construct the entire transition probability matrix needed as input for multistate life table generation. Second, rather than using posterior predictive simulation and computing the proportion of our draws that fall in various regions of the latent distribution, we will compute these probabilities directly using bivariate normal integration. Third, one of our covariates— whether an individual is healthy or unhealthy in 1987—is important for computing transition probabilities appropriately, and so, we will need to change this covariate's value in order to obtain all the needed transition probabilities for a given age.

The age-specific transition probability matrices for this three-state model (healthy, unhealthy, dead) are 3×3. The first row contains the conditional probabilities of transitioning from the healthy state to the healthy state (retention probability), from the healthy state to the unhealthy state, and from the healthy state to the deceased state. These probabilities can be obtained from the model parameter samples by setting the starting state covariate to 0 and all other covariates to predetermined, desired values, and then computing predicted values for each age $[X\beta(1)$ in the health dimension; $X\beta(2)$ in the mortality dimension]. We can then integrate a 0-mean bivariate normal distribution with appropriate correlation from the Gibbs sampler over the appropriate regions to obtain the desired transition probabilities for the first row of the transition probability matrix. These integrals are:

$$p_{12} = \int_{-\infty}^{X\beta(1)} \int_{X\beta(2)}^{\infty} BVN(0, \rho)$$

$$p_{13} = \int_{-\infty}^{\infty} \int_{-\infty}^{X\beta(2)} BVN(0, \rho)$$

$$p_{11} = 1 - (p_{12} + p_{13}).$$

To obtain the transition probabilities for the unhealthy starting state, we simply need to change the starting state covariate to 1 (to represent an unhealthy starting state) and recompute these integrals as follows:

$$p_{22} = \int_{-\infty}^{X\beta(1)} \int_{X\beta(2)}^{\infty} BVN(0, \rho)$$

$$p_{23} = \int_{-\infty}^{\infty} \int_{-\infty}^{X\beta(2)} BVN(0, \rho)$$

$$p_{21} = 1 - (p_{22} + p_{23}).$$

The final row of each transition probability matrix is fixed to $[0 \quad 0 \quad 1]$ to represent that no transitions out of the deceased state can occur.

Below is an R program that performs these computations and then converts the transition probability matrices into multistate life tables:

```
ageints=9; n=5
cv=matrix(c(0,1,1,1,16),ageints,5,byrow=T)
x=matrix(1,ageints,9); x[,2]=seq(0,ageints); x[,5:9]=cv
g<-as.matrix(read.table("c:\\mshaz.out"))
b=matrix(0,9,2)

radix=c(.848,.152,0)

mpower<-function(mat,power)
 {ma<-diag(3);for(i in 1:power){ma=ma%*%mat};return(ma)}

for(m in 1001:2000){
#read in parameter sample
b[(1:9),1]=g[m,(2:10)]; b[(1:9),2]=g[m,(11:19)]
rho=g[m,21]
sig=matrix(c(1,rho,rho,1),2,2)

#compute predicted values for transitions: start h
x[,3]=0; x[,4]=0; hfb=x%*%b

#compute predicted values for transitions: start u
x[,3]=1; x[,4]=x[,2]; ufb=x%*%b

#establish life table variables
l<-array(0,c(ageints,3,3)); l[1,,]=diag(3)*radix
bl<-matrix(0,ageints,2); tl<-matrix(0,ageints,2)

#compute transition probabilities matrices
for(a in 1:ageints){
pmat[1,2]=pmvnorm(lower=c(-Inf,hfb[a,2]),upper=c(hfb[a,1],+Inf),
                  mean=c(0,0),corr=sig)
pmat[1,3]=pmvnorm(lower=c(-Inf,-Inf),upper=c(+Inf,hfb[a,2]),
```

```
                   mean=c(0,0),corr=sig)
pmat[2,2]=pmvnorm(lower=c(-Inf,ufb[a,2]),upper=c(ufb[a,1],+Inf),
                   mean=c(0,0),corr=sig)
pmat[2,3]=pmvnorm(lower=c(-Inf,-Inf),upper=c(+Inf,ufb[a,2]),
                   mean=c(0,0),corr=sig)
pmat[1,1]=1-(pmat[1,2]+pmat[1,3])
pmat[2,1]=1-(pmat[2,2]+pmat[2,3])

#convert tp to m via Sylvester's formula
mmat=0
lam2=(pmat[2,2]+pmat[1,1]+
     sqrt((pmat[2,2]+pmat[1,1])^2-
          4*(pmat[1,1]*pmat[2,2]-pmat[1,2]*pmat[2,1])))/2
lam3=(pmat[2,2]+pmat[1,1]-
     sqrt((pmat[2,2]+pmat[1,1])^2-
          4*(pmat[1,1]*pmat[2,2]-pmat[1,2]*pmat[2,1])))/2
mmat= (log(lam2)/((lam2-1)*(lam2-lam3)))*
((pmat-diag(3))%*%(pmat-lam3*diag(3)))+
(log(lam3)/((lam3-1)*(lam3-lam2)))*
((pmat-diag(3))%*%(pmat-lam2*diag(3)))
mmat=-mmat

#compute lx and Lx for next age group
if(a<ageints)
{
expm=diag(3);pyr=diag(3)
for(j in 1:20)
{
expm=expm + ((-1)^j)*mpower(mmat,j)/factorial(j);
pyr=pyr  + ((-1)^j)*mpower(mmat,j)/factorial(j+1);
}

lx=l[a,,]%*%(expm)
l[a+1,1,1]=sum(lx[,1]); l[a+1,2,2]=sum(lx[,2]); l[a+1,3,3]=0;
blx=n*(l[a,,]%*%pyr)
bl[a,1]=sum(blx[,1]); bl[a,2]=sum(blx[,2])
}

if(a==ageints)
{
blx=l[a,1:2,1:2]%*%solve(mmat[1:2,1:2])
bl[a,1]=sum(blx[,1]); bl[a,2]=sum(blx[,2])
}
}

le<-matrix(NA,ageints,2)
for(a in 1:ageints){
tl[a,1]=sum(bl[a:ageints,1]); tl[a,2]=sum(bl[a:ageints,2])
le[a,]=tl[a,]/sum(l[a,,])
```

```
}
write(c(t(le)),file="c:\\lifetab.out",append=T,ncolumns=(2*ageints))
print(c(m,le[1,1],le[1,2]))
}
```

This program is fairly lengthy, and I will not discuss it in great depth. A number of variables are defined at the beginning, including the number of age intervals (9), the number of years in each age interval (5), and the values of the five fixed covariates (male, nonwhite, South, married, and years of schooling). These covariate values are repeated for nine lines in the x matrix, which contains incremented values of age. Next, the parameter file is read. Finally, the radix is established. The radix is the number or proportion of individuals in each state at the beginning of the first age in the life table.

After defining a function that computes a matrix raised to a specified power, the loop begins to generate a life table for each post-burn-in sample from the Gibbs sampler. The parameters are read in one sample at a time and are combined with the covariate matrix, first with the starting state set to 0 (to produce hfb) and then with the starting state set to 1 (to produce ufb).

After obtaining these two 9×2 matrices of predicted values, several life table variables are established before the computation of the life tables begins. A loop across age is established to produce the life table. First, the age-specific transition probability matrix is computed. Second, this matrix is transformed into the hazard rate matrix using Sylvester's formula to compute its log (see Singer and Spilerman 1976). The remainder of the program proceeds with typical steps in computing the number of individuals transitioning between states over the age interval and the number of person-years lived in each state during the interval (see Schoen 1988).

As an example, I ran this program to produce life tables for married nonwhite females from the South with 16 years of education. The radix was established by predicting the starting state (healthy/unhealthy) using age, sex, race, region, marital status, and education, and then computing the predicted score, based on the covariate profile just described. Figure 10.9 shows trace plots of HLE, ULE, TLE, and the proportion of remaining life that can be expected to be lived healthy (HLE/TLE). These trace plots suggest that the life table quantities converged and mixed thoroughly, just as the parameters in the original Gibbs sampler did. Figure 10.10 shows histograms of these same quantities; all appear approximately normal.

The samples of life table quantities can be summarized just as we would summarize other sample data. Mean TLE at age 45 for a person with the given covariate profile is 33.1 years, with a standard deviation of 1.5 years; an empirical interval estimate is [30.0, 35.9] years. The expected number of years remaining health was 25.4 years, with a standard deviation of 1.9 years; an empirical interval estimate is [21.7, 29.2] years. The remaining proportion of life to be spent healthy, based on these results, is .77, with an empirical interval estimate of [.68, .84]. If we wished to compare these results with those for a person with a different covariate profile, we would simply rerun the R

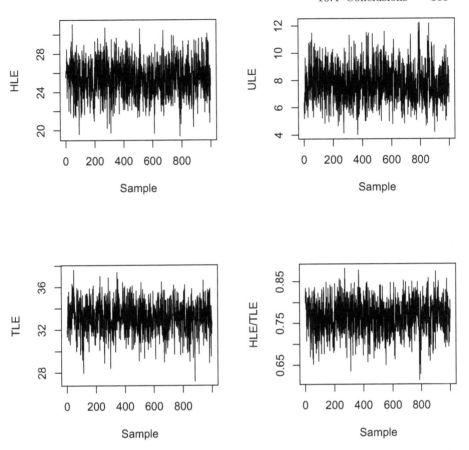

Fig. 10.9. Trace plots of life table quantities computed from Gibbs samples of bivariate probit model parameters.

program for a different covariate profile and then perform whatever sort of comparison we would like, treating the samples of life table quantities as we would a sample of parameters or a sample of data.

10.4 Conclusions

In this chapter, I have described the multivariate linear regression model and the multivariate probit model, perhaps two of the most important multivariate models that may be used in social science. Multivariate models are mathematically and computationally more complex than univariate models, and so I have paid particular attention to the reasons for using such models. As I

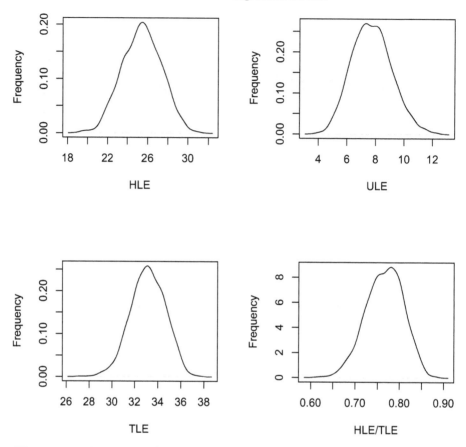

Fig. 10.10. Histograms of life table quantitities computed from Gibbs samples of bivariate probit model parameters.

have shown, the Bayesian approach to these particular models offers several benefits over a classical approach, especially when inference for auxilliary parameters is of interest.

This chapter should be considered simply an introduction to multivariate regression models, however, because we have not discussed many additional common and useful multivariate models like the multinomial probit model and simultaneous/structural equation models. Although simultaneous/structural equation models are substantially more difficult than the models presented here, the multinomial probit model is not inherently more difficult than the multivariate probit model (see Exercises). I recommend reading Bollen (1989), Hayduk (1987), Kaplan (2000) and Maruyama (1998) for an introduction to these models from a classical perspective. I recommend Lee and Zhu (2000) and Song and Lee (2002) for a Bayesian approach.

10.5 Exercises

1. Develop a simple rejection sampling scheme for sampling from selected regions of the three-dimensional (trivariate) normal distribution.
2. Develop a Gibbs sampler for a multivariate model in which some of the outcomes are continuous and some are ordinal. How difficult is this process relative to constructing a full multivariate probit sampling algorithm?
3. A polychoric correlation matrix is the correlation matrix between the latent variables in a multivariate probit model with no covariates. This type of matrix is commonly used as input for structural equation models when ordinal data are present. How could the Gibbs sampler for the multivariate probit model be modified to obtain the polychoric correlation matrix rather than regression coefficients and an error correlation matrix?
4. The multinomial probit model differs only slightly from the multivariate probit model. In the multinomial probit model, the outcomes in each dimension are all dichotomous and are mutually exclusive; that is, an individual can only take a 1 on (at most) a single outcome variable. The model is generally used in social sciences for predicting a nominal level outcome—the outcome variable is broken into a series of dummy variables with one omitted as the reference. The mutual exclusivity constraint leads to only two differences between the multinomial probit and the multivariate probit we have already discussed. First, a slightly different approach to sampling the latent data thought to underlie the observed response must be undertaken. Second, only one of the diagonal elements of the error covariance matrix must be constrained to 1 to identify the model. Regarding the simulation of the latent data, individuals are assumed to have latent traits, the maximum of which is the one for which the respondent's observed outcome is "1." That latent trait must be above 0. Latent traits for the other outcomes may also be above 0 but cannot be larger than that one. If an individual does not take a "1" value on any of the outcomes (i.e., his/her response is the reference outcome), all latent traits must be sampled from below 0. Develop a multinomial probit model algorithm and compare the results with those obtained using a multinomial logit procedure in another software package (see Imai and van Dyk 2005 for an in-depth consideration of various extant MCMC approaches to this model).

11

Conclusion

The goal of this book has been to describe a Bayesian approach to statistics, including the process of estimating parameters via Markov chain Monte Carlo (MCMC) methods, applied to models that are relatively common in social science research. Throughout the text, I have referenced a small portion of a much larger body of literature on Bayesian theory, Bayesian modeling, and MCMC methodology that has emerged over the last two decades. I have largely limited these references to sources that I have found to be invaluable in my studies and that were the most important and directly relevant sources to the topic being addressed. Yet, I have barely scratched the surface of potential sources. In this concluding chapter, I present a number of books and articles that I recommend reading to gain a more in-depth understanding of the topics I have discussed throughout the book, as well as some topics that I have not addressed. Some of these references I have presented in previous chapters; some I have not. Here, I provide a condensed summary.

As we have seen, the Bayesian approach to statistics involves (1) setting up a research question; (2) establishing a probability model for the data we intend to use to answer the question; (3) incorporating prior knowledge via the development of a prior distribution; (4) deriving the posterior distribution for the parameters, given the data and prior knowledge; (5) simulating samples of model parameters using MCMC methods; (6) evaluating the fit of the model and perhaps choosing a "best" model from among a variety of models; and (7) summarizing the parameter samples—including some that were derived from the original parameters—using basic descriptive statistics.

From these steps it is clear that understanding the Bayesian approach and implementing it requires a solid understanding of probability theory, and so the second chapter of this book covered the foundations of probability theory and the mathematical approach to statistics required to complete a Bayesian analysis. As I stated in Chapter 2, my coverage of this material was sufficient for our purposes, but I recommend DeGroot (1986) and Rudas (2004) for a more in-depth presentation. Both of these texts are thorough, yet very readable, and present a much broader view of probability theory than covered in this text.

The latter part of Chapter 2 reviewed the classical approach to statistics, from a probability-theory standpoint, involving maximum likelihood estimation. Most graduate statistics courses and books present the basics of this estimation method, but I recommend Edwards (1992) for a more theoretical discussion of this approach (and a rejection of the Bayesian one!) and Eliason (1993) for greater detail on the actual mechanics involved in producing ML estimates.

Chapter 3 provided a detailed presentation of Bayes' Theorem for both point probabilities and probability distributions. In this process, I covered some of the key arguments that have been presented historically against the Bayesian approach to statistics. I am personally convinced that many of these arguments have been adquately resolved over the last few decades, if not the last century. Nonetheless, I recommend reading Jeffreys (1961) and, again, Edwards (1992) for the theoretical bases for and against the Bayesian paradigm. One of the key arguments against the Bayesian approach has centered on the use of prior distributions. I strongly recommend Gelman et al. (1995) and Gill (2002) for lengthier discussions of prior distributions, including how to make them noninformative so as to avoid the argument that priors corrupt results by introducing too much subjectivity into the model. In this book, I have largely avoided using highly informative priors. As I said in Chapter 3, most Bayesian analyses to date, especially in social science research, have used such noninformative priors to avoid the subjectivity criticism. I think this is an appropriate strategy, but I also believe that the use of informative priors will be useful in the future in formalizing the current state of knowledge and incorporating it into the model so as to make social science research truly cumulative. From my view, social science research currently incorporates prior knowledge informally via the literature review in the hypothesis construction and model selection process, but we often see the same hypotheses tested again and again, leading to a broadening of research questions and findings rather than an accumulation of them.

Once one has decided to undertake a Bayesian analysis and has obtained a posterior distribution, the next step in the analysis is to summarize it. The summarization process is the primary area in which tremendous advances have been made in Bayesian statistics in the last few decades. Prior to 1990, Bayesian analyses often required extensive knowledge of numerical methods to approximate integrals necessary for adequately summarizing posterior densities. The emergence of the use of MCMC methods in statistics replaced the need for a stong background in numerical methods with a need for a background in simulation methods. The goal of Chapters 4 through 6 was to provide an introduction to these methods, specifically the Gibbs sampler and the random walk Metropolis algorithm. For an introduction to general simulation methods, I first recommend Ripley (1987). Next, I strongly recommend Gilks, Richardson, and Spiegelhalter (1996), the first major book introducing

MCMC methods in great detail. A number of additional books have appeared since then providing much more technical and theoretical detail specifically regarding the implementation of MCMC (and related) methods. Along these lines, I recommend Chen, Shao, and Ibrahim (2000), Liu (2001), and Robert and Casella (1999). These books are extremely detailed and provide advanced discussion of simulation approaches for various models. I also recommend Casella and George (1992) and Smith and Gelfand (1992) for concise, readable discussions of MCMC methods.

The actual summarization of the posterior distribution for the model parameters, once a sample from it has been obtained or it has been determined that the density is a known form from which integrals can be analytically derived, is a straightforward process. In this book, we began describing the summarization of the posterior distribution in Chapter 3, and we continued throughout the remainder of the book as we covered some of the most common classes of models used in social science research.

There is a large and growing market of introductory books on Bayesian statistics, and every one of them covers the process of Bayesian analysis from Bayesian model development through the process of summarization of the posterior distribution. Each introductory book, however, tends to have a different selection of models covered as well as a slightly different emphasis. In this book, I have attempted to cover models that are most likely to be used by social science researchers using observational data on humans collected through social surveys. Nonetheless, such are not the only data analyzed by social scientists, and the models I discussed do not constitute an exhaustive set. Additionally, this book does not exhaust the possible approaches to introducing Bayesian statistics, and therefore, I suggest a number of additional introductory books.

First, I recommend Gill (2002), which, to my knowledge is the only other extant book written for social scientists. Second, I cannot recommend Gelman et al. (1995) strongly enough. That book is now a classic text on Bayesian statistics and covers much more ground than I covered here, albeit at a more advanced level. I recommend Box and Tiao (1973) as a classic introductory book written at an advanced level focused primarily on Bayesian theory. Along those lines, I recommend Lee (1989), and Robert (1994), which are also somewhat theoretical but written at a less advanced level. In addition to these books, I suggest Congdon (2001 and 2003) for highly applied introductions written at an advanced level. Finally, I recommend Leonard and Hsu (1999) and Sivia (1996), both of which are very readable introductions to the Bayesian approach to statistics.

Noticeably absent from this book is an introduction to time series analysis, despite the fact that several of my examples suggested (if not begged for) a time series modeling approach. With the growth in the availability of longitudinal data, both in terms of panel data and repeated cross-sectional data, time series analyses have become increasingly important in social science over the last several decades. I recommend Hamilton (1994) for an exposition of the classical approach to time series analysis. Additionally, I recommend Alho and Spencer (2005) for a statistical demographic approach to time series, and I suggest Pole, West, and Harrison (1994) for a Bayesian appproach to time series models.

Although this book has been written as an introduction to Bayesian statistics, many of the models presented can be—and generally are!—estimated via maximum likelihood. In many cases I have compared Bayesian results with those that would be obtained via maximum likelihood approaches. The point of the book has been to show the flexibility and advantages of the Bayesian approach using models that are familiar to social scientists. As we have seen, the primary advantages of a Bayesian approach to modeling include the flexibility of altering the model to suit your needs, the ease of estimating quantities that are not directly estimated in the model, the ease of conducting inference and interpreting the results, and the ability to diagnose problems in models in which maximum likelihood solutions are neither satisfactory nor sufficient. I hope that now, after having read this book, you will agree with these conclusions and begin to explore the vast and growing literature on Bayesian statistics and consider using a Bayesian approach in your own research.

A

Background Mathematics

Although mathematics and statistics are different disciplines, a general background in mathematics and mathematical concepts is important for a solid understanding of statistics. In this appendix, I summarize the basic concepts from calculus and matrix algebra that are necessary to understand mathematical statistics. In addition to the basic summary of calculus presented below, I recommend Thompson 1946, a classic, condensed calculus text. In addition to my summary of matrix algebra, I recommend Harville 1997. For additional math commonly used throughout the book, I recommend Hagle 1996.

A.1 Summary of calculus

Calculus can be divided into two halves: differential and integral calculus. In a nutshell, differential calculus is concerned with slopes of curves and rates of change. Integral calculus, on the other hand, is concerned with area under and between curves.

A.1.1 Limits

Central to both branches of calculus is the notion of "limits." A limit is the result a function returns as some quantity in the function approaches some value. For example, the limit of the function $f(x) = 1/x$ as x approaches infinity is 0. In calculus notation we write this expression as:

$$\lim_{x \to \infty} \frac{1}{x} = 0. \tag{A.1}$$

The concept of a limit is fairly intuitive. If we imagine in this example that $x = 1$, then the function value is 1. If $x = 2$, then the function value is smaller, at $1/2$. As x gets larger, the fraction gets smaller, so that, as x approaches the largest value possible (∞), the fraction's value approaches 0. Evaluating limits can be quite difficult, and a good part of a first course in calculus is spent learning how to determine limits when expressions are more complex. For example, imagine if the limit in Equation A.1 were taken as $x \to 0$.

A.1.2 Differential calculus

With the basic concept of a limit defined, the two main branches of calculus can be developed. Differential calculus is essentially concerned with slopes of curves. When one considers the slope of a line, one is referring to a constant: A line has a given slope, and that slope does not change regardless of the location on the line at which the slope is evaluated. In contrast, the slope of a curve varies depending on the point on the curve where the slope is evaluated. In defining the slope of a curve, it is thus necessary to define a tangent line. A tangent line is a line that intersects a curve at a single point (see Figure A.1).

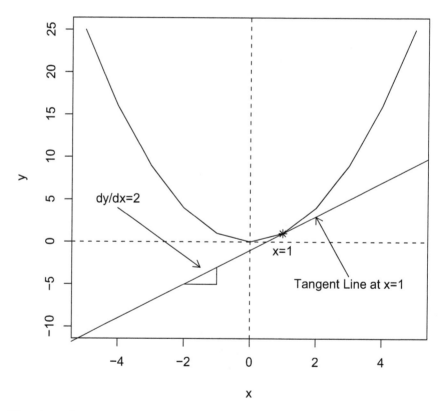

Fig. A.1. Generic depiction of a curve and a tangent line at an arbitrary point.

When we want to determine the slope of a curve, we are referring to the slope of the tangent line at that point. Recall from basic algebra that a line (and, consequently, its slope) is determined by two points. Imagine, then, that we want to evaluate the slope of a curve, say the curve $y = x^2$, at the location $x = 1$ (thus, $y = 1$). The curve $y = x^2$ is a parabola, centered at the origin and increasing as x moves away from 0. In order to determine the slope of the curve, we could begin by taking two points on the curve, say where $x = 0$ and $x = 2$, and then evaluating the slope of the line determined by these points. This approach would give an approximation to the slope of the curve at $x = 1$. Where $x = 0$, $y = 0$, and where $x = 2$, $y = 4$. The slope of a line can be computed by taking the ratio of the change in y to the change in x. Such changes can be denoted as Δy and Δx, respectively, with the ratio being expressed as dy/dx in calculus. Thus, the slope of this line is $dy/dx = 2$. However, what two coordinates should we use to determine the slope of the curve at a point? If we change coordinates, we will most likely change the estimate of the slope of the tangent line at the point of interest. It makes sense that the further we get away from the x coordinate we are examining, the worse the estimate will be; hence, perhaps we should get as close to the desired x coordinate as possible (i.e., move from $x = 0$ and $x = 2$ to $x = .99$ and $x = 1.01$). In calculus, using limits, we can define this "closing in on x" as:

$$\text{slope of curve at x} \equiv \frac{dy}{dx} = \lim_{\Delta x \to 0} \frac{f(x + \Delta x) - f(x)}{\Delta x}. \qquad \text{(A.2)}$$

Equation A.2 says that the slope of the curve—called a derivative—evaluated at x is the limit of the slope of the line created by taking two points on either side of x, as those points get infinitely close to x. This equation is intuitively simple—it is simply a generic slope formula—but it may be analytically complex. In this equation, for example, without some additional contortions, if Δx goes to 0, the equation explodes, given the division by 0 problem. Thus, a fair amount of differential calculus is spent learning "tricks" to manipulate equations so that this limit can be evaluated. Fortunately, for many common functions, there are simple rules for taking derivatives. For example, the derivative of a constant C is 0 (which makes sense, because $y = C$ is a flat line with slope 0). Another common rule is that the derivative of the function $f(x) = x^n$ is nx^{n-1} (see the end of this section for the proof). Thus, using calculus notation, the equation for the slope of our example curve $y = x^2$ is:

$$\frac{dy}{dx} \equiv \frac{df(x)}{dx} = 2x.$$

The expressions on the left of the equal sign are interchangeable and are simply a slope formula (change in y over change in x). Notice how the derivative here was taken by placing the exponent in front of x and reducing the exponent by 1 ($x^1 = x$). Notice also that this equation for the slope is general to this curve: All one must do to determine the slope of this curve is to substitute an x value. The derivative function will return the slope of the curve at that point. If our original equation were for a line, $y = mx + b$, then the derivative would be m, which is the slope of the line (recall the slope-intercept form from algebra), and the m is constant across all values of x. This result should be intuitive: As stated above, the slope of a line is constant regardless of where it is evaluated.

This "first" derivative of a curve can not only be considered a slope of the curve, but it can also be considered a rate of change, since the slope tells the rate of change in y per unit change in x. There are higher order rates of change (i.e., change in the rate of change—also called acceleration). Differential calculus involves not only first derivatives, but also higher order derivatives, which are computed by taking the derivative of a derivative. In theory, there is virtually no limit to the number of derivatives of a function that can be taken, except often second, third, and higher order derivatives are constant.

Differential calculus in dimensions greater than two is also concerned with "partial" derivatives, or the slope of a curve in one of the multiple dimensions. Partial derivatives tend to be fairly simple to compute, because when taking a partial derivative, one treats the variables representing other dimensions as constants. Whereas full derivatives are denoted using dy/dx, partial derivatives are denoted using the ∂ symbol: $\partial y/\partial x$.

Derivatives are a fundamental part of likelihood analysis in statistics. Maximizing a likelihood function requires finding the point at which the likelihood curve's derivative is 0, because a tangent line with slope 0 indicates a flat line, implying a point on the curve that is either a maximum or a minimum. In the parabola example, the minimum is reached where $x = 0$.

Second derivatives are also useful in classical statistics. The second derivative represents the rate of curvature in a curve. Given that the density function for a probability distribution is simply a mathematical curve, the second derivative reveals whether the curve has steep or shallow curvature, implying either smaller or greater variance (see Chapter 2).

A.1.3 Integral calculus

The other branch of calculus, integral calculus, is concerned in general with finding area under and between curves. In probability modeling, finding the area under curves is crucial. Indeed, the key requirement for a mathematical curve to constitute a probability density function is that the area under the entire curve totals 1.

Finding the area under a line segment is easy, because there are simple formulas for computing areas of rectangles and triangles. However, finding the area under a curve is more difficult, because there are no simple algebraic formulas for areas involving most curves. Imagine, for example, that one is presented with the curve $y = -x^2 + 3$ and wishes to find the area under it. This curve is an inverted parabola, with its vertex located at (0,3). The curve intersects the x axis in two places (where $y = 0$, $x = \pm\sqrt{3} \approx 1.73$).

We could divide the curve into two halves, create rectangles that closely fit the area under the curve, and approximate the area under the curve using the area of the rectangles (see Figure A.2 for a depiction of this curve). This estimated area would approximate the area under the curve, but there would be considerable error. The rectangles, if they joined at $x = 0$ with a height of 3, would include a considerable amount of area that is above the curve where $x < 0$ and $x > 0$. Thus, an alternative might be to consider breaking the curve into more than two sections and adjusting the height of each rectangle to more closely match the height of the curve at the rectangle's position on the x axis. However, unless the rectangles are infinitely small, there would always been some overestimation or underestimation of the area. Again, refer to Figure A.2. The upper plot shows this inverted parabola with its area under the curve being approximated using two rectangles. With two rectangles, there is considerable overestimation of the area under the curve. The middle plot shows the approximation with four rectangles; here there is substantially less overestimation. Finally, the bottom plot shows the approximation with eight rectangles. There is substantially less overestimation of the area with eight rectangles than with four.

Once again, the notion of a limit is crucial. If we let the rectangles get infinitely small, then we can reduce the error in approximation to 0. Hence, a solution to finding the area under the curve is to use the following formula:

$$\lim_{n \to \infty} \sum_{i=1}^{n} A_i,$$

where A_i is the area of the ith rectangle under the curve.[1] In this expression, as n approaches infinity, the sum becomes called an "integral," and is denoted with the symbol $\int$. Thus, integrals can be considered the continuous analog of discrete summation using $\sum$. Area under curves can be computed for the entire curve, or they can be computed for only sections of a curve. For example, the expression:

$$\int_0^{\sqrt{3}} (-x^2 + 3)dx$$

implies that we are interested in the area under the curve between the limits of $x = 0$ and $x = \sqrt{3}$. Notice the "dx" placed at the end of the expression—this quantity is the width of the rectangles being summed, and the remainder of the expression is the height.

The fundamental theorem of calculus relates integrals and derivatives, showing that they are inverse functions of one another. In brief, the theorem says:

$$\frac{d \int f(x)}{dx} = f(x). \tag{A.3}$$

---

[1] In fact, one can achieve closer approximation with a finite n if one uses trapezoids or other shapes that more closely match the shape of the curve at x.

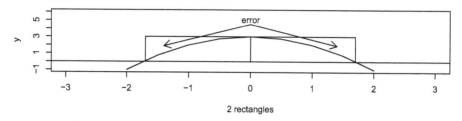

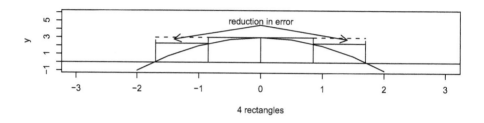

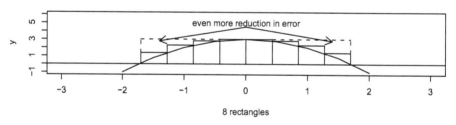

Fig. A.2. Finding successive approximations to the area under a curve using rectangles.

In other words, the derivative of an integral of a function is simply the function itself. Thus, if we know the derivative of some function, we also know the integral of some other function. For example, above we saw that the derivative of x^n was nx^{n-1}. Using the fundamental theorem, we can invert this process and find that the integral of x^n is $x^{n+1}/(n+1)$. Technically, the integral also involves adding a constant C, because, given that the derivative of a constant is 0, we never know what constant should be added when inverting the derivative (that is, taking an integral).

Without going into all the details of integration, we evaluate integrals by (1) taking the integral and (2) evaluating the integral at the limits of integration. In our current example:

$$\int_0^{\sqrt{3}} (-x^2 + 3)\, dx = \left.\frac{-x^3}{3} + 3x\right|_0^{\sqrt{3}}$$

$$= \frac{-\left(\sqrt{3}\right)^3}{3} + 3\left(\sqrt{3}\right) - 0$$

$$= 2\sqrt{3}.$$

The first line shows the integral of the function. The bar to the right indicates that these are the limits at which to evaluate this integral. The third expression shows the value of the function after evaluating it at these limits, and the final expression is the area under the curve between 0 and the $\sqrt{3}$. Notice how the function value at the lower limit of integration is subtracted from the value of the function at the upper limit of integration. This result should make sense: If you imagine taking all the area under the curve to the left of $\sqrt{3}$ and then subtracting all the area under the curve to the left of 0, what remains is the area between the two points. This result should be somewhat familiar, if you have taken a basic statistics course and worked with finding the area (or probability) under the standard normal (z) curve between two points via subtraction.

Integrals can become very complex, especially when dealing with curves of high dimension (e.g., as are used in multivariate probability distributions). Just as there are partial derivatives, there are partial integrals. Integrals can also become complex when there is not a simple expression for the integral. Indeed, some curves have no analytically tractable integrals (for example, the normal distribution curve has no closed form solution for its integral). In these cases, other methods must be used to evaluate the integral, including using sums of the area of tiny rectangles (or trapezoids).

A.1.4 Finding a general rule for a derivative

Above, I said that the derivative of $y = x^n$ is nx^{n-1}. We know this result is true generally by applying Equation A.2. Suppose our equation is $y = x^n + C$, where C is an arbitrary constant. Derivatives of sums are equal to the sum of the derivatives, so we can take the derivative of x^n separately from that of C. Since the derivative of a constant is 0, we can disregard it and focus only on x^n. Following Equation A.2, we have:

$$\frac{dy}{dx} = \lim_{\Delta x \to 0} \frac{(x + \Delta x)^n - x^n}{\Delta x}. \tag{A.4}$$

Using the rule for binomial expansion, $(x + \Delta x)^n$ can be expanded as:

$$\binom{n}{0} x^n \Delta x^0 + \binom{n}{1} x^{n-1} \Delta x^1 + \ldots + \binom{n}{n-1} x^1 \Delta x^{n-1} + \binom{n}{n} x^0 \Delta x^n.$$

Notice that the first term of this expression reduces to x^n, and thus, when it is included in Equation A.4, it cancels the x^n that is subtracted at the end in the numerator. So, we are left with a series of terms containing powers of Δx:

$$\frac{dy}{dx} = \lim_{\Delta x \to 0} \frac{\binom{n}{1} x^{n-1} \Delta x^1 + \ldots + \binom{n}{n} x^0 \Delta x^n}{\Delta x}.$$

Because all the terms in the numerator contain at least one Δx, we can factor out one from each part of the numerator and cancel it with the denominator, and we are left with:

$$\frac{dy}{dx} = \lim_{\Delta x \to 0} \binom{n}{1} x^{n-1} + \ldots + \binom{n}{n} x^0 \Delta x^{n-1}. \tag{A.5}$$

Allowing Δx to go to 0 in Equation A.5 eliminates all the terms in the equation except for the first term, which is nx^{n-1}, the rule presented above. Other general rules for derivatives are derived in a similar fashion and are usually presented in a table in a calculus text.

A.2 Summary of matrix algebra

Matrix algebra is a form of mathematics that allows compact notation for, and mathematical manipulation of, high-dimensional expressions and equations. For the purposes of this book, only a relatively simple exposition is required in order to understand the notation for multivariate equations and calculations.

A.2.1 Matrix notation

The basic unit in matrix algebra is a matrix, generally expressed as:

$$\mathbf{A} = \begin{bmatrix} a_{11} & a_{12} & a_{13} \\ a_{21} & a_{22} & a_{23} \\ a_{31} & a_{32} & a_{33} \end{bmatrix}.$$

Here, the matrix $\mathbf{A}$ is denoted as a matrix by the boldfaced type. Throughout the text, however, I use capitalized letters to denote matrices, rather than boldface, for the sake of appearance. Matrices can be of any dimension; in this example, the matrix is a "3-by-3" or "3 × 3" matrix. The number of rows is listed first; the number of columns is listed second. The subscripts of the matrix elements (a's) clarify this: The third item in the second row is element

a_{23}. A matrix with only one element (i.e., 1×1 dimension) is called a "scalar." A matrix with only a single column is called a column vector; a matrix with only a single row is called a row vector. The term "vector" also has meaning in analytic geometry, referring to a line segment that originates at the origin $(0, 0, \ldots, 0)$ and terminates at the coordinates listed in the k dimensions. For example, you are already familiar with the Cartesian coordinate $(4, 5)$, which is located 4 units from 0 in the x dimension and 5 units from 0 in the y dimension. The vector $[4, 5]$, then, is the line segment formed by taking a straight line from $(0, 0)$ to $(4, 5)$.

A.2.2 Matrix operations

The first important operation that can be performed on a matrix (or vector) is the transpose function, which is denoted as: A' or A^T. The transpose function reverses the rows and columns of a matrix so that if $B = A^T$:

$$b_{ij} = a_{ji}, \forall \, i, j. \qquad (A.6)$$

This equation says that the ij^{th} element of the transposed matrix is the ji^{th} element of the original matrix for all $i = 1 \ldots I$ and $j = 1 \ldots J$ elements. The dimensionality of a transposed matrix, therefore, is the opposite of the original matrix. For example, if matrix B is 3×2, then matrix B^T will be of dimension 2×3. The transpose of the multiple of two matrices, say $(AB)^T$, is simply the multiple of the transposes of the original matrices, only in reverse. Thus, $(AB)^T = B^T A^T$.

With this basic function developed, we can now discuss other matrix operations, including matrix addition, subtraction, and multiplication (including division). Matrix addition and subtraction are relatively simple. Provided two matrices have the same dimensionality (i.e., they "conform" for addition), adding or subtracting two matrices is performed by simply adding and subtracting corresponding elements in the two matrices:

$$A + B = \begin{bmatrix} a_{11} & a_{12} \\ a_{21} & a_{22} \end{bmatrix} + \begin{bmatrix} b_{11} & b_{12} \\ b_{21} & b_{22} \end{bmatrix} = \begin{bmatrix} (a_{11} + b_{11}) & (a_{12} + b_{12}) \\ (a_{21} + b_{21}) & (a_{22} + b_{22}) \end{bmatrix}. \qquad (A.7)$$

The commutative property of addition and subtraction that holds in scalar algebra also holds in matrix algebra: The order in which matrices are added (or subtracted) makes no difference to the outcome, so that $A + B + C = C + B + A$.

Matrix multiplication is slightly more difficult than addition and subtraction, unless one is multiplying a matrix by a scalar. In that case, the scalar is distributed to each element in the matrix, and multiplication is carried out element by element:

$$k \begin{bmatrix} a_{11} & a_{12} \\ a_{21} & a_{22} \end{bmatrix} = \begin{bmatrix} ka_{11} & ka_{12} \\ ka_{21} & ka_{22} \end{bmatrix}. \qquad (A.8)$$

In the event two matrices are being multiplied, before multiplying, one must make sure the matrices conform for multiplication, where "conform" means that the number of columns in the first matrix must equal the number of rows in the second matrix. For example, one cannot post-multiply a 2×3 matrix A by another 2×3 matrix B, because the number of columns in A is 3, while the number of rows in B is 2. One could, however, multiply A by a 3×2 matrix C. The matrix that results from multiplying A and C would have dimension 2×2 (the same number of rows as the first matrix and the same number of columns as the second matrix).

The general rule for matrix multiplication is as follows: If one is multiplying $A \times C$ to obtain matrix D, then:

$$d_{ij} = \sum_{k=1}^{K} a_{ik} c_{kj}, \ \forall \, i, j. \tag{A.9}$$

That is, the ij^{th} element of matrix D is equal to the sum of the multiple of the elements in row i of A and the column j of C. Matrix multiplication is therefore a fairly tedious process. As an example, assume A is 2×3 and C is 3×2, with the following elements:

$$A = \begin{bmatrix} 1 & 2 & 3 \\ 4 & 5 & 6 \end{bmatrix}, \ C = \begin{bmatrix} 1 & 2 \\ 3 & 4 \\ 5 & 6 \end{bmatrix}.$$

Then, element $d_{11} = (1 \times 1) + (2 \times 3) + (3 \times 5) = 22$, and the entire D matrix is (solve this yourself):

$$D = \begin{bmatrix} 22 & 28 \\ 49 & 64 \end{bmatrix}.$$

Notice that matrix D is 2×2.

Unlike matrix addition and subtraction, in which the order of the matrices is irrelevant, order matters for multiplication. Obviously, given the conformability requirement, reversing the order of matrices may make multiplication impossible (e.g., although a 3×2 matrix can be post-multiplied by a 2×4 matrix, the 2×4 matrix cannot be post-multiplied by the 3×2 matrix). However, even if matrices are conformable for multiplication after reversing their order, the resulting matrices will not generally be identical. For example, a $1 \times k$ row vector multiplied by a $k \times 1$ column vector will yield a scalar (1×1), but if we reverse the order of multiplication, we will obtain a $k \times k$ matrix.

Some additional functions that apply to matrices and are commonly used in statistics include the trace operator [the trace of A is denoted as $\text{tr}(A)$], the determinant, and the inverse. The trace of a matrix is simply the sum of the diagonal elements of the matrix. The determinant is more difficult. Technically, the determinant is the sum of the signed multiples of all the permutations of a matrix, where the term "permutations" refers to the unique combinations of a single element from each row and column, for all rows and columns. If d denotes the dimensionality of a matrix, then there are $d!$ permutations for the matrix. For example, in a 3×3 matrix, there are a total of 6 permutations ($3! = 3 \times 2 \times 1 = 6$): (a_{11}, a_{22}, a_{33}), (a_{12}, a_{23}, a_{31}), (a_{13}, a_{21}, a_{32}), (a_{13}, a_{22}, a_{31}), (a_{11}, a_{23}, a_{32}), (a_{12}, a_{21}, a_{33}). Notice how for each combination, there is one element from each row and column. The signing of each permutation is determined by the column position of each element in all the pairs that can be constructed using the elements of the permutation, and the subscript of element at each position in each pair. For example, the permutation (a_{11}, a_{22}, a_{33}) has elements from columns 1, 2, and 3. The possible ordered (i, j) pairs that can come from this permutation include $(1, 2)$, $(1, 3)$, and $(2, 3)$ (based on the column position). If there are an even number of (i, j) pairs in which $i > j$, then the permutation is considered "even" and takes a positive sign. Otherwise, the permutation is considered "odd" and takes a negative sign. In this example, there are 0 pairs in which $i > j$, so the permutation is even (0 is even). However, in the permutation (a_{13}, a_{22}, a_{31}), the pairs are $(3, 2)$, $(3, 1)$, and $(2, 1)$. In this set, all three pairs are such that $i > j$; hence this permutation is odd and takes a negative sign. The determinant is denoted using absolute value bars on either side of the matrix name: for instance, the determinant of A is denoted as $|A|$, or often, $\det(A)$.

For 2×2 and 3×3 matrices, determinants can be calculated fairly easily. For example, the determinant of a 2×2 matrix A is: $det(A) = a_{11}a_{22} - a_{12}a_{21}$. However, for larger matrices, the number of permutations becomes large rapidly. Fortunately, several rules simplify the process. First, if any row or column in a matrix is a vector of 0, then the determinant is 0. In that case, the matrix is said not to be of full rank. Second, the same is true if any two rows or columns is identical. Third, for a diagonal matrix (i.e., there are 0's everywhere but the main diagonal—the 11, 22, 33,... positions), the determinant is only the multiple of the diagonal elements. There are additional rules, but they are not necessary for this brief introduction. I note that the determinant is essentially a measure of the area/volume/hypervolume spanned by the vectors of the matrix. This helps, I think, to clarify why matrices with 0 vectors in them have determinant 0: Just as in two dimensions a line has no area, when we have a 0 vector in a matrix, the dimensionality of the figure spanned by the vectors of a matrix is reduced by a dimension (because one vector does not pass the origin), and hence the hypervolume is necessarily 0.

Finally, a very important function in matrix algebra is the inverse function. The inverse function allows the matrix equivalent of division. In a sense, just as 5 times its inverse $1/5 = 1$, a matrix A times its inverse—denoted A^{-1}—equals I, where I is the "identity matrix." An identity matrix is a diagonal matrix with ones along the diagonal, and it is the matrix equivalent of "1." Some simple algebraic rules follow from the discussion of inverses and the identity matrix:

$$AA^{-1} = A^{-1}A = I. \tag{A.10}$$

Furthermore,

$$AI = IA = A. \tag{A.11}$$

Given the commutability implicit in the above rules, it stands that inverses only exist for square matrices, and that all identity matrices are square matrices. For that matter, the determinant function can only apply to square matrices also.

Computing the inverse of matrices is a difficult task, and there are several methods by which to derive them. The simplest method to compute an inverse is to use the following formula:

$$A^{-1} = \frac{1}{|A|} \text{adj } A \tag{A.12}$$

The only new element in this formula is "adj A," which means "adjoint of A." The adjoint of a matrix is the transpose of its matrix of cofactors, where a cofactor is the signed determinant of the "minor" of an element of a matrix. The minor of element i, j is the matrix the remains after deleting the ith row and j^{th} column of the original matrix. For example, the minor of element a_{11} of the matrix A shown at the beginning of this matrix algebra summary is:

$$\begin{bmatrix} a_{22} & a_{23} \\ a_{32} & a_{33} \end{bmatrix}.$$

Taking its determinant leaves one with a scalar that is then multiplied by -1^{i+j}. This latter process is called "signing." In this case, we obtain $(-1)^2(a_{22}a_{33} - a_{23}a_{32})$ as the cofactor for element a_{11}. If one replaces every element in matrix A with its cofactor (called "expansion by cofactors"), then transposes the result, one will obtain the adjoint of A. Multiplying this by $1/|A|$ (a scalar) will yield the inverse of A.

Cofactors can also be used to find determinants. Simply take each element in *any* row *or* column and multiply it by its cofactor, and then sum these results together for all the elements in the row/column. Obviously, effort is saved if one chooses a row or column with several 0's, because the determinants of those elements' minors do not need to be calculated. (They will ultimately be multiplied by 0 and will drop from the calculation).

Even using cofactors, the process of finding determinants and inverses is tedious. Fortunately, computer packages tend to have determinant and inversion routines built into them, and there are plenty of inversion algorithms available if you are designing your own software, so that we generally need not worry. It is worth mentioning that, if a matrix has a 0 determinant, it does not have an inverse. There are many additional matrix algebra rules and tricks that one may need to know; however, they are also beyond the scope of this introduction.

A.3 Exercises

A.3.1 Calculus exercises

Evaluate the following limits. If a limit does not exist, indicate such. You should graph the expression to see whether the limit exists.

1. $\lim_{x\to\infty} \frac{1}{x}$.
2. $\lim_{x\to 0} \frac{1}{x}$.
3. $\lim_{x\to\infty} \frac{x^2+5}{3}$.
4. $\lim_{x\to 0} \frac{x^2-1}{5}$.
5. $\lim_{x\to\infty} \exp(-x)$.
6. $\lim_{x\to 0} \exp(-x)$.
7. $\lim_{x\to\infty} \frac{x}{2x}$.
8. $\lim_{\sigma\to\infty} \frac{1}{\sigma\sqrt{2\pi}} \exp\left\{\frac{-(x-\mu)^2}{2\sigma^2}\right\}$.

Using the following rules for derivatives, find the slope of the curve below at $x = 3$.

(power rule)	(constant rule)	(addition rule)
$\frac{d}{dx}[u^n] = nu^{n-1}du$	$\frac{d}{dx}[cu] = c \times \frac{d}{dx}[u]du$	$\frac{d}{dx}[u+v] = \frac{d}{dx}[u]du + \frac{d}{dx}[v]dv$

9. $y = 3x^3 + 5x^2 + 2x + 10$.
10. Using the fundamental theorem of calculus and the rules above, find the area under the curve (the integral) of the curve above between 0 and 5.

A.3.2 Matrix algebra exercises

Perform the various calculations on the matrices below. If an operation is not possible for an item, indicate this and explain why. Don't forget steps: Expansion by cofactors involves a sign function that depends on i and j, where i and j index the rows and columns. Also, the adjoint matrix is the transpose of the matrix of cofactors.

$$
\begin{array}{ccccc}
A & B & C & D & E
\end{array}
$$

$$
\begin{bmatrix} 3 & 2 \\ -1 & 3 \end{bmatrix} \quad
\begin{bmatrix} 3 & 1 & -1 \\ 4 & 3 & 5 \\ 10 & 4 & 1 \end{bmatrix} \quad
\begin{bmatrix} 1 & 7 & 4 \end{bmatrix} \quad
\begin{bmatrix} 2 \\ 9 \\ 3 \end{bmatrix} \quad
\begin{bmatrix} 4 & 1 & 3 \\ 7 & 1 & 8 \\ 6 & 8 & 7 \end{bmatrix}
$$

1. Find $B + E$.
2. Find $E - B$.
3. Find AB.
4. Find CD.
5. Find DC.
6. Find DE.
7. Find E^T.
8. Find $\det(A)$.
9. Find $\det(B)$.
10. Find E^{-1} (Hint: Use expansion by cofactors).
11. Find $\text{tr}(B)$.
12. If the determinant represents area, volume, or hypervolume from a geometric perspective, then what is the hypervolume of a six-dimensional identity matrix?

B

The Central Limit Theorem, Confidence Intervals, and Hypothesis Tests

The classical approach to statistical inference relies heavily on the Central Limit Theorem (CLT), a key result of which is:

$$f(\bar{x}|\mu_x, \sigma_x, n) \overset{asy}{\sim} N\left(\mu_x, \frac{\sigma_x}{\sqrt{n}}\right). \tag{B.1}$$

In English, this expression says that, as sample sizes get larger, the *sampling distribution* $f()$ for a statistic, here $\bar{x}$, approaches a normal distribution with a mean equal to the population mean of x (μ_x) and a standard deviation equal to the population standard deviation of x (σ_x) divided by the square root of the sample size (n) used to compute $\bar{x}$. It is important to note that the theorem does not require the distribution of the original variable x from which the statistic $\bar{x}$ was generated to be normal: Regardless of the distribution of the data, the *asymptotic* sampling distribution of a statistic will be normal.

What is a sampling distribution? Consider that, when we take a random sample of size n individuals, this sample is only one of many possible samples of size n that could be drawn from the population. Certainly, if we took a second random sample of the same size, we would not end up with the same collection of respondents, and consequently, the value of any statistic (like the mean) we calculate from one sample will most likely differ from the value obtained in another. The CLT, however, says that, if we were to take all possible random samples of a given size from the population and compute the value of the statistic of interest (e.g., the mean) for each one, the distribution of these statistics—the sampling distribution—would be normal, assuming the sample size is large enough.

B.1 A simulation study

To demonstrate the theorem, I display the results of a brief simulation that followed the following structure:

1. I drew 1,000 samples each of sizes $n = 1, 2, 30$, and 100 from a $U(0, 1)$ distribution. The mean and standard deviation of a $U(a, b)$ distribution are $\frac{b+a}{2}$ and $\sqrt{\frac{(b-a)^2}{12}}$, respectively. Here, those values are .5 and .2887 (variance $= .0833$).

2. I computed the mean for each of the 1,000 samples for each sample size and computed the standard deviation for each sample also. The collection of the means from each of the 1,000 samples of a given sample size represents the sampling distribution of the mean for that sample size.

3. I computed the mean of all the sample means computed from Step 2 for each sample size, and I computed the standard deviation (and variances) of these distributions of means.

Figure B.1 shows the distribution of these $1,000$ sample means (the sampling distribution) for all four sample sizes. The figure shows that the means are distributed across the $[0, 1]$ interval for samples size $n = 1$, basically reflecting that samples of this size are nothing more than draws from the original distribution. As the sample size increases, the means become more clustered around the true mean of .5.

Figure B.2 shows what happens to the standard deviation of the sampling distribution of the mean as the sample sizes get larger. The figure depicts the empirical standard deviation of the sampling distribution for each of the sample sizes (the standard deviation of the 1,000 sample means), as well as the theoretical standard deviation claimed by the CLT. Notice how the empirical and theoretical standard deviations almost perfectly coincide, illustrating the theorem.

Figure B.3 shows the distribution of the variances for samples size $n = 2$, $n = 30$, and $n = 100$. (Note: The variances for the samples of size $n = 1$ are 0, which is why they are not plotted.) The sampling distribution for the variances at $n = 2$ is truncated at 0 and highly right-skewed (in fact, the distribution of variances is an inverse gamma distribution; see Chapter 3). The distribution is also very broad. As the sample sizes increase, the distribution becomes more and more symmetric in shape and narrower. The mean of each of these distributions of the variance is equal to approximately .08, the correct variance $(\sqrt{1/12}^2)$. These results suggest that larger samples are also better at pinpointing the true population variance/standard deviation.

B.2 Classical inference

Classical statistical inference relies on the CLT as exemplified by the simulation results. When we draw a random sample of size n from a population, we can imagine that we are really sampling a sample mean, variance, regression parameter, or some other statistic from its sampling distribution. From that perspective, if we know that large samples have a normal sampling distribution for a statistic $(\hat{\theta})$, and we let the sample statistic (e.g., mean, variance,

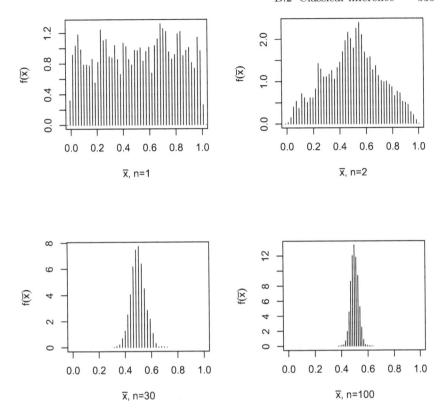

Fig. B.1. Distributions of sample means for four sample sizes ($n = 1$, 2, 30, and 100).

regression parameter) be our best guess for the true population parameter (θ), then we can use what we know about normal distributions to make inference about the likely value of the true population parameter. Two strategies are commonly used in classical inference: hypothesis testing and confidence interval construction.

B.2.1 Hypothesis testing

Under the hypothesis testing approach, we hypothesize some value for θ (H_0; the "null hypothesis"), and we compare our sample statistic to our hypothesized value of the parameter and decide whether our observed estimate is sufficiently different from the hypothesized value that we should reject the hypothesized value.

How do we determine whether the sample statistic is "sufficiently different" from H_0? By the CLT, we know that the sampling distribution for $\hat{\theta}$ is normal, and so we can standardize $\hat{\theta}$ by subtracting off H_0 and dividing by the standard deviation of the sampling distribution ($\sigma/\sqrt{n}$; called the "standard error").

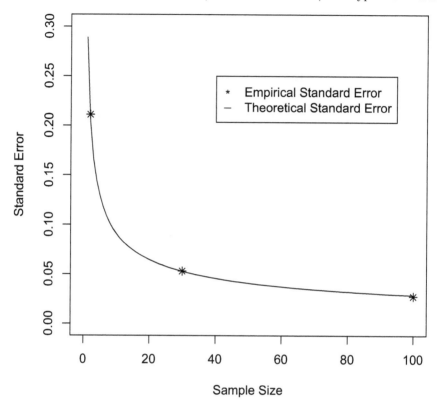

Fig. B.2. Empirical versus theoretical standard deviations of sample means under the CLT.

Given the normality of the sampling distribution, with σ known, the result is a z score:

$$z = \frac{\hat{\theta} - H_0}{\sigma/\sqrt{n}}.$$

We can therefore use this z score to assess the probability of observing $\hat{\theta}$ if H_0 were true—that is, if the true sampling distribution for $\hat{\theta}$ were centered over our hypothesized value for the parameter. If observing an estimate as extreme as $\hat{\theta}$ or moreso would be a rare event if H_0 were true, we conclude that H_0 is not true. In social science research, we generally consider an estimate that would occur with probability .05 or less under H_0 to be sufficient evidence to reject H_0. We call this level the "critical level" (denoted α), and we call our observed probability of obtaining the estimate we did under the null hypothesis a "p-value."

Although the sampling distribution for a statistic is asymptotically normal according to the CLT, we generally do not know σ (and therefore $\sigma/\sqrt{n}$) with

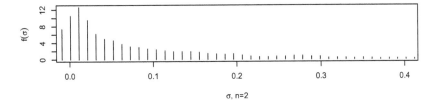

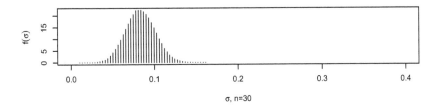

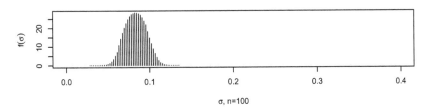

Fig. B.3. Sampling distributions of variances in the simulation.

certainty. Instead, we usually estimate σ with the sample estimate s $(\hat{\sigma})$. Recall, however, from the previous figure that the variance (hence, standard deviation) also has a distribution and that this distribution is fairly broad for small n. This means that our sample estimate of the population standard deviation has some uncertainty built into it. As a result, we must compensate for this uncertainty by using the t distribution, rather than the z distribution in constructing our standardized score:

$$t = \frac{\hat{\theta} - H_0}{\hat{\sigma}/\sqrt{n}}.$$

Technically, the t distribution is the marginal distribution for the mean when σ is unknown, and so this calculation compensates for the uncertainty inherent in using $\hat{\sigma}$ to estimate σ.

Recall also from the figure that, as n gets larger, our uncertainty about the true value of that population standard deviation shrinks, allowing us to use distributions that look more and more normal. Thus, when n is large enough, the t distribution converges on the normal distribution, and we often simply use the normal distribution for inference.

B.2.2 Confidence intervals

An alternative method of performing statistical inference is to construct a "confidence interval" around a sample estimate in order to state, with some level of "confidence," where we suspect the parameter θ falls. When σ is known, we compute intervals using the z distribution; when σ is not known, we compute intervals using the t distribution, for the same reason discussed in the previous section. These intervals are computed as:

$$(1 - \alpha)\%C.I. = \hat{\theta} \pm z_{\frac{\alpha}{2}} \left(\frac{\sigma}{\sqrt{n}} \right),$$

and

$$(1 - \alpha)\%C.I. = \hat{\theta} \pm t_{\frac{\alpha}{2}} \left(\frac{\hat{\sigma}}{\sqrt{n}} \right),$$

respectively, where $(1 - \alpha)\%$ is the level of confidence, $z_{\frac{\alpha}{2}}$ (or $t_{\frac{\alpha}{2}}$) is the number of standard errors we must add/subtract from our sample estimate $\hat{\theta}$ to obtain the desired level of confidence, and $\sigma/\sqrt{n}$ (or $\hat{\sigma}/\sqrt{n}$) is the size of the standard error. Just as we commonly use a critical level of $\alpha = .05$ under the hypothesis testing approach to inference, we often construct 95% (1-.05) confidence intervals, and so I will discuss such intervals here.

The correct interpretation of a 95% confidence interval is that 95% of the confidence intervals that could be drawn from the sampling distribution for $\hat{\theta}$ would capture θ. In order to understand why, consider, once again, that the sampling distribution for $\hat{\theta}$ is normal and centered over θ with a standard deviation of $\sigma/\sqrt{n}$. Then (assuming σ is known), 95% of all possible values of $\hat{\theta}$ will fall within 1.96 standard errors of θ. If this is true, then if we add (and subtract) 1.96 standard errors to (from) all possible estimates $\hat{\theta}$, 95% of the resulting intervals would contain θ. The ones that do not will be the intervals constructed around values of $\hat{\theta}$ that fall in the tails of the sampling distribution. As before, if σ is not known and is estimated with $\hat{\sigma}$, our interval should be constructed using the t distribution.

Figure B.4 shows a collection of 95% confidence intervals *based on the z distribution* for the simulated samples of size $n = 2$, $n = 30$, and $n = 100$. The intervals are vertical, with the true population parameter value (.5) represented by a horizontal line. Notice how these intervals are much more consistent in width and generally narrower for the larger size samples than the $n = 2$ sized samples. Also notice that some of the confidence intervals for the samples sized $n = 2$ are extremely narrow. This result reflects the uncertainty in σ^2 (and thus σ^2/n) inherent in having small samples.

Table B.1 shows the percent of the confidence intervals (out of 1,000 for each sample size) that, in fact, capture the true mean. In the table, I have

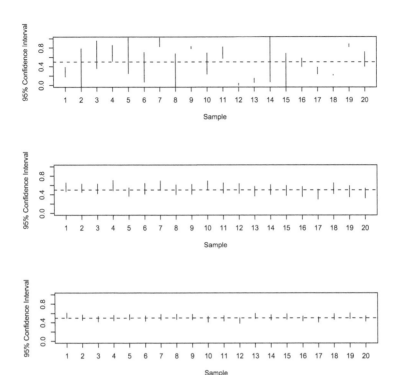

Fig. B.4. z-based confidence intervals for the mean: Top plot shows intervals for samples of size $n = 2$; second plot shows intervals for samples of size $n = 30$; third plot shows intervals for samples of size $n = 100$.

computed these percentages using both 1.96 (the critical value for the z distribution) and using the appropriate t critical value, given the degrees of freedom $(n - 1)$ for each size sample. Notice how the z distribution works well for the larger samples, but not for the small n samples. Also observe how well the t-based intervals perform.

Table B.1. Percentage of confidence intervals capturing the true mean in simulation.

Sample Size	z-based intervals	t-based intervals
$n = 2$	.639	.915
$n = 30$	.933	.948
$n = 100$	.957	.960

B.2.3 Some final notes

With classical statistics and inference, there are a few things to keep in mind. First, the interpretation of both the confidence intervals and the test statistics is tedious. We cannot say that our confidence intervals in Table B.1 suggest that the true mean falls within those limits with probability .95. The parameter, from a classical standpoint, is fixed. Only the interval itself is random. Similarly, if we reject a null hypothesis we cannot say that there is a 95% probability the null is wrong, and we cannot say that we are 95% confident that some alternate hypothesis is true, either. We can only say that, under the assumption the null hypothesis were true, the data would be extremely rare. This leads us to believe that the null is not true, but it does not disprove the null nor prove an alternative.

Second, as stated above, the justification of the classical approach to inference rests on the CLT. The CLT, however, claims that sampling distributions for a statistic are only *asymptotically* normal, meaning that sample sizes must be large in order to invoke the CLT as a justification for classical confidence intervals and hypothesis tests. When sample sizes are small, the theorem does not hold, and hence, confidence intervals and hypothesis tests are suspect. We can see this result in Table B.1. For samples of size $n = 2$ the supposed 95% z-based intervals only capture the true mean in 63.9% of the cases. Even after adjusting for uncertainty in the estimate of σ by constructing intervals based on the t distribution, the supposed 95% intervals only capture the true mean 91.5% of the time.

For this appendix, I do not provide exercises. Instead, please see Chapter 2 for relevant exercises involving the classical statistical approach.

****

References

Albert, J.H. (1992). "Bayesian Estimation of the Polychoric Correlation Coefficient." *Journal of Computation and Simulation* 44:47-61.

Albert, J.H. and S. Chib. (1993). "Bayesian Analysis of Binary and Polychotomous Response Data." *Journal of the American Statistical Association* 88(422):669-679.

Alho, J.M. and B.D. Spencer. (2005). *Statistical Demography and Forecasting.* New York: Springer.

Allison, P.D. (1984). *Event History Analysis: Regression for Longitudinal Event Data.* Sage University Paper Series on Quantitative Applications in the Social Sciences, 07-46. Thousand Oaks, CA: Sage.

Allison, P.D. (2003). *Missing Data.* Sage University Paper Series on Quantitative Applications in the Social Sciences, 07-136. Thousand Oaks, CA: Sage.

Billingsley, P. (1995). *Probability and Measure.* 3rd ed. New York: Wiley.

Bollen, K.A. (1989). *Structural Equations with Latent Variables.* New York: Wiley.

Bollen, K.A. and P.J. Curran. (2006). *Latent Curve Models: A Structural Equation Perspective.* Hoboken, NJ: Wiley.

Box, G.E.P. and G.C. Tiao. (1973). *Bayesian Inference in Statistical Analysis.* Reading, MA: Addison-Wesley.

Bremaud, P. (1999). *Markov Chains, Gibbs Fields, Monte Carlo Simulation, and Queues.* New York: Springer-Verlag.

Carlin, B.P. and T.A. Louis. (2000). *Bayes and Empirical Bayes Methods for Data Analysis.* 2nd ed. Boca Raton, FL: Chapman & Hall/CRC.

Casella, G. and E.I. George. (1992). "Explaining the Gibbs Sampler." *The American Statistician* 46(3):167-174.

Chen, M-H., Q-M. Shao, and J.G. Ibrahim. (2000) *Monte Carlo Methods in Bayesian Computation.* New York: Springer-Verlag.

Chib, S. and E. Greenberg. (1998). "Analysis of Multivariate Probit Models." *Biometrika* 85(2):347-361.

Chung, K.L. and F. AitSahlia. (2003). *Elementary Probability Theory: With Stochastic Processes and an Introduction to Mathematical Finance.* 4th ed. New York: Springer-Verlag.

Congdon, P. (2003). *Applied Bayesian Modelling.* West Sussex, England: Wiley.

Congdon, P. (2001). *Bayesian Statistical Modeling.* West Sussex, England: Wiley.

Cowles, M.K. (1996). "Accelerating Monte Carlo Markov Chain Convergence for Cumulative-Link Generalized Linear Models." *Statistics and Computing* 6:101-110.

Cox, D.R. (1972). "Regression Models and Life Tables." *Journal of the Royal Statistical Society,* Series B34:187-220.

Crimmins, E.M., Y. Saito, and D. Ingegneri. (1997). "Trends in Disability-Free Life Expectancy in the United States, 1970-90." *Population and Development Review* 23(3):555-572.

DeGroot, M.H. (1986). *Probability and Statistics. (Second Ed.)* Reading, MA: Addison-Wesley.

DiMaggio, P., J. Evans, and B. Bryson. (1996). "Have Americans' Social Attitudes Become More Polarized?" *American Journal of Sociology* 102(3):690-755.

Drezner, Z. (1992). "Computation of the Multivariate Normal Integral." *ACM Transactions on Mathematical Software* 18(4):470-480.

Durkheim, E. (1984). *The Division of Labor in Society.* New York: The Free Press.

Edwards, A.W.F. (1992). *Likelihood.* Expanded Edition. Baltimore: Johns Hopkins University University Press.

Eliason, S.R. (1993). *Maximum Likelihood Estimation: Logic and Practice.* Sage University Paper Series on Quantitative Applications in the Social Sciences, 07-96. Thousand Oaks, CA: Sage.

Elo, I.T. and S.H. Preston. (1994). "Estimating African-American Mortality from Inaccurate Data." *Demography* 31(3):427-458.

Evans, M., N. Hastings, and B. Peacock. (2000). *Statistical Distributions.* 3rd ed. New York: Wiley.

Ezell, M.E., K.C. Land, and L.E. Cohen. (2003). "Modeling Multiple Failure Time Data: A Survey of Variance-Corrected Proportional Hazards Models with Empirical Applications to Arrest Data." *Sociological Methodology* 33:111-167.

Fox, J. (1997). *Applied Regression Analysis, Linear Models, and Related Methods.* Thousand Oaks, CA: Sage.

Gelfand, A.E. and A.F.M. Smith. (1990). "Sampling-Based Approaches to Calculating Marginal Densities." *Journal of the American Statistical Association* 85:398-409.

Gelman, A. (1996). "Inference and Monitoring Convergence." Pp. 131-144 in Gilks, W.R., S. Richardson, and D.J. Spiegelhalter (eds.) *Markov Chain Monte Carlo in Practice*. London: Chapman and Hall.

Gelman, A., J.B. Carlin, H.S. Stern, and D.B. Rubin. (1995). *Bayesian Data Analysis*. London: Chapman and Hall.

Gelman, A. and D.B. Rubin. (1995). "Avoiding Model Selection in Bayesian Social Research." *Sociological Methodology* 25:165–74.

Gelman, A., X-L. Meng, and H.S. Stern. (1996). "Posterior Predictive Assessment of Model Fitness via Realized Discrepancies." *Statistica Sinica* 6:733–807.

Gilks, W.R. (1996). "Full Conditional Distributions." Pp. 59-88 in Gilks, W.R., S. Richardson, and D.J. Spiegelhalter (eds.). *Markov Chain Monte Carlo in Practice*. London: Chapman and Hall.

Gilks, W.R., S. Richardson, and D.J. Spiegelhalter (eds.). (1996). *Markov Chain Monte Carlo in Practice*. London: Chapman and Hall.

Gilks, W.R. and G.O. Roberts. (1996). "Strategies for Improving MCMC." Pp. 89-110 in Gilks, W.R., S. Richardson, and D.J. Spiegelhalter (eds.). *Markov Chain Monte Carlo in Practice*. London: Chapman and Hall.

Gill, J. (2002). *Bayesian Methods: A Social and Behavioral Sciences Approach*. Boca Raton, FL: Chapman & Hall/CRC.

Hagle, T.M. (1996) *Basic Math for Social Scientists: Problems and Solutions*. Sage University Paper Series on Quantitative Applications in the Social Sciences, 07-108. Thousand Oaks, CA: Sage.

Hamilton, J.D. (1994). *Time Series Analysis*. Princeton: Princeton University Press.

Harville, D.A. (1997). *Matrix Algebra from a Statisticians Perspective*. New York: Springer-Verlag.

Hastings, W.K. (1970). "Monte Carlo Sampling Methods Using Markov Chains and Their Applications." *Biometrika* 57:97-109.

Hayduk, L.A. (1987). *Structural Equation Modeling with LISREL*. Baltimore, MD: The Johns Hopkins University Press.

Heckman, J.J. (1979). "Sample Selection Bias as a Specification Error." *Econometrica* 47(1):153-161.

Hoeting, J.A., D. Madigan, A.E. Raftery, and C.T. Volinsky. (1999). "Bayesian Model Averaging: A Tutorial." *Statistical Science* 14(4):382-417.

Hosmer, D.W. and S. Lemeshow. (1989). *Applied Logistic Regression*. New York: Wiley.

Hosmer, D.W. and S. Lemeshow. (1999). *Applied Survival Analysis: Regression Modeling of Time to Event Data*. New York: Wiley.

House, J.S., J.M. Lepkowski, A.M. Kinney, R.P. Mero, R.C. Kessler, and A.R. Herzog. (1994). "The Social Stratification of Aging and Health." *Journal of Health and Social Behavior* 35(September):213-234.

Hubbard, R. and M.J. Bayarri. (2003). "Confusion Over Measures of Evidence (p's) Versus Errors (α's) in Classical Stastistical Testing." *The American Statistician* 57(3):171-182.

Imai, K. and D.A. van Dyk. (2005). "A Bayesian Analysis of the Multinomial Probit Model Using Marginal Data Augmentation." *Journal of Econometrics* 124:311-334.

Jeffreys, Sir H.. (1961). *Theory of Probability.* 3rd ed. New York: Oxford University Press.

Johnson, V.E. and J.H. Albert. (1999). *Ordinal Data Modeling.* New York: Springer-Verlag.

Judge, G.G., W.E. Griffiths, R.C. Hill, H. Lutkepoohl, and T-C. Lee. (1985). *The Theory and Practice of Econometrics.* 2nd ed. New York: Wiley.

Kaplan, D. (2000). *Structural Equation Modeling: Foundations and Extensions.* Thousands Oaks, CA: Sage.

Kass, R.E. and A.E. Raftery. (1995). "Bayes Factors." *Journal of the American Statistical Association* 90(430):773-795.

Laditka, S.B. and D.A. Wolf. (1998). "New Methods for Analyzing Active Life Expectancy." *Journal of Aging and Health* 10(2):214-241.

Land, K.C., J.M. Guralnik, and D.G. Blazer. (1994). "Estimating Increment-Decrement Life Tables with Multiple Covariates from Panel Data: The Case of Active Life Expectancy." *Demography* 31(2):297-319.

Land, K.C., P.L. McCall, and D.S. Nagin. (1996). "A Comparison of Poisson, Negative Binomial, and Semiparametric Mixed Poisson Regression Models with Empirical Applications to Criminal Careers Research." *Sociological Methods & Research* 24:387-442.

Lee, P.M. (1989). *Bayesian Statistics: An Introduction.* New York: Oxford University Press.

Lee, S-Y. and H-T. Zhu. (2000). "Statistical Analysis of Nonlinear Structural Equation Models with Continuous and Polytomous Data." *British Journal of Mathematical and Statistical Psychology* 53:209-232.

Leonard, T. and J.S.J. Hsu. (1999). *Bayesian Methods: An Analysis for Statisticians and Interdisciplinary Researchers.* Cambridge, UK: Cambridge University Press.

Liao, T.F. (1994). *Interpreting Probability Models: Logit, Probit, and Other Generalized Linear Models.* Sage University Paper Series on Quantitative Applications in the Social Sciences, 07-101. Thousand Oaks, CA: Sage.

Little, R.J.A. and D.B. Rubin. (1987). *Statistical Analysis with Missing Data.* New York: Wiley.

Liu, J.S. (2001). *Monte Carlo Strategies in Scientific Computing.* New York: Springer-Verlag.

Long, J.S. (1997). *Regression Models for Categorical and Limited Dependent Variables.* Thousand Oaks, CA: Sage.

Long, J.S. and J. Freese. (2003). *Regression Models for Categorical Dependent Variables Using Stata.* College Station, TX: Stata Press.

Lynch, S.M. (2003). "Cohort and Life Course Patterns in the Relationship Between Education and Health: A Hierarchical Approach." *Demography* 40(2):309-331.

Lynch, S.M. and J.S. Brown. (2005). "A New Approach to Estimating Life Tables with Covariates and Constructing Interval Estimates of Life Table Quantities." *Sociological Methodology* 35:177-225.

Lynch, S.M., J.S. Brown, and K.G. Harmsen. (2003). "Black-White Differences in Mortality Deceleration and Compression and the Mortality Crossover Reconsidered." *Research on Aging* 25(5):456-483.

Lynch, S.M. and B. Western. (2004). "Bayesian Posterior Predictive Checks for Complex Models." *Sociological Methods & Research* 32(3):301-335.

Markides, K.S. and S.A. Black. (1996). "Race, Ethnicity and Aging: The Impact of Inequality." Pp. 153-170 in R.H. Binstock and L.K. George (eds.). *Handbook of Aging and the Social Sciences* 4th ed. San Diego, CA: San Diego Academic Press.

Maruyama, G.M. (1998). *Basics of Structural Equation Modeling.* Thousand Oaks, CA: Sage.

McArdle, J.J. and D. Epstein. (1987). "Latent Growth Curves within Developmental Structural Equation Models." *Child Development* 58:110-133.

Mehta, P.D. and S.G. West. (2000). "Putting the Individual Back into Individual Growth Curves." *Psychological Methods* 5(1):23-43.

Menken, J., J. Trussell, D. Stempel, and O. Babakol. (1981). "Proportional Hazards Life Table Models: An Illustrative Analysis of Socio-Demographic Influences on Marriage Dissolution in the United States." *Demography* 18(2):181-200.

Meredith, W. and J. Tisak. (1990). "Latent Curve Analysis." *Psychometrika* 31:59-72.

Neter, J., M.H. Kutner, C.J. Nachtsheim, and W. Wasserman. (1996). *Applied Linear Regression Models.* 3rd ed. Chicago: Irwin.

Olsson, U. (1979). "Maximum Likelihood Estimation of the Polychoric Correlation Coefficient." *Psychometrika* 44(4):443-458.

Olsson, U., F. Drasgow, and N. J. Dorans. (1982). "The Polyserial Correlation Coefficient." *Psychometrika* 47(3):337-347.

Pole, A., M. West, and J. Harrison. (1994). *Applied Bayesian Forecasting and Time Series Analysis.* Boca Raton, FL: Chapman & Hall/CRC.

Poon, W-Y. and S-Y. Lee. (1987). "Maximum Likelihood Estimation of Multivariate Polyserial and Polychoric Correlation Coefficients." *Psychometrika* 52(3):409-430.

Powers, D.A. and Y. Xie. (2000). *Statistical Models for Categorical Data Analysis.* San Diego, CA: Academic Press.

Press, W.H., S.A. Teukolsky, W.T. Vetterling, and B.P. Flannery. (2002). *Numerical Recipes in C: The Art of Scientific Computing.* 2nd ed. New York: Cambridge University Press.

Preston, S.H., I.T. Elo, I. Rosenwaike, and M. Hill. (1996). "African-American Mortality at Older Ages: Results of a Matching Study." *Demography* 33:193-209.

Preston, S.H., P. Heuveline, and M. Guillot. (2001). *Demography: Measuring and Modeling Population Processes.* Oxford: Blackwell.

Raftery, A.E. (1995). "Bayesian Model Selection in Social Research." *Sociological Methodology* 25:111-164.

Raudenbush, S.W. and A.S. Bryk. (2002). *Hierarchical Linear Models: Applications and Data Analysis Methods.* 2nd ed. Thousand Oaks, CA: Sage.

Ripley, B.D. (1987). *Stochastic Simulation.* New York: Wiley.

Robert, C.P. (1994). *The Bayesian Choice: A Decision-Theoretic Motivation.* New York: Springer.

Robert, C.P. (1995). "Simulation of Truncated Normal Variables." *Statistics and Computing* 5(2):121-125.

Robert, C.P. and G. Casella. (1999). *Monte Carlo Statistical Methods.* New York: Springer-Verlag.

Rogosa, D.R. and J.B. Willett. (1985). "Understanding Correlates of Change by Modeling Individual Differences in Growth." *Psychometrika* 50:203-228.

Rubin, D.B. 1984. " Bayesianly Justifiable and Relevant Frequency Calculations for the Applied Statistician." *Annals of Statistics* 12:1151–1172.

Rudas, T. (2004). *Probability Theory: A Primer.* Sage University Paper Series on Quantitative Applications in the Social Sciences, 07-142. Thousand Oaks, CA: Sage.

Schervish, M.J. (1984). "Multivariate Normal Probabilities with Error Bound." *Applied Statistics* 33:81-94.

Schoen, R. (1988). *Modeling Multigroup Populations.* New York: Plenum.

Singer, B. and Spilerman, S. (1976), "The Representation of Social Processes by Markov Models." *American Journal of Sociology* 82:1-54.

Sivia, D.S. (1996). *Data Analysis: A Bayesian Tutorial.* New York: Oxford University Press.

Smith, A.F.M. and A.E. Gelfand. (1992). "Bayesian Statistics without Tears: A Sampling-Resampling Perspective." *The American Statistician* 46(2): 84-88.

Snedecor, G.W. and W.G. Cochran. (1980). *Statistical Methods* 7th ed. Ames, IA: The Iowa State University Press.

Snijders, T. and R. Bosker. (1999). *Multilevel Analysis: An Introduction to Basic and Advanced Multilevel Modeling.* London: Sage.

Song, X-Y. and S-Y. Lee. (2002). "Bayesian Estimation and Model Selection of Multivariate Linear Models with Polytomous Variables." *Multivariate Behavioral Research* 37(4):453-477.

Spiegelhalter, D.J., N.G. Best, W.R. Gilks, and H. Inskip. (1996). "Hepatitis B: A Case Study in MCMC Methods." Pp. 21-43 in W.R. Gilks, S. Richardson, and D.J. Spiegelhalter (eds.). *Markov Chain Monte Carlo in Practice.* Boca Raton, FL: Chapman and Hall/CRC.

Thompson, S.P. (1946). *Calculus Made Easy.* 3rd ed. Hong Kong: MacMillan Press Ltd.

Tierney, L. 1996. "Introduction to General State-Space Markov Chain Theory." Pp. 59-74 in W.R. Gilks, S. Richardson, and D.J. Spiegelhalter (eds.). *Markov Chain Monte Carlo in Practice.* Boca Raton, FL: Chapman and Hall/CRC.

Venables, W.N. and B.D. Ripley. (1999). *Modern Applied Statistics with S-Plus.* 3rd ed. New York: Springer-Verlag.

Venables, W.N. and B.D. Ripley. (2000). *S Programming.* New York: Springer-Verlag.

Willett, J.B. and A.G. Sayer. (1994). "Using Covariance Structure Analysis to Detect Correlates and Predictors of Individual Change Over Time." *Psychological Bulletin* 16:363-381.

Yamaguchi, K. (1991). *Even History Analysis..* Newbury Park, CA: Sage.

Zellner, A. (1962). "An Efficient Method of Estimating Seemingly Unrelated Regressions and Tests for Aggregation Bias." *Journal of the American Statistical Association* 57(298):348-368.

Zhang, T. (1997). *Sams Teach Yourself C in 24 Hours.* Indianapolis, IN: Sams Publishing.

Index

Monte Carlo Statistical Methods
Second Edition

Christian P. Robert and George Casella

The second edition has been revised towards a coherent and flowing coverage of these simulation techniques. This is a textbook intended for a second year graduate course, but someone who either wants to apply simulation techniques for the resolution of practical problems or wishes to grasp the fundamental principles behind those methods can also use it. Chapters 1–5 cover non-Markov Monte Carlo techniques for integration and optimization, while Chapters 7—12 provide a complete coverage of Markov chain Monte Carlo (MCMC) methods. Chapters 13 and 14 provide a path to more recent developments.

2004. 645 pp. (Springer Texts in Statistics) Hardcover
ISBN 978-0-387-21239-5

Bayesian Core: A Practical Approach to Computational Bayesian Statistics

Jean-Michel Marin and Christian P. Robert

This Bayesian modeling book is intended for practitioners and applied statisticians looking for a self-contained entry to computational Bayesian statistics. Focusing on standard statistical models and backed up by discussed real datasets available from the book website, it provides an operational methodology for conducting Bayesian inference, rather than focusing on its theoretical justifications. Special attention is paid to the derivation of prior distributions in each case and specific reference solutions are given for each of the models.

2007. 270 pp. (Springer Texts in Statistics) Hardcover
ISBN 978-0-387-38979-0

Introductory Statistics with R

Peter Dalgaard

This book provides an elementary-level introduction to R, targeting both non-statistician scientists in various fields and students of statistics. The main mode of presentation is via code examples with liberal commenting of the code and the output, from the computational as well as the statistical viewpoint. Brief sections introduce the statistical methods before they are used. A supplementary R package can be downloaded and contains the data sets. All examples are directly runnable and all graphics in the text are generated from the examples.

2002. 267 pp. (Statistics and Computing) Hardcover ISBN 978-0-387-95475-2

Easy Ways to Order▶ Call: Toll-Free 1-800-SPRINGER • E-mail: orders-ny@springer.com • Write: Springer, Dept. S8113, PO Box 2485, Secaucus, NJ 07096-2485 • Visit: Your local scientific bookstore or urge your librarian to order.

CPSIA information can be obtained
at www.ICGtesting.com
Printed in the USA
LVHW021443161218
600667LV00006B/25/P